CUSTER
AND THE
EPIC OF DEFEAT

CUSTER
AND THE
EPIC OF DEFEAT

Bruce A. Rosenberg

The Pennsylvania State University Press
University Park and London

Library of Congress Cataloging in Publication Data

Rosenberg, Bruce A
  Custer and the epic of defeat.

    1. Custer, George Armstrong, 1839-1876. 2. Heroes.
3. Legends—History and criticism. I. Title.
E83.876.C983R67   973.8'1'0924 [B]   74-14631
ISBN 0-271-01172-6

Frontispiece: Drawing by Leonard Baskin from *Custer Battlefield*,
a National Park Service Handbook by Robert M. Utley.

For All Champion
Custerphiles and Custerphobes
But Especially
Seth, Eric, and Gunner

Contents

Illustrations and Acknowledgments   ix

Encomia   xi

1   The Custer of Our Dreams   1

2   The Last Stand: A Critical Approximation   21

3   The Legend   49

4   So Fell Custer, the Brave Cavalier   85

5   Custer's Apotheosis   109

6   Instant Heroic Epics   133

7   The Martyred Heroes   155

8   The Making of a Legend   217

9   Laws of Contrast   253

Notes   287

Index   303

Illustrations and Acknowledgments

Page 27   Campaign map. From *Custer Battlefield*, a National Park
Service Handbook by Robert M. Utley.

31   Custer Battlefield map. From *Custer Battlefield*.

36   *Custer's Fight* by Amos Bad Heart Bull. From *A Pictographic
History of the Oglala Sioux,* University of Nebraska Press.

42   Custer Battlefield, markers. Photo: the author.

51   *The Last Battle of General Custer* by H. Bencke, lithograph,
1882. The Library of Congress.

58   *Custer's Last Stand* by Edgar S. Paxson, 1899. Courtesy of
Whitney Gallery of Western Art, Cody, Wyoming.

59   *Custer's Last Fight* by Otto Becker, 1895. Photo: Anheuser-
Busch, Inc.

61   Errol Flynn as Custer in *They Died With Their Boots On.*
Photo: Museum of Modern Art.

80   Front page. *Bismarck Tribune*, 6 July, 1876.

114   General Custer. Brady photo about 1865. U.S. Signal Corps
photo in the National Archives.

156   Mt. Gilboa. Photo: the author.

161   *Death of Saul* by Gustave Doré from La Sainte Bible Selon la
Vulgate, 1866. Photo: Pattee Library, The Pennsylvania
State University.

164   Masada. Photo: El Al Israel Airlines.

168   Statute of Leonidas at Thermopylae. Photo: Greek Tourist
Information Service.

171   The pass at Thermopylae. Photo: the author.

176   Roland at Roncesvalles. From *La Chanson de Roland*, ed. Leon Gautier, 1872. Photo: Pattee Library, The Pennsylvania State University.

199   Lázar. Seventeenth-century Serbian woodcut. Photo: Father Mateja Matejic, reproduced in *The Path of Orthodoxy*.

205   Walls of Constantinople. Photo: the author.

222   *The Custer Fight* by William Herbert Dunton. Courtesy of Whitney Gallery of Western Art, Cody, Wyoming.

Encomia

My view of Custer as America's "Roland of the Plains" originated in a seminar on the *Chanson* where, with the heroic help of Professor Gerard Brault, I was struggling to keep abreast of scholarship in Old French. Graduate student Kenneth Kane composed a paper on the death of Roland; and while I was listening to his analysis of this epic event the ghost of Custer rode into my collective consciousness and could not be dislodged. The battle was on. James Madison, now at West Point, complicated matters with his seminar report on other *Chansons de Geste*. And the idea refused to shut itself off. If Custer was a "Roland of the Plains," he was also a "Saul of the Steppes," a latter-day Leonidas, a Lázar of the Little Bighorn. I desperately needed reinforcements, and they were not slow in coming to my rescue. Sam Bayard and Robert W. Frank, Jr., who had rescued me many times in the past, came again with more help—on Saul and the Middle English material. Donald K. Fry let me know what he thought about tactics at *Maldon*. Eugene Borza of Penn State University's History Department and Walter Donlan of the Classics Department assisted in the problems of understanding Herodotus. Constantine Patrides, Chairman of the English Department at York University, introduced me to Constantine Paleologus. You are to be congratulated, gentlemen, on jobs well done.

Still, more aid was needed, and three institutions made it possible for me to put this strategy into operation. The Newberry Library awarded a Grant-in-Aid for the summer of 1971; I am proud to render a salute to the Ayer Collection and the library's efficient and genial staff. A National Endowment for the Humanities Senior Fellowship allowed an impossible dream to materialize: I visited Kóssovo, Thermopylae, Constantinople, and Gilboa (and Masada). And the NEH made possible the free time in which to record this now complex idea. The Research Office of Penn State's College of the Liberal Arts supported trips to the Library of Congress, the Library at West Point, and to THE shrine at the Little Bighorn, where I was given enthusiastic help by Arthur Abell and L. Clifford Soubier of the Custer Battlefield National Monument. Thanks, men.

Still, the battle was not over. As analogues kept appearing over the ridge so did the tactics for dealing with them. John Buck passed on to me some valuable psychological ammunition; Charles Cofer of Penn State's Psychology Department made sure that I used it correctly in some of my biggest guns. Alan Jabbour at the Library of Congress kept me well supplied with the folklore materials of Custeriana, and Milton Kaplan of the Prints and Photographic Section assisted with graphics. Walton Lord of Penn State's Art History Department had some hearty laughs over my posters and prints and suggested what I should think about them. Above and beyond the call of Duty!

For Dov Noy of the Hebrew University of Jerusalem, the Last Stand survived in the legend of the Negev's "35." James Rambeau gave his all for this idea, and went down with all guns blazing. Robert Frank read early essays, preliminary drafts, copies of papers, and like the "Rock of Chicamauga" never lost a battle or gave a false command. And throughout all the confusion of the struggle I remembered the wisdom of Francis Lee Utley, and I hope his sagacity runs uncontrolled through these pages. As Custer said of Sitting Bull, while on his way to Custer Ridge, everything I am today I owe to him.

These men have all made contributions and sacrifices for this cause. Now, if I am to meet my own hilltop fate, it has not been their fault; they warned me.

I am grateful also to the editors of four journals for permission to reprint, though often with substantial alterations, essays which have appeared in their journals: *The Georgia Review,* the *Journal of the Folklore Institute, Interdisciplinary Essays,* and *Parameters.*

*   *   *   *   *

On 8 March 1974, after the above tribute was glibly penned, Frances Lee Utley died. The tribute I paid him facetiously was sincerely meant, and so I have let it stand. This book had already been dedicated; but I cannot fail to honor my debt to him in these few, sober words.

... why does the name of Custer still stand in the mind
of the average American as that of a great hero?

Karl Menninger

Did you ever read about a frog who dreamed of being a king?
And then became one?
Well, except for the names and a few other changes,
They could talk about me, the story's the same one.

From "I am, I said" by Neil Diamond

The pathos of courage, contempt of death, and self-sacrifice
is nowhere praised more gloriously than precisely in these two
poems about defeat (the *Chanson de Roland* and *Bjarkamál*).

Jan de Vries

Vivas to those who have failed!
And to those whose war-vessels sank in the sea!
And to those themselves who sank in the sea!
And to all generals who lost engagements, and all overcome heroes!
And to the numberless unknown heroes equal to the greatest heroes
        known!

Walt Whitman

1

The Custer of Our Dreams

This book is about losers. But it is not about the commonplace, banal losers of everyday life, who might be interesting to a few psychologists and sociologists, and to members of their immediate families. No; I am going to write about losers we can admire for their defeat rather than those we pity. The losers who interest us are not pathetic—they are magnificent, for they lose with memorable dignity and *élan*. An aura of sublime glory gathers about their names and deeds while forgetful mists enshroud those who defeat them; disadvantaged on the field, these losers rise above the immediate chagrin of defeat and eventually above the victors. Defeat itself becomes the medium by which the majesty of these vanquished is manifested; and such men are worth knowing about.

Thus we are interested in the most distinctive of heroes, members of a very special club. Each is a hero who has only a small army with him, and though they fight on with great tenacity, they are eventually worn down by the copious numbers ranged against them. The hero's men know that they are fighting for nothing less than their way of life; because their enemy, usually brute savages from a culturally inferior land, are racial (or national) aliens sworn to destroy the hero's people.

As the one-sided battle grinds on, the hero and his men know what the outcome must inevitably be. Their situation is hopeless, further fighting is useless, yet because he is the man he is, and they are the loyal followers they are, they steel themselves to make the enemy pay dearly for each of their lives. In the last few minutes of life left to them, the hero and a few survivors, weary yet determined as ever, withdraw to a hilltop to make their final stand. And it is here, when all of his men have been cut down, that their commander wrings out the last ounce of retaliation against his inexorable foe.

But not everyone has died on that hilltop; one man, an unimportant spear-carrier who stands inconspicuously near the wings of the spectacular grand finale, makes his escape from the carnage and carries his tale to the waiting world. This lone survivor will shortly be forgotten, but his story will outlive him, and it is his story which rouses his countrymen to a fury of vengeful energy, and with the memory of their fallen hero alive in their hearts they drive the barbarians away in terror and confusion. Then, when the dust has settled, they realize that not even the great multitude of the enemy could strike their hero down had he not been betrayed.

This is the legend to which this book is dedicated; but who are the *dramatis personae?* Who is the hero and who are his men? What people are the cunning enemy from another land? Why was this battle fought at all? And why will the countrymen of the slain commander revere this memorable loss in their history from that day forward? To respond is an ambitious task: each question has many answers, and it is best to take them singly and to begin by sorting out particulars. Readers of medieval European literature know that this scenario describes the death of Roland in the twelfth-century *Chanson de Roland.* Those who know Scripture, or who are Israelis, recognize the story as that of the first book of Samuel account of Saul's death on Mt. Gilboa. A Greek knows at once that the tale is of the struggle of the Spartans against the Persian hordes at Thermopylae, except that King Leonidas did not die last. Neither did the hero of the tenth-century Old English poem *The Battle of Maldon,* Byrhtnoth; yet enough of the other details are present to make the pattern recognizable.

In 1360 the alliterative *Morte Arthure*[1] used the same details to relate Sir Gawain's defeat, although here the battle site is not the customary hilltop but a beach. (Yet Gawain was successful in seizing a hill, only to foolishly abandon it to die in the melee at its foot.) Serbs will recognize the same hopeless struggle against impossible odds as the defeat of King Lázar by the Turks on the plains of Kóssovo in 1389. To the Scots the paradigm describes the destruction of James IV and his army at Flodden; and the Welsh Mynyddog, king of Gododdin, with his 300 died in an attack on the English in A.D. 600 under the same circumstances. Moved from the hilltop to an enclosed area this might be the defense of Lejre by Bjarki against the traitorous attack of Hjarvarth and his hirelings, or the defense of the St. Romanos Gate at Constantinople by the last Byzantine emperor, in 1453, or it might be the Alamo. But all Americans, even those who "remember the Alamo," know that the story is really (and also) about George Armstrong Custer and his "Last Stand," also a battle in which the hero gets himself and his men surrounded and finally annihilated.

What has interested most writers on the battle of the Little Bighorn is the fate of Custer and the 212 men with him in their last minutes; what will interest us here is that, despite the fact that all we know of what happened to

Custer and his battalion on the afternoon of 25 June 1876 is that they all perished, the stories about him—the popular legends—as they emerge in biographies, dime novels, movies, paintings, TV serials, popular poems, jokes, and antiwar posters bear a striking resemblance to the other heroic legends we have just mentioned. It does not matter that there was no such knight as Sir Gawain, that we do not know at what point in the battle the Persians killed Leonidas or the vikings slew Byrhtnoth, that we do not know who died last when the Alamo was captured by the Mexicans: even though there really was a Custer and he made a "Last Stand" of sorts, and we know enough about him and that "Stand" to know that many of the legends are not true, what is important here is that his story has been made over in a traditional and recognizable heroic pattern.

When the details of the popular legend of Custer's Last Stand are abstracted, its similarities to other heroic fiction (and history) is clearer: the few against the multitude, the fight to the death on the hilltop, the lone survivor, the traitor, and the desperate eleventh-hour call for help. Except for the names and a few other changes the story is the same all over the world. We have already noted that unlike Custer (or Saul, or Mathô, or Constantine, or Bjarki, or Roland), Leonidas and Byrhtnoth are not the last of their men to succumb. Occasionally the battlefield is a plain (as at Kóssovo), or a beach (as at Maldon). Or disaster may befall the hero and his men in an attack rather than in a defensive posture. No one may live to tell his tale; and aid may never be summoned. Yet these variations are slight and serve to modify, by addition, deletion, or substitution, rather than refute, the basic structure of the legend. As folklorists are able to produce a workable composite by studying hundreds of variants of one folktale collected from all over the world at varying times, so we can compare our heroes on their hilltops as siblings from the same family.

The distinctive features of events otherwise alike are more glaring than those of entirely dissimilar entities; and they tell us more. Those stories that glorify the hero (rather than his comrades) usually place his death at the end of the narrative; moving it forward in the chronology puts emphasis on other facets: the loyalty (or cowardice) of his men and the testing of their vows under dire stress. Bjarki warming his hands by the fire while the enemy is at the gates tells us something about the conception of the Danish poet's sense of drama, just as Lázar's "decision" to choose heaven over victory at Kóssovo tells us much about the ethos of the Serbian songs commemorating this battle. So too with the deaths of Roland and Byrhtnoth: the Frank with a prayer of forgiveness, the Saxon with a plea to his God that his soul be saved.

The last stand has no generic favorites. Variants of the legend appear in "histories" as diverse in quality (and as widely separated in time) as that of Herodotus and Frederick Whittaker's *The Life of General George A. Custer*. The first book of Samuel, a history of quite another sort, has its own version. Flaubert retells the story for his own purposes in *Salammbô*. Although this is not Flaubert's best work, it is interesting because we know his source and we know, consequently, that he reinvented this legend out of the resources of his own imagination. Many popular, although lesser writers— not mute, but certainly inglorious Flauberts—had very similar conceptions. Their works will never appear in the *Oxford Anthology of English Literature* (or its analogue in world literature); yet their doggerel, their stories, their dime novels, their essays tell much the same tale.

Flaubert and his imitators wrote their legends into novels, but this is not the only form taken by the epic of defeat. Throughout this book a great number of literary and subliterary genres are discussed. They are treated as though they were equals, but it should be understood that this leveling is meant in only a few respects—and none of those aesthetic. A work from the Old Testament is compared with a classical history, with heroic poems of several medieval cultures, heroic folk ballads from the Balkan peninsula, alliterative poetry of the late fourteenth century, a nineteenth-century novel, and an American folk legend of roughly the same period. Obviously these works (and nonworks) are not aesthetic equals, but that is precisely one of the arguments of this comparison. In only a very limited sense has the inspiration for all of these narratives been the same: when they are in oral tradition, when they are common, popular property, the events in most of these stories are startlingly similar. If we needed such a demonstration—and we do not—we are shown once again that the narrative elements of plot, important though they may be, are not enough to make a common story a great one. For that, aesthetic qualities are needed which are beyond the scope of this book to discuss. What we want to decide here is the principle that guides the skillful artist when he molds his Venus from slimy clay, and not the art inherent in the completed work.

Custer and his last stand (the origin, the development, the transmission of the legend) is a suitable model because, despite the known facts of the event, our understanding of it assumed an ordered, traditional form. We know enough about the battle to be able to refute nearly all of the legends about it. This development from fact into fiction can also be traced in the *Chanson de Roland,* in *Salammbô,* in the popular legends of the emperor at the fall of Constantinople. That is, battles which had little in common (an ambush in the pass of the Pyrenees, an emperor rushing to the spot in the walls of his city where the enemy has just broken through, a column of cavalry ambushed as it emerges from a ravine on the prairie) became remarkably similar when "processed" in oral tradition. The important similarities of the finished products are not related simply to the fact of events becoming fictionalized, but to the processes themselves, necessarily psychological, which made a coherent, purposefully structured story of an actual event.

Much of any argument by analogy is by nature speculative and heuristic rather than definitive; but a study of Custer's legendizing will at least show how much (or more accurately how little) time is necessary for any legend to begin, a matter of interest to some. In the past we have had to rely almost entirely on the date of the event and an approximate date of the earliest record of the event; in the case of the *Roland* (luckily) the battle has been well established at 778. The defeat was recorded quite unheroically by Einhard in his life of Charlemagne written between 814 and 821. But more than two centuries elapse, two inconveniently silent centuries, before the finished legend appears in the Oxford manuscript. We have simply no way of telling whether the legendizing process took two weeks or two hundred years. With Custer we can tell.

And with Custer we can tell who makes legends. We do not have to rely on written records alone, or those particularly skillful narratives which have survived through the dint of their excellence. To know how a legend is spread we want to follow the story's myriad traces among ordinary people, not only its manifestations in literary masterpieces. Such a thorough search is impossible for a legend of the tenth and eleventh centuries; it is fairly easy for a nineteenth-century event. So it is much easier to evaluate the circumstances in which modern legends arise. Again, proximity is important; those recent conveniences, the telegraph and the newspaper, used to glorify Custer alone of all heroes, are crucial.

Beyond folklore, our investigations (if we are at all curious) will lead into and beyond psychology. People invent legends because they want to believe in them; others perpetuate them for the same reason. If we study the legend and the man who inspired the legend, we also want to know as much as possible about the people (those whom ethnologists call "the folk") who make legends happen, and when, and why. We want to know how deeply people are involved; to distinguish, in other words, heroic legend (the story itself) from heroic song (the composition of the admired and recognizable artist who takes the legend which is his legacy, too, and makes of it a narrative—or a eulogy— which we study, reverentially, when our reading is serious).

And we go beyond psychology: as Custer's Last Stand was made an artful fiction, so was Roland's, Lázar's, Constantine's, and Leonidas'. But are these the only events restructured in the process of memory? Is there something about the way we remember, the way in which we store information and later retrieve it, that exceeds and subsumes such matters as last stands—which are themselves only demonstrations of a more general epistemological phenomenon? To try to find the answer to all of these questions is a worthy goal: it is the next logical step beyond our thrill (or perhaps revulsion, if you will) when we hear or see or read yet another story about the Little Bighorn.

Custer and his legend, then, are of supreme interest. How did this heroic fantasy come about? In the answer to this question is an understanding of the legendizing process. Why did this legend take this particular form? The answer will give us an insight into a fundamental aspect of human psychology, the inclination to dramatize reality. Why was Custer chosen for this apotheosis? In the answer to that puzzle lies much of the psychology, and politics, and ethos of America in the nineteenth century, and much of America today. If we can understand why Custer was deified, we may also know much about Roland and his elevation, about Leonidas and Byrhtnoth and the others, and the reasons for their legendizing. Custer, then, shall be our model not only that we may learn more about him, and us, and our relation to him, but that we will be able to learn more about the legendizing process in the Western world in the last twenty-five centuries. Just as Custer's Last Stand has not been forgotten a century after the guns cooled, neither did its story begin in 1876, or in the nineteenth century, or even in America.

Custer has been carefully ignored by professional historians and students of military tactics and belittled by our generation in its sympathy for the American Indian. The battle in which he lost life and gained an undying fame was a small one militarily, involving only one regiment of cavalry, about 600 men. It did not decide a campaign or the war against the Sioux. Army war colleges now study Custer's tactics mainly to profit by his mistakes; yet despite all this, despite the debunking his memory sustained in Frederic F. Van de Water's acerbic biography, *Glory-Hunter*,[2] and the many books derivative of it, despite the symbol he has become of white suppression of the American Indian, he survives, and he remains far and away the most celebrated military hero of the American people.

More artistic effort—most of it noticeably poor—has been lavished on that one brief skirmish, which is minuscule compared to the epic bloodshedding of the then recent Civil War, than has been expended on San Juan Hill, Chateau-Thierry, D-Day, Iwo-Jima, and Khe Sahn combined.[3] This may be hyperbole and therefore questionable because it is impossible to prove statistically, but I cannot think of a more popular military subject. Don Russell's *Custer's List*[4] documents 967 paintings and illustrations of Custer and his last battle, and more are reproduced almost daily. Fred Dustin's bibliography,[5] compiled in the early 1950s, has over 640 entries, but poetry and fiction—which would easily triple that already distended number—are not included. More than a score of motion pictures concern Custer prominently or else mention him in some important connection; the best known are *They Died With Their Boots On, Sitting Bull, Two Flags West,* and most recently *Little Big Man.*

The television series "Branded" told of a disgraced officer's odyssey to social reinstatement, an old theme in westerns (as it is in the literature of Western civilization generally), retold in 1906 in Randall Parrish's *Bob Hampton of Placer* and filmed in 1921 by Marshall Neilan. A contemptible Custer was portrayed in the movies *Sitting Bull* (1954) and *The Great Sioux Massacre* (1965). Walt Disney was no kinder in *Tonka* (1958), while almost succeeding in making Captain Keogh's horse, Comanche, the hero of the debacle. *Warpath* (based on Frank Gruber's "Broken Lance") was more favorable to the boy general, much as was *7th Cavalry* (based on the Glendon Swarthout short story "A Horse for Mrs. Custer"). *Custer of the West* (the title alone suggests this could hardly be unfavorable) was one of the last (1968) sympathetic portraits, though no more artistically distinguished than previous efforts. At least three films, insignificant by any artistic standard, bear the title of *Custer's Last Stand* or *Custer's Last Fight.* Several television productions, in single entertainments or serials (like the fifteen-episode movie sequence, also named "Custer's Last Stand"), have also been about him directly; those that have utilized the story of the Little Bighorn include "Custer," "Branded," "Time Tunnel," and "Cheyenne."

The national park which was built on the site of the battle is rare in being named for the man and not the place or the event: it is, after all, Custer Battlefield National Monument, and not "Little Bighorn National Park" or "Sitting Bull National Monument."   The pigeons of America can straddle statues of Custer at West Point, at Monroe, Michigan (the home of his late adolescence and the residence of his wife's family), and at New Rumley, Ohio—his birthplace. Towns in North and South Dakota as well as Montana are named for him, to no one's surprise; but "Custer" is also on the map in Washington, Kentucky, Wisconsin, and Michigan. Georgia has its Custer Terrace, Pennsylvania its Custer City (as does Oklahoma), and Illinois its Custer Park. Streets, schools, and army camps have been named for him: a park in Hardin, Montana; the Air Force station at Monroe, Michigan; a reservoir in Colorado; a national forest in Montana and North Dakota; to say nothing of Custer Ridge, Washington, Custer Creek, Montana, state parks, and national highways. Much of southeastern Montana is named for him and his last battle: Garryowen, Reno Creek, Custer City. Dozens of settlements and highway markers proclaim that "Custer Marched Here" or that "Custer Camped Here," a popularity which rivals that of any hero, American or European.

And he lives in our everyday expressions, in our jokes, and on our bumper stickers. If there is any consistent pattern to these varied and multitudinous Custer allusions and references, it is to the implication that the Last Stand was lost because of the overwhelming number of the Indians; Custer remains in our memory the great soldier who found himself confronting too many of the enemy, even for him. His last words are imagined to be, "Where did all the Indians come from?" or "Remember, men, take no prisoners." One waggish observation has Custer and his men wearing Arrow Shirts.

Comedian Bill Cosby visualizes the Last Stand as a metaphysical football game in which he—as the referee—tells "Custer" to take his ten men and go to one end of the field, and then tells "Sitting Bull," the opposing captain, to take his ten thousand braves and go to the other end. Bumper stickers have tended more toward social protest. Vine Deloria's treatise provided the inspiration for one sticker, "Custer Died for Your Sins," and car owners from the Far West are fond of "Custer Had It Coming." A recent antiwar poster from Berkeley, California, shows the 1865 Matthew Brady portrait of "Yellow Hair" with his arms akimbo; the assumption is that everyone will immediately recognize him and his most famous encounter with the enemy and as quickly draw the conclusions the analogy intends: "Let's Win This War and Get The Hell Out." Out of respect for the sensibilities of my readers, I omit the numerous obscene jokes.

But what of the real Custer and his Last Stand? The unhappy fact is that little is known of the events which led to the destruction of Lieutenant Colonel (Brevet Major General) George A. Custer and the five companies of the Seventh Cavalry under his immediate command on 25 June 1876; but where there are no ascertainable facts, or few, Americans have supplied the missing data and in a few cases contradicted known details with an invented narrative.

Nearly all of the more than 950 paintings and illustrations show Custer with a sword, but the regiment did not carry this particular weapon into combat on 25 June 1876, and there is good evidence that it had not been used in battle since the Civil War.[6] Rather, the Seventh was armed with pistols and carbines. In the Warner Brothers film *They Died With Their Boots On* saber-wearing Errol Flynn is the last of his command to die, for the director placed him, defiant and undaunted, amid a field strewn with "dead" extras; but testimony we have from the Indians suggests something else.[7] When the firing had died down and the braves moved forward to count coup, several troopers are said to have leaped over the barricade they had formed with the bodies of their dead horses, and to have made a frantic dash for the river. They were clubbed down before they could escape; but these, and not the dead men on the hill, would have been the last whites alive on the field. Custer's body was found on the hill.

The battle of the Little Bighorn was probably the easiest and most one-sided victory for the Indians in their plains wars with whites. Yet contemporary newspaper accounts placed the Sioux loss at well over 200, and others, including Captain Benteen (the regiment's third-in-command) believed that Custer's battalion had taken more than their own number of the enemy with them.[8] But reconstructions, based on careful interviews with surviving chiefs, have put the Indian loss at about 45 killed, though many more were wounded.[9]

Custer's refusal to accept Gatling guns or the support of a battalion of the Second Cavalry is now famous. But another story, not as widely circulated, insists that in the final moments he sent for aid when the battle was all but lost, and the J. K. Ralston painting captures that imagined moment: Custer and about thirty men have already shot their horses and are organizing a defense at the northern end of "Custer Ridge." Meanwhile, in the right rear of the painting, heading southeast, Sergeant Butler (whose body was found several hundred yards in that direction) rides for help. But again there is no evidence that Butler or anyone else was sent for aid, or even that Custer had time to think about such a move: most of the reliable Indians thought that the battle lasted about thirty to forty-five minutes,[10] and Benteen saw on the field what were to him unmistakable signs of "panic and rout." In any event, the direction of Butler's route in Ralston's painting would have led him directly into the path of Gall's attacking braves who had at that moment, so far as we can tell, just overrun Keogh's and Calhoun's position to Custer's rear. And how would Butler have known where to ride? Custer had ordered Benteen to scour the valleys well south of the village, and so far as was known Reno was still fighting in the valley. Custer had no way of knowing that Reno had been driven to some bluffs across the river, or that Benteen had accidentally found him there.

In the wake of disaster, stories of treachery were rife; for example, various Crow scouts had from time to time been said to have betrayed the column to their ancient and hereditary enemies, the Sioux. When the news of the defeat fell upon the United States, General Alfred Terry, Custer's immediate commander, was accused of incompetence, but swiftly the public's accusations shifted to Captain Benteen, though they came finally to rest on the regiment's second-in-command, Major Marcus A. Reno. Frederick Whittaker, dime novelist of some distinction and popularity, one time captain of the army, and full-time accuser of Reno, through the inexorable force of his will, his writing, and his lobbying, brought such public and congressional pressure to bear on that unhappy officer that Reno finally asked for, and was granted, a Board of Inquiry to investigate his conduct on the field. The Board exonerated him.[11] Nevertheless, many today still believe that Reno permitted Custer to ride to this death, out of cowardice and hatred, and then, knowing that his commander was surrounded, withheld assistance. The crime would be all the more heinous if true, since it means that a spiteful Reno would have allowed more than 200 of his friends and comrades to ride to their deaths with Custer.

Probably the most widely circulated legend about the battle was that of the lone survivor. He was supposed to have lived through the entire conflict, to have seen all, and to have given the details of the fighting to the waiting world. But historians are positive that this detail also is not true. The man most often identified as the lone survivor was a Crow scout named Curly, but he saw only the first shots fired and never claimed to have witnessed very much.[12] However, a lone survivor was a convenience for newspaper reporters who needed an "authority" for their imaginative accounts of the battle, and for other (more complicated reasons) as well, and the legend long outlived the denial.

Finally, Custer is supposed to have been on the very top of the ridge when he was killed, as many paintings place him. Exactly where Custer or any of his men fell is impossible to know, for nearly all of the bodies were stripped and mutilated, and certainly the Indians were not careful to replace the corpses in their original positions after they had removed their uniforms. The bodies were buried shallowly two days later and reinterred a year later. At that time wooden stakes were placed on the gravesites, but after several years the troopers were again reburied atop the hill under a marble monument, the officers were removed for private burial, and marble markers were put in the place of the fallen men. But by that time the chance for miscalculation had been compounded several times. Custer's marker is about fifty feet down the slope; this may not be the exact spot where he fell, but it is the only evidence we have.

Such is the fame and respect that the American people have afforded Custer that they have placed him in a very exclusive Valhalla usually reserved for only one man in a culture's history. And a further tribute to the hold this man has on the imagination of his countrymen, even a century after his death, is the great number and variety of traditional stories which have been told about him, and the comparisons implicit in those stories. Out of the numberless multitude of these tales, I relate here only a few of those which, though of great antiquity themselves, were applied to Custer after 1876. In them we can see how an existing tradition has a life of its own and attaches itself to heroes as they appear: the legend is father to the man. And their association with Custer is further indication of his fame.

One of the most interesting tales concerns the young Colonel Custer and a comely Cheyenne maiden, Mo-nah-se-tah. She is said to have been at the battle with her family and tribe and to have gone to the top of Custer Ridge when the shooting stopped. It was there, while her tribesmen and allies were stripping and ceremonially mutilating the fallen soldiers, that she recognized Custer—the father of her child of several years earlier—and saved his body from a horrible dismemberment. Custer's body was one of the few found on the ridge which was not mutilated, and almost immediately fanciful reasons were given to explain this happy exception: that Mo-nah-se-tah had saved him from this final indignity, that the Sioux had too great a respect for their fallen foe, and that Custer had shot himself to avoid capture, so that his corpse was bad medicine for the Indians.

The Mo-nah-se-tah story was supposed to have begun during the Seventh's raid on Black Kettle's village in 1868. To achieve surprise, Custer ordered the regiment to attack at dawn during mid-winter, about the only time that an Indian village would be vulnerable. The intention of the cavalry was to round up or destroy the herd of ponies, thus immobilizing the fighting men, and to capture the women and children of the village. These noncombatants were to be brought to a secure reservation in the expectation that the able-bodied husbands and sons who were left behind would eventually follow them in. As the sun labored up over the frozen horizon the Seventh busied itself in these objectives. But as the morning wore on, many of the warriors who had escaped the first assault and who managed to flee to neighboring villages began returning with reinforcements. Major Joel Elliott, whose company had been ordered to block one of the escape routes, led a small detachment off in pursuit of several fugitives who had filtered through their lines, but they soon found themselves cut off from their unit and were destroyed. In the meantime the pressure on the main body of the attacking troops was such that Custer was forced to withdraw by early evening. A number of squaws who were seized as hostages were taken by the regiment back to Camp Supply. Mo-nah-se-tah was among them. But so great was the haste to withdraw that Major Elliott and his men were left to their fates.

This campaign became momentous in Custer's life, quite apart from any alleged romantic involvement on his part. The raid got a good press; and although Custer was not one who needed to be spurred by that last infirmity of noble mind, fame, it came to him with even greater abundance after the Washita attack. It was there, more than in any other action, that the Seventh and its commander achieved their reputation as Indian fighters *par excellence*. Consequently, a great victory was expected of them on the Little Bighorn. When in imminent contact with the enemy in 1876, the success which he had achieved eight years earlier in Oklahoma must have been in Custer's mind: his initial battle plan had been to rest the regiment during the afternoon and evening of 25 June, then, as on the Washita, to launch a dawn attack the following day. Only when his tactical surprise had been compromised did he decide to engage the enemy at once on that afternoon. It would not be another Washita after all. But if Washita was Custer's glory, it was also to be his undoing; for several of the officers with Reno and Benteen, late in the battle, had no thoughts of going to their general's "rescue" because they thought, first, that the five companies with him were powerful enough to take care of any force the Indians could field against him, and second, that he may well have deserted them to fortune, as he had abandoned Major Elliott several years before.

The fate of Major Joel Elliott and the small detachment that shared his fate on the Washita is a good example of history imitating art. When his small detachment was cut off, the Indians closed in on Elliott, who had chosen for his defensive position a little knoll covered with a tall, reedy grass. He could hardly have chosen worse; the Indians could not be seen by the troopers through the grass, and they, in turn, had only to loft arrows onto the knoll until all its occupants had been struck. Elliott could not escape; and several weeks later his body and those of his fifteen-odd men were found, probably lying as they fell, defending the indefensible grassy knoll. Here was a last stand in miniature: a small unit detached from the main force, initially on the attack but quickly forced to the defensive, hemmed in, and slaughtered at will. If history is purposeful, here was a symbolic anticipation of the famous "Last Stand" from the same regiment: if this were literature, Elliott's disaster would prepare us for the climax of the drama. And, ironically enough, at the Little Bighorn the surviving officers remembered Elliott and saw their fate in his. Yet the final irony is not realized: Custer had not deserted them; they would not die. Instead, they would themselves one day be accused of deserting him. If Custer could have been saved, which appears doubtful, his own past conspired against him when his subordinates, thinking themselves deserted, hesitated to come to his "rescue."

During the months following the Washita raid, Mo-nah-se-tah became an interpreter at the post, and allegedly much more than that to Custer. But as with so many stories that have arisen about him there is simply no evidence that he became her lover, let alone the father of her child—if she ever had one. All is hearsay and anecdote. Custer apologists claim that he would never have done such a thing, so great was his love for Elizabeth, surely the most conjectural and naive kind of argument.[13] One cannot even be certain that Mo-nah-se-tah bore a child in captivity, despite the respectability given the story by Mari Sandoz.[14] Complicating the story is the existence of a variant of this legend: Kate Bighead tells of two Cheyenne women who saved Custer's body from mutilation. But Kate did not identify either of them as Mo-nah-se-tah; and as usual all that remains is speculation and fantasy.[15]

Custer's body was found supine, stripped of his uniform, in an attitude of repose. So many of those around him had been badly dismembered and maimed that his fate did seem special: why not a Mo-nah-se-tah, who carried not only the white man's son but a lasting love for its father? The story, after all, is an old one; only a few details are changed from the salvation of John Smith by Pocahontas in Colonial America. In the Custer version the hero is now dead, and the Cheyenne maiden cannot save his life: but she can preserve his body and the memory of what he was in life. This is surely a variant of the John Smith legend: what one maudlin poem described of the Colonial version could well have been, with only a change of names, said of the later story:

> Then the maiden Pocahontas
> Rushes forward, none can stop her,
> Throws her arms about the captive
> Cries,—"oh spare him! Spare the Paleface!"[16]

Nausicaa saved the life of the stranger Odysseus, though not by interposing her lovely head between the poised clubs and the head of the stranger; and Aeneas had a similar encounter with Lavinia, who dreamed that her husband would come to her from across the seas. Medievalists have named the Pocahontas-Mo-nah-se-tah figure "The Enamored Moslem Princess," as again and again in the medieval romances she saves the life of the Christian captive of her pagan father. The story was told all over central Europe and made its way down through Turkey and the Balkan peninsula. The *Gesta*

Romanorum, a tremendously popular collection of moral tales which entertained centuries of medieval people, includes a variant called "Of Fidelity." The story came, as we know, to the New World as well; but whether it was reinvented or merely perpetuated by people who already knew its outlines does not matter so much as the reason for its popularity: it is a simple tale, just an episode really, which has touched on some fundamental center in the millions who have heard and read and retold it.[17] If the Mo-nah-se-tah story had not been modeled on well-known lines, it might well have been reinvented coincidentally along those same lines.

Those who had not heard of the alleged affair between Custer and his Pocahontas of the plains invented another, perhaps equally romantic, explanation for his unmutilated body, a story that reflected glory upon Custer but also praised the nobility of his assailants: the Sioux and Cheyenne left his body undefiled out of their great admiration for their fallen antagonist. This story was widely circulated at the time and though less popular now, it is with us still. But that any of the Indians knew that their attacker was Custer is doubtful. The warrior most frequently accused of killing Custer, Rain-in-the-Face, denied in his most reliable interview that any of the Indians knew of Custer's presence with the soldiers, and said that no Indian knew who had killed him.[18] The evidence, then, strongly indicates that Custer's body was untouched by chance, not choice.

Yet the stories of the Indian's nobility toward the body of their fallen foe continued to be as popular as other accounts of his mutilation. On the one hand it was desirable to imagine the enemy as savage and ruthless: it increased the desire for revenge and reinforced the idea that Custer was at least morally superior to the enemy who had physically defeated him. The sympathetic stories too showed the same qualities: even his mortal enemies recognized in Custer a great warrior after they had beaten him. Unconsciously or not, however, some of the nobility was bound to be reflected on the Sioux, who had had the grace, after all, to honor Custer, enemy or not. One such account, which shows more imagination than most, fantasizes Sitting Bull walking up to Custer Ridge when the fighting had stopped, and kneeling by the side of his slain enemy. Sitting Bull lamented, and then placed a cloth over the white man's face: "This handkerchief will guard your features against the desert's blackening heat. Farewell, great Custer, till we meet!"[19]

Like T.S. Eliot, who is said to have immortalized a discredited scholarly thesis with his great poem *The Waste Land,* Henry Wadsworth Longfellow immortalized a discredited anecdote: in revenge for previous indignities, Rain-in-the-Face cut Custer's heart out of his body and ate it. If the story is not as good as Jessie Weston's book which inspired Eliot, neither is Longfellow's poem as good as Eliot's. Three excerpted stanzas from this nineteenth-century work tell the grizzly story:

> In his war paint and his beads,
> Like a bison among the reeds,
>   In ambush the Sitting Bull
> Lay with three thousand braves
> Crouched in the clefts and caves,
>   Savage, Unmerciful!
>
> Into the fatal snare
> The white chief with yellow hair
>   And his three hundred men
> Dashed headlong, sword in hand;
> But of that gallant band
>   Not one returned again.
>
> But the foemen fled in the night,
> And Rain-in-the-Face, in his flight,
>   Uplifted high in air
> As a ghastly trophy bore
> The brave heart, that beat nor more,
>   Of the white chief with yellow hair.[20]

Nearly every major newspaper in the country had carried the story shortly after the first news of the battle. Rain-in-the-Face, allegedly humiliated several years before when Custer arrested him at a reservation trading post and he was subsequently imprisoned, had sworn revenge. At the Little Bighorn, according to this story, revenge was his.

One version had it that Rain-in-the-Face cut out Custer's heart and danced around a victory bonfire with the heart impaled on the end of his lance. In still other versions the victim of revenge was not George A. Custer but his brother Tom, who commanded Company C, and who fell several feet from his brother down the slope of Custer Ridge. Reports of the actual condition of Tom Custer's body vary, one version even going to the extent of quoting—allegedly—Major Reno on the degree of mutilation.[21]

Again, we are confronted with a very old belief which became attached, in the nineteenth century, to the popular life of Custer. From the earliest times the blood was thought to be the vehicle of the soul and the heart its seat.[22] The primitive warrior saw that as the blood ran from the wounds of the fallen, the strength, and finally the life, also left the body. As the vehicle of the soul, the blood carries with it the characteristics of its host. Thus to gain the strength of the bear Hjalti swallowed a bear's heart and drank its blood. Old Norse Ingiald emboldened himself by eating a wolf's heart, a principle also employed by Hagen in the Middle High German *Kudrun*. Siegfried—the Achilles of the Teutons—had made himself invulnerable, except in one part of his body, by bathing in dragon's blood. To heal the Fisher King of his wounds the blood of a pelican—a bird known for its excess of maternal love—was rubbed on them, though in this case the hapless king had no success. To eat the heart of man or beast ensures the eternal death of the owner, and it also imparts his quality to the eater. When Rain-in-the-Face allegedly ate Custer's heart he was making sure that his fallen foe would never rise again, and that Custer's spirit would not come back from the grave to harm him or his fellow Sioux. Custer's heart was in fact buried with him, though the spirit to avenge Custer would plague his killers.

Another story that gained currency with those who wished to praise Custer as well as with those who wished to defame him related his suicide. This tale, like the preceding stories, was invented to explain why the Indians had not violated his body: suicides were supposed to be powerful medicine to the Sioux, and having seen Custer take his own life, none of the attacking braves would risk violating his corpse. The apologists took an entirely different stand based on the same "fact," that Custer had obeyed an unwritten "law of the West" and of Indian-fighting by saving the last bullet for himself. Capture at the hands of the Indians, whose hearts we know to have been "bad" that day, would have been far worse than death. The story also allows Custer to die, like Roland, undefeated: no Indian could kill him (just as Roland's temples burst from blowing the Oliphant too vigorously), and so he died in a very important sense triumphant.

The other side of the story depicts Custer the coward or perhaps even Custer the psychotic who ends his military career not by tenaciously fighting the enemy but in an act of shame. Custer was right-handed, yet the two wounds found on his body by the burial detail were on the left side—one in his chest and one his temple. To have killed himself Custer would have had to have done so with considerable perverse flair, with a highly developed sense of irony, to say nothing of phenomenal dexterity. Under fire from several hundred howling Indians, he would have to reach his revolver across his body to his left side, squeezed off one round, and then reached up to the temple to finish the job. Surely there were easier ways. But the story had grown to such proportions and significance that Captain E. S. Godfrey, who survived with Reno and had been with the burial detail, found it necessary to comment on the rumor explicitly: "There was no sign for the justification of the theory, insinuation or assertion that he committed suicide."[23]

So strong was the medicine of Custer that while the battle raged, his spiritual presence was as powerful as his physical being. In 1938 the *Bismarck Tribune* carried a story about an alleged scene at Fort Lincoln, several hundred miles to the east of the Little Bighorn, which is supposed to have occurred while the battle was being fought. A Reverend Wainwright was leading a service in the Custer home for Elizabeth and the wives of the regiment's officers. At the very moment that the battle was blazing, the little congregation sang "Nearer My God to Thee,"[24] the Welsh hymn later sung—according to another legend—by those who were left aboard the *Titanic* when she went down in the Atlantic on her maiden voyage. So too in this great calamity, God visited the widows of the regiment and, unconscious even to them, inspired this favorite hymn.

People frequently claim or are said to have barely missed disasters—the people we hear about who failed to catch a fatal jetliner because their taxicab got caught in traffic, or those who decided to stay an extra day on business or vacation and who canceled their fated reservations at the last minute. The Custer disaster also had its share—the lone survivors—as we have seen. And it also had its portion of omens which always seem, in retrospect, to anticipate major calamities. For instance, several days before the battle, after an officer's call, Custer's personal guidon fell over in the dust. The other officers took it to be an omen of bad luck. Custer's manner impressed Lieutenant Wallace so much that he soon after remarked to Godfrey (the same officer in the burial detail) that he thought that Custer would soon die.[25] And still others are said to have made out their wills as though they had a presentiment of their fate. Even the hero himself is said to have foreseen the end: in a remark made to a friend he lamented that it would take "another Fort Phil Kearny" defeat to arouse Congress sufficiently to appropriate more funds.[26] His subsequent defeat did, in fact, arouse Congress as he had anticipated.

Today the legendary aspects of Custer retain much of their potency, despite methodical efforts to debunk and belittle him, despite the analyses of later psychologists to "explain" him away, despite our attempts to establish the facts about the man and his most famous battle. He is, in nearly every respect, regarded by many as a hero—in the classical sense. A very active cult celebrates the memory of his life and the fields of his conflicts, vowing "To seek and preserve the truth about the Battle of the Little Big Horn and all of Custeriana." The cult is nationwide, has official annual meetings in the home town of Custer's adolescence (Monroe, Michigan), and has lobbyed for such legislation as the expansion of National Park Service jurisdiction over land adjacent to the Little Bighorn battlefield.

Custer's cult, the "Little Big Horn Associates," publishes a monthly newsletter for the faithful and a quarterly *Research Review,* a rather uncritical and unskeptical hagiography. The Associates do not sponsor trips to Montana, but the newsletter makes it clear that many of the members make yearly pilgrimages to the shrine. These journeys have all the earmarks of the conventional pilgrimage: the shrine regularly visited, the seasonal character of the pilgrimage, and the recreation of the battle by local Crow Indians and National Park Service employees.

Within the shrine the hero's relics are preserved under glass. The Custer Battlefield National Monument maintains, in addition to the usual assortment of carbines, bows and arrows, and clothing, Custer's boots, a handsomely beaded buckskin jacket he once wore, personal letters, the last message from him (dictated to his adjutant and given to the trumpeter for delivery),[27] and other memorabilia. Another shrine, in Monroe, reveres yet another buckskin jacket ("once worn by General Custer ..."), a campaign trunk, and a lock of his hair.

Frederick Whittaker—and he was not alone in this conception—bestowed upon Custer a martyr's death, raising him above the level of ordinary mortals, even of ordinary military heroes. For Whittaker, Custer Ridge was the fighting man's Calvary; in the final act all that remained of the five companies were the general and a "little group of men." Curly, the faithful Crow scout, approached Custer during a lull in the fighting while the encircling Indians gathered for one final charge and offered "Yellow Hair" a chance to escape. A moment's reflection:

> In that moment, Custer looked at Curly, waved him away and rode back to the little group of men, to die with them. How many thoughts must have crossed that noble soul in that brief moment. There was no hope of victory if he stayed, nothing but certain death. With the scout he was nearly certain to escape. His horse was a thoroughbred and his way sure. He might have balanced the value of a leader's life against those of his men, and sought his safety. Why did he go back to certain death?

> Because he felt that such a death as that which that little band of heroes was about to die, was worth the lives of all the general officers in the world.[28]

The role of ritual, of which the annual recreation of the battle is only the most obvious aspect, should not be underestimated; far more people than the membership of the Associates (or other Custer buffs) attend the yearly play battle, making it one of Montana's leading tourist attractions. Among many of these tourists something much deeper than their historical interest is involved, as the startling popularity of the Custer legend itself attests. This man's act symbolizes the ultimate act of defiance against all our enemies, against all our frustrations which arise simply by living in human society, against all the circumstances, which may or may not have hostile causes, but that nevertheless thwart our desires. Custer is our idealization of defiance ennobled, on both a personal and a national scale, the embodiment of the wish that regardless of the cost we can remain true to our convictions and our principles, that we shall continue to exert our will in the face of society's pressures and counterdesires.

Consciously we may condemn the tragic hero's rashness, as the press, when the news of the battle was first known, condemned Custer. But in that he succumbs easily to his impulses he receives our sanction, because such impulses are something we can, on a level other than consciousness, empathize with: we want the hero to yield to his impulses so that we can relish his "transgressions." His courage and dauntlessness reveal the hero's spiritual value and replenish ours. Obviously, one needs great moral strength to face death without flinching; the hero rises to meet his fate, and in so doing he proves himself the master of it. The Indians killed Custer but, white America wanted to believe, he was impervious to their slings and arrows in a higher sense. His calamity tested to the utmost his inner strength.

We admire the brave loser more than the winner. As only one illustration of this principle we should note that many more men win the Congressional Medal of Honor posthumously than live to receive it. This is probably because we tend to think that if a man has given his "all," he has given the fullest measure of his devotion which, paradoxically, does not quite seem true of the live hero. This is another point that will receive fuller discussion later.

Such is the Custer of our commonplace thoughts and expressions, the dashing cavalryman who, through pride or foolishness or ambition, fought a battle against an irresistible tide of Indians—and lost. However, in the century since that small battle was fought, an oral tradition—only a fraction of which has even been hinted at—has given a distinctive shape to the events of 25 June 1876. That fictional shape of the battle of the Little Bighorn is what will interest us shortly; but to decide what is fiction we must first ascertain, as best we can, what happened to the Seventh U.S. Cavalry in its most famous encounter with an enemy.

2

The Last Stand:
A Critical Approximation

The Fort Laramie Treaty of 1868 temporarily ended the decades-old sporadic guerrilla fighting between westward-moving white settlers and their most aggressive Indian antagonists; several forts in the Dakota and Montana territories were abandoned, the Powder River country was guaranteed to the Indians as hunting grounds, and all of what is now South Dakota was to be preserved as a Sioux reservation. Many Indians, however, chose not to live on reservations under the control and domination of whites and continued to roam the territory freely. Notable among them was Sitting Bull, one of the most prominent leaders of the "hostiles."

In 1874 Lieutenant Colonel George Armstrong Custer led a reconnaissance in force into the Dakota Territory with the intent of mapping the land for future roads. But during this expedition, several of his men found gold in the Black Hills of South Dakota, land that was thriving with game, and land which happened to be sacred to the Sioux. Not very much gold was ever taken out of these hills, but for several years the promise of rich strikes drew thousands to this new country. The *Cheyenne Weekly Leader,* for instance, for over a year (1876) carried a full-page map directing settlers to the gold fields and their "urban" center, Custer City.

The great influx of prospectors into the Dakota badlands heightened the tensions already latent in the situation. The Sioux felt cheated because their promised lands were being occupied by greedy whites; in addition, there were many complaints about the food and clothing provided by the Bureau of Indian Affairs. The whites, on their part, were incensed by Indian raids on their settlements, which cost them heavily in horses, cattle, and lives. The situation soon became intolerable to the United States government, so that in the fall of 1875 the Departments of the Interior and of War made plans to end Indian depredations and hoped to coerce the Indians into selling the Black Hills.

But the major news during the spring of 1876 was not the forthcoming campaign against the Indians, and certainly not Custer; bigger news, juicier events, riper culture for more virulent sensationalism held the nation's morbid attention. The centennial celebrations were in the center ring, of course. But stealing the show, by turns, were the Whiskey Scandal, the Blaine investigation, the Turkish war in the Balkans, the imminent Presidential nominating conventions, and miscellaneous government scandals. As with Watergate a century later, the newspapers were able to stage their revelations, neither bunching nor scattering them, nursing the public's craving for sensation with a carefully programmed diet.

Three strands of fate showed occasionally among those splashier hues but were overlooked by readers whose eyes were dazzled by the glare. The tribes of the West were gathering; their depredations were increasing in number; and the aggressive reaction of white Americans was making a bloody confrontation inevitable. If many people thought about this coming collision, they did not think it very dangerous: local (Chicago) election scandals, the national ones still lingering in Washington, the opening of the Exposition in Philadelphia, even New York gossip: these baubles entertained the readers of the "news." Yet in obscure corners—at the bottoms of columns and on back pages of the *Chicago Tribune*—one can follow, almost daily, the tautening strands.

3 April	The settlers of Fort Pease complained to the *Chicago Tribune* by letter of constant Indian pillaging, attacks, and an occasional murder.
7 April	Two miners in Deadwood Creek, Nebraska, "massacred" by Sioux.
10 April	From an editorial titled "The War with the Sioux—Indian Arrogance Fed by Government Weakness": "They believed that the Government feared their prowess in battle; and believing this, their arrogance, insolence, and aggressiveness were increased beyond measure.... They never had observed their part of the treaty of 1868."
13 April	A rumor was brought to Fort Laramie that "Indians or half-breeds had murdered several men."
21 April	After more Indian robberies, it was reported that the able-bodied men at the Red Cloud and Spotted Tail agencies had joined Sitting Bull and Crazy Horse on the warpath.
3 May	In a skirmish with Indians in Nebraska one man was killed on each side.

9 May   Several reports of Indian attacks on various settlers led to an editori-
             al on "the Indian business": "Why the people of the West do not
             rise up and assert their rights, is a mystery. They have all along been
             deluded by the humanitarians of the East, who know nothing of the
             real Indian character."
17 May   In a raid on a stage in the Black Hills five men were killed and
             scalped.
18 May   A U.S. Mail carrier was killed near Fort Laramie, and the Sioux
             were said to be leaving their reservations in large numbers in antici-
             pation of a summer war.
19 May   Reports of four murders and scalpings from Bismarck and three
             more from Fort Leavenworth under the headline "Indians/Savage
             Pastimes."
30 May   Several more stories of atrocities by "the devils in human form."
             Meanwhile, Cheyenne reported that an attack by 600 warriors had
             been beaten off, the attackers then heading north to join Sitting Bull.
             Omaha reported that all the young warriors had left the Red Cloud
             Agency.
5 June   Amid more reports of Indian killings, Colonel Lounsberry (editor of
             the *Bismarck Tribune)* denied any "wholesale" murders but ad-
             mitted that stragglers were constantly being ambushed.
7 June   Large numbers of Cheyenne and Arapahoe were seen heading north,
             supposedly to join the Sioux.
8 June   Spotted Tail Agency reported sighting about 1,700 lodges heading
             north, "spoiling for a fight." Another report from Cheyenne es-
             timated another 1,200 lodges near the mouth of the Tongue River.
9 June   Indian raids reported near Cheyenne.
19 June   An additional 3,000 warriors said to have deserted Red Cloud
             Agency and headed north.
22 June   Four men "massacred" in the Black Hills.

On 25 June 1876 Custer rode into battle, though the news of the defeat was
not carried by the nation's newspapers until 6 July. Meanwhile (on 27 June)
General Logan's speech to the Senate was widely circulated: "It is our sacred
duty to civilize and Christianize Indians." On the same day the *Chicago
Tribune* realized that General Crook's recent encounter with the Sioux, which
first appeared to be a victory, was in fact a defeat; and the *Tribune* blamed
Crook for allegedly sending a cavalry force into a ravine while the bluffs above
swarmed with the enemy.

28 June   General William T. Sherman declared: "Forebearance has ceased to
           be a virtue toward these Indians, and only a severe and persistent
           chastisement will bring them to a sense of submission."
1 July   A dispatch from Fort Laramie reported that Indians returning to
           Red Cloud Agency were gossiping about a fight with cavalry.

The year before, as a result of worsening conditions, the Commissioner of Indian Affairs had ordered the Powder River Indians to report in to their assigned reservations. Messengers went out in December 1875, but many of the free-roaming Indians had no intention of surrendering their freedom. On 1 February 1876, those Indians who were not domiciled on the reservations were termed "hostiles," and plans for dealing with them were left to the jurisdiction of the War Department for appropriate action. The result was the campaign of 1876, in which Custer was to play so prominent a part.

The Powder River country fell under the jurisdiction of Civil War hero Lieutenant General Philip Sheridan, who planned a three-column attack on the recalcitrant Sioux and their allies. General George Crook was to lead about 800 cavalry and infantry north from Fort Fetterman, Wyoming. Colonel John Gibbon, at the same time, directed a second force of about 450 men of the Second Cavalry and Seventh Infantry regiments in an eastward movement from Fort Ellis, near Bozeman, Montana. The Dakota column completed the army; composed of twelve companies of the Seventh Cavalry and three companies of infantry with Gatling guns, it left garrison at Fort Lincoln, near Bismarck, Dakota territory, on 17 May and moved westward down the Yellowstone.

General Alfred Terry, the field commander, established his headquarters at the junction of the Yellowstone and Powder rivers aboard the side-paddle steamer *Far West*. Here he learned from Gibbon's scouts of an Indian concentration in the valley of the Tongue. Major Marcus A. Reno, who was later to figure prominently in the controversy that followed the battle, was given six companies of the Seventh to scout the enemy and determine their position. Reno's battalion moved south along the Powder River, then swung west and moved cross-country until it crested the valley of the Tongue. Reno had not been instructed to proceed further; but acting on his own authority he ordered his unit across that stream as far west as the Rosebud, where he found a fresh Indian trail heading south. He followed this for a short time (not long enough, thought some; too long, thought others, in that he let the Indians know cavalry were in the area but did not engage them), then wheeled and rejoined the command, which had moved by that time (20 June) to the confluence of the Yellowstone and the Rosebud. Reno had located the enemy, but not without criticism in the *Chicago*

Tribune: in a story dated St. Paul, 25 June, he was reported to have returned from his assignment and to have been "censured for not fully obeying instructions."

With Reno's information in hand, Terry then dispatched Custer with twelve companies of the Seventh to explore the Rosebud River. The young colonel—Custer was then thirty-seven—was offered a detachment of Crow scouts, which he accepted. But a battalion of the Second Cavalry and a pair of Gatling guns were refused. On the morning of 22 June, the Seventh Cavalry struck out on its own, deeper into hostile territory.

Custer's written orders from Terry, which have since become controversial, are quoted fully here:

> Camp at Mouth of Rosebud River
> Montana Territory, June 22, 1876

> Lieut.-Col. Custer, 7th Cavalry
> Colonel:
> The Brigadier-General Commanding directs that, as soon as your regiment can be made ready for the march, you will proceed up the Rosebud in pursuit of the Indians whose trail was discovered by Major Reno a few days since. It is, of course, impossible to give you any definite instructions in regard to this movement, and were it not impossible to do so, the Department Commander places too much confidence in your zeal, energy, and ability to wish to impose upon you precise orders which might hamper your action when nearly in contact with the enemy. He will, however, indicate to you his own views of what your action should be, and he desires that you should conform to them unless you shall see sufficient reason for departing from them. He thinks that you should proceed up the Rosebud until you ascertain definitely the direction in which the trail above spoken of leads. Should it be found (as it appears almost certain that it will be found) to turn towards the Little Horn, he thinks that you should still proceed southward, perhaps as far as the headwaters of the Tongue, and then turn towards the Little Horn, feeling constantly, however, to your left, so as to preclude the possibility of the escape of the Indians to the south or southeast by passing around your left flank. The column of Colonel Gibbon is now in motion for the mouth of the Big Horn. As soon as it reaches that point it will cross the Yellowstone and move up at least as far as the forks of the Big and Little

Horns. Of course its future movements must be controlled by circumstances as they arise, but it is hoped that the Indians, if upon the Little Horn, may be so nearly inclosed by the two columns that their escape will be impossible.

The Department Commander desires that on your way up the Rosebud you should thoroughly examine the upper part of Tullock's Creek, and that you should endeavor to send a scout through to Colonel Gibbon's column, with information of the result of your examination. The lower part of the creek will be examined by a detachment from Colonel Gibbon's command. The supply steamer will be pushed up the Big Horn as far as the forks of the river is found to be navigable for that distance, and the Department Commander, who will accompany the column of Colonel Gibbon, desires you to report to him there not later than the expiration of the time for which your troops are rationed, unless in the meantime you receive further orders.

> Very respectfully,
> Your obedient servant,
> E. W. Smith, Captain, 18th Infantry,
> Acting Assistant Adjutant-General.[1]

The controversy was part of the argument over whether Custer had disobeyed orders, which arose almost immediately after the battle. Those who supported him have pointed to one passage: "the Department Commander places too much confidence in your zeal, energy, and ability to wish to impose upon you precise orders which might hamper your action when nearly in contact with the enemy." Those who hold this view dismiss as suggestions rather than orders the passage that begins with "he will, however, indicate to you his own views."

But others point out that such phrases as "the Department Commander desires" are the military man's style of expressing direct orders, and that Custer did not proceed far enough southward to be able to examine the headwaters of the Tongue.[2] When he came across the trail of the Indians heading due west toward the Big Horn, he followed it; was this a situation in which he was "nearly in contact with the enemy," justifying his departure from the written orders? A scout, George Herendeen, had been supplied Custer for the purpose of informing "Colonel Gibbon's column, with information of the result of your examination"; Herendeen was never sent anywhere and spent 25, 26, and 27 June with Major Reno, under siege.

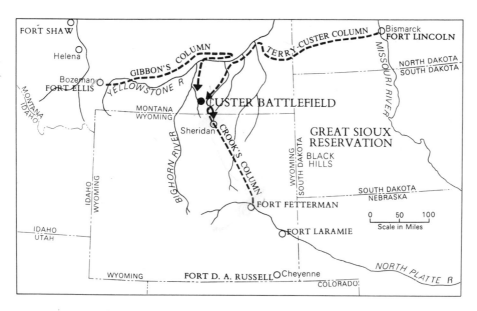

Three-Pronged Movements in the Sioux Campaign of 1876

All during June 1876, events and Custer's own mistakes conspired against him. Experience in the plains wars indicated that the problem in fighting the Indians was not so much defeating them as it was getting them to stand and fight at all. This was one of Custer's major worries. Moreover, he had been led to believe by the Bureau of Indian Affairs not to expect more than 800 hostile braves; in fact he was probably confronted by over 4,000. Finally, he was not aware that many of his future foes were armed with Winchester repeating carbines, whereas his own men were equipped with single-shot Springfields. Thus of the three major aspects of military intelligence—the number of the enemy, their willingness to fight, and their armament—Custer was ignorant and unprepared.[3]

As soon as the westward swing of Custer's march began, his Crow and Arikara scouts detected signs of a great many more Sioux and Cheyenne than had been expected, and they reported this information to the officers. For whatever reason, however—for mistrust of his men or overconfidence— Custer thought that the Crows were overestimating the force of the hostiles, and he increased the rate of his march, from twelve miles a day on 22 June to thirty on 23 June, and the same number on the next day as well. But the width of the trail, the extent of horse droppings, and the number of campsites did finally, despite all his initial optimism, force him to raise his estimate of the enemy's strength to about 1,500.[4] Still, he felt as he always had: the Seventh Cavalry was equal to any assignment given; it alone could defeat all the Indians of the plains.

That his scouts felt differently is obvious from snatches of conversation reported after the battle. Bloody Knife, who was killed in the valley with Reno, was notably pessimistic about the chances of the expedition when he saw the extent of the trail left by the Sioux he was following:

> It is as I have told Long Hair: this gathering of the enemy tribes is too many for us. But he will not believe me. He is bound to lead us against them. They are not far away; just over this ridge, they are all encamped and waiting for us. Crazy Horse and Sitting Bull are not men-without-sense; they have their scouts out, and some of them surely have their eyes on us. Well, tomorrow we are going to have a big fight, a losing fight.[5]

This passage, often quoted by those who wished to prove that Custer's strategy was extremely foolish in everyone's eyes but his own, should be carefully weighed before it is accepted. The remarks were repeated, several years after the fact, by a man who probably agreed with their intent. And, in subsequent years, when the outcome of the battle justified Bloody Knife's fears, he might (however unconsciously) have been made to appear more the prophet than he actually was—one who died in the battle he had predicted would be a fatal one. The nature of the battle indeed was such that the second-guessing was easy to come by; had Custer won, it would never have been so prolific. Nevertheless, after all these questions have been raised, we should not necessarily disbelieve that several of the Indians had doubts about the success of the mission; or that the famous scout Charlie Reynolds (who also, unfortunately, died the next day) was entirely misquoted when he is alleged to have agreed with Bloody Knife: "I feel as he does: tomorrow will be the end for me, too."[6]

If the scouts were morbid about their chances against the Sioux, their pessimism seems not to have infected the soldiers in the regiment. Sergeant Charles A. Windolph, who later fought alongside Benteen on Reno Hill, remembered with some clarity the confusion of night marches and the exhaustion he felt as the men neared contact with the enemy:

I think we must have stumbled along in the dark for around three hours, when a halt was ordered. None of us had had much sleep for several days, so we were glad to lie down and grab a little rest. When daylight came around 3 o'clock we made coffee, but the water was so alkaline we almost gagged on it.

It was around 8 o'clock when we got orders to saddle up. We marched about ten miles, when we were halted in a sort of ravine. We'd been told to make as little noise as possible and light no fires. There'd been no bugle calls for a day or two.[7]

On the evening of 24 June, still some miles from the Indian village, Custer's plan of action was to ride to the summit of a divide which commanded the Little Bighorn valley, rest his regiment and the pack train there during 25 June, and then ride into battle at dawn of 26 June. No doubt he recalled the great success he had in a dawn raid on the Cheyenne village of Black Kettle several years earlier. Lieutenant Charles A. Varnum, the officer in charge of the scouts, was sent with a few Crows to a high point of ground fifteen miles southeast of the eventual battlefield, called the Crow's Nest, from which the valley, and the river the Indians called "Greasy Grass," and the ridge beyond could be seen through the scorching summer haze. From this point the scouts could make out the stands of woods which lined the Little Bighorn, and on the far bench the largest encampment they had ever seen on the plains: it stretched for about three and one-half miles in length, clinging to the contours of the snaking stream, and sprawled across the valley floor, at points perhaps one-half mile to the west. In this village—really a small portable city—were representatives of all the Teton Sioux: Hunkpapas, Oglalas, Miniconjou, Sans Arc, Blackfoot, and Brule; there were also northern Cheyenne and several eastern Sioux. And beyond the village swarmed a gigantic pony herd.

Curiously, Lieutenant Varnum could not himself see anything of the village his scouts reported to him, nor could Custer when he was summoned to the Crow's Nest. The land is very dry and dusty, and any slight breeze is likely to stir up a fog of alkaline dust. But whether he could see the village or not, Custer realized that he must be near it. This aggravated the disagreement between the general and his scouts, although the discussion was a brief one since Custer was not one to tolerate opposition. Again, this exchange is frequently cited as yet a further instance of Custer's refusal to see the truth, though it lay much larger than life before him on the sprawling plains. Mitch Bouyer is said to have told Custer, atop the Crow's Nest: "General, we have discovered the camp, down there on the Little Horn. It is a big one! Too big for you to tackle! Why, there are thousands and thousands of Sioux and Cheyennes down there." But Custer is said (in this tale) to have been unimpressed, and like the Custer of the Arthur Penn movie, to have replied, "I shall attack them! If you are afraid, Bruyer [*sic*]—." Mitch was not afraid, and he is supposed to have replied, with petulant reluctance, "I guess I can go wherever you do."[8]

Small parties of Sioux were seen shortly, and when one of the sergeants went back over the trail to recover a box of rations that had fallen from a mule, he found several braves prying it open. Clearly the regiment had been discovered, and Custer made another of the several fateful decisions he was to make during that march: with the likelihood, as it must have seemed, that the Indian village would soon disperse, he decided not to wait until 26 June but to attack at once. It was then the morning of 25 June 1876.

The regiment mounted and moved forward to reconnoitre the village and to attack it. Trooper William Slaper, at that time a young soldier who was to see his first action later that day with Reno's battalion, remembered some of the hardships of frontier soldiering on that morning:

> As I recall, it was about daylight when we halted and made coffee. I remember this very distinctly, because I did not get any of the coffee, having dropped down under a tree and fallen asleep, holding on to the bridle-rein of my horse, and I did not awaken until called into line. We did not unsaddle at this halt, so the animals secured but little rest.[9]

By noon the regiment had crested a divide at a point about twelve to fifteen miles southeast of the village, and here Custer paused to divide the command. Until that moment he had kept personal control over all of the men; now he assigned Captain Frederick Benteen one battalion composed of companies H, D, and K—about 125 men in all—and directed him to break from the trail heading due west and to explore the valley, the ridge beyond, and the valley beyond that. At a subsequent Board of Inquiry Benteen referred to these orders as "valley hunting *ad infinitum*."[10] In his private papers, apparently written before the Board convened, Benteen elaborated:

> From my orders, I might have gone on twenty miles without finding a valley. Still, I was to go on to the first valley, and if I did not find any Indians, I was to go on to the next valley. Those were the exact words of my order—no interpretation at all.... We knew there were eight or ten thousand Indians on the trail we were following.[11]

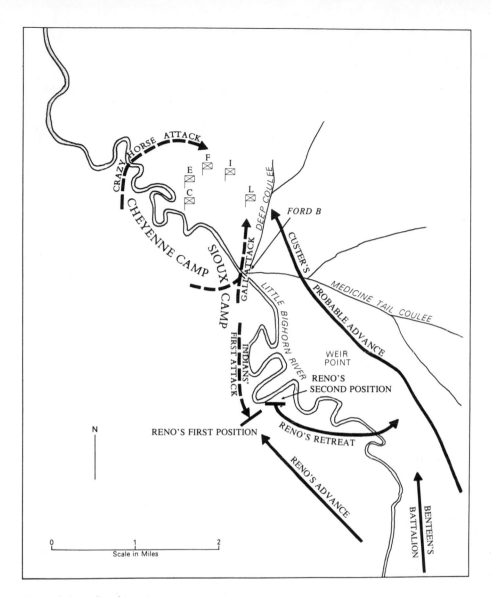

CRAZY HORSE ATTACK

F

I

E

C

L

CHEYENNE CAMP

SIOUX CAMP

GALL ATTACK

DEEP COULEE

FORD B

CUSTER'S

MEDICINE TAIL COULEE

PROBABLE ADVANCE

LITTLE BIGHORN RIVER

INDIANS' FIRST ATTACK

WEIR POINT

RENO'S SECOND POSITION

RENO'S FIRST POSITION

RENO'S RETREAT

N

RENO'S ADVANCE

BENTEEN'S BATTALION

0   1   2
Scale in Miles

Custer's Last Battle

But in an official letter to Reno just after the battle, he said that it was his understanding that if no Indians were seen he was, on his own judgment, to return to the regiment.[12]

Although this reasoning may be senseless, Benteen was a good soldier who was nearly in combat. His commanding officer seldom bothered to explain his decisions to his subordinates; he expected them merely to obey. And obey Benteen did, though his heart was not in it:

> But through the whole oblique to left, the impression went with me that all of that hard detour was for nought, as the ground was too awfully rugged for sane Indians to choose to go that way to hunt a camp—or, for that matter, to hunt anything else but game.
>
> I knew that I had to come to some decision speedily, when I had given up the idea of further hunting for a valley being thoroughly impregnated with the belief that the trail Custer was on would yield quite a sufficiency of Indians.... My real, Simon-pure, straight orders were to *hunt that valley*; but I didn't know where the valley was, and thought that perhaps an opportunity might happen later to search for it.... So, shouldering the responsibility of not having found the valley, I pitched off with the battalion at a right oblique to reach the trail Custer's column had followed.[13]

Sergeant Windolph was with Benteen's battalion as it turned off the trail at a left oblique, and his impression of the country and of the value of the mission approximated his commander's:

> It was rough, rolling country we were going over, and it was hard on the horses.... Even to the troopers in the ranks, it looked as if we were on a wild-goose chase.... I suppose we must have been going up and down those rugged hills for the best part of two hours before we turned back on the Custer trail. I think we covered somewhere around seven or eight miles.[14]

With the regiment thus weakened, Custer advanced with the remaining nine companies to a point within clear sight of the valley and the village, which loomed to his scouts like a small but very ominous city. About four miles south of it he then detached his second-in-command, Major Marcus Reno, with three companies (A, G, and M, about 140 men) and ordered him to charge the near (southern) end of the village. Later Reno recalled that Custer assured him that he would be "supported by the whole outfit."

Reno's battalion moved out, crossed over to the left bank of what is now called Reno Creek, and then felt its way down the sloping bluffs to a ford of the Little Bighorn. It was then about 2:30 P.M. The companies paused at the ford to water their horses and to tighten up their formation. Several Indians had been seen fleeing across the valley floor toward the village, and since the soldiers' basic assumption was that the Indians would try to escape, Reno had been ordered to charge. Of this moment, the Oglala chief Low Dog has said:

> I was asleep in my lodge at the time. The sun was about noon (pointing with his finger). I heard the alarm, but I did not believe it. I thought it was a false alarm. I did not think it possible that any white men would attack us, so strong as we were. We had in camp the Cheyennes, Arapahoes, and seven different tribes of the Teton Sioux—a countless number. Although I did not believe it was a true alarm, I lost no time getting ready. When I got my gun and came out of my lodge the attack had begun at the end of the camp where Sitting Bull and the Uncpapas were. The Indians held their ground to give the women and children time to get out of the way.[15]

Once across the river and into the valley, however, dust swirls made it clear to Reno that the Indians, rather than retreating, were advancing toward his men to attack. For trooper William Slaper it was his first combat:

> Soon commenced the rattle of rifle fire, and bullets began to whistle about us. I remember that I ducked my head and tried to dodge bullets which I could hear whizzing through the air. This was my first experience under fire. I know that for a time I was frightened, and far more so when I got my first glimpse of the Indians riding about in all directions, firing at us and yelling and whooping like incarnate fiends, all seemingly naked as the day they were born.[16]

Interpreter Fred Girard was sent back to notify Custer of this unexpectedly brisk resistance. Reno deployed the battalion into line and advanced at a trot; with contact imminent the troopers were ordered into a gallop. But within sight of the first tepees of the village through the swirling dust the numbers of the Indians became so great—Reno later said—and the firing so heavy, that a halt was ordered, and the companies dismounted and deployed as skirmishers. Lieutenant Varnum, detached from Company A to command the scouts, soon became separated from them; whether they fled when the firing became heavy or in other ways lost Varnum is not known for certain, but whatever the reason the lieutenant found himself alone:

> When the skirmish line was formed I saw a good many excited men shooting right up in the air.... Reynolds was very anxious to get a drink of whiskey out of his flask, and, to tell the truth, I was paying more attention to that than I was to the Indians.... The heavy firing came from these Indians in the front, and it was so rapid that there were bullets in the air all the time. As a rule, the Indians fired from their ponies; they were just scampering around us and pumping those Winchester rifles into us as fast as they could.[17]

First Sergeant John Ryan of Company M recalled the following scene:

> When we got to the timber we rode down an embankment and dismounted. This was where the channel of the river changed and was probably several feet lower than the level of the prairie. We dismounted in haste, number four of each set of four holding the horses.
>
> We came up onto higher ground forming a skirmish line from the timber towards the bluffs on the other side of the valley and facing down stream in the direction of the Indian camp. This was our first view of the Indian camp from the skirmish line. Some of the men laid down while the others knelt down.
>
> At this particular place there was a prairie dog town and we used the mounds for temporary breast works. We got the skirmish line formed and here the Indians made their first charge. There were probably 500 of them coming from the direction of their village. They were well mounted and well armed. They tried to cut through our skirmish line. We fired volleys into them repulsing their charge and emptying a number of their saddles.... Finally when they could not cut through us, they strung out in single file, lying on the opposite side of their ponies from us, and then they commenced to circle. They overlapped our skirmish line on the left and were closing in on the rear to complete the circle.[18]

Reno had understood his commander to mean that support would soon follow from where he had just ridden through his own command, and he frequently looked back to the line of bluffs across the Little Bighorn for the support from "the whole outfit" which he assumed would be forthcoming. But in the meantime his already weak position on the valley floor was deteriorating further. The battalion's right flank, where Sergeant Ryan was fighting, was anchored in the woods that lined the river and was soon under fire from Indians who used the brush for cover from which to rake it; the left, which was never sufficiently well-manned to extend across the valley, was easily outflanked as Sioux and Cheyenne horsemen circled around and began attacking the battalion's rear. Few men were actually lost, but the situation quickly became so dangerous that Reno ordered the line swung counterclockwise until it rested against the stand of trees. By the time this maneuver was effected it was probably close to 3 P.M.

Hundreds of screaming Sioux and Cheyenne continued the attack across the valley at Reno's front and through the woods at his rear, and their attack was pressed so vigorously that within half an hour in the woods yet another withdrawal was ordered. Although this move was, in subsequent and calmer moments, called a charge (albeit to the rear), semantics could not disguise the loss of control by Reno over his men in the timber and the hurried mounting and flight toward the river and the bluffs beyond. So confused was the execution of this maneuver that several men were left in the wood, never having heard the command to mount. The battalion formed a column, and as it rode back toward the river, Reno at the head, the Indians swarmed around them, picking off troopers whose guns were empty, clubbing down stragglers, and waiting at the ford to slaughter the troopers whose horses wallowed in the river bottoms. Sergeant Ryan recalled, "As we cut through them the fighting was hand to hand, and it was death to any man who fell from his horse, or was wounded and was not able to keep up with the command."[19] Most of the men made it safely to the far bank and, spurred no doubt by fright, speedily scrambled up the steep bluffs.

On the other side, Chief Two Moon had mixed impressions of blurs of massed and confused men and horses, and of individual tableaux:

> I got on my horse and rode out into my camp. I called out to the people all running about: "I am Two Moon, your chief. Don't run away. Stay here and fight. You must stay and fight the white soldiers. I shall stay even if I am to be killed."

The winner's portrayal is much like Indian narrative accounts: the actions of individuals do not seem to be subordinated to any overriding motif, yet in the confused welter of soldier, Indian, and horse, the swarming incoherence of battle is conveyed. Amos Bad Heart Bull, like all of the victors, is ignorant of the white chief's identity.

I rode swiftly toward Sitting Bull's camp. There I saw the white soldiers fighting in a line. Indians covered the flat. They began to drive the soldiers all mixed up—Sioux, then soldiers, then more Sioux, and all shooting. The air was full of smoke and dust. I saw the soldiers fall back and drop into the river-bed like buffalo fleeing. They had no time to look for a crossing.[20]

In his personal papers made public only after his death, Reno gave a fairly full account of his withdrawal from the stand of timber. In Reno's own account the retreat was more orderly and controlled. His remarks were written nearly ten years after the event, when the actions of his men were likely to seem more militarily disciplined than others remembered them:

I mounted my command and charged through the reds in a solid body. As we cut our way through them, the fighting was hand to hand and it was instant death to him who fell from his saddle, or was wounded. As we dashed through them, my men were so close to the Indians that they could discharge their pistols right into the breasts of the savages, then throw them away and seize their carbines, not having time to replace their revolvers in their holsters.... Our horses were on the dead run with, in many instances, two and three men on one animal. We plunged into the Little Big Horn and began the climb of the opposite bluffs. This incline was the steepest that I have ever seen horse or mule ascend.... In this narrow place (the ford) there were necessarily much crowding and confusion and many of the men were compelled to cling to the horses' necks and tails for support, to prevent their being trampled to death or falling back into the river. Into the mass of men and horses, the Indians poured a continuous fire and the Little Big Horn was transferred into a seeming river of human blood.[21]

For trooper Slaper the ford crossing was one of the traumatic highlights of the battle; it was where the regiment, aside from Custer Ridge, suffered the heaviest casualties:

I did not strike the river at the regular ford, so was compelled to jump my horse into the stream at a point where the bank was about six or eight feet high. My animal nearly lost his footing when he struck the water. As I glanced about me, the first thing that engaged my attention was trumpeter Henry Fisher of M Troop, riding in the river some distance up, with Lieut. Benny Hodgson hanging to one stirrup.... As Fisher gained the opposite bank, dragging Hodgson at the end of his stirrup, and the latter was trying to struggle up the incline, another shot rang out and Hodgson dropped. I did not see him move again, and suppose he was killed right there.[22]

Slaper's details were subsequently found to be at odds with other eyewitnesses to the same event, but he was right in the essential fact: Lieutenant Hodgson did die in the stream.

Meanwhile Benteen, having found his "valley hunting" mission fruitless, and having carried out his orders to the letter at least, returned to the trail of the regiment and followed it to the bluffs where he discovered Reno and his exhausted command, sorely beleaguered, their ammunition nearly gone. The time was probably around 4 P.M., and Benteen's men stopped to solidify the defensive position to which Reno had been so hastily driven, and to share their cartridges. Reno's battalion had lost more than thirty men, and the rest were demoralized. Benteen's accidental arrival was, for the salvation of the entire command, fortunate. The officers then speculated about the whereabouts of Custer; the location of his five companies, and certainly their fate, was unknown and unimagined. Neither Reno nor Benteen dreamed that their commander was already fighting desperately for his life, perhaps at that moment already dead.

Some firing was still heard from upstream, and impatient with what he felt to be Reno's lethargy, Captain Thomas B. Weir on his own authority ordered his own company (D) in the direction of the firing—from "Custer Ridge." He and his men advanced about one mile to a pointed and precipitous hill that now bears his name, Weir Point; from there he later reported that with his service issue binoculars he could see Indians riding around on ponies, dragging objects behind them which Weir could not make out. Whatever Weir's precise intention may have been—it was in general to head in the direction of the firing and to support Custer—swarms of Indians soon massed at this front and on his flanks so that he had no alternative but to retreat. Other elements of the Reno-Benteen command arrived to support and protect his withdrawal, and by nightfall the remnants of the Seventh Cavalry clung for their lives to the bluffs, where they remained for the next thirty-six hours.

In reconstructing the battle, Captain Benteen recalled the fighting on the hill in quite specific terms, and with the experienced eye of a professional soldier:

After our line was formed, it was about as lively a fire as you would like to stand up under. You had only to show a hat or a head, or anything, to get a volley. It was about 5:30 when we got our line finished, or maybe later. We were under fire from two and a half to three hours.

The Indians had picnic parties as large as a regiment standing around in the river bottom, looking on. There was no place to put them. Fully two thousand were around us, waiting for a place to shoot from!

The Indians close to us did not expose themselves. The only thing you could see would be the flash of a gun. They came so close that they threw arrows and dirt over at us with their hands, and touched one of the dead men with a coup stick.[23]

In later years the survivors remembered Benteen walking cooly up and down their lines, encouraging them, cautioning them to save ammunition, directing their fire. For Sergeant Windolph, lying on his face in the sand, the picture was less heroic:

My buddy, a young fellow named Jones, who hailed from Milwaukee, was lying alongside of me. Together we had scooped out a wide shallow trench and piled up the dirt to make a little breastwork in front of us. It was plumb light now [on the morning of 26 June] and sharpshooters on the knob of a hill south of us and maybe a thousand yards away, were taking pot shots at us.

Jones said something about taking off his overcoat, and he started to roll on his side so that he could get his arms and shoulders out, without exposing himself to fire. Suddenly I heard him cry out. He had been shot straight through the heart.

The lead kept spitting around where I lay. Up on the hilltop I could see a figure firing at me from a prone position. Looked like he was resting his long-range rifle on a bleached buffalo head. I tried my best to reach him with my Springfield carbine but it simply wouldn't carry that far....

Somehow I always figured that the sharpshooter who had killed Jones ... must have been a renegade white man.... He could shoot too well to have been a full-blooded Indian.[24]

During that time there was further opportunity to reflect on the movements and fate of Custer and the five companies with him. Where were they? Several men thought that their commander had abandoned Reno just as he did not or could not rescue his subordinate, Major Joel Elliott, several years before in the Washita battle. Reno had expected Custer to "support him" by following him into the valley. Why Custer did not, if he ever intended to, is not known. One of the more charitable suggestions is that of Colonel William A. Graham, who speculated that Custer, on seeing the great number of braves riding to meet Reno, may have assumed that most or perhaps even all of the Sioux were already in action, and so decided to attack the village in flank or in its rear. Thus, this speculation goes, Custer continued along the bluffs opposite the village until he reached the ridge where his men still lie.

Even the route Custer took from a point opposite Reno's valley position, where he was seen to wave his hat as if in encouragement to those below, to the ridge of the Last Stand is unknown and a matter of controversy. It is known that Custer's men fired heavily from behind Nye-Cartright ridge, about a mile to the east of Custer Ridge, in the direction of the ford in the middle of the village (Ford B),[25] across which Gall led his Sioux in an attack. From this point the battalion arrived at or may have been driven to the ridge where it was annihilated. There were no human survivors: no officer, soldier, scout, or civilian lived through his portion of the battle. The Indians survived, of course; but they were not interested in what was happening on the hill in terms that would interest future white historians. They were concerned, rather, with the enemy directly in front of them; each brave moved about as he wished, and fought an individual war with the cavalry, as he had fought every other battle in his experience. This is clear from Two Moon's description of the attack on Custer's battalion:

> Then the Sioux rode up the ridge on all sides, riding very fast. The Cheyennes went up the left way. Then the shooting was quick, quick. Pop-pop-pop very fast. Some of the soldiers were down on their knees, some standing. Officers all in front. The smoke was like a great cloud, and everywhere the Sioux went the dust rose like smoke. We circled all around them—swirling like water around a stone. We shoot, we ride fast, we shoot again. Soldiers drop, and horses fall on them. Soldiers in line drop, but one man rides up and down the line—all the time shouting. He rode a sorrel horse, with white legs and white forelegs. I don't know who he was. He was a brave man.
>
> Indians keep swirling round and round, and the soldiers killed only a few. Many soldiers fell. At last all horses killed but five. Once in a while some man would break out and run toward the river, but he would fall.

> At last about a hundred men and five horsemen stood on the hill all hunched together. All along the bugler kept blowing his commands.... And then the five horsemen and the bunch of men started toward the river. Then man on sorrel horse led them, shouting all the time. He wore a buckskin shirt and had long black hair and moustache.... One man all alone ran down toward the river, then round up over the hill. I thought he was going to escape, but a Sioux fired and hit him in the head. He was the last man. He wore braid on his arms.[26]

The might of the Sioux and Cheyenne was overwhelming, devastating, and complete. None of Custer's party lived to tell of their fall; yet it has been just this absence of known facts that has encouraged America's collective imagination.

One of the most frequently used clues as to the movements of the five companies on Custer Ridge is the two-foot marble markers which are said to show where each officer and trooper fell. A detail from the seven surviving companies buried the dead. But the regiment had only two shovels, and the makeshift implements they found were really inadequate for a deep burial. A year later, a newly formed Company I returned to the field to reinter the enlisted men and to remove the bones of the officers for reburial elsewhere. They found that many of the skeletons had become exposed. Some bodies had been dug up by wolves, others pillaged by human scavengers. A stake was driven in the ground near the head of each soldier. Later, marble markers were placed where the wooden stakes protruded.[27]

These markers may be the best indication we have as to final position of the troops under Custer's command, but even they are not to be trusted. It should be remembered that it was the Indian's custom to strip and sometimes to mutilate their foe's bodies. Such indecencies were perpetrated upon Custer's men; why should we assume that the soldiers' bodies were left in the position where they had been found? Why would an Indian be meticulous about replacing a body in its original spot after it had been tossed about to remove the clothing? And then, Captain Weir said that he saw Indians on ponies riding around in circles, dragging unidentified objects on the ground: were they bodies? When Captain C. K. Sanderson, commander of the 1877 burial detail, reported many of the bodies uncovered, how careful was he about replacing the bodies where they were originally buried? More important, would he have known where they had been originally buried or where they originally fell? The bodies were exposed for a year; wolves and men had scavenged them; rains and snows had come and gone (and Montana has an

Custer was not fool enough to fight from the hilltop. His marker—with those of his brother, several officers, and several troopers of Company F—is down the slope of the ridge facing the Little Big Horn. Here, where the markers are huddled closest, the "Last Stand" was probably made. Custer's marker, in the middle of a cluster of three, stands in the center of this photograph; several markers are above it.

abundance of both), and nearly all the men died on the slopes of the hill: how had rain, and melting snow, and storms affected the exposed bones? We will never know, but our ignorance in this matter should also caution us about drawing too many hard conclusions from the position of the markers. These marble stones came last, after the bones of the enlisted men had been reburied once again under the monument which sits atop Custer Ridge. Finally, how carefully and accurately were the marble stones set relative to the wooden stakes?

Despite the multiple possibilities for error, a few details may be reasonably surmised. It has been assumed from the direction of the regiment's march that the first Indian assault crashed upon companies I and L, defending the southeast portion of the ridge. The position of the soldiers' bodies and the proximity of their officers suggests an organized defense, and it seems that though these men had little time to prepare for their defense, they were more brilliantly led than the others. Captain Myles Keogh and Lieutenant James Calhoun commanded. Fragments of C, E, and F troops were scattered over a wide area between Custer's final position and the river, some of the men having been slain nearly 2,500 feet from the site of Custer's body. It is generally assumed that these companies could not offer effective resistance and were haphazardly, though entirely, wiped out.[28]

From personal experience at the battlefield I think it just as likely that companies C and E were with Custer at the crest of the ridge and were ordered to attack the village (immediately to their front), but after advancing about 2,000 feet were halted by heavy firing from their front and from a rise on their right flank. Recent discoveries of expended Indian cartridges on the flank support—indeed, inspired—this view. From many positions on the field amid the marble markers of the men of C and E companies the monument atop Custer Ridge is not even visible. Furthermore, a ravine about ten to fifteen feet deep flanked E Company's position, and my guess is that the men of this company very suddenly found themselves overwhelmed—by Indians pouring out of the ravine (in which several troopers' bodies were found) and by those firing on them from the rise on their right and front. Cut off from their commander and the rest of the battalion (F Company remained on the hill, and Calhoun and Keogh were then fighting for their lives, out of sight and more than 3,000 feet in the rear), it would be surprising if the men did not panic. That their officers, Tom Custer, Captain Yates, and Lieutenant Smith, were found among the bodies around their colonel suggests that it is at least possible that when the companies were overrun the officers fled for their lives back in the direction they had last seen Custer's guidon. Obviously they found him, and there, near the crest of the ridge, they joined him in death.

According to an alternative reconstruction by Jerome Greene,[29] when Custer's five companies reached a point opposite the middle of the village, a further division into two battalions was made: C and E companies were ordered to attack with F, I, and L in reserve to the rear. The attacking battalion was quickly repulsed, though supported by the companies on Nye-Cartright ridge, which explains the many cartridge finds there. But from that moment on, the action was a divided one: F, I, and L moved rapidly to Custer Ridge, where the latter two units had a few seconds to prepare a defense. The assault battalion, further to the south because of the momentum of their attack, retreated toward the summit of the ridge at an angle, the angle to the crest of the ridge in which their bodies were found. Unlike many conjectures about the battle, Greene's is plausible, was conceived after a careful study of shells and bones found on the field and in the area, and does not have a pet thesis or a reputation to defend. In this respect Greene is in select company, for after the battle had ended, even before the Seventh could be refitted, one of the most intense and celebrated controversies in American history had begun.

Many people analyzed the decisions and actions of Custer himself, and Reno's behavior was closely scrutinized by almost as many: had he done all that he should have in the valley attack, and shortly after, when he ordered the disastrous retreat from the woods? Should he and his men have sallied forth from their hilltop fortifications in the direction of the firing they heard downstream? Reno was accused of incompetence in the valley, cowardice when he withdrew, even of treason on the hill. He was also said to be drunk (by a civilian mule driver) and to have suggested a running withdrawal, abandoning the wounded (by Benteen, in private). But even in the matter of the controversy, Reno was only second to his commander.

The controversy swirling around the memory of Custer mainly concerned two questions: his alleged disobedience of orders in being at the Little Bighorn on 25 June in the first place, and his disposition of troops when contact with the enemy was imminent. As with nearly every other facet of this fascinating chain of events, no one is to be trusted implicitly. Everyone directly involved in the event also had his own interests to preserve. General Alfred Terry, Custer's commander and the expedition's senior officer, had a distinguished Civil War record but was—even by his own admission—relatively green when it came to fighting that entirely different enemy, the Indian. He was an intelligent man, a pleasant, self-sacrificing officer who inspired the love of his subordinates (Major James Brisbin once said to him: "You have more sense in your little finger than Custer has in his whole body. You underrate your own ability and overrate Custer's"); but most impressive of all, he was modest. He knew that with his limited experience in the plains wars he should rely heavily on the judgment of those of his subordinate officers who had seen previous action. After the debacle became known, Terry was one of the first men blamed by the public which thought, as reflected in some newspapers, that Custer divided his force on Terry's orders. This we know was not true; yet Terry's statements would still be held suspect by those who felt that he was shifting blame for the disaster from his own shoulders to those of his dead subordinate: had not Terry allowed Custer to exercise his judgment when "nearly in contact with the enemy," and was it not Terry's plan to attack an Indian force, whose whereabouts were not exactly known, from three angles?

Terry explained his plan of action in his official report to his Departmental Commander, Civil War paladin Philip Sheridan:

> This plan was founded on the belief that at some point on the Little Big Horn a body of hostile Sioux would be found; and that although it was impossible to make movements in perfect concert, as might have been done had there been a known fixed objective to be reached, yet, by the judicious use of excellent guides and scouts which we possessed, the two columns might be brought within co-operating distance of each other, so that either of them which should be first engaged might be a "waiting fight"—give time for the other to come up. At the same time it was thought that a double attack would very much diminish the chances of a successful retreat by the Sioux, should they be disinclined to fight.[30]

Colonel John Gibbon, marching from Fort Ellis in western Montana toward the Terry-Custer forces with whom he would cooperate, had a similar understanding of the operation. Of the role of his counterpart in the action Gibbon wrote:

> Lieutenant Colonel Custer was instructed to keep constantly feeling toward his left, well up toward the mountains, so as to prevent the Indians escaping in that direction, and to strike the Little Big Horn, if possible above (south) of the supposed location of the camp.... The department commander strongly impressed upon him the propriety of not pressing his march too rapidly.[31]

Custer's responsibility for carrying out these plans was nowhere condemned as sharply as in a letter from Major James Brisbin to Captain Edward Godfrey. Brisbin was a great admirer of General Terry and held Custer, as it happens, in great contempt. It was Brisbin's battalion of the Second Cavalry which Custer refused to allow to accompany the Seventh in its march up Tullock's Creek. The occasion of his letter (now famous to Custer buffs and historians of the battle) was a reply to Godfrey's recent article in the January 1892 issue of *Century* magazine, which gave that officer's account of the battle. "Now, my dear Godfrey," Brisbin began, "you, as well as I and all of us, know that Custer did disobey his orders, if not in letter, then in spirit, and I think, and have ever thought, in letter as well as in spirit."[32]

Brisbin did not always recall the events of June 1876 with impeccable accuracy; so although his word is (again) not to be taken without question, his citations of events and conversations to which others were a party are convincing. Brisbin felt strongly that Custer should have continued his march south along Tullock's Creek rather than swinging west when he struck the Indian Trail. To Brisbin, Custer had taken much too liberally the instructions he had from Terry allowing him to depart from the plan if he saw "sufficient reason" for doing so.

The scout Herendeen (Brisbin wrote to Godfrey) had been attached to Custer's column specifically for liaison; when the Seventh reached Tullock's Creek, Herendeen was to leave and notify Gibbon. And, Brisbin insisted, this is exactly what the scout intended to do. He rode up to Custer at the head of the column and said, "General, this is the Tullock, and here is where I am to leave you and go down it to the other command." But the general gave Herendeen no reply; and after a while, "seeing he was not wanted, he fell back and followed along, nor did Custer ever speak to him again, though he knew Herendeen was there to go down the Tullock and communicate with us by Terry's orders."

Brisbin—it was then sixteen years after the battle—attributed Custer's fall to those reasons that were by then commonplace. At what point Brisbin reached these conclusions is not known; but in the letter to Godfrey he claimed that Custer was "jealous of Gibbon," had "just made an ass of himself by his groundless attack on Belknap" and was "smarting under the rebuke of the President" for it, and that, finally, Custer refused the assistance of the Second Cavalry and the Gatling guns because (quoting Custer in a conversation with the Sixth Infantry's John Carland), "I want all the glory for the 7th." Brisbin's comment about this alleged conversation says as much about his relationship with Custer as anything: "The insufferable ass got it!":

That Custer knew the strength of the Indians I know.... Gibbon had sent Bradley over in the night with scouts... and Bradley had done so.... Their camp was seven miles long up the Rosebud, and we all put them at 1,000 to a mile, or 7,000 souls, with 3,000 fighting men.... All this Custer knew, for I told him all about it, and cautioned him to be careful.

One of the final remarks in this very damaging letter might well serve as a memorial to the Seventh Cavalry: after dispatching Custer, Terry was said (again by Brisbin) to have had second thoughts, and so he ordered his own forces to advance rapidly toward the Little Bighorn because he was said to be "uneasy about him and his command." On the evening of 25 June the Little Bighorn was still several miles away, but Terry's exhausted infantry could move no further. Brisbin remembered Terry approaching him, inquiring about the condition of his cavalry, and then saying, "you know I promised Custer we would be in the Little Big Horn valley on the 26th of June."

Benteen agreed that Custer had disobeyed orders. And while one should be skeptical about any of that acerbic officer's opinions of his commander, bitter as was the animosity between them, the early date of this letter (4 July 1876) indicates that it was Benteen's first, and decidedly genuine, impression. Sincerity is not necessarily truth; but at the very least the captain reflected the clear feeling among the officers of the regiment in the aftermath of their defeat:

> Had Custer carried out the orders he got from General Terry the commands would have formed a junction exactly at the village, and have captured the whole outfit of teepees, etc., but Custer disobeyed orders from the fact of not wanting any other command—or body to have a finger in the pie—and thereby lost his life.[33]

When Benteen wrote this letter to his wife he was in the field near the *Far West*. He had met with Major Brisbin at the Little Bighorn battlefield, and he may have conversed with him further at the *Far West* base camp; it would be unusual if he had not. Is it possible that the idea of Custer's disobedience was spread here from one officer to the other (but from whom to whom?); but the question can only be posed, not answered.

In any event, when General Sherman wrote his official report on the battle, the matter of alleged disobedience was not raised; rather, the man who once

thought that war was hell and that the only good Indian was a dead one sum-
marized the battle in purely tactical terms:

> Had the Seventh Cavalry been kept together, it is my belief it would
> have been able to handle the Indians on the Little Big Horn, and
> under any circumstances it could have at least defended itself; but,
> separated as it was into three distinct detachments, the Indians had
> largely the advantage, in addition to their overwhelming numbers. If
> Custer had not come upon the village so suddenly, the warriors would
> have gone to meet him, in order to give time to the women and
> children to get out of the way, as they did with Crook only a few days
> before, and there would have been, as with Crook, what might be
> designated a rear-guard fight, a fight to get their valuables out of the
> way, or, in other words, to cover the escape of their women, children
> and lodges.[34]

3

The Legend

When Colonel Gibbon's relief column from the north joined forces, on 27 June, with the survivors of the Seventh Cavalry's disastrous encounter with the Indians, one of the first duties was to bury the dead. This most disheartening of military obligations was performed during the late afternoon, nearly forty-eight hours after the cessation of firing on Custer Ridge. Digging graves for the regiment's slain was difficult not only psychologically but physically as well because only two shovels could be found at hand, and the powdery soil of the plains caved in as soon as it was scooped out. Emotionally it was much worse: all of the rescuers as well as the survivors were shocked to learn that five companies of regular cavalry had been wiped out by the Indians, none more surprised and shocked than Reno and Benteen and their men, though their position for nearly two days had been only a scant four miles away.

The bodies of Custer and his battalion—only 202 were found of the approximately 215 who had ridden into battle with him—had been lying under the broiling sun for nearly two days. Many of the men had been badly mutilated. Others had been killed with hatchets and clubs and their condition was indistinguishable from those who had been more systematically maimed. And nearly all had been stripped of their clothing and arms. Repellent though the scene was, the location of the bodies on the field was historically valuable in that it provided some of the little evidence of what happened in the battle, for from the location and position of the already rotting and maggot-eaten corpses one might guess, at least in very broad outline, at the course and nature of the battle.

Custer's third-in-command, Captain Frederick Benteen, hero of the defense of the hill to the south, was among the burial detail; his description of the field and his impressions of it are among the most articulate:

> I arrived at the conclusion then as I have now that it was a rout, a panic, till the last man was killed; that there was no line formed. There was no line on the battlefield; you can take a handful of corn and scatter it over the floor and make just such lines. There were none; the only approach

> to a line was where five or six horses were found at equal distances like
> skirmishers.... Only where Custer was found were there any evidences of
> a stand. The five or six men I spoke of were where Capt. Calhoun's
> body was.... The position of the bodies on the Custer battlefield in-
> dicated that the officers did not die with their companies.... That shows
> they did not fight as companies. All the officers, except Col. Keogh,
> Capt. Calhoun, and Lt. Crittenden were on the line with Custer. That
> would not be the fact if the command was overwhelmed while making a
> stand.[1]

The field has surprising little dips and rises, though one would generally
describe it as undulating, and it is covered with scrub and sagebrush. Some
gnarled oak grow in a ravine several hundred feet to the front of Custer's
final position, and cottonwoods edge the Little Bighorn River, but otherwise
there is little natural cover. The area is not a good one for defensive actions,
especially for cavalry under attack by dismounted warriors; Custer's position
on the slope of the ridge was exposed and, as Lieutenant Wallace (who had
fought with Reno in the valley) later pointed out, "There was no way [for
Custer] to protect himself."[2]

Yet the first description of the battlefield, allegedly by an eyewitness, told a
somewhat different story. Although the account cited below was from an editorial in the *Chicago Tribune,* it tells essentially the same narrative as nearly
every other newspaper in the country, having been received from the wire
services:

> Since the murder of Gen. Canby by the Modocs the country has not
> been more startled than it was by the announcement that Gen. Custer
> and five companies of his regiment, the Seventh Cavalry, had been
> massacred by the Sioux Indians in a ravine ... the Indians outnum-
> bering our troops ten to one. Gen. Custer had personal and soldierly
> traits which commended him to the people. He was an officer who did
> not know the word fear, and, as is often the case with soldiers of this
> stamp, he was reckless, hasty, and impulsive, preferring to make a
> dare-devil rush and take risks rather than to move slower and with
> more certainty. He was a brave, brilliant soldier, handsome and
> dashing, with all the attributes to make him beloved of women and ad-
> mired of men; but these qualities, however admirable they may be,
> should not blind our eyes to the fact that it was his own madcap haste,

Some aspects of the legend—in this case the sword—appeared early. The Bencke
lithograph is one of the first illustrations of Custer at the Little Big Horn.

rashness, and love of fame that cost him his own life, and cost the service the loss of many brave officers and gallant men....

They drew him into an ambuscaded ravine.... In this instance, three hundred troops were instantly surrounded by 3,000 Indians, and the fatal ravine became a slaughter-pen from which but a few escaped.... No account seems to have been taken of numbers, of the leadership of the Sioux, of their record of courage and military skill. (7 July 1876, p. 4)

Why this particular version of the battle was written we will never know for certain. A ravine, about fifteen feet deep in places, does point from the Little Bighorn toward the center of Custer's position. Several soldiers of E Company were found in it; they had been dragged there or they had fled to it, but by no means could it be imagined that any sizable portion of the five companies were "ambuscaded" there. One possibility lies in the well-known Indian liking for ambushes; they had frequently been able to draw soldiers as well as civilians into them, and stories of ambushed whites were quite common in those days. Just a few days before General Crook, in the "battle of the Rosebud," had been criticized by the press for sending his cavalry into a ravine whose commanding hills swarmed with Indians. Plausibly, newsmen who had never seen the field might well imagine that Custer had fallen for the old Indian ruse, certainly an explanation which the American public had been conditioned to accept.

Within a very short time yet another account of the battle emerged, whose author was equally imaginative and equally ignorant of both the terrain and the position of the fallen troopers. But this account was to survive, almost to this day:

All along the slopes and ridges and in the ravines, lying as they had fought, line behind line, showing where defensive positions had been successively taken up and held till none were left to fight, lay the bodies of the fallen soldiers; then huddled in a narrow compass horses and men were piled promiscuously.

At the highest point of the ridge lay General Custer, surrounded by a chosen band.... Here behind Colonel Yates' company, the last stand had been made, and here, one after another, these last survivors of General Custer's five companies had met their death. The companies had successively thrown themselves across the path of the advancing enemy and had been annihilated. Not a man has escaped to tell the tale, but the story was enscribed on the surface of the barren hills in a language more eloquent than words.[3]

Which version was right? The only authentic survivor was Captain Myles Keogh's horse, Comanche; the Indians had scattered over Canada or else had returned to reservations and were understandably reticent about their role in the battle; and the barren hills were silent. Chief Low Dog, who did survive the battle and who in fact had participated in the fighting on Custer Ridge, said that "no white man or Indian ever fought as bravely as Custer and his men."[4] But Thomas B. Marquis quoted another Indian eyewitness as thanking "the everywhere spirit" who "caused the white men to go crazy and turn their guns upon themselves."[5]

More than any single man or collective legend, writer Frederick Whittaker greatly expanded and romanticized the fight. He had met Custer several years before in the New York offices of *Galaxy* magazine, for whom the general was serializing his *Life on the Plains*. Whittaker, a Civil War officer in a New York volunteer cavalry regiment, became an ardent admirer of Custer's thereafter, devoting most of his energies of the next ten years not only to deifying Custer but to assailing the surviving officers of the Seventh. Whittaker had not been within 2,000 miles of the battlefield, and so he drew upon newspaper accounts for his description of the fight. It shows his romantic imagination at its most inventive, this man who wrote over one hundred nickel and dime novels (with such exotic titles as *Bel Rubio, Old Double Sword,* and *The Russian Spy)*. Custer's Last Stand as Whittaker envisioned it is worth quoting at length for its details as well as for the spirit of this immensely influential biography:

> *The men lay dead in an irregular line, Calhoun and Crittenden in place in rear.* This is the order of the tactics, the officers watching and moving along their line, within a few feet. There they fell, every man in his place. They were ordered to stay and be killed, to save the day, and they obeyed orders. Who then was Calhoun, that he was the first ordered to die?... He was Custer's dearest of all friends on earth; he was the bravest and gentlest of men.... Did Calhoun murmur—did he question the order?...
>
> Not a murmur came from that one, and the other showed by this first sacrifice that he placed the country above all his earthly loves. "The country needs; I give her a man who will do his duty to the death: I give them my first brother. I leave my best loved sister a widow, that so the day may be saved. Farewell."

Well did Calhoun redeem that trust. Every man in his place, no faltering, no going back, Calhoun's company kept on firing till the last cartridge was gone, and one by one dropped dead in his tracks under the fire of the swarms of Indians that kept dashing to and fro before them, firing volley after volley. Down they went, one after another, cheered up by this grand figure of DUTY, young Calhoun encouraging them to the last.... Calhoun, with his forty men, had done on an open field, what Reno, with a hundred and forty, could not do defending a wood. He died like a hero, and America will remember him, while she remembers heroes....

The sight of Calhoun's men, dying as they did, had nerved Keogh's men to the same pitch of sublime heroism. Every man realized that it was his last fight, and was resolved to die game. Down they went, *slaughtered in position,* man after man dropping in his place, the survivors contracting their line to close the gaps. We read of such things in history, and call them exaggerations. The silent witness of those dead bodies of heroes in that mountain pass cannot lie.[6]

Sioux chief Red Horse, who was at the battle, had quite a different version:

The soldiers charged the Sioux camp about noon. The soldiers were divided, one party charging right into the camp. After driving these soldiers across the river, the Sioux charged the different soldiers [i.e., Custer's] below, and drove them in confusion; these soldiers became foolish, many throwing away their guns and raising their hands, saying, "Sioux, pity us; take us prisoners."[7]

What really happened? Benteen was there, but his testimony may have been colored by his long and deep hatred for Custer, which he did not conceal in later years. And perhaps there was some truth to the claim that at the Reno Board of Inquiry, three years after the battle, the regiment's officers "closed ranks" to protect the survivors and the reputation of the regiment. If Custer's battalion was quickly slaughtered, it weakened the charge against Reno that he failed to come to his chief's rescue. Whittaker, on the other hand, had no ostensible stake in the battle or its aftermath, but for reasons which are not now known, he cherished Custer and his memory with fanatic jealousy. Custer could do not wrong; Reno, or Benteen for that matter, could do no right.

For anyone who would know the course of the battle the Indian accounts offer as little help as the white man's. When considering them, it should be borne in mind that nearly all of them were rendered many years after the battle and that there are several good reasons, besides faulty memory, why they would be distorted. Many Indians felt that if they admitted being in the battle or killing white soldiers they would be punished. Others used the opportunity to brag about their imagined adventures, such as the dozen or so Indians who each subsequently claimed to have killed Custer. Still others found it an advantage to tell reporters and interviewers what they thought their white questioners wanted to hear.

From the point of view of the white men, however, the absence of any facts or accurate accounts enabled them to see the battle as they chose, as they wished it had happened. For example, Lieutenant Lee, the recorder at the Reno Board of Inquiry, summed up the "prosecution's" case, in part, with the thoughts that must have reflected those of nearly all white America; Captain Benteen's description of the battle as a probable "panic" and "rout" grated several already inflamed nerve endings:

> The well-known capacity, tenacity and bravery of Gen. Custer and the officers and men who died with him forbid the supposition of a panic and a rout. There was a desperate and sanguinary struggle in which the Indians must have suffered heavily. From the evidence that has been spread before this Court it is manifest that Gen. Custer and his comrades died a death so heroic that it has but few parallels in history. Fighting to the last and against overwhelming odds, they fell on the field of glory. Let no stigma of rout and panic tarnish their blood-bought fame. Their deeds of heroism will ever live in the hearts of the American people, and the painter and poet will vie with each other in commemorating the world-wide fame of Custer and his men.[8]

One of the ways in which painters vied with each other to depict a glorious Custer was to show him with a sword in his hand, brandishing it above his head, about to slash the nearest Indian. Actually, sabers were rarely used in combat by American cavalry after the Civil War, even though they were still issued. They were next to useless in combat, having been made obsolete by projectile warfare. They were heavy and bulky; cavalrymen used them mainly to tether their horses in the absence of picket lines. In 1864 alone over 90,000 sabers were "lost" by their owners, a practice that was halted only when the War Department held soldiers pecuniarily responsible for their "losses."[9] There is some evidence that the Seventh used this weapon in its raid on the Cheyenne at the Washita in 1868, but little testimony that sabers were used at the Little Bighorn campaign of 1876.

Yet countless illustrations, most popularly the Anheuser-Busch lithograph, show Custer armed with a sword; it is one of the most "romantic" of weapons, indelibly associated with cavalry, with glamour, with *eclat* and heroism. It remained the symbol of the cavalry long after the carbine and pistol had replaced it; and when the tank replaced the horse and cavalry units became known as "armored cavalry," the crossed sabers remained as the service's insignia, superimposed on the frontal silhouette of a tank. Shaw's sensible and unromantic hero Bluntschli is challenged to a duel and chooses machine guns rather than swords: he is the practical soldier, not the romantic. And Hemingway's Catherine Barkley explained about her late fiancé, "...I remember having a silly idea he might come to the hospital where I was. With a sabre cut, I suppose, and a bandage around his head.... Something picturesque." Frederick Henry replied that Italy "is the picturesque front."

"Yes," she said. "People can't realize what France is like. If they did, it couldn't all go on. He didn't have a sabre cut. They blew him all to bits."[10]

For such a hero as Custer, a saber was the only acceptable weapon.

And it was just as necessary that his destruction be on a hilltop. Again, the painters have done the most to perpetuate this detail of the legend, but unlike the detail of the sabers, there is an element of truth here. Custer's Last Stand was made on a steep ridge, but unlike the battle of the artists, Custer did not stand on the summit. He and about thirty men who were found with him appear to have been surrounded, a large number of Sioux under Crazy Horse having circled behind him to support the frontal attack of Gall. Under those circumstances it was natural for him to have sought high ground, but it would have been inexcusably inept, even suicidal, for him to have stood on the top of the hill to give the attacking Indians a 360-degree field of fire. The situation was desperate enough, being under fire from the enemy in front and on both flanks. The placement of the marble markers are, we know, unreliable, but Custer's is about fifty feet down the slope from the summit, and it is not the highest on the hill: eight or nine others are higher up. The markers are carelessly sited; but they are the only evidence we have concerning the position of Custer's body, and the burden of proof is on those who depict him on the hilltop.

Our associations with hill and mountain tops range far beyond the death of the glorious vanquished. Raglan's heroes die on elevations also. Hemingway found the air in the mountains pure and cool. It is also closer to heaven; thus Jesus prayed "The Lord's Prayer" from a hilltop, and Moses received the Ten Commandments while similarly elevated. It was upon this tradition that

Martin Luther King, Jr., based his last sermon, "I Have Been to the Mountaintop." And the flag-raising at Iwo-Jima, perhaps the most famous battle photograph of World War II, was no doubt enhanced because of its hilltop setting. That this stirring picture was posed merely illustrates that its photographer had an eye for appropriately heroic surroundings.

To a certain extent, the visual elevation of Custer was almost inevitable. Edgar Paxson's famous painting, *Custer's Last Stand,* is a good example of how terrain is used to support meaning. Fanatic attention was paid to every historical detail of the battle. The troopers are armed with Springfield carbines and Colt pistols, the Indians with authentic clubs and hatchets. The uniforms are historically correct, even the horses are branded "U.S." Custer is in the center of the painting dressed as he was on his last day: in a fringed buckskin jacket and trousers, cavalry boots and gauntlets, and the red kerchief of his own design.

Custer stands in the center of the canvas, slightly above the horizontal, conspicuous in his bright buckskins from the darker objects in cavalry blue and war paint around him. He is also conspicuous because he is standing upright, whereas all around him his soldiers are kneeling, or sitting, or lying outstretched. And all of the figures in this crowded painting are gazing, firing, or charging either toward or away from the central focus he represents. Above his bare head stretches Montana's big sky, blotched by smoke and dust.

Custer had had his famous flowing shoulder-length locks cut before the Little Bighorn expedition, and this too is shown by Paxson, clearly as Custer's head and shoulders are outlined against the clouds and smoke of battle. The painting is in the tradition of those two famous portrayers of Napoleonic martial and battle scenes, the Baron Gros and Meissonier, especially in Paxson's treatment of sky and smoke. But in his lack of splendor or magnificence, in his disorderly composition, in his concern for realism, Paxson is very much his own man.

Poised above Custer's head the blue and gold regimental standards are carried aloft, their staffs angling away from the central figure while drawing further attention to it. Even without these flags Custer is the main object of Paxson's work: in the relative brightness of his costume, in his stance itself, in that he is the center of the canvas, he is by far the most important figure. The flags highlight his importance further. Unfortunately for the realism of the scene, at that precise moment in the hero's life, the standards were several miles to the rear, furled in their casings with the pack train. Even the most scrupulous attempts at realism seem, for artistic reasons alone, to result in the glorification they sought to minimize.

Accurate in most details, Edgar Paxson framed the scene's hero with the regiment's standards. Actually, they were several miles away, furled in their cases, when Custer died. But to present this striking visual effect, Paxson compromised truth for the sake of art.

More Americans know Custer and his Last Stand through the F. Otto Becker
depiction than through any other medium. Anheuser-Busch has produced nearly
one million copies of Becker's work, a number that rivals the *Mona Lisa* or the *Last
Supper*.

Paxson's Custer is the most prominent figure at the "moment" in the battle when the depicted scene takes place, but it is not certain that he will be the last to die. He seems to be clutching a wound in his left side (Custer was actually wounded there), but in such a way that even this gesture is defiant: with his other hand he levels his pistol at the onrushing Indians. The ground is cluttered with individual scenes: a trumpeter blows some call (charge?) while a soldier near him holds his hand to his ear. Other soldiers are reloading their guns, or firing them, or are caught in the instant of being struck down. The scene is a confused welter of bodies, red and white, living and dead. Here again Paxson's realism gets in the way of art: there are no compositional lines of movement, there is no motion in the structure of the painting; rather, we are induced to examine each figure separately as he struggles around Custer who, if not the last to die, will be among a very small group which holds out to the end.

In the most famous illustration of the Last Stand, F. Otto Becker's *Custer's Last Fight*, he is again the center of the action, and again probably the last soldier to keep his feet. The source of inspiration of this version, made popular by the Anheuser-Busch Company in barrooms around the country, was an 1886 painting by Cassilly Adams. It did not enjoy a great success, hanging in a St. Louis barroom for several years until the owner died and the beer manufacturer confiscated it as a creditor's asset—at least according to one story.[11] Becker copied this composition in 1895 but made many changes on his own. Adams had his Custer on a small ledge at the foot of several puny hills, which Becker changed to a more realistic representation of Custer Ridge. In the big blue Montana sky float cotton clouds, each a gigantic cumulus moustache. Most important for the scene's realism, Becker added many figures and enlarged the scope of the scene. But still Custer is prominent, in the middle of the composition, heroic in the gold of his buckskins, eye-catching in his flowing red scarf and emerald undershirt, a trace of which shows from under the jacket. He raises over his head a sword from which three Indians are already reeling: Frederick Whittaker has been felt here too. All around Custer his men are dead (some already stripped and scalped), dying, or about to be killed. Custer will be last. Becker's work has nothing to recommend it aesthetically, yet over one million copies of it have been circulated by the Anheuser-Busch Company, which says much about the fame and romance of the scene depicted.

Perhaps the most widely viewed version of the Last Stand in which Custer is the last man to be struck down is not in a painting at all but in the Warner Brothers movie of 1941, *They Died With Their Boots On*. The dashing Errol Flynn was appropriately cast as the "Boy General," which alone was

Flynn is Custer. No actor was ever better cast as the "Boy General." Though others, particularly Wayne Maunder, looked more like the original, none have had Flynn's flair, audacity, or panache. Custer himself could not have chosen better.

enough to ensure the movie's popularity. It does not take much belaboring to realize that Flynn was much like Custer. This vaguely biographical film was widely reviewed and widely seen: *Life* magazine devoted several pages to it, together with still pictures taken from the film, the last of which shows Flynn standing amid a thick circle of "Indian" and "cavalry" extras, alone in his defiance of the enemy. Moments later, as Flynn stands with one hand on the regimental guidon and the other holding his sword, a Sioux bullet strikes him to the ground.

The idea that the General should be the last of his command to be slain had occurred to others much earlier. The *New York Herald* of 26 July 1876, in a story datelined Bismarck, North Dakota, gave the account of an Indian scout who was said to have seen the battle, and to have seen Custer die nearly last. Several different writers attributed this detail to "an Indian scout," probably the young Crow, Curly, who had quickly become famous as the "lone survivor." J. C. Talman wrote that Custer was among five men left on the hilltop before the Indian's final rush, and that "Yellow Hair" was not scalped out of the Sioux' respect for a great opponent; F. A. Kinsey also quoted Curly, who said in this version, quite specifically, "General Custer was the last man to be killed." And another "survivor," white scout Alfred L. Chapman, confided to Kinsey that he had watched the battle from a nearby hill and had seen Custer fall last.[12] And this is just a brief sample.

The most tactless self-proclaimed "lone survivor" was Willard Carlisle, who, in a moment of glaring insensitivity, wrote to Custer's widow, Elizabeth, of his fantasy:

> When the red-skins made their rush down the valley that morning, I did not know what was going on, but I climbed a hill and there in full sight was the terrible battle going on. The Indians road [*sic*] around in a circle and kept picking off the horses first.
>
> After they had shot all the horses, killed or wounded them, then they started to close in on the men, and they done it slow too.
>
> Custer and his men then retreated to a small rise of ground, and there made their last stand.
>
> Those of the red-skins who had lost their horses, closed in on foot and slowly but surely they picked off the white men, one by one, until at last only the brave General Custer was left with his comrades dead around him.
>
> One sweep of the saber and an Indians head was split in two, one flash of his revolver, his last shot, and a red-skin got the bullet between the

eyes, then he fell with a bullet in the breast, the last of that brave band.

I saw him within 15 minutes after he was shot, and there was still a smile on his face. Perhaps he was thinking of his home, his beloved wife or Mother. Who can tell.[13]

How could the last of the soldiers to fall be determined? We should understand that such a determination cannot be made, but that in the absence of facts or knowledge we have recreated the story of the Last Stand according to our imaginations. As it happens, Indian accounts of the battle indicate that Custer could not have been the last to fall. Kate Bighead, who saw much of the fighting, has already been cited. And what of the man in "braids" whom Low Dog said nearly escaped? Or the five men on horses who dashed for the river when all of their comrades had fallen? Of course it might also be true that Custer was killed early in the fight as he led his men in an attack on Ford B, and that several Cheyennes carried his body to the top of the hill, presumably to glorify him; that story is still told by the tribal historian of the Crows, Joe Medicine Crow, at Crow Agency, Montana.

Major Will A. Logan, former superintendent of Glacier National Park, claimed to have been the first white man to see the Custer battlefield, recalling that an "Irish or Irish-American" officer was the last to die; perhaps it was Captain Myles Keogh, commander of I Company:

> ... and now—at last—the unconquerable white warrior chieftain fought and bled ... alone. A dramatic situation beyond human conception.[14]

The Indians held a council during a lull in the fighting; some were for letting this last soldier alive go free, but he merely leveled his blazing pistol at them in reply to their entreaties. The Indians attacked in "charge after charge," but he killed so many of them that they believed that his position was filled with "ghost troopers." In a final charge he shot six Indians with his last six bullets: "In his right hand gleamed a cavalry saber, his left gripped the butt of an empty six-shooter." He killed three more with his saber before the Indians swept over him. Logan claimed, unhandsomely, that Custer took his own life in the early stages.

The brave Red Top insisted that he killed the last soldier, a man who was alive and resisting long after Custer had been killed.[15] About a dozen of the men who rode with Custer to the ridge on 25 June were never found, and Indian testimony has it that a small detachment bolted for freedom and succeeded in riding several miles from the field before they were overtaken and killed:[16] were they the last? Or was it First Sergeant Butler, whose body was found several hundred feet west of the ridge? We are not certain whether Butler was a messenger sent for help, the last man alive who nearly made good his escape, or simply a soldier slain far from his unit for reasons we cannot evaluate.

The last man might even have been Lieutenant Harrington, one of the minor, yet most fascinating, mysteries of the battle. Several Indians reported that when Custer's battalion had been nearly finished off, an officer (a soldier with braid on his shoulder) broke through the lines in a desperate attempt to escape. He rode for several miles, a few braves in pursuit, but they finally gave it up as hopeless. At the moment when they decided to return to the battle, they saw "Lieutenant Harrington" rein in his horse and, although he had made good his escape, he drew his revolver and put a bullet through his brain.

Lieutenant Harrington's body was never found, and he has frequently been identified as this suicide. The usual explanation is that although fear drove him to attempt escape, his pride and honor (he was a newly graduated West Pointer) prevented his continuing to live in disgrace—for having deserted his comrades, and for his "cowardice." These reasons have the advantage of being obvious, and thus believable, but why did "Harrington" shoot himself so soon? One would expect guilt or shame to act slowly upon him, not having so compelling an effect for several days or perhaps even months. This man shot himself while still in the excitement of the escape when, if fear had driven him to flee in the first place, fear should still have been controlling him; the Sioux who were following him had just given up the chase and he had only seconds, presumably, to reflect upon the consequences of his now successful escape.

Another alternative is more interesting though perhaps no more convincing. Experiments with rats dropped into large tanks of water show that their heartbeat rates decrease, rather than increase, until they die. It appears as though they expect to die, and then, in despair, do so. Voodoo curses are based on the same psychological principles: the "cursed" person expects the magic to have a mortal effect and slowly "kills" himself in the expectation of inevitably dying.

Hospital patients who have been told that they may die on the operating table during major surgery often respond to successful surgery strangely. They may experience a sense of omnipotence and feel that having survived the surgery nothing more can harm them. Other such patients are quickly given to fits of severe depression; even suicide is a possibility several days after the successful completion of dangerous surgery. Before the operation the patient expected to die and had prepared himself to give up his life; when the operation ends and he is still alive, he cannot cope with the situation and "decides" nevertheless to give the life which he had been prepared, in great anguish, to sacrifice all along. Was this the fate of the "Harrington" at the Little Bighorn? Like the obvious explanations offered earlier, this one suffers from the time element: hospital patients have days to think over their fates, and Harrington had seconds. But perhaps aspects of both are involved: prepared to lose his life, he nevertheless escaped; and then guilt and shame overcame this young West Pointer, and so he gave the life he thought he would lose earlier, gave it to make up for his having left his comrades on a field of hopeless slaughter. We will never know—we may never even know who this man was—but his fate is one of the most fascinating sidelights of the battle.

Another aspect of this legend is the great number of enemy killed by the hero. Thus before Custer and his remaining men succumb, they take with them into Valhalla a frightful toll of the enemy. This part of the story is revealed early: in a letter to his wife dated only ten days after the battle, Captain Benteen assured her that Custer's men killed more than their own number of the enemy. He says that he knows because a Crow scout has survived the battle and has reported this consoling detail. Reporter John Finerty also quoted Curly, who was supposed to have seen "that the field was thickly strewn with the dead bodies of the Sioux who fell in the attack—in number considerably more than the force of soldiers engaged." Curly "was satisfied that their loss exceeded 200 killed, besides an immense number wounded."[17]

The truth is that the number of Indian casualties could never be accurately determined, neither at this battle nor at any one in which the red men were allowed to recapture their own dead and wounded. The main reason lies in the nature of Indian warfare. They did not fight in a line and they hardly fought as units as European and American armies knew that concept. To a large extent each Indian brave was on his own in a fight. His chief had a vague military responsibility over him: at the beginning of Reno's attack, for instance, Sioux and Cheyenne chiefs had to rouse and round up the able-bodied men in their tribes and urge them into battle. Areas of responsibility were never precisely defined. Braves followed their chiefs in the broader aspects of tactics such as attack and retreat, but the detailed execution of such maneuvers was left to the individual. The Indian did not need a highly organized military organization to perform superbly.

Indians were trained to fight from the time they were old enough to ride and shoot. Hunting and raiding comprised a great portion of their way of life, and survival on the plains depended on their individual ability. Ranged against them, the whites were not nearly as well prepared. Thirty to forty percent of the Seventh who rode into combat on 25 June were recruits who had never heard, let alone fired, shots in anger.[18] The others may have been veterans, but "veteran" did not imply the degree of proficiency it does today. Many troops went into battle during the Civil War without having fired their weapon in training (although ammunition was more plentiful then). Moreover, many veterans of the frontier had little or no experience fighting Indians, and perhaps little experience with their weapons.

Army efficiency took other forms. The trooper did have his sergeant, who was responsible to an officer; casualties could be counted, and noted, and recorded. On the Indian side, a reconstruction of casualties depended on the memory of the chief. But from these recollections, the number of Indians killed was nothing like 200. Kill Eagle estimated the loss at 14 men to Reno and 39 to Custer with 14 more dying shortly after in camp, but he also placed the number of wounded at a very high 600. Crazy Horse put the number of killed at 58, the wounded at 60; Crow King remembered that from 30 to 50 died, and Low Dog thought it was 38.[19] The most careful reconstructions of the battle by white historians, taking these numbers into account, place the Indian loss at around 35,[20] making it the easiest and most one-sided victory in the plains wars.

One of fantasies to emerge from the battle was Custer's alleged call for help. Sergeant Butler, whose body was found well west of the field, was one of the many thought to have been the last man to die, though he is better known as the battalion's messenger sent with a desperate S.O.S. to Reno and Benteen. There is no evidence for such a belief. At about the time that the Reno fight had begun, Custer sent Sergeant Daniel Kanipe back to the pack train to urge that Captain McDougall rush forward with the mules. A little later, as the battalion rode down Medicine Tail Coulee, trumpeter Giovanni Martini was given a note, written by adjutant W. W. Cooke: "Benteen, Come on. Big village. Be quick. Bring packs. W. W. Cooke. P.S. Bring pacs." No other message or messenger got through to the remainder of the regiment, but again, in the absence of facts or evidence, a legend has been created.

A second story that has gained some currency has far more imagination and entertainment value. According to this version, Custer had time to write a far lengthier note than the one given to Martini; this message never got through but was found on the body of a trooper much later, "stained with blood and with bullet holes through it." The text follows:

```
                    Reno
for god's sake send help
I am surrounded and can't
break through I have only
40 troopers left and can't hold
out another minute I          nt
send          lan to you as he's
dead          enough bucks
   evacuate you          osition
   join me for gods sake
hurry. Am entrenched along
the Big Horn Basin
                    Custer.
```

Incredible as this "last message" is, in terms of its style, in terms of length by a presumably desperately beleaguered Custer, it had wide circulation. The *Cadiz* (Ohio) *Republican* published it on 23 June 1932 in its "Custer Memorial Dedication Supplement," and it had previously appeared in Don C. Seitz' *The Dreadful Decade,* as well as Milton Ronsheim's *The Life of General Custer.* And Colonel Graham reprinted it in *The Custer Myth.*[21]

Of all the legends and fantasies that developed about the battle, none were as destructive of the reputations of survivors as persistent claims of cowardice or treachery on the part of various members of the command. Before details of the battle were known, the public turned to the "natural" villains in such a disaster—"traitorous" Indian scouts—even though such villains had no existence. A story that was current almost immediately following the battle told of one of Custer's Arikara scouts, a young man named Billy Cross, who throughout the expedition was in constant and secret communication with the Sioux, and who double-crossed the cavalry by leading them through a specially prepared field where the prairie grass had been knotted by squaws to trip up the horses.[22] Cross was said to have deserted shortly after the fight began, after having informed Custer that the Indian village was small and the fight would be easy. The informant, allegedly a sergeant in the Sixth Infantry (with Gibbon), said that the Indians concealed their village with wicker breastworks. This sergeant then went on to describe the Indian dead, "piled up like cordwood, so effective was the fire of the soldiers." And then the final fantasy: he reported a large number of white men with the Indians, and he claimed that English was spoken on both sides.

One of the hostiles who had been shot was masked; when the mask was removed a white face with "a long, gray, patriarchal beard" was revealed. Finally, the bugle calls on the Indian side that were heard during the fight were thought to have been performed by a trumpeter discharged dishonorably from the Second Infantry in 1868.

Stories of renegades who either betrayed Custer or helped Sitting Bull were also common; renegades are, after all, a kind of traitor. The *Chicago Tribune* (31 July 1876, p. 5) cited information given them by former Indian Agent Charles Jones reporting that Sitting Bull had been planning a war against the whites as far back as 1872, and he was being assisted—even directed—by "a very talented white man, a Mexican, whom the Indians know by the name of Frank," and who was believed to have been the "presiding genius over the movements on the field" at the Little Big Horn. The stories of Indian betrayals are with us yet; in 1952, Everett E. McVey published a four-page pamphlet called *The Crow Scout Who Killed Custer,* a title that adequately describes the content.[23]

No doubt many personal and patriotic needs demanded the story that such a hero as Custer, and such a regiment as the Seventh, in combat with "savages," should be betrayed; it would be much harder to believe that they had met their deaths in a fair fight. This is nothing more than scapegoating. The situation clearly demanded a traitor, or at the very least a coward, and the man eventually convicted by the public's opinion—Custer's second-in-command, Major Marcus Reno—was personally destroyed, first by public and personal venom, later by a dishonorable discharge.[24]

When the first vague outline of the events of the battle became known to the public, anger and frustration were initially directed against Custer's immediate commander, Brigadier General Alfred Terry, and his ultimate commander, President Ulysses S. Grant, but soon the public's hatred was directed at Captain Frederick Benteen. Finally, and lastingly, it settled on Reno. That Custer's supporters and admirers should decide that the battle was lost through treason or cowardice was probably inevitable; that Reno was selected as scapegoat was less so, though circumstances had conspired against him too. The idea may have begun before the battle was ever fought, though the reaction was not reported until later: on 13 July, a week after news of the disaster reached the newspapers, the *New York Herald* printed a lengthy article on Reno's scouting mission, which preceded Custer's attack by several days. The reporter felt that Reno had both gone too far and not gone far enough. He, and six companies of his regiment, had been ordered to scout the Powder and Tongue rivers for the hostiles known to be in the general area. But once on their trail he proceeded as far west as the Rosebud, nearly endangering the security of the entire command by giving warning to the Indians that a large body of soldiers was in the area. Nevertheless, having scouted so far in excess of his orders, Reno failed to follow the trail to the Indian camp and then into battle: his "determination forsook him" because of his "faint heart." Rumors of a court-martial, the article continued, were rife at headquarters.

As far as the public was concerned Reno then made the fatal error of standing to fight in the valley, then leading an orderly retreat to the edge of the timber, then another, though less orderly, to the bluffs at his rear. And to the public, his last fatal error was in not rushing away from his hill position to the sound of the guns downstream. Perhaps, in later life, when everything and everyone had turned against him, Reno might have agreed that he should have charged. But who is to know what might have been done that day? The Indians were whipping up dust clouds and the troopers could not see very clearly through them. Sergeant Ryan thought that the enemy numbered 500; Reno himself put the figure at 800 to 1,000. The hostiles swarmed around his left flank and the firing was intense. Yet in the first thirty minutes or so, Reno suffered only three casualties, and two of them because the soldiers' horses bolted into the Indian "lines." A thousand men banging, and whizzing, and clubbing away, and only three men hit!

There is further conjecture about his position in the woods. Reno saw himself outnumbered and the enemy creeping steadily closer through the brush, setting it afire, killing the scout Bloody Knife at his side, splattering his brains over Reno's own uniform. Antagonists like Whittaker thought that Reno might have held the woods forever, despite his depleted ammunition. The most dispassionate view (though not necessarily the one nearest the truth) is that of Colonel Graham:

> ... some thought Reno lost his head, and Custer with it: some thought he should have marched at once to the sound of the guns, without waiting for the ammunition packs. But those most critical of his conduct in the valley were not with him in the valley; and those who held that he should have marched at once ignored his lack of ammunition.
>
> But when these same men took the witness stand and swore to tell the truth, all, as good soldiers, even the more experienced Benteen, to whom Reno himself looked for advice and counsel, recognized and acknowledged that it was Reno and not one of them who was the Commanding Officer; that it was he, not they, upon whom rested the duty and responsibility of decision.... And not one of them, not even the unfriendly

Godfrey, was able to put his finger on any act that he was willing to stigmatize upon his oath, as cowardice.[25]

Still controversial are the characterizations of Reno's deportment on the hill: was he terrified or merely excited (as most men would be under the circumstances) or, as Colonel Graham himself put it, were "his overwrought nerves still in the ascendant, his self-control gone?"[26] Benteen arrived at the very last minute; he ordered the ammunition divided among all the men while Custer was at that moment dying—or was he already dead? The impatient Captain Weir rode off in the direction of Custer's firing but got no nearer than three miles when the force of the enemy drove him back. Could Custer, by that time, have really been saved?

On 8 July, General T. L. Rosser, C.S.A., former classmate of Custer's at West Point and Civil War opponent in the Valley campaign, wrote a public letter which was reprinted in the *Chicago Tribune:*

> I feel that Custer would have succeeded had Reno with all the reserve of seven companies passed through and joined Custer after the first repulse. I think it quite certain that Gen. Custer had agreed with Reno upon a place of junction in case of a repulse of either or both of the detachments, and instead of an effort being made by Reno for such a junction as soon as he encountered heavy resistance he took refuge in the hills, and abandoned Custer and his gallant comrades to their fate...
>
> As a soldier I would sooner today lie in the grave of Gen. Custer and his gallant comrades alone in that distant wilderness, that when the last trumpet sounds I could rise to judgment from my post of duty, than to live in the place of the survivors of the siege on the hills. (P. 5)

Rosser had little idea of how the battle was fought. He imagines Reno with all of the remaining companies of the regiment, standing aloof on a distant hilltop, not the actual shattered three companies in the valley, nor the reinforced six after Benteen arrived. The seventh company, guarding the pack train, did not arrive until even later. And where is this "place of junction" to which the separate columns were to retreat after an initial repulse? It is all in Rosser's imagination. Reno replied personally, was rebuffed by further imagination and heady patriotism ("I would sooner today lie ...") and wisely replied no more.

Accuracy in evaluating the battle was bound to suffer because of Reno's role as "foil." If Custer fought bravely on the hilltop, why did Reno not fight (and die?) as bravely in the valley? Custer had hurled headlong into the assault; Reno had first withdrawn to the timber, then fled to the hills. If one was to say that Custer was a rash fool, then by contrast Reno could be called a prudent one. But if one assumed that Custer was brave, dashing, and gallant, then Reno's "prudent" retreats were acts of cowardice, perhaps even treason. It was almost inevitable in evaluations of the battle that heightening the bravery of one man necessitated detracting from the other. People could not think that both men were brave, or that one was foolish and the other timid; the public wanted a simple foil, a sharp, clear, contrast.

Their voluble and articulate spokesman was Frederick Whittaker, he of the envenomed pen, whose ardent admiration for Custer was part of the inspiration of his campaign against Reno. In a public letter to Wyoming Territory Delegate W. W. Corlett he charged disobedience and cowardice:

> Having been called upon to prepare the biography of the late Brevet Major General George A. Custer, U.S.A., a great amount of evidence, oral and written, came into my hands tending to prove that the sacrifice of his life and the lives of his immediate command at the battle of the Little Big Horn was useless, and owing to the cowardice of his subordinates.... First: Information coming to me from participants in the battle ... is to the effect that gross cowardice was displayed therein by Major Marcus A. Reno ... and that owing to such cowardice, the orders of Lieut. Col. Custer, commanding officer, to said Reno, to execute a certain attack, were not made.
>
> That the failure of this movement, owing to his cowardice and disobedience, caused the defeat of the United States forces on the day in question; and that had Custer's orders been obeyed, the troops would probably have defeated the Indians.
>
> That after Major Reno's cowardly flight, he was joined by Captain Benteen, ... and that he remained idle with this force while his superior officer was fighting against the whole force of the Indians, the battle being within his knowledge, the sound of firing audible from his position, and his forces out of immediate danger from the enemy.
>
> That the consequences of this second exhibition of cowardice and incompetency was the massacre of Lieut. Col. Custer and five companies of the Seventh United States Cavalry.[27]

Unfortunately for Reno, Whittaker wrote well and influenced people, many in high places. Public pressure on him grew so great that Reno requested and was granted a Board of Inquiry, which convened in the winter of 1879. The Board exonerated him, but the reaction of many was predictable: it was a "whitewash" to save the face of the Seventh and the service, and the officers were alleged to have said one thing in private but to have testified to quite another thing on the stand. Whittaker's influence survives to this day: custodians at the Monroe County Historical Association still tell visitors to the Custer Room that Reno permitted Custer to ride to his death and intentionally withheld assistance, ignoring the fact that in doing so he and Benteen would also be letting over 200 of their friends and comrades ride to their deaths as well.

While the foil bears the brunt of the public's wrath, the hero's motivations are usually more gently treated. Leonidas is praised for his loyalty to his men, his country, and his sense of honor; Roland is praised for his pride in his family, for his sense of personal honor, for his pride in himself and his men, but he is rarely condemned for his *hybris*. With Custer, public sentiment went through two distinct stages. The first response was to blame Custer himself, at a time when none of the facts of the battle were known and before other scapegoats could be found. The *New York Times'* response was typical, gently censuring the recently defeated general:

> The facts as now understood dispose most people here to lay blame for the slaughter upon Gen. Custer's imprudence and probably disobedience of orders. But criticism is kindly and charitable in tone, as it would not be had he not fallen with his command in the thickest of the battle. (8 July 1876, p. 1)

Frank Leslie's Illustrated Newspaper, in its first editorial coverage of the battle, noted "the vaulting ambition of General Custer—in the excess of his personal bravery over his good judgment."[28] But before a month had passed, the mood and attitude of the American people toward Custer had changed. Terry was no longer blamed, as already mentioned, for dividing the command into three. The rancor against Grant subsided, probably because it was hard to blame Washington for a tactical defeat in Montana. For the *New York Herald* as for the rest of the nation, Custer emerged from the shadow of imprudence and disobedience, in a few weeks, to the warm radiance of epic heroism:

The underlying thought in this massacre of Custer and his command is duty and valor.... The story that comes to us today with so much horror, with so much pathos, will become a part of our national life.... The deeds of our young captain and his little band are worthy of as much honor as those of Leonidas, and will be remembered as long ... as the charge of the Light Brigade has an eternal freshness in the memory of Englishmen.... They remember only that an English Brigade in the high pursuit of duty did not hesitate to ride into the batteries of an army! "This is magnificent," said Bosquet, looking on, "But it is not war." It was something higher than war. It was the utter consecration of one's life to his duty, the sublimest thing a man can do.... The charge of Cardigan was not as daring a deed as the charge of Custer.... The charge on the Yellowstone was victory or death. (12 July 1876, p. 6)

Eventually, though contemporaries thought that he "was smarting under recent criticism, and more determined than ever to make a glorious record," and "counting on his former successes, and underrating the enemy," Custer was also felt at first to be a "victim to his own rash gallantry."[29] But a man's pride is his glory as well as his defeat:

Throughout he was the same dashing cavalryman, whether upon the plains or in the charge down the Shenandoah. The Murat of our Service, fearless, reckless of the odds against him, and confident of success against almost any odds by the *elan* with which he bore down upon an opposing column.... Added to his dauntless courage was the loftiest ambition, that made him eager to seize upon any and every opportunity to distinguish himself in the field.[30]

Could a higher tribute have been paid to Roland? Or Leonidas? Or Robert E. Lee?

One of the elements in the heroic legend in which the public could actively participate was the lone survivor. This mass pretense was possible because of the mysterious circumstances surrounding the fate of Custer's battalion. Newspaper reporters needed a witness to whom they could ascribe their imaginative accounts; the public wanted reliable assurance that the Seventh did in fact "fight like tigers," and the military needed its own vindication. And so at first a trickle, and then a flood of "lone survivors" came forth and delivered their exclusive accounts of the battle to the public.

The *St. Paul Pioneer-Press and Tribune* (8 September 1876, p. 5) published one of the first accounts of these self-proclaimed survivors, and to this day one of the most original. An old trapper named Ridgely claimed to have been a prisoner of Sitting Bull on 25 June and to have seen the entire battle from the Indian's camp. A little over twenty years later the same idea was used as the basis for a boy's novel.[31] The youthful hero is Jack Huntingdon, who, while visiting friends in Sitting Bull's camp, hears Rain-in-the-Face's vow to cut out Tom Custer's heart. Later, Jack (always the lucky boy in the lucky place at the lucky time) is sitting in Gall's tent when the battle on Custer Ridge begins. As the Indians rush into the action, he flees to Reno's position in the hills. But the real-life Ridgely saw more than this, though his observations were no more real than Jack Huntingdon's. Ridgely said that he and his three friends were well treated because they claimed to be Canadian. From the camp, then, they could see the Indians prepare for battle after having observed all of Custer's movements. The Indians positioned themselves in Custer's line of march, and at Ford B about 1,500 to 2,000 of them, "in regular order of battle," moved with perfect military precision. Ridgely's Custer was felled from his horse during the first onslaught—not on Custer Ridge—and the battle was over forty-five minutes later. Six prisoners were taken, Ridgely claimed, but they were soon burned at the stake. Captains Yates and Keogh were the last to die. Ridgely then made his escape when the Indians overindulged in fire water during their victory celebration.

Newspapers in those days would publish almost any story bearing on the Custer disaster. Many captured Indians later swore that no white men lived in their camp; all the reliable Indian testimony indicates they did not know in advance that they would be attacked, certainly not on 25 June; the Indians did not prepare an ambush along Custer's line of march, and they certainly did not maneuver or fight with precise movements as units; it is not likely that Custer died near Ford B; by the best accounts the battle began some three to four hours past noon; the Indians all insisted that they took no prisoners because their enemy's hearts "were bad"; and, finally, Yates and Keogh may have been the last to die but since their bodies were found half a mile apart, and their commands farther, it would be difficult for one man in one place to determine the time of death of both. But the story got printed and has become another page of American folklore.

But these were just the earliest stories. When W. J. Baily died in 1920, it was announced in his home town, Omaha, Nebraska, that he had escaped the slaughter because he was sent for medical supplies. The following year George Yee passed away in Sitka, Alaska, having claimed through his life that he had escaped the massacre because he had been assigned to look after the officers' baggage. In Wichita, Kansas, that same year, lone survivor John C. Lockwood died; he was known to be the carrier of the last message from Custer. "Sergeant Jim" Flannagan died in Mandan, North Dakota, also in 1921, claiming to have been the last surviving scout of Custer's frontier years. And to round out the year, in Rugby, North Dakota, Charles Mitchell—one of the few survivors of the Custer battle—also died.

The obituary of Charles Hayward of McKee City, New Jersey, had a slightly different angle; he survived when his horse fell and he hit his head, causing Hayward to lose his memory for twenty-four years. Three years later, in 1926, it was noted of John Poppe that when his company was surrounded at the Little Bighorn, he volunteered to ride for some more ammunition; later he rescued a wounded lieutenant from certain death, for which he was awarded the Medal of Honor by a special act of Congress. One year after Poppe's exploits became public, Willard Carlisle told his own distinctive tale. In 1929 at Antlers, Oklahoma, W. B. Hicks, a sole survivor, told how he had escaped from the doomed battalion when dispatched to Reno for aid; he dressed and painted himself in the manner of the Sioux, and as he rode from Custer Ridge he turned in time to see Custer shot down. The following year, 1930, in Baxter Springs, Kansas, a W. R. Hicks (nicknamed Curley) died, having for several years identified himself as Custer's scout Curly. In Baltimore several months later Samuel Thomas died, having claimed more modestly that he had been a scout for Custer and Buffalo Bill. Ossining, New York, had a William Osborne who, while a member of the Sixth Infantry, had witnessed the aftermath of the battle; Osborne died in 1936.

Even into the fifth decade of our century lone survivors kept appearing. The year 1940 saw the death of another Omaha resident, Alexander McDonnell, who was known locally as the man who took the first scalp from an Indian at the Little Bighorn; he later helped to bury Custer. Jacob Horner died four years later in Bismarck, North Dakota, his local paper reporting that he was "one of the two known survivors of General Custer's defeat at the Little Bighorn." James Snepp died at the age of 92 in Rochester, Indiana, in 1946; he was believed to be the last survivor of the battle, saved when General Custer sent him "back" for reinforcements. And in 1948 in Lisbon, Texas, Frank Dalton passed away after a rich life: he was not only part of a column which arrived too late to rescue Custer and his men on the night of 25 June, but was the uncle of the famous outlaw Daltons.[32]

The temptation to be a lone survivor was too great for several semipro-fessional liars. Frank Finkel, of Dayton, Washington, who never admitted that he was inventing history, and "Old Ed" Ryan, self-billed as "the biggest liar in Wyoming and South Dakota," are among the most inventive and enter-taining. Finkel said that he enlisted in the Seventh Cavalry under the name of "Hall" and was assigned to Cheyenne, Wyoming. When the battle on the Little Bighorn raged its most fiercely, Finkel was on the line with C Company; he was wounded, first in the forehead, then in the side, finally in the right foot. He remembered seeing a solid stream of Indians pour across a ford in endless waves and thinking "we were trapped like rats." When he was wounded his horse reared and panicked, bolting through the wild melee of trooper and Indian alike. He outdistanced the Indian ponies pursuing him, who turned back to the river with a parting shot.

After traveling several more miles he rested his horse and fashioned a tourniquet from a strip of saddle blanket, then rode on. Later that night he collapsed from exhaustion near a stream, but it was alkaline and neither he nor his horse could drink from it. Out of the dark came two riders with war bonnets; they dismounted, kicked him a few times, and, convinced that he was dead, re-turned to their horses. With their backs turned, Finkel whipped out his revolver and shot one of the unsuspecting Indians, but the other escaped. The next morn-ing Finkel was back in the saddle again, and he soon approached a wooded area. He entered it and came upon a clearing where a man was chopping wood. There was a moment of mutual suspicion and fear; the man drew his gun. Finkel fell from his horse, exhausted. But "Bill" carried Finkel to his cabin and there nursed him back to health, using natural remedies such as pine pitch to heal the wounds. Finally Finkel decided to leave his woodland paradise and return to the army, a Rip Van Finkel in cavalry blue. But the cynical officer at Fort Benton did not believe his story and wanted to court-martial the returned prodigal, so Finkel once more deserted, finding his way eventually back to Dayton.

"Old Ed" Ryan had a great fictive imagination, but his Custer story is not up to his usual standards. The *Chicago Daily News* and *Billings Gazette* carried a feature article about him on 8 and 9 August 1951, and no doubt other papers in the West did too. The scene was a roadside souvenir stand. Ed sat near the doorway, and as tourists entered, he began telling the reporter about his pet fish. While he was taking her for a walk that morning she slipped off a bridge and drowned: "Forgot how to swim, I guess." Outside the store rests a headstone with the name "Johnny Pommer" inscribed. When asked about it, Ed recalls that he and Johnny were fellow troopers in the old Seventh when his friend "fell sick of fever," and Custer ordered "Old Ed" to stay behind until he got well, when both boys should rejoin the unit. But Johnny died, and was buried outside of Ryan's store, saving Ed from the fate of the Seventh. Since that day, Ed claims, he has been AWOL for seventy-five years, the longest stretch on record.

But Ed Ryan tried to play his game two ways: he admitted to reporters that he was a liar, pointing out that "it don't hurt nobody none," yet he could also take himself seriously, or at least ask other people to. In a letter dated 3 March 1953 he wrote to Captain Edward S. Luce, superintendent of the Custer Battle-field National Monument:

> Dear Mr. Luce
>
> I would like very much to receive a copy (reprint) of the Bismark Tribune Bismark Dakota Territory July 6th 1876   My name is on that. List of Soldiers who fell in the Battle of the Little Big Horn Corporal Ryan is the way it is listed according to records I was one of the fallen I am very much alive and enjoying My 96 years if There is a charge for This Paper Please let me know and I will send any amount you state I am very anxious to secure This Paper and a Tourist advised me you could supply same
>
> Yours Very Truly
Ed Ryan
Custer South Dak.[33]

Old Ed was about fifty-six at the time and obviously enjoying every year of it.

But by far the most widely accepted and most famous of the "lone sur-vivors" was the Crow scout Curly. Unlike the others, Curly never claimed to have seen the battle, or to have been in it, or to have survived—at least at first. Most of the stories were invented for him, usually by imaginative news-paper reporters, and ascribed to him for "authenticity," although after a while there is some indication that he did tell white interviewers what he thought they might want to hear.

Curly was seventeen years old at the time of the battle when he and his three tribesmen, Hairy Moccasin, Goes Ahead, and White-Man-Runs-Him, rode with Custer. When combat was imminent for Custer's column the Crows were allowed to withdraw since their job was scouting, not fighting. Curly may have seen the opening stages of the battle from a distant hill, but beyond the first shots, he saw nothing. He apparently rejoined Reno's com-mand on its hill position, but later that night, having had enough of white man's battles—and losing battles at that—he rode off in the general direction of home. Before he got there, however, he found Terry's floating headquarters, the steamer *Far West,* at the mouth of the Bighorn near the Yellowstone, where he was welcomed aboard and fed. The event is celebrated in the painting *The Crow Scout Curley Reaches the Steamboat Far West— June 28, 1876.* When Curly was taken aboard he was questioned about the battle, but he had little to say. Sergeant James E. Wilson, on duty on the *Far West,* made the following report:

> An Indian scout named Curly, known to have been with General Custer, arrived about noon with information of a battle, but there being no interpreter on board very little reliable information was obtained. He wore an exceedingly dejected countenance, but his appetite proved to be in first class order.[34]

Also on board the *Far West* was at least one reporter from the *St. Paul Pioneer-Press* and James Coleman, a local trader. Subsequently, incredible stories began to flow forth from these men. After the battle the wounded from Reno's command were carried downstream on litters and placed on the decks of the boat. Benteen was in the vicinity of the steamer with the other survivors. Captain Grant Marsh—a figure legendary enough to merit a book-length biography[35]—then piloted his craft back up the Yellowstone to Bismarck, arriving in record time on 5 July. The news of the disaster roared out like a prairie fire. Clement A. Lounsberry, the editor and publisher of the *Bismarck Tribune* and special correspondent to the *New York Herald,* published a special edition of the *Tribune* and for the next twenty-four hours kept the telegraph lines open as he flashed the news to New York and Chicago.

His story was the most complete, but it was not a scoop. When Colonel Gibbon's column arrived at the battlefield, a scout was detached to report the news to Fort Ellis, at Bozeman, Montana. Muggins Taylor left camp near the battlefield on 28 June and arrived at the *Far West* the next day. He left the steamer on 1 July on his ride to Bozeman, 175 miles to the west. On the next day he rode into Stillwater, where he talked to a reporter from the *Helena Herald,* W. H. Norton. By the next day Muggins had brought the news of the disaster to the *Bozeman Times.* The *Herald,* meanwhile, published a special edition on the battle on 4 July, then telegraphed the news to the *Salt Lake City Tribune,* which carried the news the next day (5 July) and then wired Chicago and New York.

The first mention of Curly appeared in the *Bismarck Tribune*'s special edition of 6 July, where Lounsberry wrote: "We said of those who went into battle with Custer none are living—one Crow scout hid himself in the field and witnessed and survived the battle. His story is plausible, and is accepted, but we have not room for it now." A curious judgment for a newspaperman! The biggest American news story of the decade, perhaps the biggest story of the West, and the paper does not have room for the account of the one eyewitness. The Curly story had modest beginnings, for two days before, at the mouth of the Bighorn, Captain Benteen had written to his wife that one Crow scout had survived the battle and had seen the cavalry kill more than their own number of Indians—but nothing more. It is likely that as the *Far West* moved upstream toward Bismarck, the story grew and expanded to include Curly's escape and details on how the battle was fought.

The "Muggins Taylor version" of the battle bore little resemblance to the version that the nation was soon to accept—in fact, little resemblance to the actual situation. On 6 July the Eastern papers described the field as "a horrible slaughter pen": "When the Indians left the battlefield it looked like a slaughter pen, as it really was, being a narrow ravine."[36] The story was very brief and could give only a few details, though it did assure the reader that the Seventh "fought like tigers." And on the basis of this brief communique, Custer was both condemned for his rashness or daring and generally censured for leading five companies into such an obvious place of ambush as a ravine.

The terrain changed substantially, however, in a more detailed story carried by the *Chicago Tribune* (and newspapers across the nation) two days later (8 July), reprinted from the *St. Paul Pioneer-Press*; it was the "line behind line" account which first used the phrase "last stand," and which was to become definitive. Once the idea of a lone survivor had been established, almost any fantasy could be asserted. The inventive reporter or novelist had then an "authority" for his own version of the battle, a non-English-speaking authority over 1,000 miles away who could not contradict anything. Many of the epic elements of the Custer legend just detailed were ascribed to Curly at one time or another. The *Chicago Tribune* printed one of the first Curly stories, datelined Bismarck:

> The Crow Indian Curly is believed to be the only survivor of the 250 men who went into action with Custer. He is very clear in his knowledge of the fight, and has made a statement.... The fight began about 2

FIRST ACCOUNT OF THE CUSTER MASSACRE.

TRIBUNE EXTRA.

Price 25 Cents.

BISMARCK, D. T., JULY 6, 1876.

MASSACRED

GEN. CUSTER AND 261 MEN

THE VICTIMS.

NO OFFICER OR MAN OF 5 COMPANIES LEFT TO TELL THE TALE.

3 Days Desperate Fighting by Maj. Reno and the Remainder of the Seventh.

Full Details of the Battle.

LIST OF KILLED AND WOUNDED.

THE BISMARCK TRIBUNE'S SPECIAL CORRESPONDENT SLAIN.

Squaws Mutilate and Rob the Dead

Victims Captured Alive Tortured in a Most Fiendish Manner.

What Will Congress Do About It?

Sioux, emptying several chambers of his revolver, each time bringing a red-skin before he was brought down—not through the heart. It was here Bloody Knife surrendered his spirit to the one who gave it fighting the natural and hereditary foes of his tribe, as well as the foes of the whites.

The Sioux dashed up beside the soldiers in some instances knocking them from their horses and killing them at their pleasure. This was the case with Lt. McIntosh, who was unhorsed early in the scuffle. He was pulled from his horse, tortured and finally murdered at the pleasure of the red devils. It was here that Fred Girard was separated from the command and lay all night secreted, expecting to be overhauled every moment by the skulking devils who resettling to his comrades within a few feet of him, and, but time will not permit us to relate the story.

Through some means succeeded in saving his black stallion in which he took so much pride. The ford was crossed and the summit of the bluffs having, Col. Smith says, the steepest sides that he ever saw ascended by a horse or mule, reached, the ascent was made under a galling fire.

The companies engaged in this affair were those of Captain Moylan, French and McIntosh. Col. Reno had gone ahead with these companies in obedience to the order of Gen. Custer, fighting most gallantly, driving back repeatedly the Indians who charged in their front, but the fire from the bluff before so galling forced the movement heretofore alluded to. Signals were given and soon Benteen with the four companies in reserve came up in time to save Reno from the fate with which Custer about this time met. The Indians charged each time repulsed with heavy slaughter by its gallant defenders. Soon, however, they reached bluffs higher than those occupied by Reno, and opened a destructive fire from the bluffs, being beard from Custer, Col. Weir was ordered to push his command along the bank of the river in the direction he was supposed to be, but he was soon driven back, retiring with difficulty. About this time the Indians received strong reinforcements, and literally swarmed the hill sides and on the plains, coming so near at times that stones were thrown into the ranks of Col. Reno's command

his remains mutilated. The squaws seem to have passed over the field and crushed the skulls of the wounded and dying with stones and clubs. The bodies of some were severed from the body, the privates of some were cut off, while others bore traces of torture; arrows were shot into their private parts while yet living, or other means of torture adopted. The officers who fell were as follows: Gen. G. A. Custer, Cols. Geo. Yates, Miles Keogh, James Calhoun; W. W. Cook, Capt. Jackson, A. E. Smith, Lieutenants Riley, Critenden, Sturgis, Harrington, Hodgson and Porter, Asst. Surgeon D Wolf. The only citizens killed were Boston Custer, Mr. Reed, Charlie Reynolds, Isiah, the interpreter from Ft. Rice, and Mark Kellogg, the correspondent of the Tribune and New York Herald. The body of Kellogg alone remained unstripped of its clothing, and was not mutilated. Perhaps as they had learned to respect the Great Chief Custer. Nor for that reason did the Indians mutilate him, but in like manner learned to respect this humble shower of the lead pencil and to that fact may be attributed this result. The wounded were sent to the rear some fourteen miles on horse litters strelling the Far West, sixty odd miles up the Big Horn which point they left on Monday at noon reaching Bismarck nine hundred miles distant at 10 p.m.

The burial of the dead was sad work but they were all decently interred Man could not be recognised: among the latter class were some of the officers. This work being done the command wended its way back to the base where Gen. Terry, awaits supplies and approval of his plans for the future campaign.

The men and arms were out with marching and fighting, and are almost wholly destitute of clothing.

The Indians numbered at least eighteen hundred lodges in their permanent camp, while those who fought Crook may have joined them, making their effective fighting force nearly four thousand. These were led by chiefs carrying flags of various colors, nine of whom were found in a burial tent on the field of battle. Many other dead were found on the field, and near it ten squaws at one point in the ravine—evidently the work of Ree or Crow scouts.

The Indian dead were great in number, as they were constantly assaulting. The camp had bore an inferior force.

KILLED.

Field and staff, George A. Custer, Brevt. Major General.

W. W. Cook, Brevt. Lt-Colonel.
Lord, Asst. Surgeon. J. M. DeWolf, Acting Asst. Surgeon.
N. C. Staf., W. W. Sharrow, Surg Major.

Henry Voss, Chief Insptr.

Philip Dallan........	Corp.
James Drinaw........	
A. G. K. King........	Privt
J. K. Armstrong........	
Wm. Moody........	
James McDonald........	
John Sullivan........	
B Benj. Hodgson........	.2d Lieut
Richard Doran........	
C George Mark........	Brevt Lt-Col
T. W. Custer........	
H. M. Harrington........	2d Lt

The body of Lt. Harrington was not found, but it is reasonably certain that he was killed.

Edwin Baba........	..1st Sergt
F. ley........	Sergt
Finkle........	
French........	Corpl
Foley........	
Ryan........	
Allen........	Privt
Orville........	
Bucknell........	
Elsman........	
Engle........	
Brightfield........	
Fanand........	
Hamel........	
Hatticell........	
Kingsout,........	
Lewis........	
Mayer........	
Philip........	
Russell........	
Rix........	
Ranter........	
Short........	
Shea........	
Shade........	

Gen. Custer, Cols. Calhoun, Yates, Capt. Smith, and Lt. Porter. The un- happy Mrs. Calhoun, loses a husband, three brothers and a nephew. Lt. Harrington also had a family, but no trace of his remains was found. We are indebted to Col. Smith for the fol- lowing list of the dead; to Mr. Porter for the list of wounded, which is also ful.

H. A. Bailey........	Blacksmith
J. E. Broadhurst........	Privt
J. Barry........	
T. P. Downing........	
J. Coubers........	
Mason........	
Blorm........	
Meyer........	
McElroy........	Trplr
Mooney........	
Eaker........	Privt
Foyle........	
Bauth........	
Cobber........	
Darling........	
Davis........	
Farrell........	
Hilky........	
Huber........	
Hime........	
Donelson........	
Henderson........	
Leddison........	
O'Conner........	
Rood........	
Reese........	
Smith 1st........	
Smith 2nd........	
Smith 3rd........	
Stella........	
Stafford........	
Smallwood........	
Schoole........	
Vaugant........	
Tarr........	
Walker........	
Bragew........	
Knight........	Capt
G. W. Yates........	2d Lt
W. Van Risley........	
Kinney........	1st Sergt
Nuvey........	Sergt
Vickory........	
Wilkinson........	
Coleman........	Capt
Feeman........	
Briscl........	
Brandon........	Farrier
Manning........	Blacksmith
Atchison........	Privt
Brown 1st........	
Brown 2nd........	
Bruce........	
Brady........	
Burnham........	
Cather........	
Carney........	
Dohman........	
Donnelly........	
Gardiner........	
Hammon........	
Kline........	
Krianth........	
Luman........	
Loose........	

Shall This Be the Beginning of the End?

It will be remembered the the Bismarck Tribune sent a special correspondent with Gen. Terry, who was the only professional correspondent with the expedition. Kellogg's last words to the writer were: "We leave the Rosebud tomorrow and by the time this reaches you we will have

MET AND FOUGHT.

the red devils, with what result remains to be seen. I go with Custer and will be at the death." How true! On the morning of the 22d Custer took up the line of march for the trail of the Indians, reported by Reno on the Rosebud. Gen. Terry, apprehending danger, urged Custer to take additional men, but Custer having full confidence in his men and in their ability to cope with the Indians in whatever force he might meet them, declined the proffered assistance and marched with his regiment alone. He was instructed to follow it until he discovered the Indians, and report by courier to Gen. Terry who would reach the mouth of Little Horn by the evening of the 26th, when he would act in concert with Custer in the final wiping out. At four o'clock, the afternoon of the 24th, Custer scouts reported the location of a village recently deserted, whereupon Custer went into camp, marching again at 11 p. m. continuing the march until daylight when he again went into camp for coffee. Custer was then fifteen miles from the village located on the Little Horn, one of the branches of the Big Horn. Forty miles above its mouth, which could be seen from the top of the divide, and after lunch General Custer pushed on. The Indians by this time had discovered his approach and soon were seen mounting in great haste, riding here and there, as he presumed in full retreat. This idea was strengthened by finding a freshly abandoned Indian camp with a deserted tepee, in which one of their dead had been left. Moving on six miles from where the battle took place, Custer with his usual vigor pushed on to making seventy-eight miles without sleep, and attacked the village near its foot with companies C, E, I, and L, of the Seventh cavalry, Reno having the mean time attacked it at its head with three companies of cavalry which, being surrounded, after a desperate hand to hand conflict, in which many were killed and wounded, cut their way to a bluff about three hundred feet high, where they were reinforced by four companies of cavalry under Col. Benteen. In gaining this position Col. Reno had to recross the Little Horn, and at the ford the hottest fight occurred. It was here where Lieutenant McIntosh, Hodgson and Dr. DeWolf fell; where Charley Reynolds fell in a hand to hand conflict with a dozen or more

by those, unarmed or out of ammunition. Charge after charge in quick succession, the fight being sometimes almost hand to hand. But they drew off finally, taking up the hills and ravines. Col. Benteen charged them from it in confusion. They evidently trusted in their numbers and did not look for so bold a movement. They were within range of the corral and were driving out the inhabitants, wounding the number, in the head, while many horses and mules were killed. Near 10 o'clock the fight closed, and the men worked all night strengthening their breastworks, making knives, cups and plates to dig, taking up the pieces of hard tack in picks, taking up the fight again in the morning. In the afternoon of the second day the desire for water became almost intolerable. The wounded were begging piteously for it; the tongues of the men were swollen and their lips parched, and from lack of rest they were almost exhausted. So a bold attempt was made for water. Men volunteered to go with canteens and camp kettles, though to go was almost certain death. The attempt succeeded though in making it one man was killed and several wounded. The men were relieved, and that night the animals were watered. The fight closed at dark, opening again next morning, and continuing until the afternoon of the 27th. Meantime the men become more and more exhausted and all wondered what had become of Custer. A panic all at once was created among the Indians and they stampeded, from the hills and from the valleys, and the village was soon deserted except for the dead Reno and men wept upon each others necks. Gen. Terry came in sight, and strong men wept upon each others necks, but no word was had from Custer. Hand shaking and congratulations were scarcely over when Gen. Terry and his men had found Custer. McGuire, Co. E. 7th cav, all perished, with one hundred and ninety cavalry men. Imagine the effect. Words cannot picture the feeling of these, his comrades and soldiers. Gen. Terry sought the spot to know if these were the brave men who followed Custer, all perished; no one lives to tell the story of the battle. Those deployed as skirmish men, lay as they fell, shot down from every side, having been entirely surrounded. Reno, in an open plain. The men in the companies fell in platoons, and like those on the skirmish line lay as they fell, with their officers behind them. In these proper positions, General Custer, who was found near, and around and near him lay the bodies of Col. Tom and Boston, his brothers-in-law, Col. Calhoun, his brother-in-law, and his nephew young Reed, who insisted on accompanying the expedition. From the position of the bodies of the non-commissioned staff all dead—all striped of their clothing and many of them with bod-

the appearance of being abandoned in haste. The most gorgeous ornaments were found on the bodies of the dead chiefs and hundreds of finely dressed robes and other finery were thrown about the camp. The Indians were certainly severely panicked.

We said of those who went into battle with Custer none are living, some Crow scout escaping, one of the number told us and and survived the battle. His story is plausible, and is accepted, but we have no room for it now. The names of the wounded are as follows:

LIST OF WOUNDED.

Private Davis Cowey, Co. 7th Cav, right leg; Frank McDonall, D. left leg; Sergt. John Paul, H. back; Priv. Michael C. Madden, K, right leg; Wm. George, H, left side, died July 3d, at 4 a. m.; 1st Sergt. Wm. Heyn, A, left knee; Privt. John McVay, C, hips; Patrick Corcoran, K, right shoulder; Max Wilke, K, left breast; Alfred Whitaker, C, right elbow; Peter Thompson, C, right hand; Jacob Deal, A, face; J. H. Meyer, M, back; Roman Rutler, M, right shoulder; Daniel Newell, M, left thigh; Jas. T. Muller, H, thigh; Elijah T. Stroude, A, left leg; Sergt. Patrick Carey, M, right hip; Privt. James E. Benett, C, body, died July 5th, at 3 o'clock; Francis Reeves, A, left side and body; James Wilbur, M, left leg; Jasper Marshall, L, left foot; Sergt. James T. Riley, F, back and left leg; Privt. John J. Phillips, H, right arm; John Dolan, both hands; Samuel Severn, H, both thighs; Frank Brunn, M, face and left thigh; Corpl. Alex B. Bishop, H, right arm; Privt. James Porter, A, right arm; W. E. Harris, M, left breast; Chas. H. Bishop, H, right arm; Fred Homsted, A, right wrist; Sergt. Chas. White, M, right ear; Privt. Thos. P. Varner, M, right shoulder; Chas. Campbell, C, right elbow; John Cooper, H, right elbow; John McGuire, C, right arm; Privt. Scott, H, right hand; Daniel McWilliams, H, right leg.

An Indian scout, name unknown, left off at Birtbold; Sergt. M. Riley, Co. I, 7th infantry, left off at Buford; Communication Privt David Atkinson, Co. E, 7th cav, left off, July 4th, at Buford. Contipation.

The total number of killed was two hundred and sixty one, wounded fifty. Thirty-eight of the wounded were brought down on the Far West; three of them died en route. The remainder are cared for at the field hospital.

De Rudio had a narrow escape, and his escape is attributed to the noise of beavers, jumping into the water disturbing the sagacious Indian to follow his retreat; Privt David, Co. A, he got out of sight, and after hiding for twelve hours or more finally reached the command in safety.

The body of Lt Hodgson did not all into the hands of the Indians; that of Lt. McIntosh did, but was buried; Lt. Crittenden, though a half-breed, was a gentleman of culture and esteemed by all who knew him. He leaves a family at Lincoln, as does

Name	Rank
Stuart.	
St. John	
Thadius	
Van Allen	
Warren	
Windham	
Wright.	
D Vincent Charley	Farrier
Patrick Golden	Privt
Edward-Hansen	
E. Sturgis.	Brevt Capt
	2d Lt
F. Hohmeyer.	1st Sergt
Egnen.	Sergt
Hagan.	
James Calhoun.	Corp
Miller.	1st Lt
Tweed.	Privt
Velker.	
Kieffer.	
Andrews.	
Crisfield.	
Harrington.	
Haugge.	
Kavangh.	
Loberlge.	
Mahoney	
Schmidt.	
Lunon.	
Semenson.	
Siebold.	
O'Connell.	
J. J. Crittenden.	20th Inf
Butler.	1st Sergt
Warren.	Corpl
Harrison.	
Gilbert.	Teptr
Seiller.	Privt
Walsh.	
Asbeck.	
Burke.	
Cheever.	
McGue.	
McCarthy.	
Maxwell.	
Scott.	
Babcock.	
Tarbox.	
Dye.	
Tessier.	
Galvin.	
Graham.	
Hamilton.	
Rodgers.	
Snow	
Hughes	
D. Whitney	1st Sergt
Hughes.	
J. J. Callahan.	Corpl
Julius Helmer.	Trptr
E. Ulet Clair.	Privt
Graham.	
Milton Jm	
Madden.	
Monroe.	
Ruddew	
Omeling.	
Sicrote.	
Sanders.	
Wanew.	
Way.	
Lerock	Farrier
Kldey	Privt
D. C. Gillette.	
C. H. Gross.	
F. P. Holcomb.	
M. E. Horn.	
Adam Hitlaner.	
Fred Lehman.	
Henry Lehman	
E. P. Lloyd.	
A. Melcharger	
J. Mitchell.	
J. Noabaug.	
J. O'Bryan.	
J. Parker.	
F. J. Pitter.	
Geo. Post.	
Jas. Quinn.	
Wm. Reed.	
J. W. Rossberg	
D. L. Lymmon.	
J. E. Troy.	
Chas. Van Bramer.	1st Lt
W. B. Whaley.	Sergt
Daniel McIntosh	
Edward Driscoll	Capt
M. Coseline.	Farrier
Benj. Wells.	Saddler
Henry Dose	Teptr
Crawford Selby.	Privt
Benj. F. Rodgers.	
Andrew J. Moore	
Edward Stanley.	
Henry Seafferman.	
John Papp.	Corpl
Geo Lee.	Corpl
Julian D. Jones.	
Thos. Meador.	Sergt
Miles F. O'Hara.	Corpl
Fred Stringer.	Privt
Henry Gordon.	
H. Klotabander.	
H. Lawrence	
W. D. Meyer	
G. E. Smith.	
D. Somers.	
J. Tanner.	
H. Teley.	
H. C. Voyt.	
Boston Custer.	Civilian
Arthur Reed.	
Mark Kellogg.	
Chas. Reynolds.	
Frank C. Mann.	

INDIAN SCOUTS.

Bloody Knife	
Bobtailed Bull.	
Stab.	

Total number of Commissioned officers killed............14
Acts aent Surg............1
Enlisted men............237
Civilians............5
Indian Scouts............3

o'clock, and lasted, Curly says, almost until the sun went down over the hills.... Curly says more Indians were killed than Custer had men. He also says the big chief (Custer) lived until nearly all his men had been killed or wounded, and went about encouraging his soldiers to fight on.... The last officer killed was a man who rode a white horse (believed to be Lieut. Cooke). (29 July 1876, p. 5)

Curly was further "quoted" about his escape in a Sioux blanket when the battle was nearly over (which will be examined later in detail); and he described the battle as desperate in the extreme. Finally, Curly said that the soldiers fought on until the last man among them fell. The language used in Curly's interviews, however, is not known.

By far the most imaginative exploiter of Curly stories was Frederick Whittaker, whose writing on the Last Stand is based largely on evidence he said he received from the Crow scout: "How that fight went, Curly the Upsaroka scout, tells us, he the only man who escaped alive."[37] According to Whittaker, Curly's testimony was taken down by an officer aboard the *Far West* through an interpreter. Much of the account is identical to that which appeared in the *Chicago Tribune*: the attempt to cross the ford, continuous charges upon all points of Custer's line, the fight from 2 o'clock until sunset, the big chief who lived until nearly all the men were casualties. At that point Curly secured a Sioux blanket (in some versions from a brave who had dismounted to mutilate an officer), put it on, and made his way through the melee (like Frank Finkel), the Sioux assuming that he was one of their own. All these details were widely repeated and published in newspapers throughout the country and circulated in the oral tradition of the West, but Whittaker added an embellishment of his own:

When he saw that the party with the General was to be overwhelmed, he went to the General and begged him to let him show him a way to escape. General Custer dropped his head on his breast in thought for a moment, in a way he had of doing. There was a lull in the fight after a charge, the encircling Indians gathering for a fresh attack. In that moment, Custer looked at Curly, waved him away and rode back to the little group of men, to die with them.... Why did he go back to certain death?[38]

Why indeed? Whittaker went on to say that Custer felt that his "little band of heroes" was worth the lives of the world's general officers. Weighing the consequences of "the lesson" of his death to America, he chose to die with his men. Whittaker should have realized—and perhaps he did—that there are enough known facts to discount almost all the fictions concerning the Little Bighorn. The Curly stories, quite aside from the Crow's admission that he saw only the first stages of the fight, are severely damaged by the circumstantial evidence. It was a very hot summer. The Chicago papers complained about the heat all through June and July, and it was probably over 100 degrees on the battlefield. The Sioux themselves wore little more than breechclouts; Curly in a blanket would have been as conspicuous on that field as a fire hydrant or a soda fountain. Yet the story was ideal in its appeal to easterners and others who knew nothing about the Indians, like Whittaker himself: the style of dress, of wearing the hair, the decorations on the moccasins, would have easily identified Curly as a Crow to all his Sioux enemies. After all, the Sioux hated the Crow and were hated in return far more intensely and for a longer time than had existed the animosity between white men and Sioux. And then Whittaker's logic stumbles over its own details. The warrior strength was said to have been around 4,000, and more than half were in action against Custer. It would take more than a slight suspension of disbelief to accept the story about a lull in the action long enough to have permitted Whittaker's scene. And where was that clearing on the field to which Custer might ride, apart from his little band of men? He and that little band were hard-pressed by aggressive warriors advancing to finish off a disadvantaged enemy; and in any event the men of Custer Ridge had shot their horses to use as barricades. Whittaker was a former cavalryman; he should have known this. The newspaper accounts mentioned it, and it was the standard tactic of cavalry caught in a "surround."

Whittaker also wrote of this scene that Custer had a real choice: "With the scout he was nearly certain to escape. His horse was a thoroughbred and his way sure." Yet how are we to believe that through those thousands of Sioux and Cheyenne—rightly called the "finest light cavalry in the world"—any horse, no matter how thorough his breeding, could have picked his way with certainty? These "last minutes" of Custer's life, we must conclude, are pure fiction.

When these narrative elements are combined into a coherent story—the sword, the hilltop, the last to die, the heavy toll of the enemy, the call for help, treachery, the hero's pride, and the one survivor, each developed and perpetrated in its own way—a legend of heroic aspect has been created. It does not matter that most, or all, of the stories are, as history, inconceivable; rather, what is important is that they are believed. Why these stories came about, and why we chose to believe in them, is the purpose of much of the rest of this book to explain.

4

So Fell Custer, the Brave Cavalier

In a regrettably brief chapter on "The Pattern of a Heroic Life," Jan de Vries mentions that the hero of world literature and legend often dies young.[1] The reader of heroic literature knows how a surprising number of *helden* are not permitted a full life: Achilles, Roland, Siegfried, Cuchulainn, for instance. At least as many others died in the fullness of their ripe years, however, demonstrating that the hero's age at the time of his death is not a fixed element. Yet it is important that some die young, and others old. For the mature men we feel a wistful sadness; it is the mellowed grief for those who have lived long and well, we have come to rely on their wisdom and their guidance, we feel at their passing the same resigned sorrow we do when our fathers die after full lives. Such men are the givers of laws, our kings: Charlemagne, Barbarossa, King Arthur, Beowulf, or Lincoln.

The others must die young because they are not cut from the same cloth: we would not want them to sit upon our thrones, but rather in saddles, and to die charging an enemy. Beowulf—the older Beowulf—should rule; not Siegfried, of whom a recent Austrian writer has said, "Like all only-children of well-to-do parents, he was a bit spoiled and bored."[2] Would many Americans, who so thrilled to the heroic tales of "Custer's Last Charge," really—upon reflection—want to see their hero in the White House? When the young man dies we are filled with anguish for the loss of what might have been; and thus we strive to create a "perfect" life, a life in which the hero's deeds are not allowed to pale or sour because the hero lived too long, and could never duplicate and certainly not exceed the glamorous accomplishments of his youth.

This is exactly what Frederick Whittaker had in mind when he wrote a panegyric on Custer's death in *Galaxy* magazine,[3] though he was no mythologist and no scholar of ancient history. He was merely a well-educated man with a flair for writing who saw the dramatic and heroic possibilities in Custer's life almost at once:

Every now and then comes a bright meteor flashing from the multitude, and vanishes as swiftly as it came, leaving behind only a legend of light. The brilliant and exceptional genius dies young or suffers sudden eclipse when the period of maturity has passed; while those who attain fame late live late to enjoy it.

Custer was in this respect (Whittaker went on to say) like Raphael the Divine, Don John of Austria, The Black Prince, Alexander, Byron, Shelley; not like Napoleon or Alcibiades, who died after their fame had been diminished. Custer's life had been rounded and perfect; and it is to Whittaker's credit that he made these evaluations on his own (much as many will regret that he made them about Custer), and that the quality of his writing took a quantum leap in this eulogy when compared to that of his dime novels:

> In his life he was the *beau sabreur* as truly as Murat; brilliant as Frederick's favorite Seidlitz, with an unfailing good fortune peculiarly his own.... To Custer alone was it given to join a romantic life of perfect success to a death of perfect heroism; to unite the splendors of Austerlitz and Thermopylae; to charge like Murat; to die like Leonidas.... He found the one thing needed to complete his character as an ideal hero of romance—a glorious and terrible death on the battlefield ... and he died the only man on record whose death in Indian warfare was as proud and heroic as that of Leonidas at the Pass of Death.

The novelist as well as the painter and the poet had vied with each other (as Lieutenant Lee, trial officer at the Reno Board of Inquiry, foresaw) to depict not only the Last Stand but Custer's last moments on earth. And such attention and lavish affection as has been spent on this glorious and terrible moment is only what such an event, after all, demands. For the young hero—a Siegfried or a Custer—death is not only the fitting and brilliant end to a short but momentous life, it also is a bright star to which the rest of the multitude is to be unfavorably compared.

To Roland's death Turoldus devoted 175 lines (depending on how the count is made; I opt for lines 2221-2396).[4] The hundreds of thousands of slain Saracens lay around him, their comrades in full and panicked retreat. The 20,000 Franks who had been the proud rear guard lay before them, alas, equally dead. And then, in laisse 149 we have a crucial episode: Roland is unconscious upon his horse near Oliver, who is bleeding and close to death.

Oliver's eyes are dimmed, so much has he bled, so that when Roland revives and approaches him, Oliver strikes out in blind fury, cleaving Roland's golden helmet, cracking the nosepiece in two. Yet Roland remains unhurt. He merely looks up and asks, "It is Roland; did you know?" Oliver then answers that now he recognizes his leader's voice and begs the count's pardon. Roland replies that he is not hurt, grants his forgiveness, and as he finishes speaking his good friend dies.

This scene is a pause in the battle, a moment of silence amid the rings of steel on steel and the shouts and cries of desperate men. And during this pause Oliver does what no enemy has been able to—strike Roland—though fortunately he is not able to wound him. And at this moment, in the midst of this terrible carnage with several hundred thousand Saracens ranged against them, we are reminded that Roland has not suffered at their hands. And at this moment, too, we see a tender loyalty in the young count which we would hardly have suspected of the proud nobleman at the epic's opening. Oliver has struck him (again, as no enemy could); and now his response is gentle: "I have always loved you. Did you intend that blow?" The question has a touching naivete about it; and when Oliver assures him that blindness was the cause, Roland forgives him, "here and in front of God," and his friend dies in peace.

If mighty Oliver can die from wounds the enemy has dealt him, what chance has Roland? That is the final consequence of this interlude: Roland's moments are numbered in heaven, though he will meet the angels without Saracen wounds. He faints from grief, recovers, and staggers to a nearby hilltop, where he faints again. A stealthy Saracen watches his faltering enemy, and when he thinks the moment right this Saracen rushes forward to steal away with the noble man's sword. But Roland revives again and, taking his prized horn Oliphant, bashes out the skulking pagan's brains: his eyes pop out (in the effusive language of the epic) and drop to the ground. Shakily, Roland feels his own sight leaving him, as Oliver's had deserted him; his life passes before his inner eyes, a grand entourage in the service of Church and lord. And, making confession for all of his sins, he turns his face toward conquered Spain and dies. The angel Gabriel descends and receives his glove.

Byrhtnoth dies perhaps halfway through his last battle; and he is not young, so that his "perfect and rounded" life is of another sort. In the Old English *Battle of Maldon*[5] we have enough variations on the basic theme to show the flexibility and adaptability of the legend's form. And yet, though we know the real Byrhtnoth's age at the time of his death, in the poem his age is not an important issue. This narrative is more concise on the English leader's death, devoting only thirty-three lines (149-182) to it, but that is as much a function of the laconic, muscular nature of Old English narrative as it is concern (or seeming lack of it) for the Saxon earl. The battle had already been joined. The English (Saxons) had been able to hold an intervening ford from the viking thrusts, but like the armies in Polybius and those of Surrey and James at Flodden who agreed to combat, the Saxons agreed to let the vikings cross over so that the matter could be settled once and for all. With a loud laugh and a prayer of thanks, the noble thanes rushed into the ranks of the reeling vikings, slashing them right and left. Many of the sea pirates fell before their whirling blades. But soon one of the invaders sent a hurtling javelin (a coward's weapon in heroic poetry because the wielder did not have to close with his opponent) through Byrhtnoth's side; the Saxon turned on him and at once struck him down, but the wound he received would soon be fatal. Another viking rushed toward the wounded earl like a jackal thinking to prey on his crippled faun, and he succeeded in slashing the hero's sword-arm. Thus defenseless before his enemy, Byrhtnoth offered a prayer to God and encouragement to his men.

Here too is the moment's pause in the wild melee which tells us all. The camera with which we have been viewing the action, which has skipped around the field—now back for a long-range panoramic view of the entire action, now zooming in for a close-up—focuses steadily on this one tableau. The combatants are almost frozen in their deadly business, and we all pause for Byrhtnoth's prayer, which we know will be his last. Now we can think back to the events that have led to this moment: his bravery in deciding to fight the foreigners, his decision to let them cross the river to fight on equal terms with him, the early success of the Saxons. And we can anticipate as well what is to come after his death, which is at this moment inevitable. Some of his men will take flight, while others will show them more clearly as cowards by their determination—against even greater odds than at first—to fight. The young Ælfwine will rally round the leader's body and recall what he had done for them and what they had promised to do for him, and being young he will vow to fight to the death, for fighting was their vow. And the older men will say that since their leader lies here now, they, though old, do not wish to leave him, and their rounded and full lives will end there too.

So too with the accounts of Custer's death. No martyred saint has been so cherished. Hundreds of paintings and illustrations and dozens of movies have sought to capture that momentous instant, but writers have felt that a thousand words are worth more than a single picture, or several celluloid frames. The climactic and dramatic center of the epic is the death of the hero;

and so upon this event the writer lavishes his greatest skills. Thus it is appropriate here that the first account be that of Frederick Whittaker,[6] who knew and admired his hero so intensely, and whose literary labors on Custer are the most distinguished:

> How that fight went, Curly the Upsaroka scout tells us, he the only man who escaped alive.... Custer had to go farther down the river and farther away from Reno than he wished on account of the steep bank along the north side; but at last he found a ford and dashed for it. The Indians met him and poured in a heavy fire from across the narrow river. Custer dismounted to fight on foot, but could not get his skirmishers over the stream. Meantime hundreds of Indians, on foot and on ponies, poured over the river, which was only about three feet deep, and filled the ravine on each side of Custer's men. Custer then fell back to some high ground behind him and seized the ravines in his immediate vicinity. The Indians completely surrounded Custer and poured in a terrible fire on all sides. They charged Custer on foot in vast numbers, but were again and again driven back. The fight began about 2 o'clock, and lasted, Curly says, almost until the sun went down over the hills. The men fought desperately, and, after the ammunition in their belts was exhausted, went to their saddlebags, got more and continued the fight. He also says the big chief (Custer) lived until nearly all his men had been killed or wounded, and went about encouraging his soldiers to fight on. Curly says when he saw Custer was hopelessly surrounded, he watched his opportunity, got a Sioux blanket, put it on, and worked up a ravine, and when the Sioux charged he got among them, and they did not know him from one of their own men. (Pp. 598-99)

The description is general, containing few particularizing details. But Whittaker says that when Curly was questioned closely by officers aboard the *Far West* he related the following anecdote, "pregnant with light," about Custer's last moments:

> When he saw that the party with the General was about to be overwhelmed, he went to the General and begged him to let him show a way to escape. General Custer dropped his head on his breast in thought for a moment, in a way he had of doing. There was a lull in the fight after a charge, the encircling Indians gathering for a fresh at-

tack. In that moment, Custer looked at Curly, waved him away and rode back to the little group of men, to die with them. How many thoughts must have crossed that noble soul in that brief moment. There was no hope of victory if he stayed, nothing but certain death. With the scout he was nearly certain to escape. His horse was a thoroughbred and his way sure. He might have balanced the value of a leader's life against those of his men, and sought his safety. Why did he go back to certain death? (P. 599)

Whittaker, like most good writers, can make the fantastic seem plausible. His style conveys a sense of reasonableness, of believability, of measured truth. Yet fictional elements abound: Curly at the battle at all, the extended fight until the ammunition belts are exhausted, and the absurdity—the Sioux blanket. And then Whittaker adds the ludicrous anecdote of Custer, conveniently given a moment of solace by the attacking Sioux, as though the scene were in some *Chanson de Custer,* dropping his head on his breast while the encircling Indians pause for the sake of the drama, while the great man decides to return to his men. What of the premise of Whittaker's story? Would any man have returned to his troops to die with them? We have cited the implausibility of his being "certain" of escape with hundreds, possibly thousands, of Indians around him, of the improbability that on that crowded field this metaphysical moment could have taken place. And what thoroughbred could be so "sure" of his way through a battlefield as though it were a Wordsworthian bridle path?

Why did he go back to certain death? Whittaker explains:

Because he felt that such a death as that which that little band of heroes was about to die, was worth the lives of all the general officers in the world. Thanks to the story of the Crow scout, we know that he had the chance to live alone, and that he deliberately accepted death with his men as the worthier. He weighed, in that brief moment of reflection, all the consequences to America of the lesson of life and the lesson of heroic death, and he chose death. (Pp. 599-600)

Custer, at this point, becomes heroic symbol as well as hero, the vehicle of the lesson of death as well as the hero on the hilltop. Moments later he is again with his band fighting for his life in language that has long outlived him: the charm of his life, the leonine ferocity and defiance:

There was the little group of men on the hill, the Indians hovering round them like hounds baying a lion, dashing up close and receding, the bullets flying like swarms of bees, the men in the little group dropping one by one. At last the charm of Custer's life was broken.

He got a shot in the left side and sat down, with his pistol in his hand. Another shot struck Custer and he fell over. The last officer killed was a man who rode a white horse.... At last they were all gone, every officer of the group. Custer fallen and Cook killed, the remaining men broke. Then the scout fled too. (P. 600)

This is idealism, yet with a touch of realism too. Custer is not the last to die, and in this version his dying seems natural, as it may well have happened in life. But Whittaker is not content to let his hero die a natural death, the one witnessed by Curly. Rather, he goes on to give him a further, and more incredible account, one which he claims to have received from several Indians who were among the victors and who later escaped to Canada. Back on American reservations, they were able to give the following accounts, supplementing that of Curly:

... it appears that when only a few of the officers were left alive, the Indians made a hand to hand charge, in which Custer fought like a tiger with his sabre when his last shot was gone, that he killed or wounded three Indians with the sabre, and that as he ran the last man through, *Rain-in-the-Face kept his oath and shot Custer.* (P. 601)

The story is amazing: Custer's saber, the last-minute slaying of three Indians, and the story of Rain-in-the-Face's oath. One wonders if and how Whittaker could believe it. Perhaps he was writing allegory or undisguised fiction to glorify his hero. And at about the time that these thoughts occur to the reader, Whittaker includes the most unusual passage of all: a calm, reasoned defense of the fantasy he has just presented:

While this account disagrees with that of Curly, I am inclined to believe it, for several reasons. Curly was some way off, the confusion was great, and the two brothers Custer were dressed alike and resembled each other closely in figure. I am inclined to believe that it was Colonel Tom Custer whom Curly saw fall as he described it. On the other hand, several Indians who were in the fight have told the same story about the sabre, and have given Big Rain or Rain-in-the-Face, as the man who shot the

General. We know Custer to have been a man of great strength and activity, one who had used the sabre freely in the Civil War; and in his last struggle such a man would have been as able to kill three Indians, as was Shaw the famous English guardsman at Waterloo, who was seen to kill *nine* French cuirassiers with his sword before he was shot. A last reason that is convincing is this. It is well known that the Indians did not mutilate Custer's body, it being the only one in that group entirely spared. The only reason for such a respect could have been a reverence for his valor. It is also well known that the Indians regard the striking of a living enemy *with a hand weapon* as the highest proof of valor possible, placing a very different estimate on shooting an enemy. All the reports of the Indians who reached the British Possessions were unanimous in saying that they dreaded the sabre more than any thing, and this is easily understood when their superstition as to hand weapons is considered. It seems certain that they would never have reverenced Custer's body as they did, had he not struck down their best men in that grim hand-to-hand fight, wherein, among all the brave and strong, he was the bravest and best swordsman of all, the other officers having but little teaching in the use of the sabre. Be that as it may, it is known that he must have died under circumstances of peculiar heroism to win such respect, and that he was only killed by the bravest Indian of the whole northwest, a man whose unflinching fortitude had enabled him to hang in the air *for four hours* in the Sun Dance.

So fell Custer, the brave cavalier, the Christian soldier, surrounded by foes, but dying in harness amid the men he loved. (Pp. 601-2)

An audience uninformed of the facts of the battle would find it hard to challenge Whittaker's account. It is reasoned and meticulous; evidence is weighed and sifted carefully. We are told in detail why some stories are to be believed whereas others are not. We are led by the hand to understand why Curly may have been mistaken, why it is likely that Custer—that handy man with a saber—could have killed three Indians in his last moment, why the account is reasonable when one considers what Shaw, that other famous swordsman, had done. However, in a careful reading Whittaker's rhetoric trips over its own boots: the field which is all confusion for Curly in the second account is calm enough for Custer to meditate on escape in the first, and then return safely to his small band. The survivors with Reno spoke at length of the dusty soil of the region; the Indians took advantage of it to cloud the area to Reno's front in the valley. Did it miraculously settle for Custer's last moments? If the Indians were so "superstitious" about hand weapons, why did they use hatchets, tomahawks, and clubs so commonly? And the great swordsman, who used his weapon so freely during the late war, is only one-third as good as Shaw, after all.

These several descriptions of Whittaker's from *The Life of General George A. Custer,* from his poem "Custer's Last Charge," and from his *Galaxy* panegyric—in fact nearly all of the accounts of the battle in popular poetry and "history" of the day—sound entirely imaginative today, for a peculiar thing happened to the writers of these genres after the Last Stand. Whittaker in particular seemed incapable of distinguishing between the products of his imagination and the events of the world around him, between what actually happened at the scene of Custer's Last Stand (as well as could be known) and what had already happened in his novels.

Whittaker's dime novels bear the romantic titles of *The Mustang-Hunters, The Grizzly-Hunters, The White Gladiator, Dick Darling, The Pony Expressman,* and *The Death's-Head Rangers.*[7] They are poorly (because rapidly) written in a flat, colorless prose, filled with melodramatic episodes (such as hair-breadth escapes, rescues from the clutches of the savages, fights to the finish against overwhelming odds), and romantic characters: conquistadores, renegades (noble of soul), gamblers, young and handsome pony expressmen. The cheap, unquestioning heroic values of the day emerge clearly in the pages of these books; and so, without much careful scanning at all, does the material which Whittaker would borrow, probably unconsciously, to describe the last fight of his hero, Custer. For Whittaker's accounts of the Last Stand are little more than his novels abstracted and draped around the figure of the Seventh Cavalry's illustrious commander.

The hero that Custer was to become appears in several of the novels. In *The Death's-Head Rangers* he is Charlton, "six feet of graceful symmetry, his chestnut curls shining in the sun" (p. 96). And Whittaker's heroes often had blond hair, as did Custer. In *The Grizzly-Hunters* this is the tint of the locks of Little Gilmore, nearly a foot shorter than Charlton, but nevertheless with "bright golden hair... curling hair long and flowing under the neat, dark-blue chasseur cap" (p. 10). Darling was what Custer would be, "a trim, handsome, young cavalier" (p. 32).

Whittaker's own experience in combat, and the serious wound he received in the Wilderness campaign, did not diminish his zest for war. On the contrary, his battle descriptions are among his best writing, and they are created with a vigor lacking in nearly all of his other material, except perhaps when he is describing an Indian princess or some "glorious beauty" like the Amazon Eulalie St. Pierre. In *The Death's-Head Rangers,* Whittaker, in the narrator's voice, remarks that "it does not require long for men in action to take the measure of a leader. Battlesmoke clears the mental vision, if it obscures the bodily sense" (p. 68). And in the attack on the enemy: "Like meteors falling from the sky, the wild Texans shot through the battery, rode over the artillerymen, and dashed pell-mell on the heavy squadrons of the enemy's cavalry in reserve" (p. 69). Exactly like the charge of the Light Brigade! Led by the English stranger on their expedition, Colonel Medhurst, the Texans charged the guns—and won. "Just as the Englishman cut at a Mexican officer, cleaving him to the teeth, the Rangers began firing with their revolvers, and in a moment more than five hundred Mexicans were fleeing, in a panic-stricken herd, before the ferocious charge of one-fifth of their number" (p. 69).

The Death's-Head Rangers is not a tale of heroic defeat but of victory. And Colonel Medhurst is actually one of the lesser heroes of this romance of the Mexican War; the real paladins are the Texas cavalrymen, whom the English Colonel effusively admires, which is all the more impressive after his own caper against the enemy: "with his long sword flashing to and fro, [he] raged like a lion in the midst of the fight" (p. 80). Whittaker does not say whether Medhurst, like Custer, killed three of the enemy with his saber; he does, however, ascribe this feat to another of his heroes, Sergeant Diaz of The White Gladiator, who, "in less time than it takes to describe it ... stabbed three men dead" (p. 90).

The prototype of "the little band of heroes" also appears in two novels, The White Gladiator, where the outnumbered Spaniards are described with nearly those same words several times (pp. 20, 91, 98, 100), and The Death's-Head Rangers, where they are a "little troop" (p. 87). The Mustang-Hunters has its own small group of two when Gilmore (the same hero of The Grizzly-Hunters) and the old mountain man, Pete Wilkins, hold off an entire party of Comanches, about seventy by Whittaker's count, on the warpath. Earlier in the same novel, those same worthies had been assisted by the greenhorn Frank Weston (who eventually got the girl, Eulalie) when they met, trapped in a narrow pass, and gunned down about twenty-five other Comanches. Yet the nearest analogue to what might have happened at the Little Bighorn occurred when the Death's-Head Rangers attacked the much larger Mexican force: it was magnifique, but was it war? "Fifty men charging two thousand, seems like madness, but it has been done before this, with success, in cavalry battles. At the sight of the Texans coming down on their flank, the whole Mexican line, already shaken by the artillery, wavered and halted, while the squadrons on the left tried to show a new front." And like

Scarlett's outnumbered squadron at Balaclava, which has received little fame for its genuinely gallant heroics in its successful charge against the Russians, the Texans are successful. For Custer, we know, the odds were simply too great.

The few against the many, the single cavalier or small band ranged against impossible odds, was a commonplace of dime novels. In *The White Gladiator* the bad Mexicans "came on like a great tidal wave" (p. 44) and from their treacherous assault only Manola escaped. Little Gilmore in *The Grizzly-Hunters* "was not the man to leave a comrade," as Custer was not the man to leave his men behind to their fates; "small as he was, his courage amounted to perfect fearlessness.... He felt that his last hour was come, but he stood firm" (p. 48). Even a skulking enemy is occasionally entitled to a determined stand; in *Dick Darling* the Utes, surrounded near the novel's end, were "clustered together, dogged and sullen, grasping their weapons to sell their lives dearly" (p. 74). Compare line 72 of Whittaker's "Custer's Last Charge": "We can but die once, boys, but sell your lives dear."[8] Dick Darling himself had earlier fought a one-sided battle against a large war party of those same Utes: "surrounded by pitiless red foes, firing into him from all sides, he neither quailed nor shrank [like the Seventh which, in Whittaker's poem, did not "flinch"], but sat up erect in his saddle, firing steadily, and felling foe after foe, regardless of his own wounds" (p. 45). As a fitting tribute to the heroism of darling Dick, he was afforded "the Custer treatment" by the Indians: "Touch not the scalp. Let the body lie.... He was a brave man and never quailed nor shut his eyes when I shot him. Let his body be honored" (p. 45). But Dick Darling's fate is kinder than Custer's; he is taken in by a novitiate who has seen the whole terrible affair, nurses him back to health, and then, putting aside her habit, takes him as her husband to live with her in the earthly bliss of sunny Santa Barbara.

For the number of the hero's band the age preferred 300, or occasionally its multiple. In the day's popular literature Custer's battalion was frequently numbered at 300, which it was not. Perhaps this was an attempt to reinforce the comparison with Leonidas' Spartans, who were not quite 300 but were closer to this number. The charge of the Light Brigade was said by several writers to have been made by Cardigan and his 600 (actually the Light Brigade at Balaclava numbered slightly over 700, with only 195 returning from that catastrophe), but there appeared no implication that Cardigan's charge was twice as good. So we are not surprised to see that the Death's-Head Rangers also numbered 300.

The disasters in Whittaker's admitted fiction had their lone survivors and their traitors just as did his "history." We have mentioned Manola's escape when her people are destroyed by their Mexican enemies. The defeat of the favorites was possible only because of the treason of one guard who allowed the enemy to approach without giving the alarm. Later, for his treason, he was made to pay the ultimate penalty. The traitor in *The Grizzly-Hunters* is Matlasca; in *The White Gladiator* it is Aguilar. The traitor's dastardly deeds always make the defeat of the hero's forces possible; and he is always punished for it in the end.

The enemy is the savage, sneaky, and ultimately cowardly fiend we would expect of the genre. In Whittaker's books he is often a Mexican, but Whittaker's Indian villains reveal much of nineteenth-century America's attitude toward the red man. In *Dick Darling* the narrator says of a certain tribe that "they were true Western Indians, of that half Mongol type which is so grim and repulsive." At this particular point they were on the warpath, yet "their army clothes, dirty and begrimed, announced them as 'reservation Indians,' whom Uncle Sam feeds and clothes, through the medium of thieving agents, till some robbery of the latter drives them to retaliation and all the wild excesses of a savage nature" (p. 17). We are hardly in the presence of humans at this point; even the "thieving agents" are not quite so despicable as the begrimed savages they plunder.

Later in *Dick Darling* the Indians become more ominous: "the Dakota was a cut-throat, by name and nature, but he made truces for trade" (p. 26). When in *The Mustang-Hunters* the Indians scatter before the charge of St. Pierre, his glorious beauty of a daughter, and Frank Weston, the old Frenchman muses aloud, "Eh, Parbleu ... but they are cowards those Indians. They must be Comanches" (p. 72). Thus in his fiction Whittaker condemns this fierce tribe on grounds that few western white men dared claim of their real antagonists. Later he speaks of Gilmore's vengeful cruelty as manifesting "a fiendish ingenuity an Indian might have admired" (p. 83), but Gilmore, being white, is soon repentant. Little humanity can be attributed to these dime novel Indians, so that Whittaker's readers probably would not expect them to be treated as humans, when they were met. This cumulative portrait makes it easy to see why Custer's defeat at their hands would be greeted with shocked surprise and would be seen shortly after as a stinging insult. Like the seventy-odd "Comanches" caught by St. Pierre, Wilkins, and Gilmore in a walled glen from which there is no escape, probably the best thing to be done with them is to fire away with repeating rifles from impregnable positions on the heights until all are dead or helplessly crippled (as on pp. 76-77).

It is as Dick Darling says: "I believe in civilization myself, and you know, Jack, we're pioneers of civilization out here" (p. 11). Jack, a pragmatic and cynical foil to the hero, scoffs at this noble assertion; yet later, when he is himself trapped by Indians, he thinks not about himself at first, "but like a true American, he thought first of his duty, and of the orders about what to do in a similar case" (p. 40). And so the wild western world of the dime novel framed its magic pictures, while on the canvas its blond, curly-haired heroes fought at "the Pass of Death" *(The Mustang-Hunters,* p. 28), themselves "like tigers" *(The White Gladiator,* p. 26), their horses "like fiends incarnate" *(The White Gladiator,* p. 25); not "a man flinched from following" *(The White Gladiator,* p. 58), while their officers raged like lions in perfect fearlessness, and their sullen, savage, and repulsive enemy died craven deaths.

Whittaker was by no means unique in his attitudes, of course. He shared these prejudices and biases with nearly all of his dime novelist colleagues, and with most white Americans. It is surprising, however, to find that the nineteenth-century historians—particularly William Prescott, John Motley, and Francis Parkman—commonly romanticized the events they were describing and analyzing. The title of David Levin's book tells their story succinctly: *History as Romantic Art.*[9]

For the first of the great American chroniclers, history was the visible manifestation of the cosmic Providential scheme in which moral laws were transitions between the ages. History was to them a moral drama—an idea that is at heart medieval—and Prescott, Motley, and Parkman gave their histories the forms of drama. For instance, Prescott thought of his own *The Conquest of Mexico* as a prose epic, a "romance of chivalry."[10] He saw in this moral drama the triumph of the forces of civilization over their cultural inferiors, Christianity triumphant over heathenism and its most repugnant practice, cannibalism; this is Prescott's story of the subjugation of the weak and indecisive Montezuma by the resourcefulness, genius, and resolute will of Cortes.

History was drama, and its great men were actors strutting upon the world's stage. And this is the way Prescott populated his work, as his journals state: "above all, keep *character,*—and especially the pervading, dominant character of the hero in view. Omit no act or word of his that can illustrate it. Interest is created out of character. All other interest is not only inferior in kind, but in degree."[11] But how could Parkman and his colleagues get all of the facts of history they needed for their dramas? What of the facts, events, and utterances of the hero which they felt did not demonstrate the character of the hero? The writing of history had to be particularly selective; and since the American people missed some details of the Little Bighorn battle, the early historians supplied them from their own sense of what was fitting and proper to drama.

To particularize a personality these historians frequently interrupted their narrative to present an anecdote about a character—often a minor functionary—through a story that would be exemplary of some trait: courage or cowardice, cruelty or generosity, devotion or betrayal. Often the actor was caught in some situation of danger where, under unusual stress, his deepest character emerged. Each tableau had to be drawn in greater detail than the encompassing panorama in which it appeared; consequently these interpolations gained significance in the narrative as a whole.

In Parkman's writing the focus was often centered on seemingly trivial yet psychologically and morally revealing aspects of the hero. In writing of battles, for instance, Parkman kept his description of the fighting general, at first giving the reader a wide perspective of the action, until the moment of crisis in the struggle; then he showed in detail how the bravery of some small group or the perception of the leader proves decisive. And though at times the bravery of the small group may demonstrate national character, the qualities of the hero were uppermost. The hero was thought to perfectly represent his people; he was the "soul" of his army or nation, he alone knew his followers perfectly, he felt in close touch with their souls, and consequently he knew when and how to lead them. The great man had always in the past risen to lead in a democracy; Americans were a "race" that had been ordained to save the world with liberty; her leaders had already come forth in response to that calling, and, by implication, more would come forth in the future.

When we look closely at these dramatized leaders created by the American historians, we realize that they represent the spirit of the heroes of the fiction of the time. Prescott's cold and patrician Ferdinand is drawn as a foil to his queen, Isabella, thought by the American to be warm of soul. And she, in turn, for her kindness, her humane warmth, her patronage of the arts, was contrasted with England's Elizabeth who—like many a dark lady of American fiction— was haughty, arrogant, and vainly selfish. He also had his mold precast for other heroes: the traditional motif of the lone hero quelling a hostile mob by riding among them is found in Prescott's early novel, *Morton's Hope,* and William of Orange repeats the episode in *The Rise of the Dutch Republic*. Motley was so intrigued by Shakespeare's Iago that he cast Cardinal Granville and Francis Aertsens in the role.

Reflecting their Protestant biases, all of these historians depicted the priests of the Catholic Church as gothic characters. Their prejudices as white Europeans were as flagrant: Parkman's *La Salle* is made to describe the Indian as some less-than-human creature, part animal, part devil, and only part man. Demonic imagery commonly evoked the Indian; the Anglo-Saxon temperament was viewed as rationally calm, in sharp contrast to the red man's savagely passionate nature; the white man's rock-like strength was a foil to the Indian's impetuous temperament. At this point and in this respect American historians and dime novelists display very similar attitudes toward settlers and Indians.

The ties between these two genres were even closer than has been suggested. More than the spirit, prejudice, and ethos of the age were shared by such seemingly disparate writers as Prescott and Whittaker; a striking similarity of descriptive detail (to give the kindest face to plagiarism) appears in the two. For instance, Prescott related the following scene of human sacrifice in *The Conquest of Mexico*:

> As the sad procession wound up the sides of the pyramid, the unhappy victim threw away his gay chaplets of flowers, and broke in pieces the musical instruments with which he had solaced the hours of captivity. On the summit he was received by six priests, whose long and matted locks flowed disorderly from their sable robes, covered with hieroglyphic scrolls of mystic import. They led him to the sacrificial stone, a huge block of jasper, with its upper surface somewhat convex. On this the prisoner was stretched. Five priests secured his head and his limbs; while the sixth, clad in a scarlet mantle, emblematic of his bloody office, dexterously opened the breast with a sharp razor of *itztli*—a volcanic substance, hard as flint,—and, inserting his hand in the wound, tore out the palpitating heart. The minister of death, first holding this up towards the sun, an object of worship throughout Anahuac, cast it at the feet of the deity to whom the temple was devoted, while the multitudes below prostrated themselves in humble adoration.[12]

The same scene, altered and amplified in ways appropriate to fiction, begins Whittaker's *The White Gladiator*:

> On the summit of the great Teocalli, a pyramid several hundred feet in hight [*sic*], stretched a platform, surrounded by massive walls, and containing a low stone temple of the War-god, in front of which the

square altar was built, on which burned the sacred fire.... Before him [the War-god] were the dark figures of the priests, in long robes, with disheveled hair; and standing at the head of the sacrificial stone, by the altar, was a graceful, youthful figure, crowned with plumes, who swung to and fro a censor.... On the summit of the Teocalli, meanwhile, a strange scene was taking place. A young girl, graceful and beautiful as a fawn, was being led forward between two priests, to the sacrificial stone.

The stone, a great block of jasper, was raised into a hillock in the middle, so that when the victim was laid thereon, the breast and heart were thrown up, the back being arched inwards.

The priests led the girl forward, crowned with flowers, and half dressed in white, the graceful bust alone exposed. The whole band raised a low, monotonous chant, to the deep accompaniment of the huge war-drum that stood by the stone....

The young prince had been standing on the head of the sacrificial stone, beating the drum. In his left hand was the flint-knife with which he was appointed to sacrifice the very victim who now appealed to him.[13]

Whittaker then returns to "the black-robed priests ... with their long hair falling over their eyes, and matted together with the blood of human sacrifice."

Most of the characters of *The White Gladiator* derive, at least in name, from Prescott as well: Cortes (of course), his mistress Doña Marina, Alvorado (who is elevated by Whittaker to heroic status in the novel), and Sandoval. One important and interesting transformation takes place: Prescott's source for much of his history was the Spanish scholar Bernal Diaz, often cited in the notes. Whittaker needed a physically strong, brave, obedient sergeant of ordinary intelligence to set off the boldness and audacious leadership of his hero Alvorado, and the character he created he gave the name of Bernal Diaz. Throughout American narrative of the nineteenth century, then, one would have been hard put to distinguish fact from legend, or history from fiction. The inspiration for the novelist as for the chronicler was chiefly the same: the art of dramatization.

For most Americans this was the world in which Custer, that other pioneer of civilization, lived, and in which he fought for the white man's destiny. The forthcoming war against the Sioux must have seemed to many, in early

1876, a matter which would be decided simply by valor and hard fighting—if ever the slippery Indian could be induced to fight at all. For Whittaker, and millions of others, once Custer had been betrayed (whether by timid or treacherous subordinates did not much matter) there remained only personal bravery and martial skill to decide the issue.

Yet not everyone pictured the outcome of the Last Stand in simple terms such as valor and hard fighting. In 1938 W. T. Dugard recalled a rather elaborate battle: somewhere on the field he approached an apparently innocent ridge, when suddenly he saw three Indians on it, pow-wowing with three cavalry officers, one of whom was Custer. (Dugard's inspiration might have been the Charles Schreyvogel painting.) The six men spoke solemnly, though Dugard could not hear them, "when suddenly a gun went off somewhere ... and one of Custer's men fell from his horse."[14] This was a signal to all the men who needed no orders to act; the result was a general battle on all sides in which all of the 246 troopers were killed. Before Custer died, Dugard recalled, he killed one last Indian with his sword. The Indian loss was immense, their bodies thickly carpeting the ridge, several lying in front of each soldier. When the firing had subsided, Dugard took the lone living survivor, Captain Keogh's horse, Comanche, and rode to Benteen on the hill.

Again, the basic conception is an old one. Malory[15] describes the final battle of King Arthur against the traitor Mordred in similar terms: the armies assemble and a temporary truce is arranged on the condition that no sword be drawn. But during negotiations one of the soldiers sees an adder creeping through the prairie grass and draws his sword to kill it; this involuntary act triggers a mass violent reaction, and a furious battle, causing thousands of casualties, ensues.

Other writers were influenced by the early newspaper accounts of the "line behind line" version. T. M. Newson imagined an orderly, methodical defense in which the cavalry was allowed sufficient time for defensive maneuvers. Lines were formed, the men firing shoulder to shoulder until cut down by enemy fire. "The brave men ... continued to close up the gaps made by the enemy, until not a living soul was left upon the field.... Three hundred men ... the most gallant cavalry officer America ever produced, had passed out of life, out of activity, out of reality, down into the shadow of death!"[16] And in the field of fire in front of the troopers' lines lay hundreds of Indians, the ghastly toll of victory.

Francis Brooks turned to rhyme to describe the epic moment:

Down the Little Big Horn
(O troop forlorn!)
Right into the camp of the Sioux
(What was the muster?)
Two hundred and sixty-two
Went into the fight with Custer,
Went out of the fight with Custer,
Went out at a breath,
Stanch to the death!
Just from the canyon emerging,
Saw they the braves of Sitting Bull surging,
Two thousand and more,
Painted and feathered, thirsting for gore,
Did they shrink and turn back
(Hear how the rifles crack!),
Did they pause for a life,
For a sweetheart or wife?

* * *

Cavalry, cavalry
(Tramp of the hoof, champ of the bit),
Horses prancing, cavorting,
Shying and snorting,
Accoutrements rattling
(Children at home are prattling),
Gallantly, gallantly,
"Company dismount!"
From the saddle they swing,
With their steeds form a ring
(Hear how the bullets sing!),
Who can their courage recount?

Do you blanch at their fate?
(Who would hesitate?)
Two hundred and sixty-two
Immortals in blue,
Standing shoulder to shoulder,
Like some granite boulder
You must blast to displace

(Were they of a valiant race?)—
Two hundred and sixty-two,
And never a man to say,
"I rode with Custer that day."
Give the savage his triumph and bluster,
Give the hero to perish with Custer
To his God and his comrades true.

Closing and closing,
Nearer the redskins creep;
With cunning disposing,
With yell and with whoop
(There are women shall weep!)
They gather and swoop,
They come like a flood,
Maddened with blood,
They shriek, plying the knife
(Was there one begged for his life?),
Where but a moment ago
Stood serried and sternly the foe,
Now fallen, mangled below.[17]

Illustrations of this battle have inspired too many attempts at literature. The Cassilly Adams painting, from which the famous Anheuser-Busch lithograph was made, is twelve feet high and thirty-two feet long, epic merely in its size. In 1886 when it was displayed in St. Louis the value placed on it was $50,000, according to the advertising material accompanying it. Such an epic painting deserved an epic narrative, and this is what its viewers got to supplement their vision of the battle. According to the artist's notes, Calhoun fell first: "Calhoun's company all dead, every man and officer's dead body found in line, shows that they fought kneeling—without hope—but not one flinched from his position among the dead and dying comrades." The account obviously derives as much from Whittaker as from the "line behind line" newspaper account. "On the next higher terrace Capt. Keogh's company was ordered to dismount and hold the savages in check, while the General and the rest of the command took still higher ground and kept their flanks open.... The brave Keogh and his noble men follow the example set by Calhoun. No panic; no group of tangled up mob. There they knelt in open order and fired at what they could see of the unmerciful foe that returned their fire from behind every crevice in the many ravines around them."

All this was alleged to have happened before the moment of the painting; all has been prologue to the grand moment of glory:

> Here the artist has represented the tableau that ensued. The men have killed what few horses are left, and used their dead bodies for protection against the leaden rain that pours around them. They are out of ammunition. A prolonged yell rends the air, such as might proceed from the choir of hell. On rush the now thickly crowded mass of savages, each intent upon the fiendish desire to bathe his hand in the blood of their defenseless victims. Fiercely rush the leaders of the Cheyennes, with tomahawk and knife in hand. "Rain-in-the-Face" is well up with his rival braves, anxious not to be out-done in courage and also to be revenged on the Custers.
>
> Like a bayed lion Custer springs forward to meet them, sabre in hand—a few bright gleams of light shoot from the sabre's blade. Down goes the foremost! Another twinkling circle and another brave goes tottering back! A momentary hesitation pervades the moving mass of men; a hundred guns are brought to bear upon Custer, but so close are they intermingled now they can not shoot. Another brave strides forward, with uplifted tomahawk, thinking to count "Coup," but the weapon is parried from his hand by the dextrous swordsman, and the steel enters his savage breast. "Rain-in-the-Face," seeing the fate of the three braves, raises his pistol and fires.
>
> This ends the career of the greatest cavalry leader America ever saw, and also ends the story of the picture.[18]

The writers of "history" books often pictured the battle in much the same way. Like so many others, they were the victims of Whittaker's florid prose and vivid imagination. J. W. Buel's account in *Heroes of the Plains* is one example:

> The day is almost done, when, look! heaven now defend him, the charm of his life is broken, for Custer has fallen; a bullet cleaves a pathway through his side, and as he falters another strikes his noble breast. Like a strong tree stricken by the lightning's bolt, shivering the mighty trunk and bending its withering branches down close to the earth, so fell Custer; but like the reacting branches, he rises partly up

again, and striking out like a fatally wounded giant lays three more Indians dead and breaks his mighty sword on the musket of a fourth; then, with useless blade and empty pistol falls back the victim of a dozen wounds. He is the last to succumb to death, and dies, too, with the glory of accomplished duty in his conscience and the benediction of a grateful country on his head.[19]

The final account to be cited here is from the verse of Laura Webb, written in the year of the battle. This commemorative poem employs a lot of the sentimentalism, the maudlin idealism, the terrible prosody of much nineteenth-century American poetry. The 1840s and 1850s have been called the age of sentiment, but this attitude survived until well into the last years of the century. Patriotism, too, was rife, bred into the youth of America partly by the homely goodness of the McGuffey readers. T.S. Eliot felt that poetry was the product of the suppression of emotion; *Custer's Immortality* wallows in it:

> Not one escaped to tell the tale
>   Of how they bled and died—
> Not one of all that little band
>   That did so bravely ride
> With gallant CUSTER at their head,
>   Forever from our view;
> Not one escaped the vengeful hate,
>   Of the revengeful Sioux.
> To sure and certain death they rode,
>   That grand, heroic band
> To all that Death holds grim and dark,
>   By the savage Indian's hand.
> Not one returned to tell how fierce,
>   How deadly was the strife,
> That ended only when each man
>   Had yielded up his life.
> An offering on his Country's shrine,
>   When came her hour of need!—
> That Country whose now sorrowing heart
>   Doth in mute anguish bleed
> O'er the new-made grave of CUSTER,
>   And his brave, heroic few,
> Who, in the path of Duty fair,
>   Were swept from mortal view.

Far off they fought, far off they died,
  Afar their fame has spread,
Until each Land beneath the sun
  Knows how our glorious dead
Rode straight "into the jaws of Death,
  Into the mouth of Hell,"
To the wild, unearthly music
  Of the Red-man's savage yell!
Yea, all the world knows how they "charged,"
  With CUSTER at their head,
And knows the dire and dread result—
  A heap of silent dead!

Knows how with fearlessness they rode
  Their last and fatal ride;—
How they were found, facing the foe,
  The CUSTERS close beside;
Has learned about the gory field
  Where stark Death claimed his own,
And sees, in Fancy, crimsoned cloak,
  Over each figure thrown.
And this the whole world knows, and more,
  For, on the scroll of Fame,
In letters of Immortal light,
  Shines CUSTER'S deathless name!

That wondrous "Charge" of CUSTER,
  So dauntless and so brave,
Is the noblest act of daring
  That History ever gave;
For CUSTER knew full well the fate
  That awaited his command,
Was, to conquer the revengeful Sioux,
  Or, sacrifice his band!

But did his heart grow faint to think
  What might, perchance, befall?
Or turn aside from Honor's path,
  At Caution's whispering call?
Did the cruel Indian's planted stake,

With faggots piled full high,
Appall the soldier's lion heart,
   Or cloud his clear, grey eye?
Did the war-dance of the savage,
   As he glided 'round the stake,
Cause CUSTER'S valiant heart to quail,
   His steady limbs to quake?
Did the torture of the barbarous foe,
   So cruelly refined,
Cause a single throb of doubt to cross
   Brave CUSTER'S peerless mind?

No; not the faintest pulse was stirred
   Of fainting in his heart;
Though, doubtless, thoughts of home and wife;
   Caused the quick tear to start;
For "the bravest *are* the tenderest,
   The loving are the daring,"
While Love and Duty, Fame, Renown,
   The soldier's thoughts are sharing;
And weakness, all unknown to fear,
   Sweeps o'er the soldier's breast,
And wakens in his warrior life
   A strange and wild unrest.
But when demands of Honor come,
   The dearest must be left,
Despite the eyes that watch and wait,
   The hearts of Light bereft
Of all that brightens life on Earth,
   Or makes it like to Heaven;
While Hope, like clouds before the wind
   To Nothingness is driven!

And this was CUSTER'S end and aim:
   His country's fame and good!
While these to purchase, pure, unstained,
   He gave his proud heart's blood!
While on the page of future Time,
   The eyes to come will see,
Upon our distant Western wilds
   A new Thermopylae![20]

Custer's Immortality is a poetic equivalent to Becker's lithograph of the Last Stand. And like that illustration, the poem achieved a certain fame, being published separately in the same year as the battle it celebrates. To the public, then as now, that poetry was finely crafted was of less concern than the sentiment in that poetry, and sentiment issued from Laura Webb in abundance.

Pathos was her mode. Almost none of the dramatic, heroic, or patriotic aspects of *Immortality* are without it. On the eve of the hopeless battle Custer and his men think not of death or the "torture of the barbarous foe" but of "home and wife," which "caused the quick tear to start." Such passions flow from the same muse who inspired "lone survivor" Willard Carlisle to find a smile on Custer's face and to assume he was thinking of his wife or mother.

The lonesome, desolate quality of Montana is exploited fully: "far off they fought, far off they died." The troopers begin "their last and fatal ride" in the "distant Western wilds," from which "not one returned." The Sioux are "revengeful," full of "vengeful hate," but we are never told why; we must assume it is because the poet needed them full of hate as a foil to the more wholesome cavalry. They, in turn, are a pathetic "little band," though little in numbers only, for they are in their courage one with their "lion heart" leader.

Custer is given more than human stature in this role as martyr: "to sure and certain death they rode," yet he consciously chose to fight: "for CUSTER knew full well the fate/ That awaited his command." His death is no mere accident, no fortune of war; it is "an offering on his country's shrine." He took "the path of Duty" for "his country's fame and good." He is like the Cardigan of legend who realizes the futility of his actions but performs them anyway for the higher purpose implicit in them. He is, in a slight way, like Christ who knows what His fate must be, and consciously proceeds along the course of history until that destiny is fulfilled in "the noblest act of daring."

Webb sees "The Charge of the Light Brigade" as an analogy; Custer's men also ride straight "into the jaws of Death,/ Into the mouth of Hell." And, putting aside a great many details of the real fight, the poetic battle becomes yet another salvation of Western civilization, "a new Thermopylae!" But, then, scores of newspapers referred to the Little Bighorn in terms of both those other disasters. Laura Webb may have been overwhelmed by her romantic imagination, but among Americans in 1876 and the years following, she was certainly not alone.

5

Custer's Apotheosis

On 21 December 1866, a decade before the battle on the Little Bighorn, Captain William Judd Fetterman rode at the head of a battle group (forty-nine infantrymen from the Eighteenth, twenty-seven cavalrymen from the Second) in what had become a frequent rescue operation around Fort Phil Kearny, Wyoming: Indians were again attacking the fort's wood train while it was conducting logging operations several miles west of the post. Two civilians, James Wheatley and Isaac Fisher, volunteered to accompany Fetterman, bringing the unit's number to eighty-one.[1] The captain's orders had been explicit enough, one would think, to avoid any misunderstanding. And so when Fetterman's detachment moved north and west, Colonel Henry B. Carrington, the post commander, assumed that his junior officer was obeying orders to "support the wood train" by swinging wide around the Sullivant hills to cut off the path of retreat usually taken by marauding Indians.

At 11:15 A.M., when the reinforced company moved out through Fort Kearny's gates, Carrington instructed Fetterman (for the second time), "do not engage or pursue Indians at its [the wood train's] expense. Under no circumstances pursue over the ridge, that is, Lodge Trail Ridge." And again, when Lieutenant Grummond led his twenty-seven men from the Second Cavalry to support Fetterman, Carrington repeated his orders: "under no circumstances must you cross Lodge Trail Ridge." The striking force's progress was not followed closely, for during the next several minutes Colonel Carrington was distracted by several Indians who suddenly appeared along the Bozeman Road, which ran past the fort. The post artillery was readied, a round of case shot was fired at them, and when the Indians dispersed, all went to lunch.

A few minutes before noon Grummond's cavalry overtook the infantry and moved ahead and to their flanks as the combined force advanced up Lodge Trail Ridge. Several Indians on swift ponies pranced toyingly in front of the blue coats, just within rifle range, retreating as Fetterman's men advanced, down the far (northern) slope, across the valley of Peno Creek, and up yet another hill to the northwest. As the braves zigzagged back and forth in front of the troops, they gestured obscenely at the soldiers, and shouted taunting insults at them. But they would not stand and fight.

Fetterman's slow-motion chase continued well beyond the limits set by his commanding officer, taking him out of sight of the fort. His troops advanced on the western valley of the Peno, where it swung around the hill they had just descended, and when all of the detachment were clear of the slope, the earth exploded into furious life. Howls and shrieks clawed the brittle air; from behind rocks and sage clumps, from out of gullies and ravines, from under every stalk of prairie grass leaped a painted brave. Sioux, Cheyenne, and Arapaho—in numbers close to 2,000—hurtled across the flats screaming for soldiers' blood. The trap which Red Cloud had so carefully baited, had planned many weeks before, sprang shut on 81 astonished men in blue.

Wheatley and Fisher and the five or six enlisted men with them in the point dismounted at once and poured such a devastating volley into the attackers that the assault was for an instant stopped dead. But there were too many Indians, and they were on too many sides. Hundreds of arrows, perhaps thousands, came whining through the air each minute; lances came hurtling, whirring into the pockets of blue; and an occasional insanely brave warrior would leap among the soldiers, slashing with his hatchet until shot down. Fetterman recovered from the shock quickly and, under the intolerable stings of shaft after shaft, moved his infantry back to the slope of the ridge, where they could find some cover among the boulders.

The cavalry lost its commander, Lieutenant Grummond, early in the fight, began to panic, but picked its way, more or less as a unit, up to the summit of the ridge, actually the only route the surrounding Indians permitted them. In several minutes the infantry lower down the slopes were overrun. The cavalry turned loose their horses and prepared themselves for a last stand. It came upon them quickly; the Indians were particularly aggressive that day, since they wanted to finish the job before help could come from the fort. So they took more casualties than they wanted in that brutal slugging match of carbine against arrow and bayonet against battle hatchet.

When Captain Ten Eyck with seventy-five officers and men marched to Fetterman's rescue, he reached some high ground north of Lodge Trail Ridge and east of Fetterman's position around 12:45 P.M. By then all the firing had stopped, and the relief column was just in time to see the last of Fetterman's command killed.

That Fetterman acted in clear and flagrant disobedience of precise and unambiguous orders is obvious. Brilliant, dashing, gallant, cocky—these are the terms which had rightly been applied to Captain Fetterman, but just as appropriate would be arrogant and impetuous. In many ways the mold that stamped Custer was marked in Fetterman. Although he knew nothing of fighting Indians (Fort Kearny had been his first plains assignment), Fetterman had also boasted that "a single company of regulars could whip a thousand Indians," and "with eighty men I could ride through the Sioux nation,"[2] almost Custer's exact words several years later.

If the similarities in the personalities of these two men seem superficial, other aspects of their last stands bear a preternatural resemblance. In disobedience of orders, or at the very least in excessively poor judgment in disregarding them, Fetterman and a relatively small group of men were overwhelmed and annihilated by a horde of Indians within a short time. Fetterman too withdrew to a ridge to defend himself, and there he and nearly all of his men (six or seven defended themselves in the Peno valley) were slaughtered. As was usual in Indian warfare, almost all of the men were mutilated and robbed. Defensive tactics also followed the pattern: a defensive circle of many men was found near the top of the ridge. As at Custer's Last Stand, the only living survivor was a horse, also badly wounded. Unlike Comanche, Dapple Dave was mercifully shot on Ten Eyck's order.

In the aftermath of the "Massacre Hill" debacle, stories of lone survivors proliferated. Because Captain Ten Eyck had not gone directly to Massacre Hill but had first sought some high ground with which to reconnoitre the area, he (like Reno) was publicly and privately charged with cowardice. And he shared the same fate, taking to drink, which led to his resignation from the army several years later. Whereas Custer had been a rumored suicide, Fetterman and Captain Fred Brown did save their last bullets for each other rather than fall into Indian hands. Their bodies were found on the slope of Massacre Hill, each with a heavily powder-burned wound in the temple.

Yet it was not an archetype of the more famous last stand: Fetterman was ambushed while being decoyed into thinking he was attacking a few Indians, and Custer was, as we know, actually on the offensive. And Fetterman had a few advantages over Custer. Though the terrain was not ideal, with enough men it would have been defensible, especially from among a number of large boulders on the slope of the hill. The Eighteenth Infantry (with the company from the Second Cavalry) were able to take a great many Indian casualties; and although there is the problem of compiling accurate statistics for Indians killed and wounded, Dee Brown thinks 60 killed on the field a reasonable number, with 100 of the 300 wounded succumbing later.

The battle impressed the professionals as well as the public: Custer is said to have remarked to a friend that it would take "another Phil Kearny" to rouse Congress enough to increase military appropriations. And in August 1867 a detachment under the command of Captain James Powell (who had been at Fort Kearny the year before) was attacked and surrounded while guarding the civilian loggers west of the fort; Powell and his men raced for the cover of several wagon beds which they had removed from their chassis and placed in a square for just this purpose, and they threw a withering fire into the Sioux. Powell had a great advantage over his former comrade; new breech-loading rifles and thousands of rounds of ammunition cost Red Cloud, in his own words, the flower of his fighting men in that "Wagon Box fight." Powell recalled later that the Fetterman disaster was very much on his mind.[3] Yet the battle on Massacre Hill never quite caught the public's imagination as did the one on Custer Ridge, and we never hear of "Fetterman's Last Stand," perhaps because of the unromantic quality of the defeated commander's name.

Yet there is much more to Custer's apotheosis than the chance happening of a suitable name. Custer had what today would be called "charisma," having been "good copy" years before his battle on the Little Bighorn. He was one of the youngest officers in the army to win a star, being twenty-three when given a battlefield promotion to Brigadier General—after having finished last in his class at West Point. At Appomattox he had already won his second star, again in the field. Throughout the Civil War he had become indelibly associated with the romance of cavalry and the flourish of sabers; it was Custer, said to have been at the head of his beloved Michigan volunteers with his golden locks cascading over his shoulders, who defeated the equally charismatic J.E.B. Stuart at Yellow Tavern, where Stuart died from his wounds. When the Grand Duke Alexis of Russia visited the United States in 1872, the grand tour of the American West was planned by General Philip Sheridan, the scouts were led by "Buffalo Bill" Cody, and the military escort was commanded by George A. Custer. It was Custer who destroyed Black Kettle's Cheyenne in a raid on the village in the dead of winter, Custer who was court-martialed for shooting deserters without a trial in Kansas, Custer who was the darling of the American public: handsome and dashing in the red kerchief of his own (unofficial) design, the hand-decorated buckskin jacket and trousers, his golden hair streaming in the breeze. Nearly a century after his death he is remembered for that hair: Dr. Norman Vincent Peale thinks that Custer's tonsorial splendor was acceptable then, though not for today's youth: "Take ... the matter of long hair on boys. Do you, as an adult, regard it with instinctive disapproval? I know *I* do! ... I tell myself that 100 years ago nobody considered that dashing cavalry leader, General George Custer, effeminate because he wore his yellow hair shoulder-length. But *still* I don't like long hair on boys!"[4] Xerxes had similar feelings about the Greeks at Thermopylae.

Custer was a star, as we today understand the word and the particular personality phenomenon behind it; and the public worshipped him as a later public would adore "Ike" Eisenhower, Babe Ruth, and Frank Sinatra. Mass media have made many more stars now and have also focused attention on the psychology of the worshipper; yet much of what may be said about the popularity of many celebrities today was true of Custer in the 1870s. We get a clearer idea of the general's "image" when viewed in modern perspectives. The motion picture industry created a sensational craze for Rudolf Valentino (particularly as *The Sheik*), Paul Newman, and Errol Flynn. The last is particularly interesting, for aside from his perfect casting as Custer in *They Died With Their Boots On* (because their public personalities were so close), Flynn's charisma persisted—perhaps was even enhanced—after a trial for rape, just as Custer's conviction in Kansas left him untarnished.

The primary psychological function of star-worship is the relief of boredom by an elopement into an exciting world. It is an escape from one's "dull" life, of course; yet almost by definition one's real life is dull by comparison with the idealized life of the star. Even senior citizens are not immune, as seen in the curious fixations of those over sixty for Englebert Humperdinck and Liberace. Custer was a "star" and was much admired. The newspapers admitted as much; the soggy poems testified to his status among the most glittering luminaries of his time.

Another factor is as least as important; we tend, today, to put great stress on the role of sexuality in all of our motives, but Custer was admired by men also. Errol Flynn, Paul Newman, Elliott Gould, George C. Scott have their male admirers. And more is involved here than an envy of the star's money, his alleged (or real) sexual accomplishments, his defiance (especially true of Scott) of the "establishment." Identification with the celebrity makes one an extension of him. The adulation that is afforded the star is, in some psychic measure, afforded the worshipper as well. It is the process of self-aggrandizement: we are one with the loved and admired person of our fantasies and thus share his radiance.

Custer's flamboyance and flair for self-publicity (he wrote *My Life on the Plains* and several articles for national magazines) was also common to such other American heroes as Davy Crockett and Ethan Allen. Crockett, for instance, was "known" for his skill as an Indian-fighter, bear-hunter, and woodsman. But as a volunteer scout in Tennessee during the Creek War he

Custer, the Roland of the American Plains, as Mathew Brady captured him.

seems only to have scouted for food, and if he killed any Indians there is no reliable record of it. He was successful in scouting turkey, squirrel, and a cow or two. It has been reliably charged that he "weaseled" his way out of the army;[5] when he lost his bid for his third term in Congress he left for Texas, deserting his wife and family, and (more to the point of the legend) proved himself totally inept with a rifle. In one recorded shooting match he missed the target cleanly, and on another occasion he missed a buffalo. Crockett claimed that he killed bear only for food, but at the same time he once boasted of 300 kills in a single year, 11 of them on one day. Once in Texas he lost his horse, got himself lost, and then was finally rounded up by some Comanches, hardly the hero of the *Autobiography* or *Colonel Crockett's Texas Exploits.*

Ethan Allen also had a great gift, not only for relating modest achievements as though they were handsome conquests, but for keeping dirty linens far out of sight. He first won fame in his raid on Fort Ticonderoga, which secured Vermont's sovereignty. His "Green Mountain Boys" suffered few casualties, but Allen became famous for his demand for surrender "in the name of the Great Jehovah and the Continental Congress." Yet his atheist inclinations were apparent subsequently in a plagiarized essay on *Reason, The Only Oracle of Man.* Though the attack on Ticonderoga had been successful, his subsequent assault on Montreal ended in defeat for his army and his own incarceration. Allen spent much of the rest of the war in an English prison, from which he not only refused to attempt escape but also prevented comrades from doing so. At one time he was accused of trying to sell out Vermont to the British, but the charge was never sustained in court, some say because of perjured witnesses.[6]

Custer also had that other concomitant of charisma, what his apologists might term "a strong personality." The regiment seemed divided between Custerphobes and Custerphiles, though it is now hard to determine in what proportions. Benteen's hatred for him was well known. In several letters written to former sergeant Theodore Goldin from 1894 to 1896,[7] Benteen called his commander a "braggart," a "villain," a "murderer," a "liar," and even insisted that he "was criminally intimate with a married woman, a wife of an officer of the garrison" at Fort Leavenworth. More than once his subordinate called Custer an "S.O.B."

Benteen did not reserve all of his bile for his commander, either. On "Reno Hill" he said that he found Company A's commander, Captain Myles Moylan, "blubbering like a whipped urchin; tears coursing down his cheeks." He found Lieutenant Edward Mathey of M Company a "nonentity" and his unit "damned" to have him at its head. Weir (commander of

D Company) he once called a "d——d liar," and Benteen challenged him to a duel, but Weir demurred. Following the battle Benteen thought that Godfrey (of Company K) was "trying to make much capital for himself." And he recalled a brawl he had once had with Reno, having "slapped his jaws ... before quite a crowd of officers."

On the other side Weir and several others were quite upset that Reno did not single them out for praise in his official report of the Little Bighorn; and Godfrey's contempt for Reno was so great that he vehemently objected to his commander's name being placed on a memorial on "Reno Hill," an objection that apparently was crucial in having the names of all men with Reno and Benteen omitted—especially those of the commanders. Godfrey's dislike for Benteen was less acute, though he did care little for his captain's "artist's temperment." All in all it would be hard to conceive of a more factional and personality-ridden regiment in the service.[8] Yet all of these strong feelings, positive and negative, which were shared by the public, by millions of people who did not know Custer and would not recognize him on the street, enhanced his reputation, his popularity, his charisma. Even the *Chicago Tribune* (7 July 1876) was enthralled by the romance of his image, as we saw earlier. This man, whose "madcap haste, rashness, and love of fame" had cost the nation the lives of more than 260 officers and men, nevertheless had many "personal and soldierly traits to recommend him." Though he was "reckless, hasty, and impulsive," he was also "brave" and brilliant. Perhaps most important, he was "handsome and dashing," did "not know the word fear," and possessed many qualities that made him "beloved of women and admired of men."

As important to the legend as Custer's personality was the setting of the battle: a very special place, the American Wild West. Much has been written in recent years about the American West as symbol and myth, and our understanding of the plains in our national consciousness has been greatly enhanced.[9] The first longings to cross the plains were expansionist. In the earliest years of the nineteenth century men of foresight and influence declaimed for westward colonization; the aim of some of them, particularly Thomas Hart Benton and Asa Whitney, was trade with Asia over an imagined northeast passage to India. Not only would a mighty American empire develop, but the American desert would bloom with the unparalleled prosperity that Asian trade would bring. Philadelphia's William Gilpin saw the American empire as a manifest proof of the theories of geographer Alexander van Humboldt: all of the great empires of the world had developed in the "isothermal zodiac." Why not add the United States, Gilpin thought, to China, India,

Persia, Greece, Rome, Spain, and Great Britain? If the United States was to join those other mighty empires, the West was the great challenge to be met. It was, in Gilpin's fine phrase, "the untransacted destiny of the American people."

Few people lived beyond the Alleghenys in those days, and where few lived there was freedom—or so it seemed to a number of writers in the "overcrowded" cities of the Eastern seaboard. The workaday farmer's life was tedious, wherever he toiled, but as Henry Nash Smith has well said: "The Wild West was by contrast an exhilarating region of adventure and comradeship in the open air. Its heroes bore none of the marks of degraded status. They were in reality not members of society at all, but noble anarchs owning no master, free denizens of a limitless wilderness."[10] From such an attitude sprang such heroes of the West as Daniel Boone, Kit Carson, and Buffalo Bill.

The Boone legend was fostered by several men whose primary political interests involved the expansion of the western frontier. As early as 1784 John Filson lauded Boone in *The Discovery, Settlement and Present State of Kentucke*, which identified the man as the embodiment of the spirit of colonization and projected him as the symbol of the ethos of the nation's territorial ambitions. In 1813 Daniel Bryan (who happened to be Boone's nephew) published *The Adventures of Daniel Boone*, whose already quasi-mythic hero was the agent of the "Spirit of Enterprise," bringing civilization to the wilderness across the Alleghenys. Other writers visualized the struggle of the forces of Civilization against those of the Wilderness as a hand-to-hand fight between Boone and an Indian.

At the same time Boone became a symbol of the American's attempted escape from encroaching and stifling civilization, a pastoral hero of the kind celebrated for centuries. Timothy Flint's widely read biography, *The Life and Adventures of Daniel Boone* (1833), depicted the Kentuckian as the restless adventurer, constantly driven to escape from the evil influences of civilization; yet at the same time Boone was the idealist-pioneer stilling the savage breast of the untamed land. A reporter for the *New York American* retold one of the many Boone anecdotes about his love of isolation when he "quoted" the settler as asserting that he "had not been two years at the licks before a d——d Yankee came, and settled down *within an hundred miles of me*."[11] Stories of this sort were legion, like the one claiming that Boone felt constrained to move on when he could no longer fell a tree and have its top branches lie more than a few yards from his door.

Daniel Boone became a hero not only through his own merits (a rarity at any time), not only because he happened to have several admirers who published eulogies to him, but because Americans saw in him a symbol of their own cultural aspirations. He was the pioneer who cleared the wilderness, yet at the same time he was the lover of the untrodden ways. As the new nation aspired to embrace the west coast and to colonize and fertilize the desert and the plains between the oceans, it quite naturally singled out certain conspicuous pioneers as its folk heroes. Daniel Boone was not only a brave and a noble man, he was also the spirit of America's westward movement. At the same time, he was represented in certain protest literature as the solitary lover of nature who had the courage and the resourcefulness to escape from the stultifying technology of the Eastern American cities; he was the romantic's Thoreau in buckskin.

So too with Kit Carson, the mountain man whose life seemed to typify the reckless freedom of the wild hills—or so Easterners imagined it. He also became the vessel of the aspirations to empire to the mid-nineteenth century that Boone had become a century earlier. But by Carson's "time"—if we measure his era in the terms of his dime novel popularity—the natural surroundings in which Kit and his friends capered were no longer benign, and the hero could no longer find Divine manifestations in rocks and stones and trees. Rather, nature now appeared savage, something to be fought against and overcome. In such an indifferent and even hostile environment the hero had to live by his wits and his cunning.

Carson the man first drew public notice from Jessie Benton Fremont's accounts of her husband's explorations of the West, but these stories were all elaborated and of course exaggerated in subsequent biographies and adventure stories. Carson was to become, in this fiction, "one of the best of those noble and original characters that have from time to time sprung up on and beyond our frontier, retreating with it to the west, and drawing from association with uncultivated nature, not the rudeness and sensualism of the savage, but the genuine simplicity and truthfulness of disposition, and generosity, bravery, and single heartedness to a degree rarely found in society."[12] It was said of Kit that even his fellow trappers, rude and uncouth as they were, recognized the "superior dignity" of the man. Kit could complain that one of his biographers, DeWitt C. Peters, "laid it on a leetle too thick," but as Americans aspired in some remote, idealized, symbolic way to be mountain men, to forge the pillars of empire while both wrestling with the demons of the wild and escaping the pollution of the cities, Kit Carson—willingly or not—was destined to become one of their heroes.

The untamed Wild West of Kit and his friends became the testing grounds of the pioneer's manliness, where men were two-fisted, red-blooded, *men*. Earlier in American history it had been thought of as another kind of testing grounds. In the minds of many of the first settlers the plains acquired many of the associations of the desert or the wilderness. The Biblical precedent was clear. The Jews had wandered in the desert for forty years, Jesus was tempted in the desert for forty days. When God gave the Israeli desert to His people, he commanded them:

> And thou shalt remember all the way which the Lord thy God led thee these forty years in the wilderness, to humble thee, and to prove thee, to know what was in thine heart, whether thou wouldest keep his commandments, or no. (Deut. 8:2)

So the Pilgrims sought a New Paradise in the New World, and the life they hoped to find there would embody a new reformation.[13] John Eliot thought it fitting that the Pilgrim went with a suffering mind into the (American) wilderness where nothing flourished and nothing was easy; his ideal was that the good Christian should be confronted with hard labor, wants and desires, and such temptations as only the wilderness afforded. The wilderness was not only savage, not only teeming with dangerous animals and reptiles, but peopled with ignorant barbarians: it was, in a word, un-Christian.

Roger Williams once likened the church to a garden, and the world to a wilderness. The walls of many monasteries surround a garden—a piece of land which has been ordered and cultivated and fertilized: within the walls all is serene and symmetrical; outside the world is capricious and chaotic. For Cotton Mather the world of the American wilderness was the empire of Antichrist, filled with dangers and demons. In *The Ecclesiastical History of New England* he set out this typological relation most clearly:

> It is written concerning our Lord Jesus Christ that he was led into the wilderness to be tempted by the devil; and the people of the Lord Jesus Christ, led into the wilderness of New England, have not only met with continual temptation of the devil there; the wilderness having always had serpents in it; but also they have had in almost every new lustre of years, a new assault of extraordinary temptation upon them; a more than common hour and power of darkness.[14]

For the Hebrews any desolate and wild country signified a region in which one could find God. This feeling was soon assimilated into Christian thought.

The wilderness, the desert, the prairie, became a testing ground where a chosen people would be made ready for the promised land through purgation and humiliation. The sinister and forbidding quality of the wilderness made it a place of purification. Thus to Christians the Indians, who were the children of the wild, were challenges to proselytization. Conquest of them and of their lands was tantamount to the expansion of Christianity.[15]

Johnny Appleseed was planting more than orchards; he was cultivating a church in the wilderness, with a spiritual seedbed. It was for this reason that stories grew up about "wild" Indians allowing him to pass through their lands unmolested, and animals lying down by his side to be soothed by his readings from Scripture. The greatest challenge of the American West was not to cowboys but to proselytizing Christians; the American Home Missionary Society worked on the assumption that revival preaching was the cultivator necessary to turn the entire American wilderness into a garden of the Lord. When Custer rode westward into Montana, then, it was already a semi-numinous land, and he was something of a white Christian paladin on a sacred mission. He has since been described in terms that typify the Western hero and make him as one with the West: "He was the kind of fighter produced only by the bone and sinew of new worlds. Tall, lean and rugged, long-haired, dominating and courageous to the point of recklessness, Custer would have had no place in a long-established civilization."[16]

Two months before his last battle, a reporter aboard the *Far West* (perhaps Mark Kellogg, who was with the regiment and was killed on Custer Ridge) sent the following musings to the *Chicago Tribune:*

> The Sioux ... will most assuredly fight to the bitter end for the country which is their favorite hunting-ground. Of course, the march of civilization cannot be impeded. The white man is destined to drive the aboriginal Indian from his haunts, his hunting-ground, and his lodge. It seems hard that this should be so, but it is the destiny of nations. The scream of the locomotive supplants the war-whoop of the warrior; and the latter, when he hears, knows well its portent. The Plow of the immigrant robs the prairie of its primeval covering, and forces from the rich, willing earth the increase guaranteed by the Great Master to those who by the sweat of their brow seek to earn an honest living; domestic cattle succeed the buffalo, the cackle of the barnyard-fowl the cry of the prairie-hen. There is ample food for moralizing out here, I can tell you. (21 April 1876, p. 7)

If the setting was perfect for a heroic sacrifice, so were the times right for the tragedy. Much of the news during 1876 had been depressing. The nation was barely rising from the trough of a recession. Promised appropriations were never voted by Congress; payments to the Indians, ratified by treaty, were defaulted; the superintendents of government buildings were ordered to conserve fuel, light, and water. And Grant's administration was riddled with corruption and scandal. The major newspapers of the country carried daily reports of the latest congressional findings on their front pages: the Postal Contract scandal, the "Naval Inquiry," the Whiskey Scandal, the Belknap investigation. The last bore directly on Custer and the Indians: alleged corruption in the awarding of post traderships on reservations and the supposedly notorious corruption of the traders after their enfranchisement drew Custer to Washington to testify. It was a tactical mistake for him, for Secretary of War William W. Belknap was a friend of President Grant's, and Custer's involvement—however much or little his own doing—angered his commander. But at that moment, in the early spring of 1876, the nation was little concerned with the testimony of George A. Custer in its desire to hear good news for a change. In 1876 the country had had enough of scandal—it wanted something it could be proud of.

That it got from the celebrations, nation-wide, of the centennial year of American independence. Every day the nation's leading newspapers carried warm accounts of the sumptuous preparations for the great event, as exhibition halls in several major cities readied for their grand openings. Royalty from Europe and the Far East streamed into America, particularly to the East Coast, to pay the tribute of their presence to the new republic. The mighty nations of the world brought their finest handicrafts—from Japanese porcelains to Krupp railroad artillery—to be exhibited in the biggest exhibition hall of all, in Philadelphia. Sidney Lanier composed a cantata, "The Centennial Meditation of Columbia"; and Richard Wagner was commissioned to write the official Centennial march. So what if the government was having trouble paying its fuel bills and having more trouble finding an honest public servant? The Centennial celebrations were something to be proud of, something to make Americans forget the mess their country was in, and it was something about America which, in the midst of defeatism, was positive:

> The great Centennial Exposition, or Fair of the World, was inaugurated yesterday in Philadelphia with imposing ceremonies, which are described elsewhere. It represents the active labor of five years, the

results of a century's progress in this country, and the current condition of the world in all its material industries and artistic growth. In the case of our own country there is an additional element of a patriotic character, from the fact that it is the Centennial of American freedom. In the celebration of that Centennial there must of necessity be more or less bosh and buncombe, for it is a national peculiarity of ours to slop over in all matters pertaining to the Star-Spangled Banner and the American Eagle. Making all allowances, however, for our national exuberance, there is an abundant reason for congratulations and rejoicing that the Republic has survived its first hundred years, and there is abundant reason to hope also, in the language of Whittier, that the new cycle cast in some diviner mold will shame the old. (*Chicago Tribune*, 11 May 1876, p. 4)

While Boss Tweed, the Erie Gang, and the Indian Ring monopolized the front pages of American newspapers, those ominous squibs and fillers quoted earlier also began appearing. There were reports of murders and scalpings, raids and ambushes, rumors that braves were leaving Red Cloud Agency or that Crazy Horse was gathering ammunition, and that large parties of Indians were seen heading north toward the Powder River country.

In May 1876 there was no doubt in the minds of white America about the outcome of the war. The most vehement complaints were against the federal government for taking so long to put an end to the pesky problem, and the only question was how soon it could be accomplished. In the West, where Indian depredations were a daily reality, hatreds were greater and impatience stronger, as this *Cheyenne Weekly Leader* editorial of 13 May shows clearly:

In about every issue of the *Leader* we are compelled to chronicle the murder of our citizens by the savages who infest our borders. Day after day the telegraph brings to us the particulars of horrible atrocities committed upon the people of Wyoming and Dakota by the fiendish and blood-seeking Indians, whom the government, under so-called treaty stipulations, is feeding and supporting with the most generous liberality.... Will not this powerful government protect its citizens against the savages? Will it not use its mighty military arm to teach these murderous devils that they cannot forever, and with impunity, rob and murder our people?... There is only one policy to be pursued, and that is to increase the military force in this department by at least one or two regiments.... If the army of the United States is not adequate to furnish the additional force, then let the government arm and equip the men on the frontier ... and we will guarantee a thorough and speedy settlement of the whole Indian question at a very small cost to the country.

As one traveled further east in those days, the approach toward the Indian question assumed increasingly milder tones. In the final analysis, however, the policy recommended was substantially the same; yet the tone in the East was slightly more conciliatory. The *Chicago Tribune*, for instance, was less strident than the *Cheyenne Leader,* assigning blame for the country's Indian troubles on the corruption in the Grant regime (always, it seems, a ready scapegoat of the time). Nevertheless, the *Tribune* felt that the final solution to the Indian problem was to be effected only by force, as seen in its editorial of 10 April (quoted in detail because it is a particularly lucid exposition of American attitudes in 1876):

By the provisions of the treaty of 1868, the Sioux portion of this country has been a region sealed against white men. The Indians have always been anxious to keep white men out of their country; and the Ring who have had charge of THE PEACE POLICY of dealing with them have been equally anxious that no disinterested eyes should be peering about the Agencies that are situated many miles away from the abodes of white men. According to the report of the Commission appointed last year to negotiate for the purchase of the Black Hills, the so-called Peace Policy, after an experimental trial of eight years, has been found to be a failure; and, they might have truthfully added, a fraud too.... In fact, there has never been any problem in this Indian business, except getting the management of Indian affairs out of the hands of a Ring, who, fortified behind Peace Commissioners, white-cravated gentlemen, and all sorts of sentimental tom-foolery, have fleeced both the Indians and the Government, and been guilty of speculation and frauds more extensive and flagrant than ever before disgraced any branch of the Government.... And, in case the present Congress transfers the management of Indian affairs to the War Department ... the country of which I am speaking will not be likely even to be troubled by its present inhabitants any more.

This analysis is good, although limited. Corruption in the Bureau of Indian Affairs was driving Indian and white apart. Supplies promised the tribes in return for their confinement to specified reservations were often appropriated by the agents. Whiskey, whose sale to the Indians was prohibited, and guns, whose sale was even more strictly proscribed, were commonly sold to them for the agent's great profit. For his part, the Indian was ill-fed and clothed, contrary to treaty, and reservation life held little attraction for him. Distrust of whites was consequently rife, and many Indians understandably left the reservations when they were hungry, or cold, or, as in 1876, angry. Away from the reservations many whites ignored the wretched way the Indians were treated and took notice only of their violence. So it was with the *Chicago Tribune,* which acknowledged the culpability of the Indian Bureau, but in conclusion turned on the Indian himself in recommending a violent solution:

> They believed that the Government feared their prowess in battle; and believing this, their arrogance, insolence, and aggressiveness were increased beyond measure.... They never have observed their part of the treaty of 1868.... The only cure is force,—force,—applied with unrelenting severity. We must fight him until his pride and power are humbled to the dust.... It is to be hoped that the humanitarians, of the class who are always ready to apologize for the horrid butcheries of the Indian, but who have no bowels of compassion for the sufferings and losses of those pioneers of civilization, the frontiersmen, will not succeed in turning aside the sword from the heads of the "cut-throat" Sioux. Let Gen. Crook alone in this matter, and the Indian question, so far as the Sioux are concerned, will be set at rest forever. (10 April 1876, p. 3)

But Crook's men were not adequate for the job, though they fared better than Custer's. And when the news of the Last Stand was carried to the nation the American people were shocked almost to disbelief; that shock was expressed in many different ways, however, and in many instances it revealed much about America and the American people in 1876. For the most part the South defended Custer against those it felt were his detractors, finally blaming President Grant's corrupt regime for the disaster.[17] The nation labored mightily for reconciliation of North and South for the centennial year, when the old sins would be washed away and a new century might be baptised in harmony. And it seemed as though the sense of nationalism, stimulated by the fact of the one-hundredth anniversary of independence, might mollify and palliate sectional hatreds.

The *Richmond Whig* declared that "the North alone shall not mourn this gallant soldier"; and the *Norfolk Virginian,* staying clear of sectional bias, put the blame on Terry (who, it thought, should be court-martialed) for dividing the force into three units just prior to the battle. But while these feelings seemed to join the spirit of the North in a mood of national grief, the constant attacks by Southern newspapers on the Grant administration and its corruption suggested a sectional bias still. Many papers in the North and West blamed Grant also, but the Southern censure of the president was combined with harping reminders of the large garrisons of federal troops still on Southern soil. Why were they occupied in oppressing their fellow Americans when they were obviously and desperately needed in combat against the Indians? And no doubt many Southerners saw in the Northern and Western hostility toward the Indian a parallel to their own attitudes about Blacks. Why, then, was the South being punished when the Westerners were themselves bent on genocide?

The Times of London, with insight aided by distance and a tradition of political acumen, understood how the American people would react to news of the disaster before the predicted reaction materialized and Americans themselves recoiled. A *Times* editorial treated the situation with remarkable insight, tact, and understanding, though its racial arrogance will seem offensive today:

> So heavy a blow has seldom, indeed, been struck at the regular troops of a civilized Power by a barbarous enemy.... It is inevitable that such a disaster should sting the American people almost more as an insult than as an injury; but though the threatened retaliation will be severe, we cannot censure it severely, or contend that it is not dictated by a natural impulse.... We cannot doubt that the recital will kindle a flame in the United States before which the Indians will be driven back upon the alternative of death or deserts more barren and distant even than those of the present "reserves." The people of the United States, and especially the men of the West, who alone in this generation have been brought into actual contact with the Red Indians, have been little under the influence of those humanitarian ideas which are found to plead so powerfully for a mollification of English policy when we have to deal with inferior races. The conduct of the American Government towards the Indians of the Plains has been neither very kindly nor very wise; but its restraining influence, not always implicitly obeyed, has

drawn loud complaints from the settlers of the frontier lands.... The borderers will certainly make the disaster to General Custer's command an excuse for forcing upon the Government a war of extermination or of expulsion. (8 July 1876, p. 11)

And so it came to pass. At Virginia City, Nevada, a company of volunteers stepped forward, prepared to fight the moment permission was granted; the Salt Lake City government offered 1,200 men to avenge the death of Custer and to exterminate the Sioux; Senator Paddock introduced a bill (on 7 July) authorizing the president to accept military volunteers from Nebraska, Wyoming, Colorado, the Dakotas, and Utah—where such men had already come forward; and a rally at Yankton, Dakota Territory, called for a regiment of mounted troops to aid in the prosecution of the Indian wars; the Keokuk, Iowa, "Veteran Guards," 100 strong, volunteered to go out "and fight the Indians"; Sioux City sent a telegram to Washington offering 1,000 men for the war, to be combat-ready in ten days; and as far away as New York, three companies of the Third Regiment packed their caissons for the trip west. The "Sherman Guards" of Springfield, Illinois, telegraphed to Washington to tender their services against the Indians, and as far away as San Francisco meetings were held to raise volunteers. We have seen that the response of the South was the same.

Newspapers in the West were hardly more restrained. Again, from the *Chicago Tribune:*

It is time to quit this Sunday-school policy, and let Sheridan recruit regiments of Western pioneer hunters and scouts, and exterminate every Indian who will not remain upon the reservations. The best use to make of an Indian who will not stay on a reservation is to kill him. It is time that the dawdling, maudlin peace-policy was abandoned. The Indian can never be subdued by Quakers, and it is certain that he will never by subdued by such madcap charges as that made by Custer. (7 July 1876, p. 4)

The day following (in a decision quite apart from the *Tribune's* editorial) the Twenty-Second Infantry Regiment was ordered into the field to reinforce General Terry; on the same day the Fifth Infantry, with the famed Indian fighter Nelson A. Miles commanding, left Fort Leavenworth for the Black Hills while several former officers which the regiment left behind offered to raise volunteer companies. The nation had indeed been stung with a galling insult, and its first reaction was an angry call for vengeance. Letters to newspapers bordered on hysteria:

> In every case where an inoffensive citizen is slain, let 100 of these red brutes feel the power of a rope properly adjusted under their chins, securely attached to the limb of a sturdy and well-formed tree, whose duty it shall be to hold them suspended in the air, at least 10 feet from the ground for a period not less than three months.[18]

In Washington General Hurlbut, a respected veteran of the Civil War, denounced the peace policy before the House of Representatives, condemning Sitting Bull in particular as "a predatory, murdering vagabond" who was beyond living up to treaties. Representative Steele (of Wyoming) attacked the Fort Laramie treaty of 1868 as "a national dishonor and a disgrace ... the foundation of all the difficulties in the Sioux country, and the cause of the death of Custer and his men." Such sentiment was gathering support at a dizzying speed, making any moderate position all but untenable. The rhetorical position of anyone urging less than extermination was difficult amid the frenzy of revenge then sweeping the nation. "Humanitarian" was for a time a derogatory slur, so hysterical had much of the nation grown, and humanitarian voices had difficulty in being heard. Still a *New York Times* editorial called for reason and justice in dealing with the Indian, whom it now conceded had to be defeated:

> It is even desirable that our defeats should impel us to wage war in the sharp, vigorous manner which is the truest mercy to friend and foe. But it is neither just nor decent that a Christian nation yield itself to homicidal frenzy, and clamor for the instant extermination of savages by whose unexpected bravery we have been so sadly baffled.
>
> All through the West there is manifested a wild desire for vengeance against the so-called murderers of our soldiers. The press echoes with more or less shamelessness the frontier theory that the only use to which an Indian can be put is to kill him. From all sides come denunciations of what is called in terms of ascending sarcasm "the peace policy," "the Quaker policy," and "the Sunday-school policy." Volunteers are eagerly offering their services "to avenge CUSTER and exterminate the Sioux," and public opinion, not only in the West, but to some extent in the East, has apparently decided that the Indians have exhausted the forebearance of heaven and earth, and must now be exterminated as though they were so many

mad dogs.... We must beat the Sioux, but we need not exterminate them. (12 July 1876, p. 4)

It should be remembered that the very first response of many had been to condemn Custer. That was when news of the battle was only a few days old, and the ire of the country could reasonably be directed against the man who—they thought—had led five companies of cavalry into an "ambuscaded ravine." We have seen that the *Chicago Tribune* of 7 July found him "reckless," hasty, and impulsive, preferring to make a daredevil rush and take risks rather than to move "slower and with more certainty." The *New York Times* (7 July) quoted unnamed "older officers" who blamed the disaster on "that foolish pride which so often results in the defeat of men." The *Times* itself editorialized the following day that "the facts as now understood dispose most people here to lay blame for the slaughter upon Gen. Custer's imprudence and probable disobedience of orders." A telegram from General Sheridan to Sherman was reported (on 9 July) to have made much the same point: "I deeply deplore the loss of Custer and his officers and men. I fear it was an unnecessary sacrifice due to misapprehension and a superabundance of courage." And *Leslie's Illustrated Newspaper* (29 July 1876, p. 338) three weeks later condemned "the vaulting ambition of General Custer—in the excess of his personal bravery over his good judgment."

But such evaluations were not to last for very long given the feeling of white America about the Indians, and given Custer's irresistible glamor. The *New York Herald* began soliciting contributions for a memorial to Custer and his men, and the project was immediately successful. Representative A. M. Waddell (of Raleigh) introduced a bill to the House asking funds for a Custer statue. The South, he thought, would vigorously support such a bill for nowhere in the country was bravery more admired than there. For whatever reason, Waddell was unsuccessful, perhaps because his proposed legislation duplicated the *Herald*'s project. As the money streamed into the New York newspaper's offices, so did some revealing letters:

I enclose ten cents (all I can spare), for a monument to the noble General Custer. I am a school girl, but can read the newspapers, and my heart was filled with pity when I read the other night for mother the account in your paper of the awful slaughter done by the Indians on General Custer and his army.... I would give the world to have had one look at the fearless General Custer; and then he was so young and, as the papers say, so handsome. I could cry tears over his sad fate.... Leave it to the school girls and a monument will soon be raised to the gallant General Custer, for he was a man.

And very soon those shocked voices began to rise again, but this time in Custer's support. No longer was he imprudent, reckless, and hasty; no longer was it his foolish pride which led to the destruction of over 250 men of the Seventh Cavalry. The great numbers of the Indians, their treachery, and the spite of President Grant became the causes of the disaster. Finally the blame shifted to Major Reno, by way of Terry and Benteen. It was hard to blame Custer for the disaster, for he himself had made the ultimate sacrifice. As the *New York Times* put it, "criticism is kindly and charitable in tone, as it would not be had he not fallen with his command in the thickest of the battle" (8 July, p. 1). But one should not think that at first everyone was spiteful, then everyone became laudatory. While the *Chicago Tribune* was condemning Custer's "rash gallantry" it also praised other aspects of Custer the man:

> Throughout he was the same dashing cavalryman, whether upon the plains or in the charge down the Shenandoah, the Murat of our Service, fearless, reckless of the odds against him, and confident of success against almost any odds by the *elan* with which he bore down upon an opposing column.... In appearance he was the very *beau ideal* of the soldier—tall, lithe and sinewy, with the free, firm carriage of the veteran of many fields, and the dashing grace of the gallant cavalier; almost foppish in costume.... But he was no stage soldier. (7 July 1876, p. 2)

And all the while Frederick Whittaker was busily writing *The Life* of his dead hero, gathering materials—as he tells us—from various oral and written sources. Nevertheless, he also had time to write a stunning eulogy, a panegyric really, which kept the Custer legend on its way skyward.[19] Parts of Whittaker's essay have been quoted earlier (it begins with the metaphor of the bright meteor flashing from the multitide) and so need only be recalled here. And the fame of Custer began to sprint like a meteor past the dark clouds of the worst disaster the U.S. Cavalry had ever suffered on the plains.

And seldom was heard a discouraging word. A few other malcontents, including Wendell Phillips, wrote letters to various newspapers and a telegram to General Sherman questioning the policy of the War Department, wondering why the battle was termed a "massacre" simply because "we" lost, and defending the peace policy while attacking the corruption under which it was conducted. The Reverend D. J. Burrell of Chicago brought up troublesome subjects in a sermon on the first Sunday following the news of the disaster: "Who shall be held responsible for this event so dark and sorrowful.... The history of our dealings with these Indian tribes from the very beginning is a record of fraud, and perjury, and uninterrupted injustice. We have made treaties, binding ourselves to the most solemn promises in the name of God, intending at that very time to hold these treaties light as air whenever our convenience should require them to be broken.... We have driven them each year further from their original homes and hunting-grounds.... We have treated them as having absolutely no rights at all.... We have made beggars of them."[20]

But the man that Custer was—his flair for the dramatic, his great personal appeal to the public—was the surest guarantee that his image would not long be tarnished. The place where he died; the manner in which he died—alternately the "Thermopylae of the Plains" (suggesting a heroic defense) and a latter-day "Charge of the Light Brigade" (suggesting an heroic assault); the great expectations aroused by the celebration of the centennial year; the hopes inspired by the frustrations of scandal and recession; and finally the territorial and economic aspirations of many—all of these factors militated against a public conception of Custer and his last battle that would be anything less than heroic. His legendary fame had yet other sources, of course: the psychological reasons for his apotheosis and for the public's preference for the Last Stand version (when little was known about what really happened) are, however, more appropriate to a following chapter.

And the mysterious nature of the battle, with all of its unanswered and unanswerable questions, has added to the intrigue and charisma of the event. Custer's movements in the last few hours of his life are not known: the route he took to "Custer Ridge," the disposition of his forces before their deaths, the alleged attack at Ford B, Custer's intentions when first in contact with the enemy (or his plan prior to contact, for that matter)—all of these puzzles have greatly added to our interest in this battle. The personal courage of the men or of Custer himself, the debate over whether he disobeyed orders by being at the Little Bighorn, and the second-guessing about dividing the regiment: these undeterminables have enabled thousands, perhaps millions, of interested citizens to enter into the battle, to make their own evaluations, to place responsibility for themselves, to imagine what really happened during those last minutes on Custer Ridge.

And the fact that the battle was lost to the Indians added luster to the public's interest. Their "savage" ways had long been of curiosity to Europeans, their life little understood by white settlers and pioneers. They could become noble savages or irretrievable demons in American fiction, but they were essentially a mystery to the public. That they were alien, of another race, and of another cultural level also made it relatively easy for the American people to identify with Custer and to overlook a number of disagreeable facts concerning repeated violations to the treaty of 1868, the presence of whites in the Black Hills and along the Yellowstone River in 1876, the very purpose of the Terry expedition.

So the Custer legend grew. Why it survived for so long is another matter. We realize that fame plays erratic tricks with a man's life. We have seen what self-publicity can do for certain men, but this is by no means a complete formula for immortality. Nor is true heroism: Ranald MacKenzie was widely acclaimed for his Indian-fighting record during the last forty years of the nineteenth century (as commander of the famed Fourth Cavalry) and is little known now. Joshua Barney was a genuine hero of epic proportions in both the Revolutionary and 1812 wars, and he has been largely forgotten. Robert Sherrod was only one of many to celebrate the heroic deeds of Lieutenant Dean Hawkins at Tarawa (the airstrip there was named for Hawkins), but the deeds and the man have been forgotten by the public. The unheroic Wyatt Earp and Doc Holliday and their circle, on the other hand, have become heroes of sorts without the benefit of self-publicity or exalted position. By way of contrast, it is the great leaders, regardless of their personal differences, who live in the legends of the Civil War. General Sherman was certainly flamboyant and often provided reporters with exciting "copy," but he did not write very much during the war when his reputation was made. General Grant, though determined, could hardly be called an exciting personality, and his writing was not published until after he had retired from the Presidency. The gallant Robert E. Lee, so much admired by both North and South, also could never be thought of as self-aggrandizing.

Fame is created by the public: Custer, like other American heroes, has remained in the hearts of his countrymen because he became the vehicle of some aspect of their aspirations: he symbolized, in other words, a part of their ethos.[21] We have seen that Daniel Boone was at the same time both the pioneer who cleared the wilderness and the lover of solitude. As the United States was drawn westward, and hardy souls were needed to clear the forests and cultivate the earth, Americans naturally made certain conspicuous pioneers their folk heroes. More than being a brave and resourceful man, Boone was a symbol of American expansionism just as he was the Easterner's personified desire to escape urban stultification. And we have seen how it was the same with Kit Carson, who was many of the things to nineteenth-century America that Boone was in the eighteenth century. Americans really did not want to live with reptiles, fight Indians, or go without bathing, but they could idealize the men who did, for such labors were the necessary effects of empire-building. In reality, a pitched tent in the backyard is enough of "out-of-doors"; in ideality, men and boys can empathize with the rugged life where men really have to be men. And we can empathize with Custer, who embodied the struggle against the Indian in white America's ambitions to colonize the plains.

6

Instant Heroic Epics

The poetry and prose written to commemorate the battle of the Little Bighorn is hardly worth detailed analysis and has so far received little, for both its historical accuracy and its literary worth are minimal. Few poems about the battle have ever been anthologized, save one essay on the "Bards of the Little Big Horn" and a volume of rhymes about American history.[1] Artistic merit was not the *rationale* for either edition. Humble scribblers (and "humble" is meant here as a poetic rather than a social or moral evaluation), pious and sentimental ladies, and a few accomplished poets were moved to commemorate the battle in verse. Whitman celebrated "Far Montana's Canyons" (and not himself), but the poem is minor and appears now only in the *Complete Works*; Longfellow's versified version of the Rain-in-the-Face legend has attained some popularity, perhaps because it is based on a ghoulish anecdote, even though the event it describes never happened; and what was one of the best of the lot, by the least known Frederick Whittaker, has become as invisible as its author.

Though the battle was a small one, it expanded in America's imagination and swelled to epic proportions in heroic poetry. Poets either genuinely believed that the battle was epic or they sought to make it bigger than life— outstripping *The Rape of the Lock*—bigger even than Montana's sky. Their rhetoric and the sentiments of the times suggest sincerity. And finally it was the overwhelming numbers of the poets which carried the day. Enough of the elements of epic were already present in the known facts of the disaster—a dashing, romantic, and youthful general and his illustrious regiment of cavalry slain to the last man, in a battle in which few details were known, against a little understood (and hence exotic) foe, set in the Wild West. And so literally before the bodies of the slain troopers had been finally interred, poem after poem appeared on the horizon, more numerous than the Sioux themselves, and just as deadly.

The actors in the epic were made grander than life, as though to provide some comparison with the colossal martial epic which had ended a little over a decade before; and the mood, the tone which pervaded nearly all of this poetry was mauve. Custer himself was described as an American Hector (sometimes Achilles), the young (tawny) lion of the plain; he was even likened to Christ. His gallant charge was "too bold," yet it upheld the loftiest principles of life and of our race, causing a new star to shine in the firmament. His foe, sometimes "wolfish" because of his cowardly custom of attacking in large packs, was said to be of Satan's company, a simile that elevated the skirmish to cosmic proportions: the Indians were the fiends incarnate who rose up out of the ravines and with deafening yells, like a chorus from Hell, fell on the little band of heroes.

The battle reaffirmed for Whitman the "old, old legends of our race"; the men of the Seventh, "like the gods of old," whose numbers were reinforced in poetry to an epicly suitable 300, fought like tigers. It became a battle for all the world to admire, braver and more daring than the Charge of the Light Brigade, our very own Thermopylae of the Plains. All the world was said to be appalled at this fight of Fame; and the leader, peerless Custer, was lofted off to Glory's height while Fame herself knelt at his shrine.

Beyond what they say about popular culture, these tributes to Custer can be used to chronicle an important phenomenon at work: the gradual, fragmentary, and at first incoherent formation of a legend. The process has long interested scholars of legend and myth;[2] but the way in which such narratives come to assume a traditional form has never been open to analysis, owing partly to their antiquity. Moreover, the people who believe in them have no interest in studying the legends analytically and the believers are reluctant to decompose their beliefs into narrative elements and to discover "sources." These are the pursuits of disinterested scholars.

But evidence on the formation of the Custer legend is plentiful. This is an important fact, when nearly all other studies are based on speculation and surmise.[3] We may be able to go a long way toward understanding the relationship between myths, legends, and folktales, toward understanding why they may share the same or similar motifs (narrative elements) and one not be a degenerate form of the other.

In the United States of 1876, we can see the spirit of a legend made flesh. Different people—newspaper reporters, soldiers at the scene, writers and poets, and other people of prestige with access to the public—all, quite independently of each other, formulated their own strikingly similar ideas of the event. Much borrowing took place, naturally; it is the task of the concluding chapters of this book to argue that the similarities of conception were no coincidence. Meanwhile, we can see that nearly all of the conceptions about the battle scenario were at first fragmentary; one man thinks that Custer was the last of his command to die but has little idea of the rest of the details: he has no further thoughts (at least he does not mention or write of any) about other aspects of the battle. If questioned closely, our hypothetical man might well work them out. At the same time others had different ideas about other aspects of the event: all of the men were killed, one man escaped, the scouts led the column into a trap, one of Custer's own men refused to come to his rescue, and so forth. It is when there is communication between people, at some date later than when they had their first ideas, that a coherent narrative begins to emerge. In 1876 the newspaper provided that function of consolidation; today it is radio and television as well as newspapers; in medieval and classical times (and up to the present) it is an oral transmission. And then, at some point one man puts together several of these fragments and a coherent narrative is formed. In 1876 that man was Whittaker.

The first such complete account of the event is not necessarily the best; in fact de Vries thinks that when the great epic is composed the tradition declines.[4] The masterpiece which culminates a tradition also seems to conclude it; in the case of the Last Stand, however, this artistic pinnacle has not yet been achieved. When the coherent tale is put together people may well think that it tells the story the way it "really" happened; they may even feel that it tells the story the way they think the events occurred, because of the way in which an impulse will cue—and bring forth—others that are related (a matter also discussed in the final pages of this book). The narrative may even have already formed on some unconscious sphere, so that on reading Whittaker's account of the battle—to remain with our example—millions felt that they "knew" that he was telling it the way it really was. Whittaker cued certain responses within the public, was himself "cued" by the various fragments which he heard about the battle from numerous sources, and thus told the story "right." In the following pages we can see the American people constructing their legend of the Last Stand, bit by bit.

Just one week after the news reached the East, the *New York Herald* (15 July 1876, p. 3) published one of the first efforts at legend-making, "Custer's Last Charge," author anonymous:

> Brother and kinsman have fallen
>   Doomed Custer stands all but alone
> A rampart of dead men around him
>   His last cry his rifle's deep tone!

This ditty, penned rapidly upon the event, almost instantly perpetuates one of the elements of the legend: Custer alone with the bodies of his brothers, nephews, brother-in-law, and command flung around him; almost immediately, then, Custer is pictured á la Flynn, heroically alive and fighting when all of his men have fallen. The other details of the poem are conventional and do not have even that slight historical interest: Custer overwhelmed by the Sioux who must trust to their numbers alone, their stealthy attack, like wolves, on his men, the rhetoric of fraternity cheers ("trusted and true"), and the naive patriotism:

> On through the smoke of battle,
>   With maddening cries on the air,
> The wild Sioux rush up from the riverside
>   Like wolves on a man in their lair.
> Like wolves, and trusting to number,
>   They sweep on the desperate few
>   Who each bade a stern adieu
>   To the tried, to the trusted and true,
> They died as they stood, ere the oncoming yell
> Of the savages lifted its chorus from hell.
> Ere their horse hoofs trampled the rampart dread
> The last of the whole command lay dead—
> A sight for the world, in pride, to scan,
> While Valor and Duty lead the van.
> They charged, they struggled, THEY DIED TO A MAN.

For several decades America's popular tastes had been sentimental, pathetically humanitarian, but above all religious and patriotic.[5] The Civil War had galvanized that feeling for the North as well as for the South; the centennial gave that sense to the reunited nation. This mood was true of both poetry and fiction. *The Man Without a Country* is one of the best demonstrations of the public's taste before the Civil War, richly sentimental and deeply patriotic. Among poems, *Paul Revere's Ride* helped make Longfellow America's best loved poet. Even Oliver Wendell Holmes, usually a bit too upper-class (that is, Bostonian) for most people's tastes, stirred the country with his stirring plea in "Old Ironsides." Emerson did the same with "Concord Bridge."

The hey-day of the sentimental female poet had, by 1876, seemingly passed. Rufus Griswold first published *The Female Poets of America* in 1849, and six years later the volume had gone through five printings. Griswold's was perhaps the most successful of such ventures, though 1848 also saw the debut of Caroline May's *The American Female Poets* and Thomas Buchanan Read's *Female Poets of America,* which both sold quite well. By the time the Last Stand was made and instantly became a topic of poetic musing, the lady poet in America had somewhat waned in popularity but was still alive and reasonably well in the hearts of her countrymen. Almost as soon as his martyrdom had been established Custer was canonized by Laura S. Webb, the same poetess who penned *Custer's Immortality.* She now composed in a "classical" vein "A Wreath of Immortelles"; one quatrain will establish the tone:

> Oh, twine a wreath of immortelles
>   Around the storied name
> Custer, dashing, daring, gay—
>   Who now belongs to Fame.[6]

Clearly, if in his life Custer had charmed the gods of battle, he had failed utterly to impress the muses of poetry. Edmund C. Stedman, several notches above these other rhymesters as a poet, nevertheless rode into a dark ravine of his own when he put the Last Stand to verse. First published on 16 July 1876 (*Chicago Tribune,* p. 2),[7] Stedman's poem began by invoking the romance of sabers, lamenting the "wolfish foe," and reminding the reader that this disaster had marred the optimism and euphoria of the Centennial. The first newspaper accounts said that the Seventh fought "like tigers," a conventional enough metaphor, but the most superficial observation of Custer's tawny mane made a leonine metaphor leap to mind: Stedman may have been the first of the literati to use it, but many after him—notably Whitman—also thought the golden-maned Custer much like a lion:

> What! shall that sudden blade
>   Leap out no more?
>   No more thy hand be laid
> Upon the sword-hilt, smiting sore?
>   O for another such
>   The charger's rein to clutch—
> One equal voice to summon victory,
>   Sounding thy battle-cry,
> Brave darling of the soldier's choice!
>   Would there were one more voice!

Stedman's muse apparently materialized right after the heat of battle while he himself was in the heat of composition (the poem is dated 10 July), when newspapers still misled Americans in believing that Custer had impetuously directed his men in a mad dash into a ravine where he had been treacherously ambushed. This same Stedman held to the highest ideals for the poet and his work. He had at one time deplored the "horrible degeneracy in public taste," feeling that the entire nation was swamped, flooded, and deluged "beneath a muddy tide of slang, vulgarity, inartistic bathos, impertinence and buffoonery that is not wit."[8] He was an important man of letters in 1876, read by the populace and intelligentsia alike:

> O gallant charge, too bold!
> O fierce, imperious greed
> To pierce the clouds that in their darkness hold
> Slaughter of man and steed!
> Now, stark and cold
> Among thy fallen braves thou liest,
> And even with thy blood defiest
> the wolfish foe;
> But ah! thou liest low,
> And all our birthday song is hushed indeed!

Yet some of the lines bear the unmistakable stamp of the poet:

> Young lion of the plain,
> Thou of the tawny mane!
> Hotly the soldiers' hearts shall beat,
> Their mouths thy death repeat
> Their vengeance seek the trail again
> Where thy red doomsmen be;
> But on the charge no more shall stream
> Thy hair—no more thy saber gleam—
> No more ring out thy battle-shout,
> Thy cry of victory!

> Not when a hero falls
> The sound a world appalls:
> For while we plant his cross
> There is a glory, even in the loss;

But when some craven heart
From honor dares to part,
Then, then, the groan, the blanching cheek,
And men in whispers speak.
Nor kith nor country dare reclaim
From the black depths his name.

Thou, wild young warrior, rest,
By all the prairie-winds caressed!
Swift was thy dying pang;
Even as the war-cry rang
Thy deathless spirit mounted high
And sought Columbia's sky:—
There, to the northward far,
Shines a new star,
And from it blazes down
The light of thy renown!

For Stedman, too, the Last Stand was a charge; and Custer, with gleaming saber which shall thrust no more, rises above his defeat by his defiance of his red doomsmen, even in death.

In that the battle pitted a relatively small number of "friendlies" against a hostile force several times their number, it was compared with Thermopylae; never mind that the Greeks were defending their homeland against the Persians who had sworn their destruction, and were not attacking these Asian aliens to deprive them of their lands. Since Americans assumed that Custer had charged into battle against an overwhelming force, analogies with "The Charge of the Light Brigade" were frequent—although the Light Brigade was never put on the defensive, hemmed in, and finally annihilated. If the Light Brigade's charge was a great moment in sentimental history (it was a disaster militarily) there was a Tennyson to celebrate it. Certainly his poem was greater than the battle it celebrated. The American people, on the other hand, had their desires and a great many poems, but very few of them were even mediocre, and none of them are remembered. Perhaps what was needed was a Tennyson, several years in which to think about the battle, and a rounded number of the slain: Cardigan's force was rounded to an even 600.

Yet one may well wonder why Americans would want to compare the Last Stand with the charge of the Light Brigade. Cecil Woodham-Smith has described Lord Cardigan as "unusually stupid; in fact, as Greville pronounced later, an ass."[9] An officer in his regiment thought he had "as much brains as my boot" (p. 213); and Major William Forrest, also on the Crimean invasion, called Cardigan a "dangerous ass," and the man who gave him the order to charge, Lord Lucan, "the cautious ass" (p. 213). Cardigan's stupidity was no closely held secret of his officers and later historians; all of England knew of it, and American newspapers had also gotten wind of his various problems: his earlier discharge from command for incompetence, his continual harrassment of his officers—especially those of lesser station—his trial before the House of Lords for dueling.

During the siege of Sebastopol Lord Cardigan lived aboard his private yacht, which was anchored in Balaclava harbor—and to which he retired after the famous "charge" for a warm bath and some champagne. The English expeditionary force was generaled by egregious incompetents, and the entire campaign was a chronicle of folly, bungling, and gentlemanly ineptness. Is this what Americans wanted to compare to Custer's last battle? The orders sent by Lord Ragland to Lord Lucan, commander of cavalry, are models of ambiguity and, because of the needless bloodshed they caused, nothing less than criminal. The whole affair was disgraceful, beginning with the incompetence of the officers right down to the details which led to the charge: Lord Raglan's ambiguous order, Lord Lucan's failure to question a seemingly impossible mission with no point, Captain Nowlan's exasperated wave of the arm vaguely toward the end of the valley as he told Lucan, "There are your guns, my Lord, there are your enemy!"

Yet the charge of the Light Brigade became instantly famous in Great Britain, and Cardigan was at first a much-honored hero. Subsequent articles in newspapers, investigations official and otherwise, tarnished Cardigan's reputation disastrously among a certain class of Englishmen, yet to the popular mind he remained a great hero—the leader of the noblest display of arms in England's history. No doubt the process was much like that which elevated Custer in America, regardless of what subsequent events and revelations and revaluations might demonstrate. There is perhaps one important difference between the fame of these two men, and that of degree: Custer's went on to dwarf the event, whereas Cardigan's has, to some extent, been overshadowed by the charge. Tennyson honors the event, not the man who led it.

In an anonymous poem in the *St. Paul Pioneer-Press* (22 July 1876, p. 9), Tennyson was clearly in the poet's mind: "The Song of Custer and His Men" had twenty-two stanzas; stanza eighteen is presented here. The few against the many, the desolation of the battlefield, have already been established as part of the legend:

Three hundred men, with thund'ring strides,
   Charg'd to the gates of hell!
Three hundred men this day have died,
   While deaf'ning devils yell!
For cold, and stiff, and still, and lone,
   Last of this bloody fray,
Upon the hills of Little Horn,
   He sleeps in crimson clay!

Another poem, "Custer: To The Heroes of The Custer Tie" (referring to Custer's homemade red kerchief?) appeared in the *Chicago Tribune*, also rather early (10 July, p. 2), and seemed to echo the popular "Old Ironsides" in phrase, tone, and meter. The work had ten stanzas; only the fifth is repeated here:

The banners were by proud foes borne,
The guns from field and fortress torn;
Where are the flags that once waved high?
Where is that dread artillery?
They now those heroes' camp adorn.

Stanza six draws much of its information, and certainly its hyperbole, from Custer's own proclamation to his division at the close of the Civil War:

Well may they shout, well may they brag
Who never lost one gun or flag,
Who never heard a hostile gun
But quickly surrounded, seized, and won,
The piece within the lines they drag.

Compare the second line with Whitman's, "after thy many battles in which never yielding up a gun or a color."

Not even Homeric similes were sacred from the Custerphiles. Frances Chamberlain Holley in 1890 composed six stanzas on "Custer's Farewell,"[10] in which the fallen general was compared to that other epic loser, Hector of Troy:

IV

"Come on, my boys! The fierce battle is won!
   We will stack our arms by the River Fair,

Here tenting we'll wait, upon Glory's height,
    And drink to the brave from her wine-cup rare."

V

As Hector, in flashing armor, called
    The Trojan sons—while the battered gate
In fragments flew like a shriven oak—
    So Custer call'd, but scal'd the walls of fate.

VI

And they lay down to sleep—not to dream,
    While radiant forms, from the unseen land,
Brood softly above them with tender wings.
    It was "Custer's Luck," with his brave command.

Clearly, this is an ambitious poem. The comparison with Hector, the epic prince of the defeated Trojans, was not often made in the nineteenth century. Shakespeare's thought-ridden hero is invoked by the first line of the sixth stanza, though Custer's men, unlike Hamlet, sleep but do not dream. The rest of stanza VI is recalled later in a poem by Hopkins, but both poems, "Custer's Farewell" and Hopkins', owe to Matthew 3:16 where the Holy Spirit is described as a dove descending to earth. Finally, the general's own coined phrase, "Custer's Luck," is invoked, as a kind of Keatsian "wine-cup rare."

But despite its erudition and allusiveness it is not a good poem. The idea of the battle "won" is intriguing, since in a very important way it was a victory for Custer and certainly for many Westerners. The arms are then stacked on the "River Fair" (Jordan?), but in the next line the tenting is on "glory's height." Custer presumably is a type of Hector, for the reasons just mentioned, but in the last line of stanza V he is scaling the "walls"; at Troy the Greeks, not the Trojans, would be scaling the walls, unless any Trojans were fleeing the battle and deserting their besieged city: is this the image Frances Holley wants? And then the "boys" lay down to sleep, but where? On the river bank, on the heights, on top of the scaled wall, or somewhere in the "unseen land," not necessarily excluding any of the first three loci? Although this poem exhibits erudition, allusiveness, and a knowledge of poetic tradition, these qualities alone do not a poem make.

Ella Wheeler Wilcox also invoked memories of Troy—this time of the somewhat more successful if not truculent Achilles—but made of the battle a cosmic war against the forces of hell.[11] The poem is very long, 107 stanzas arranged in three books, as is perhaps befitting an epic, but only a few stanzas and fewer particularly memorable lines are quoted:

Book I,1   All valor died not on the plain of Troy.
            Awake, my muse, awake! be thine the joy
            To sing of deeds as dauntless and as brave
            As e're lent luster to a warrior's grave.
            Sing of that noble soldier, nobler man,
            Dear to the heart of each American
            Sound forth his praise from sea to listening sea—
            Greece her Achilles, immortal Custer, we.

III, 30   Ah, grand as rash was that last fatal raid
            The little group of daring heroes made.
            Two hundred and two score intrepid men
            Rode out to war; not one came back again.
            Like fiends incarnate from the depths of hell
            Five thousand foemen rose with deafening yell,
            And swept that vale as with a simoon's breath,
            But like the gods of old, each martyr met his death.

The identification with Achilles is distinctive, but hardly appropriate; probably this is why few others used it. We are annoyed by the pretentiousness of the hyperbole, the self-conscious invocation of the "muse," the "praise" sounding from sea to sea. Unlike "Custer's Farewell," Wilcox' "Custer" has little originality. All the metaphors (the fiends incarnate, the depths of hell), the rhetoric (the little group, the five thousand foemen, the deafening yell) are drearily familiar; all the figures had been used often before to describe the Last Stand, even by those purveyors of phrases outworn, the newspapers, even by some of the soldiers themselves in their memoirs. But the most derivative stanza is in book III, line 32, which sounds almost exactly like Whittaker's conception of the last moments:

> When Curly saw that the party with the General was to be overwhelmed, he went to the General and begged him to let him show him a way to escape. General Custer dropped his head on his breast in thought for a moment, in a way he had of doing.... In that moment, Custer looked at Curly, waved him away and rode back to the little

group of men, to die with them. How many thoughts must have crossed that noble soul in that brief moment.... Why did he go back to certain death?

Because he felt that such a death as that which that little band of heroes was about to die, was worth the lives of all the general officers in the world.

Thus Wilcox:

A second's silence. Custer dropped his head,
His lips slow moving as when prayers are said—
Two words he breathed—"God and Elizabeth,"
Then shook his long locks in the face of death,
And with a final gesture turned away
To join that fated few who stood at bay.
Ah! deeds like that the Christ in man reveal.
Let Fame descend her throne at Custer's shrine to kneel.

We would not be doing the poet full justice, however, without citing her closing lines:

Cast down thy lyre, oh Muse! thy song is done!
Let tears complete the tale of him who failed, yet won.

In a more populist vein, Captain Jack, the poet scout, provided the perfect counterpoint to all the "high-falutin'" business about Muses, lyres, and the plains of Troy. But, more ominously, Captain Jack also overtly expressed many of the coarser sentiments Americans were feeling. The Captain's gods were not meter and rhyme but revenge. His poem, "Custer's Death,"[12] widely circulated on the backs of "Wild West Show" programs, is in ten stanzas; only three of them and part of the last one are presented here:

I

"Did I hear the news from Custer?
    Well, I reckon I did, old pard;
It was like a streak of lightnin',
    And, you bet, it hit me hard.
I ain't no hand to blubber,
    And the briny ain't run for years;

But chalk me down for a lubber,
  If I didn't shed regular tears.

VII

Never mind that two hundred thousand
  But give us a hundred instead;
Send five thousand men towards Reno,
  And soon we won't leave a red.
It will save Uncle Sam lots of money,
  In fortress we need not invest,
Jest wallop the devils this summer,
  And the miners will do all the rest.

IX

They talk about peace with these demons,
  By feeding and clothing them well:
I'd as soon think an angel from heaven
  Would reign with contentment in h—l.
And some day these quakers will answer
  Before the great judge of us all,
For the death of the daring young Custer,
  And the boys who around him did fall.

X
* * *

But I tell you the day is approaching—
  The boys are beginning to muster—
That day of the great retribution,
  The day of revenge for our Custer.

Dozens of poets used as many formulas, but none was poetic and none succeeded—either with the muse of poetry or with the gods of time. John Neihardt tried several innovations: he told the story from the Indian's point of view and he tried to make his account "historical." Neither technique was a guarantee of good poetry, though it is more readable than most history.[13] And as literature about the Last Stand, it is better than most.

... the troopers ... heading down a swale
By fours, with guidons streaming in the gale,

> Approached the ford. 'Twas Custer with the grays,
> A sorrel troop and thrice as many bays—
>
> Grown dimmer in the falling battle-night,
> The stormy guidon of the troopers tossed,
> Retreating upwards, lessened and were lost
> Amid a whirling cloud that topped the hill.
> ... then a shout
> Enringed the battle, and the scene went out
> In rumbling dust—as though a mine were lit
> Beneath the summit and the belch of it
> Gloomed bellowing. A windy gloaming spread
> Across the ridges flicked with errant lead
> And wayward arrows groping for a mark.
> And horses, hurtled from the central dark,
> With empty saddles charged upon the day.

The central images are effective, although not brilliant. The gathering storm is apparent in the "stormy guidon" "streaming in the gale." They become lost "amid a whirling cloud" on Custer Ridge. Then the furious death struggle on the hill is a scene going out "in rumbling dust," as though a great mine had exploded under the earth, under the feet of Custer, and from the ridge flickers "errant lead" and riderless horses hurtle. Not memorable, but not bad.

But history is not necessarily poetry, though William Gesell, a portion of whose work follows, is a more convincing exemplar of that aphorism than is Neihardt. As Wordsworth learned in his later years, specificity and details can actually get in the way of poetry:

> Eighteen hundred seventy-six the horror news arrived,
> The massacre of the Custer brigade, not one of them survived.
> Two hundred and forty-five enlisted men, in this onslaught,
> And Custer with his twenty officers, the battle to death here fought.[14]

The meter of just these four lines is a disaster, the melody a catastrophe—particularly in the third and fourth lines. Even the syntax is knotted to wring out a rhyme from the limp line: "the battle to death here fought." And finally, as if further comment were necessary, even the facts are wrong: 265 officers and men did not perish with Custer on the ridge. We may move on without commenting on the absence of imagery.

Because the Last Stand caught the popular fancy of America, it also caught the imagination of popular poets. And even though a number of poets of talent and reputation wrote about the battle and its aftermath, for the most part the poetic results were little better. Longfellow was interested in the revenge of Rain-in-the-Face and did more than oral tradition to perpetuate this legend. Yet his poem is not a very good one; it has even been called "awful," though it is nevertheless better than those of the newspaper craftsmen. The story is told[15] that when a Major Kossuth Elder translated Longfellow's poem for the benefit of Sitting Bull, that great chief—always a bit surly on the subject of whites—was heard to state a preference for Negroes:

> In that desolate land and lone,
> Where the Big Horn and Yellowstone
>   Roar down their mountain path,
> By their fires the Sioux chiefs
> Muttered their woes and griefs
>   And the menace of their wrath.

Perhaps he should not have tried to rhyme "Yellowstone"; and certainly he should not have tried to portray Indians if he could not make them more than cigar store ornaments, however murderous their intentions in the poem. Longfellow ends with a characteristic Easterner's apostrophe, a questioning of white motives, and an ironic lament that this had happened in the centennial year:

> Whose was the right and wrong
> Sing it, O funeral song,
>   With a voice that is full of tears,
> And say that our broken faith
> Wrought all this ruin and scathe,
>   In the Year of a Hundred Years.

Longfellow's quiet melancholy and cheery optimism reflected the taste of the public during the 1870s, as he had for decades. And while his tear-stained voices sang for the nation's broken faith, Whittier was more interested in converting the savages. When it was reported that Rain-in-the-Face had applied for admission to the Hampton Institute in 1886, professing himself a man of peace desirous of learning the white man's ways, Whittier rejoiced at this happy vindication of humanity. Of the original nine stanzas, three are repeated here:

> The years are but half a score,
> And the war-whoop sounds no more
>   With the blast of bugles, where
> Straight into a slaughter pen,
> With his doomed three hundred men,
>   Rode the chief with the yellow hair.[16]

The slaughter pen image was the language used by the first newspaper accounts; "the chief with the yellow hair" is from Longfellow:

> His war-paint is washed away,
> His hands have forgotten to slay;
>   He seeks for himself and his race
> The arts of peace and the love
> That give to the skilled hand more
>   Than the spoils of war and chase.

>   VI
> The hands that have done the wrong
> To right the wronged are strong,
>   And the voice of a nation saith:
> "Enough of the war of swords,
> Enough of the lying words
>   And shame of a broken faith!"

Walt Whitman, who wrote some respectable poems about the Civil War, also tried his hand at the Last Stand. The result is good; it is characteristically Whitmanesque with its catalogues, its romantic diction, and its flamboyant rhetoric. Yet it does not quite succeed as great poetry:

> From Far Dakota's canyons
> Lands of the wild ravine, the dusky Sioux, the lonesome stretch,
>   the silence,

Haply to-day a mournful wail, haply a trumpet-note for Heroes.
The battle-bulletin,
The Indian ambuscade, the craft, the fatal environment,
The cavalry companies fighting to the last in sternest heroism,
In the midst of their little circle, with their slaughter'd
    horses for breastworks,
The fall of Custer and all his officers and men.

Continues yet the old, old legend of our race,
The loftiest of life upheld by death,
The ancient banner perfectly maintain'd,
O lesson opportune, O how I welcome thee!

As sitting in dark days,
Lone, sulky, through the time's thick murk looking in vain for
    light, for hope,
From unsuspected parts a fierce and momentary proof,
(The sun there at the centre though conceal'd,
Electric life forever at the centre,)
Breaks forth in a lightning flash.

Thou of the tawny flowing hair in battle,
I erewhile saw, with erect head, pressing ever in front,
    bearing a bright sword in thy hand,
Now ending well in death the splendid fever of thy deeds,
(I bring no dirge for it or thee, I bring a glad triumphal
    sonnet,)
Desperate and glorious, aye in defeat most desperate, most
    glorious,
After thy many battles in which never yielding up a gun or a
    color,
Leaving behind thee a memory sweet to soldiers,
Thou yieldest up thyself.[17]

Less than great, as it is rightly considered, the poem is still clearly the work of a fine poet; his considerable talents permeate this work. The emotion is not forced as in "How sad, amid the festal days/Of our Memorial year,/A Nation all should turn to weep/Beside poor CUSTER'S bier!" More honest feeling is carried by the simple telegraphic lines, "The Indian ambuscade, the craft, the fatal environment,/The cavalry companies fighting to the last in sternest heroism."

Whitman reverses our expectations: he will not have the nation mourn for Custer "asleep" in crimson clay "in this onslaught." The news of the defeat is brought by the battle-bulletin (telling of the Indian ambuscade, their craft, and the fatal environment) from out of far Dakota's canyons, the lonesome stretch, the silence. It sounds in his ears, by chance, like a trumpet-note for heroes. The third stanza presents a visual analogue: the persona sits, looking in vain for light or hope (lone, sulky, in dark days), much like the silent lonesome stretches of the first stanza. And then, from the center—much as the trumpet-note had sounded forth from its vortex—the lightning flash breaks out, as though from the sun, concealed.

The movement of this poem is achieved by the succession of these concentric metaphors. From the lonesome stretches of the West sounds forth a trumpet; this physical image gives way to the symbolic sun breaking forth from a thick murk across the vain and hopeless vacuum of space. Custer the martial saint has at last brought hope, reviving the oldest legend of the race; Custer, true to his sainthood, displays the "loftiest of life" by his death, head erect, pressing ever in front, bearing a bright sword. In the last few lines the spirit is again made flesh: we are with the cavalry companies again, desperate and glorious, fighting to the last. And Custer, who on earth never lost a gun or color, loses himself to this world to gain a higher reward, trailing clouds of glory, leaving behind a memory that is sweet to soldiers.

Like other poets, Whitman saw that the Last Stand was a classical tragedy, that though the battle had been lost on earth, ultimately "the fierce battle is won!" Frances Chamberlain Holley would feel the same. And like Whittaker, Whitman saw that death was the fitting end (perhaps the only fitting end) for the "splendid fever" of Custer's deeds, and that for the tragic hero not a dirge but "a glad triumphal sonnet" was demanded. Custer yields up himself ritually in a sacred recreation of the old legend of his race. But unlike other poets, Whitman said so in hard, tearless lines, the truest tribute to Custer and his last charge.

Another of the best poems celebrating the Last Stand is relatively unknown, written by a man little known but to Custer buffs: Frederick Whittaker. It is anapestic, like his other battle poem, "The Column of Death." It is fictional, but it is after all a poem, not history. Yet his imagery is effective, the allusions appropriate, and as a heroic lay it is ambitious. All the standard images are here: the ringlets of light, the fated 300, the lion, the circle of fire, the fight like tigers, and the hero's words of encouragement. This is a competent poem, and a poem rarely read. As de Vries guesses, great epics are anticipated by decades of oral tradition during which many "lesser" lays may be composed. "Custer's Last Charge"[18] is just such a heroic lay, competent in itself, awaiting the moment of its epic fulfillment:

> "Dead! is it possible? He, the bold rider,
> Custer, our hero, the first in the fight,
> Charming the bullets of yore to fly wider,
> Shunning our battle-king's ringlets of light!
> 5   Dead! our young chieftain, and dead all forsaken!
> No one to tell us the way of his fall!
> Slain in the desert, and never to waken,
> Never, not even to victory's call?"
>
> Comrades, he's gone, but ye need not be grieving,
> 10   No, may my death be like his when I die!
> No regret wasted on worlds I am leaving,
> Falling with brave men, and face to the sky.
> Death's but a journey, the greatest must take it:
> Fame is eternal and better than all:
> 15   Gold though the bowl be, 'tis fate that must break it,
> Glory can hallow the fragments that fall.
>
> Proud for his fame that last day that he met them!
> All the night long he had been on their track,
> Scorning their traps and the men that had set them,
> 20   Wild for a charge that should never give back.
> There on the hilltop he halted, and saw them,
> Lodges all loosened and ready to fly:
> Hurrying scouts, with the tidings to awe them,
> Told of his coming before he was nigh.
>
> 25   All the wide valley was full of their forces,
> Gathered to cover the lodge's retreat;
> Warriors running in haste to their horses,
> Thousands of enemies close to his feet!
> Down in the valleys the ages had hollowed,
> 30   There lay the SITTING BULL'S camp for a prey!
> Numbers! What recked he? What recked those who followed!
> Men who had fought ten to one ere that day?

Out swept the squadrons, the fated three hundred,
Into the battle line steady and full;
35   Then down the hillside exultingly thundered,
Into the hordes of the Old SITTING BULL!
Wild Ogalallah, Arapahoe, Cheyenne,
Wild Horse's braves and the rest of their crew,
Shrank from that charge like a herd from a lion,
40   Then closed around the great hell of wild Sioux.

Right to their centre he charged, and then facing—
Hark to those yells! and around them, oh! see!
Over the hilltops the devils came racing,
Coming as fast as the waves of the sea!
45   Red was the circle of fire about them:
No hope of victory, no ray of light,
Shot through that terrible black cloud without them,
Brooding in death over Custer's last fight.

Then, DID HE BLENCH! Did he die like a craven,
50   Begging those torturing fields for his life?
Was there a soldier who carried the SEVEN
Flinched like a coward or fled from the strife?
No, by the blood of our CUSTER, no quailing!
There in the midst of the devils they close,
50   Hemmed in by thousands but ever assailing,
Fighting like tigers, all bayed amid foes!

Thicker and thicker the bullets came singing,
Down go the horses and riders and all,
Swiftly the warriors round them were ringing,
60   Circling like buzzards awaiting their fall.
See the wild steeds of the mountain and prairie,
Savage eyes gleaming from forests of mane,
Quivering lances with pennons so airy,
War painted warriors charging amain.

65   Backward again and again they were driven,
Shrinking to close with the little lost band;
Never a cap that had worn the bright SEVEN

Bowed till its wearer was dead on the strand.
Closer and closer the death circle growing,
70   Ever the leader's voice, clarion clear,
Rang out his words of encouragement glowing:—
"We can but die once, boys, but SELL YOUR LIVES DEAR."

Dearly they sold them, like Berserkers raging,
Facing the death that encircled them round;
75   Death's bitter pangs by their vengeance assuaging,
Marking their tracks by their dead on the ground.
Comrades, our children shall yet tell their story,
CUSTER'S last charge on the Old SITTING BULL;
And ages shall swear that the cup of his glory
80   Needed but that death to render it full.

Pathos was the mode of Whittaker's contemporaries, but he chose to engage his readers with a tale of heroism, albeit exaggerated and romanticized. Scott and Byron were very popular too, and Whittaker's kinship is with them rather than with the mawkish ladies of Griswold's collection. Wilcox, Holley, and Webb bid us drown ourselves in tears of pity; Whittaker tries to arouse our sympathy and admiration for Custer without mourning him sorrowfully. That is the significant difference between them: our admiration. What we feel in the ever-narrowing circle of the Indians and the unflinching Seventh in its anaconda coil is tension and a sense of heroic fulfillment.

Whittaker is not writing history in this poem, just as he did not depict reality in his prose about the battle. Yet we forgive him that in poetry—a form of expression not to be literally believed, as Plato saw—though we may not be so charitable regarding the biography. Custer had not "all the night long" been "on their track" (1.18), but he had encamped on the far side of the Crow's Nest. No traps had been set for him to scorn (1.19). Several of the regiment's men were veterans, but one can hardly believe thay had ever fought odds of ten to one before that day (1.32). Three hundred seemed the most popular number for the size of Custer's force in the newspapers—perhaps because that was the number of Leonidas' men, perhaps because it was half the size of Cardigan's "Light Brigade"—but the actual number was somewhat less. If a battle line was formed (1.34), it appears not to have been on Custer Ridge, and if several Indian assaults were repulsed (1.65), no one remembered it. Did Custer call out, "We can but die once, boys, but SELL YOUR LIVES DEAR" (1.72)? Only Whittaker appears to have known.

"Custer's Last Charge" is in the tradition of the heroic lay, employing many of the elements of *The Battle of Maldon,* the alliterative *Morte Arthure,* even the *Song of Roland.* Like those poems (and many others) the fight begins at long range, the warring armies approach each other rapidly and then, dismounted, they fight close at hand. Like Roland, and Byrhtnoth, and Sir Gawain, Custer has an initial success: "backward again and again they were driven" (1.65). But inevitably the battle goes badly, and the situation grows desperate. The epic hero urges his men on to brave deeds of heroism in the face of inevitable death, and Custer is no different, his words closely echoing those of Roland: "But cursed be he who sells his life cheaply."[19]

Whittaker has structured his poem as a question and response. The first stanza asks, "dead? is it possible!"; the rest of the poem answers that it is true, all too true. But these nine stanzas do not merely reply, they do not merely describe the circumstances of the hero's fall, they offer consolation (as does the elegy) to Custer's comrades by reminding them that death takes everyone (1.13) and that "fame is eternal and better than all" (1.14). Glory has hallowed his death, so, comrades, "ye need not be grieving" (1.9).

Custer becomes the epic hero of yore, charming the bullets to fly wider, shunning his ringlets of light, while he and his men fight like raging Berserkers. Yet Whittaker achieves this epic elevation without an invocation of the Muse, without stacking arms by the River Fair, without the thundering demons of hell for his foes ("devils" of the plains are formidable enough). The enemy are numbered in hordes coming as the waves of the sea, which can be readily accepted. The Seventh is again said to have fought like tigers, a hyperbole no more imaginative than what was found in contemporary newspapers. And Whittaker would have us think that none ever flinched. We can forgive him this wishful flight of fancy just as we can forgive him the heroic words he gives his "young chieftain," for it is heroic poetry that he is writing, and we should be disappointed if he had not composed it in this way, if he had not had his "Custer" act in just this way. We forgive Whittaker because it is the function of poetry to communicate a transcendent truth as the poet sees it, regardless of the objective facts. Thus in heroic poetry the hero, whoever he is, must be made to seem truly heroic. In this, at least, Whittaker has succeeded.

7

The Martyred Heroes

Custer's is not the only last stand of this book, but to us it is the best known. The hero who dies with panache has more than a score of facets to interest us. Custer fascinates us because we know so much about him; the others interest us because we know so little about them. With Custer as our model, then, we may be able to deduce much about the origin and development of the heroic legends of other peoples. Saul was the first; and so with the son of Kish we begin.

On a windy and treeless mountain Israel's first anointed king stood amid his small but loyal band of subjects and prepared to defend his kingdom—and their homeland—against the enemy. The hostile army was one accustomed to victory, and in the impending battle the Philistines were far more numerous. Saul's situation was desperate: he had defeated these same people, as well as several other oppressors of his people, just a few years before, yet now, in 1013 B.C., they had reappeared, their brandished spears and gleaming swords threatening to return the young nation to vassalage. The vast army of the Philistines, numbering in the thousands,[1] had lumbered westward toward Mt. Gilboa, across the Jordan River, very near the edge of the former Jordanian bulge. The Israelites prepared to defend the heights and the plains below while Saul, caught suddenly in a fit of uncertainty and doubt over God's failure to appear as his guide, rode to the neighboring village of Ein Dor where he had heard dwelled a witch with the power to conjure. Saul, all of his composure and control gone, sought to invoke the spirit of Samuel from whom he desperately needed advice.

Mt. Gilboa is a chain of hills and ridges north of the present Beit Alfa kibbutz. One can only guess at the site of the battlefield; residents of the kibbutz will not even do that, though they do point to one crest, out of sight in the distant north, which their children call "Saul's throne." Haifa is the nearest major city; buses leave hourly for Afula, and from this dusty farming settlement still other buses travel the now fertile valleys to Beit Alfa and Beit She'an, where Saul's body was at first taken. The landscape could be that of central California. The hills leap up precipitously from the flat valley

Mt. Gilboa is a series of steep ridges, and the exact spot where Saul fell is not known. The ridge pictured is near the battlefield; in its contrast of rock and soft moss, of sand and desert flowers, in its unrelieved exposure to the sun, this scene is much like many others above Beit Alpha.

benches and seem to have been piled haphazardly on top of each other. When one mound is traversed, another appears. When a hill is finally, and laboriously, topped, yet another is there to be climbed. Each ridge gives way to one yet higher, each hill to one beyond. The ground is sandy (like Montana's) and only scrub brush, and thistles, and desert flowers grow there. No clouds interfere with the incessant sun; and nothing interferes with the swarms of hungry desert flies. The only relief is afforded by the unrelenting desert wind sweeping across the broiling Jordanian plains. It is little enough relief, especially for soldiers marching, or fighting, or dying.[2]

Israel's first king was subject to fits of depression. The Old Testament says that "the spirit of the Lord departed from Saul, and an evil spirit from the Lord troubled him" (1 Sam. 17:14); the *Interpreter's Bible* assessed his major problem as extreme egoism (II, 1039-40); and Bailey and Kent used the more modern concept of "mental illness."[3] It is now commonplace to criticize Saul for lacking sagacity, for whatever his problems—psychological or theological—his reign was flawed, and he was at times an irresponsible tyrant.[4] Yet something in his personality commanded the respect and the loyalty of nearly all those who knew him; during Saul's life David alone, of all the prominent Israelites, broke with him openly. And when Saul had fallen and the news was brought to David, it was he who lamented most eloquently:

> The beauty of Israel is slain upon the high places: how are the mighty fallen!
>
> (2 Sam. 1:19)

We are not sure of the tactics used on the field that day thirty centuries ago. Some versions have it that the Israelites defended Mt. Gilboa successfully for a time, but that faintness of heart and lack of faith in their erratic leader caused them to abandon their positions in the mountains to the enemy and to flee for their lives.[5] A more honorable version has the battle storming back and forth for nearly all the day, the Israelites fighting bravely but finally being worn down by the cavalry and chariots of the Philistines.[6]

The Old Testament gives no details of the battle or of the conduct of the Israelite warriors, but rather is almost exclusively concerned with their leader. His death is made truly heroic, surprisingly so since Saul has not fared well at the hands of the poets and scribes. As Samuel, book 1, chapter 31 has it, nearly all the men[7] of Israel were killed on Mt. Gilboa before the Philistines fell heavily upon the survivors, finally slaying Saul's three sons, Jonathan, Abinadab, and Malchishua, with their arrows. At the end only the wounded

king remained, with his faithful armor-bearer.[8] The battle now hopeless, Saul
would neither flee nor allow himself to be captured, but chose instead to die
what Graetz has aptly termed "a death worthy of a king"[9]: he ordered his
armor-bearer to kill him, but that loyal servant could not bring himself to slay
God's anointed. Finally, Saul fell upon his own sword. The servant followed
his master.

Then:

> It came to pass on the third day, that, behold, a man came out of camp
> from Saul with his clothes rent, and earth upon his head: and so it was,
> when he came to David, that he fell to the earth, and did obeisance.

When David bade him rise and speak, the unnamed Amalekite answered:

> ... the people are fled from the battle, and many of the people also are
> fallen and dead; and Saul and Jonathan his son are dead also.
>
> (2 Sam. 1:2-4)

When asked by David how he knew this dreadful news, the man answered that
he met Saul alone on the battlefield and that the king begged to be killed. The
man said that he then killed Saul, and he showed the royal crown and bracelet as
proof. We remember the righteous anger of David, as fierce as his lament was
bitter:

> Ye mountains of Gilboa, let there be no dew, neither let there be rain,
> upon you, nor fields of offerings: for there the shield of the mighty is
> vilely cast away, the shield of Saul, as though he had not been anointed
> with oil.
>
> (2 Sam. 1:21)

The contrast which the Old Testament writers made between Saul and
Samuel was as clear as it was instructive: old and young, spiritual and physical, wise and strong, prophet and warrior. If the contrast was new then, it has
certainly become a cliché in the subsequent centuries. To the modern critic it
has the feel of a literary device, and it may well have been heightened in the
centuries preceding the transcription of the books of Samuel. Despite the
scribes' dislike of Saul, Jewish secular legends admire his modesty, his in-
nocence, and his unusual beauty. If he had any drawback in popular legend, it
was his great mildness.[10] Scholars carp about his alleged shortcomings—his

lack of sagacity, his lack of a deep spiritual insight, and his temperament; but all acknowledge that he was a first-rate soldier.

He was physically strong ("stronger than lions") and had great personal courage. He was outstanding as a soldier and as a general and, judging from the loyalty of his subordinates, inspired the confidence of nearly all his subjects. He was an imposing figure, "from his shoulders and upward he was higher than any of the people" (1 Sam. 9:2), and this too was a facet of his leadership. However ineffective and tyrannical he is alleged to have been as Israel's first king, it is primarily as a warrior and military leader that he is best known. When he died, David lamented the passing of a great soldier: "How are the mighty fallen, and the weapons of war perished" (2 Sam. 1:27).

This fearless and compelling leader was the ideal martyred hero to make his last stand on a hilltop. Whatever the writers of the Old Testament may have thought of King Saul, the oral tradition which transmitted the account of his last battle has been kind. No hero in the West—not Roland, not Custer—is said to have died more gloriously. His men were outnumbered by the fierce, arrogant Philistines. The situation was crucial, for on the outcome was to rest the fate of Israel, or so thought Saul and his men. The battle is said to have been a bitter one; in the last moments only Saul and his servant were left alive on the field. Some Israelites may have fled (perhaps these are "the people" whom the Amalekite said "are fled from the battle"); but these may just as easily have been civilians in the immediate region. Saul's three sons fell, presumably near the end.

The traitor in this account does not compromise the safety of command, since the battle is lost anyway, but appears as the Amalekite who robs Saul's body of its crown and claims to David to have killed the king.[11] And he is also the lone survivor, an insignificant figure in the fighting itself, but the one man who had seen the battle and who carried the news to David. He is also a clearly defined foil to Saul's faithful armor-bearer, who had refused to kill his master, even on command. He is a Cornwall to Saul's Kent. And Saul, as is fitting, dies last, and by his own hand. Like Roland, no enemy could strike him down; like Custer, said by some to have saved the last bullet for himself, true to the so-called Code of the West.

The death of Saul on Mt. Gilboa is well told. Saul's early uncertainty both heightens the drama and prepares us for his subsequent loss. So even before the battle is joined we are anxious about the result. Shakespeare used the same scheme for the last act of Macbeth, when the Scottish king, also uncertain of the outcome, like Saul, faces his fate with dignity and heroism. The biblical antagonists are counterbalanced as in a well-constructed drama: the small band of Israelite peasants and shepherds are fighting for their homes and their new country against the hordes of bellicose barbarians seeking to enslave them. Saul's men and then his own sons fight and die bravely on the mountaintop; his armor-bearer is loyal to the end. Finally the cowardly and treacherous Amalekite defiles God's anointed, and when he brings the news of Saul's death to David expecting a reward, he is instead slain. In all it is a skillful story, appropriate to the death of a great national hero, though it has not achieved the renown of many others whose narrative is much the same. Perhaps the Old Testament writers were successful in deflating Saul's character; perhaps we do not normally turn to the Bible for this sort of tale of heroism.

The idea that in the historical books of the Old Testament the narrative has been arranged is no more heretical than what many biblical scholars have long thought and written.[12] One of the most recent studies, for instance, argues that the books of Samuel are chiastically structured:[13] the reigns of Saul and of David divide at the end of the first book, while the story of each man's reign is also told in two halves, the first part relating each king's successes, the second part his failure. The turning point in each man's life is placed in the middle of his narrative, Saul's in his war against Amalek (1 Sam. 15), David's in the affair with Bathsheba. Even if one cannot agree with this author in his view of the intricate nature of the chiastic structure—down to the level of single lines and even, in some instances, individual words—the evidence is strong that in the Samuels we have a "planned narrative."

With the configuration of the narrative elements in these books so discernible, their strict historicity is questionable; they were written not as history in the modern sense, but as pedagogical treatises. David's involvement with Bathsheba and Saul's war with the Amalekites, who were the traditional embodiments of evil, are instructions to other and future princes on the principles of political and moral leadership. The same observations have been made of the Homeric epics, even of *Beowulf*. Yet Saul's death may or may not have been narrated for a pedagogical purpose; the point is not important for our understanding of the structure of the Samuels. Certainly the story's form, its attention to drama, its balancing of character types, its striking similarity to the other heroic tales we shall soon discuss, all argue strongly that whether through intention or the "natural" shaping of oral tradition, a planned literary account has emerged. For the limited purpose of appraising Saul's heroism we will do best to examine his life as a carefully wrought narrative.

A nineteenth-century French engraving perpetuates the legend of Saul, the last of
his men alive near the summit of Gilboa, taking his own life. The horizon swarms
with the enemy's horsemen.

Not only are the characters in the final act established to counterbalance each other and to highlight their traits, not only is the structure chiastic (if one is to accept the above reading), but the events of Saul's life leading up to the defeat at Gilboa are carefully structured as are the events of David's life afterward. When Saul goes into battle at Gilboa several echoes reverberate in our memories. He had earlier defeated these same Philistines in a spectacular upset at Michmash. Seriously outnumbered, he had thought of withdrawing from his position when Jonathan and his armor-bearer, unnoticed and alone, suprised the enemy outposts and after killing the guards put the entire Philistine garrison to rout. The Israelites, numbering only about 600 and armed with neither swords nor spears, charged into the fleeing army which had in its host 30,000 chariots, 6,000 horsemen, and people "as the sand which is on the sea shore in multitude" (1 Sam. 13:5). As a reward for his piety in the Philistine wars an angel brought him a sword, the only sword in his army.[14] And shortly after Saul would gather a much larger army to make war on Amalek, which he also, though less spectacularly, defeated.

But in those days God was on the side of Saul, even though at the battle of Michmash Saul disobeyed God's commandment, and Samuel reproached him, and told him that as a result his children would not establish a kingdom in Israel forever. And when he prepared to go to war with Amalek Samuel came to him again and said, "Now go and smite Amalek, and utterly destroy all that they have, and spare them not; but slay both man and woman, infant and suckling, ox and sheep, camel and ass" (1 Sam. 15:3). But Saul disobeyed again: he captured the Amalekite king Agag alive[15] and spared the best of the captured sheep and oxen to sacrifice to the Lord. So the Lord sent Samuel to tell Saul of his rejection. Immediately after that (1 Sam. 16) Samuel went to Jesse to anoint his son David; and the Lord sent an evil spirit to trouble Saul.

Saul had relied on the Lord in those days, and the Lord had given him great and impressive victories with a meager band of ill-armed farmers. At Gilboa the Lord turned his back on Saul, and with Samuel dead, the Israelite king had nowhere to turn, except, he believed, to the witch of Ein Dor. Saul himself, on Samuel's command, had outlawed witchcraft and conjury, but in his hour of fear and trembling he turned to the witch for help. His fate on Gilboa was in this sense decided even before the battle began, as it was foreshadowed by David's anointing and subsequent rise in power and prestige. David, too, had begun to win impressive victories beginning with his unexpected slaying of Goliath. David also learned from some of Saul's mistakes. For example, after Michmash Saul commanded that his people not eat of the sheep or oxen or any of the food which they had taken as spoils; Jonathan, who had not heard the order, tasted some honey which he had found on the ground. Saul felt obliged to sacrifice him, his eldest son, but the people pleaded on behalf of their hero and Saul recanted, and so Jonathan was saved. But in the process, many Philistines escaped from the Israelites, who were weakened from hunger. Later, David and 400 followers fell upon an Amalekite army which had sacked Ziklag, and the Israelites destroyed nearly all of them; but David ordered that the spoils be divided among his people.

Saul had invoked God's displeasure because of his disobedience. Though the Lord had given him victory after victory, Saul did not carry out His commandments fully. And so, on the eve of Gilboa, he went into battle deserted spiritually, all but helpless with his small band of men—about the same number which had given him victory at Michmash. Yet if Saul is pathetic at this moment, if he is to be condemned by the Old Testament scribes for his disobedience and for his jealousy of David and for his evil spirits, there is something noble about this great warrior nevertheless. Faced with certain defeat, deserted by his Lord, desolated by Samuel's death, he nevertheless went into battle bravely and fought fiercely.[16] In a struggle in which defeat and death were certain, Saul fought with the valor and dignity of the great king he must have been; in that way he rose above his own fate. If we can admire Camus' Sisyphus, laughing as the boulder crashes once more to the bottom of the hill, we must also concede a greatness of heart to Saul, determined that if he must die he will do so like God's anointed.[17]

The last stand most remembered by Israelis today did not take place on Mt. Gilboa, however, but at Masada. The defense of this mountain fortress near the banks of the Dead Sea has become a symbol of modern Israel's determination to survive, as is poignantly clear in the motto, "Masada Shall Not Fall Again." On the flattened, almost perpendicular mountain, nearly 1,000 Jewish zealots killed their families and then themselves rather than fall into the hands of the attacking Roman soldiers. We do not know who died last, though Josephus notes that the zealots were led by Eleazar, whom he calls "a man of influence."[18]

The Romans attacked the fortress by storming its wooden walls across an earthen ramp they had constructed next to the mountain. When it was clear to the defenders that they could no longer hold their positions, under Eleazar's urging they destroyed their stores and then themselves. When the legionnaires secured the fortress and discovered the masses of slain, "instead of exulting as over enemies, they admired the nobility of their resolve and the contempt of death displayed by so many in carrying it, unwavering, into execution."[19]

The defense of Masada is a living reality for Israelis today: "Masada Shall Not Fall Again." The site of the last stand of the first revolt, where more than 900 Jewish patriots chose, in the words of their leader, a "death of glory to a life of infamy. . . . We shall remain free men." The remains of Herod's palace are visible on the tiers of the escarpment.

Two women and five children escaped by hiding themselves in underground aquaducts while their comrades and kin were destroyed in the slaughter.

The question of Josephus' knowledge of the events of the siege and his historical accuracy are not being questioned here. The problems of the chronicler are much the same as those faced by the historian of Thermopylae; thus for economy, they are considered together. Chronology is also important; Josephus lived many years after Herodotus and may have been influenced by him. It is important for our understanding of the legendizing process that we pay closer attention to those narratives that are not derivative.

Some five centuries after Saul died on Mt. Gilboa defending his nation and his honor, at about the time when the Old Testament was first being written down, Herodotus was gathering information from peasants in the area of the battlefield which was to become the most illustrious in Greek, and perhaps all Western history: the stand of Leonidas and his Spartans at the pass of Thermopylae. The battle was still within the living memory of many who had known of the fight or had heard accounts of it from other witnesses. From these informants Herodotus is said to have compiled his data within forty years of the conflict and then to have recorded it in his *History*. It would not be overly dramatic or sentimental to say that he "immortalized" it, for few other "Last Stands" have so caught the imagination of all who have heard of them as has the story of Leonidas and his men at the pass. Even Custer's Last Stand was called by some of his contemporaries in their wildest chauvinistic exuberance the "Thermopylae of the Plains."

More than history, Herodotus' account[20] is also stirring narrative. The invading Persian horde, more than one hundred times the numerical strength of the Greek contingent,[21] had massed at the western end of the Thermopylae pass on the plain of Anthela. To their right was the seemingly inpenetrable Mt. Callidromon; to their left, the Gulf of Malis. All that stood between the Persian Emperor Xerxes and the plains above Athens was a small allied army of Thebans, Thespians, and a few others, and Leonidas, king of the Spartans, with 300 men which Herodotus says "the law assigned him" (p. 200). Later, Athenians would criticize the small number of their allies and rivals, resenting Sparta for not contributing more to the war effort, while others would quibble about the battle itself, arguing that it was not intended to be a mere holding action (to allow Athens to evacuate) but was itself the last line of defense.[22]

For Xerxes at that moment, however, no such pedantic trifles disturbed his imperial mind. Only a seemingly impotent handful of armed men lay between him and the conquest of the Balkan peninsula, and when his scouts reported that they had seen the Greeks engaged in their morning calisthenics and others casually combing their long hair, his confidence in victory was reconfirmed. He is reported to have thought it laughable that his enemy should be engaged in such occupations on the eve of battle (p. 202). He called for his advisor and claimant to the Spartan throne, Demaratus; and he then learned to his surprise that these were the normal preparations of Greek men readying for war, and furthermore that the men they would shortly confront were actually the best in all of Greece. But Xerxes was not to be dissuaded or even forewarned, and he shortly launched his Medes and Cissians against the Greek position, with confident orders to bring the captives before him directly.

However, when the men of Xerxes rushed forward in their vast numbers to attack the Greeks, the defenders not only held firm but actually slew a great many of them with slight loss to themselves. Reinforcements were then thrown into that meatgrinder, but they too were sent reeling with a heavy loss. The emperor became disgusted with his soldiers' poor showing, and withdrew the Medes, replacing them with an elite unit led by an officer named Hydarnes, whose fortune was no better. The Greeks were defending a narrow pass where the numbers of the Persians could be neutralized, since only a few of them could come into action against the defenders at any one time; the Greeks had the advantage of longer spears and used them to kill off the Persians, never coming within range of their enemy's hand-held weapons.

Herodotus also noted with pride that the Lacedaemonians fought with cunning as well as ferocity, occasionally seeming to flee the enemy, waiting for the Persians to rush after them "with much noise and shouting," and then wheeling about sharply to catch the overconfident enemy in their trap. In these ways were "vast numbers" of Persians destroyed while "very few" of the Spartans fell.[23] Herodotus reported that at the sight of this slaughter Xerxes, who just a little earlier had scoffed at the hair-combing of the Greeks, thrice leaped from the throne from which he watched the battle, in fear for his army.

And so the battle continued in the same one-sided way on the next day, the allied Greek contingents repeatedly driving off the headlong assaults of the Persians. So skillful and determined was the defense that the pass might have been held indefinitely. But then one of the residents of the area, a man named Ephialtes, went to Xerxes and, apparently in hopes of a reward (like the Amalekite at Mt. Gilboa), told him of a pathway known to the shepherds of Malis (now commonly identified as the Anopaea Track), which wound through the mountains and debouched into the pass at the Melampygou rock behind the Greek position. Ephialtes' treason would lead to the destruction of the Greek forces. And like so many traitors in such stories, he met a pitiless destiny: fearing the Lacedaemonians, he fled into Thessaly with a price on his head. Some time later he returned from exile to Anticyra, where he was slain.

Meanwhile Xerxes, delighted at the information, sent Hydarnes at the head of some 10,000 crack troops to follow the path through the night. At dawn (of the third day) the Persians emerged from the mountains and surprised a large body of Phocian guards, who quickly retreated to defensive positions on the crest of a nearby mountain; and so they, in effect, removed themselves from the battle, while Hydarnes led his men past them and rushed unhindered onto the Greek positions in the pass.

A council of the Greek leaders was hastily convened: what should they do in this perilous situation? Some of the contingents immediately prepared to march for home, whether on their own authority or on Leonidas' command was not known; Herodotus thought the latter. The Spartan king determined to stay with his men, however, and to defend the pass to the last. This decision, so fraught with drama and heroism, has been the cause of much subsequent speculation. Herodotus recalled that at the beginning of the war when the Spartans consulted their oracle, they were told that either Sparta must be overthrown by the barbarians, or one of their kings must perish: "O ye men who dwell in the streets of broad Lacedaemon!/Either your glorious town shall be sacked by the children of Persia/Or, in exchange, must all through the whole Laconian country/Mourn for the loss of a king, descendant of great Heracles" (p. 206). G. B. Grundy[24] thought little of the prophecy and its alleged effect on Leonidas but felt rather that the practical Spartan king must have thought that he had a chance to defend the pass successfully. The traditional view is that the battle was a holding action to allow time for the evacuation of Athens (recent archeological findings support this posture), and that Leonidas was a Spartan, whose warrior code galvanized his sense of duty: he would die to save another's city.

Whatever his motives, he stayed, with his 300[25] and with a detachment of Thespians who refused to retreat and so shared his heroic death. Meanwhile, the Persians under Hydarnes poured down out of the mountains, the officers urging their men forward onto the Spartan fortifications. Many were trampled to death by their own men; many others were crowded into the sea, but still they drove on to the Greek defenses. The Thespians and Spartans, on their part, fought on desperately, knowing that their destruction was imminent, and "exerted themselves with the most furious valour against the barbarians" (p. 207).

One warrior in particular was singled out for his poise in the face of this overwhelming enemy: a Spartan named Dieneces. When one of his allies

A statue of Leonidas now guards the pass at Thermopylae, facing the Kolonos and the impenetrable Callidromus mountains. In 480 B.C. the Gulf of Malis would have covered the monument.

exclaimed that "such was the number of the barbarians, that when they shot forth their arrows the sun would be darkened by the multitude," the Spartan answered with the laconic, understated bravado characteristic of his country, "if the Medes darken the sun, we shall have our fight in the shade" (p. 208).

As the sun rose on that third day the Persians attacked with their swords, hacking away at the Greek spears until most of them were splintered, and the Spartans and Thespians were soon forced to defend themselves with their own swords. It was at this point, with both armies fighting closely, that Leonidas fell, "together with many other famous Spartans," two sons of Darius, and two brothers of Xerxes (p. 207). Herodotus tells us that a fierce struggle arose over the body of Leonidas in which the Spartans four times drove back the onrushing Persians and at last, through their courage and ferocity, succeeded in safely bearing away his body. With it they slowly withdrew to the east where they made their final stand on a hillock, Kolonos, about two miles west of the east gate village of Alpeni:

> Here they defended themselves to the last, those as still had swords using them, and the others resisting with their hands and teeth; till the barbarians, who in part had pulled down the wall and attacked them in front, in part gone round and now encircled them upon every side, overwhelmed and buried the remnant which was left beneath showers of missile weapons. (P. 208)

For the "lone survivor" we have our choice of two men. One of the famous anecdotes of Herodotus about the battle tells of two Spartans who lay wounded in Alpeni on the third day with "a disease of the eyes." Both had been ordered by Leonidas to leave the Greek camp. But when news of the Persian flanking attack reached their village, Eurytus ordered his Helot to lead him to the fighting; the other wounded man, Aristodemus, chose to remain at Alpeni, and he later escaped with the retreating allies. Eurytus was led to the thickest part of the fighting and died in the battle with his countrymen; but when Aristodemus returned to Lacedaemon he was held in such disgrace that death would have been preferable, and he soon chose that course at the battle of Plataea (p. 210). The other, far less dramatic "lone survivor" Herodotus does not mention until book 8 (chap. 21) of the *Histories:* Abronichus, son of Lysicles. Perhaps he is not mentioned in book 7 because his story is hardly as dramatic (or didactic) as that of Eurytus and Aristodemus, and he is rarely mentioned as a possible informant for Herodotus. But however authentic was

Abronichus' tale—Herodotus does not comment on it—he was an Athenian observer stationed with the Spartans, and he kept a small boat handy. When the battle was hopelessly lost, he is said to have fled to his craft and to have brought the hard news to Athens.[26]

Thus ended one of the great acts of collective heroism in the West. Leonidas was the Spartan leader and his name is mentioned most prominently in Herodotus' account, yet unlike most of the other heroic last stands he does not stand out quite as conspicuously above his men as does Saul, or Roland, or Custer. Leonidas, unlike those other heroes, did not die last; we are told specifically that he fell before the retreat to the hillock. But we are also told that a furious struggle arose over his body, and whether the actual moment of his death was known to Herodotus or not (who among the combatants had lived to tell him?), his comments concerning it are important.

Herodotus seems to have more in mind in his narrative than glorifying the Spartan king. We are told that when Leonidas was slain his men increased their energies to save his body from defilement when in the possession of the enemy; they recaptured it to keep it in "safe" hands, and when it was finally taken by the Persians it was over their own dead bodies on the Kolonos. The lesson is clear: not only did Leonidas make a heroic decision to stay at the pass of Thermopylae, but his men also were bravely determined to fight. Even more important, during the most desperate moments of the struggle his warriors showed their loyalty and kept their obligation to their king by the fierceness of their struggle to save his remains, like the fierce struggle over the body of Patroclus. Not only their bravery and their skill at war but their unflinching loyalty is thus commended. That is one of the most important messages Herodotus seems to be conveying.

The visitor to the battlefield may well be astonished at the geography if he has read Herodotus recently. The national highway that runs past the battlefield today is somewhat north of the actual site, in an area that was in 480 B.C. under the waters of the Gulf of Malis. In those days the pass ran well to the south of the national road, on the far side of Kolonos and the hillock supporting the Phocian wall, site of the Greek camp. The plain of Anthela remains as well, but it is hardly spacious enough for the more than 5 million persons Xerxes is said to have commanded (7. 185-86), of whom more than 2½ million were fighting men, unless we imagine that they were encamped in bunks six or seven deep. And we certainly cannot believe that the rugged and massed hills around the second Thermopylae pass, particularly in the area of the Phocian wall and Kolonos, supported anything like the 14,200 warriors Kontorlis claims comprised the defending army.

The Thermopylae pass as it appears today, looking westward toward the position of
the Persian armies.

Yet even allowing for some exaggeration, other questions immediately perplex the battlefield visitor. Herodotus did not identify the path used by Hydarnes to outflank the Greek position, but modern scholars have. Whether the path which is pointed out to the visitor is the one actually used by the Persians is moot; but one thing seems sure: The Anopaea Track is narrow for much of its course and the mountain is steep. As on Mt. Gilboa few trees grow here, and those that do are stunted. The brush, however, and low-lying vegetation are thick, the soil sugary and strewn with rocks and boulders. It taxes our understanding to be told that 10,000 troops, carrying arms and armor, made their way along this path on the night of the second day of battle, and then descended this path on the morning of the third, when they formed for battle. In many places the path hardly seems wide enough for two men to scramble abreast, and they would have had to scramble to top the rise and descend upon the Melampygou rock to the east of the Greek camp.[27]

That armed men could perform this maneuver quietly—the Phocians were said to have been caught sleeping and thus were surprised—and could then descend that mountain path without a great deal of stumbling, falling, and confusion seems incredible. Where on the sharply undulating topography they could assemble in formation is an even greater enigma. Imagine, for instance, that the Persians were able to march along the track four abreast, a generous breadth; allowing about two feet between ranks—rather close quarters—or a yard for each rank, the Persian column would stretch out for 2,500 yards, or more than a mile. The van would be coming into action against the Phocians while nearly all of the column was still lumbering through the brush. The position of the Phocians should then have been as advantageous as that of their allies in the pass to the west; why then did the thousand of them retreat to another hill to defend themselves? Either the Anopaea Track in 480 was as broad as an autobahn today, or the Persian forces were not nearly as large as Herodotus' informants indicated, or the Greeks at the pass of Thermopylae were undone for reasons that can only be subject to speculation.

And what are we to make of the remaining struggles in the battle? Having swept past the Phocians without stopping to fight, Hydarnes and his 10,000 fell upon the rear of the Greek position. The Melampygou rock was named by Herodotus, but of course he could not locate it exactly, nor did he feel a need to. Which "rock" it was (or is) is a matter of tradition and scholarly conjecture. But let us assume that Kontorlis and his colleagues are correct in their identification; that would place Hydarnes and his Immortals astride the third Thermopylae pass about 10 A.M. on the third day, moving toward the rear of the Greek position. The Melampygou rock was about two kilometers away, and the

Persians—even Persians tired from their hike along the Anopaea Track—could cover this distance in several minutes. Yet we are told that the Greeks held a council to decide on their strategy in this dire circumstance, and that part of the Greek force decided to return home.

But at that point where could they go? Xerxes and his millions were to their front, the west, and now 10,000 crack troops blocked their escape to the east, or so one would think. Herodotus is silent on this point. He does not say how various Greek contingents managed their withdrawal, and he also does not say that they had to fight their way through Hydarnes' men. His silence here is not in the interest of clarity. Meanwhile, Leonidas led his men in an assault on the main Persian force in the area of the modern thermal baths, at least 1,500 yards west of Kolonos. Then, when these men learned that Hydarnes and his Immortals had arrived, they are said by Kontorlis to have withdrawn to Kolonos. But at this point they should have been surrounded, unless we assume that by "arrived" the Melampygou rock is meant, or that the Persians, unhindered, moved more slowly over two kilometers than did the Spartans, who—while fighting off Xerxes' men to their front—moved over 1,500 yards backward, carrying and defending the lifeless body of Leonidas.

If this discussion of Herodotus' account of the defense at Thermopylae suggests that he has written, like the Old Testament writers of the books of Samuel, a "planned" narrative, then it is only an extension of what has been said elsewhere.[28] Herodotus is thought not to have placed great strategic importance on this battle; like General J. F. C. Fuller in recent years, he may have considered that its importance lay in halting the Persian army and forcing the Persian fleet to fight.[29] Rather, the Ionian historian is said to have invested it with symbolic and moral significance. In the former sense, he alternated his description of the Spartan stand with accounts of the battles at sea, where the war was finally decided. In its moral aspect, the battle presents Leonidas as the "typical representative" of the citizen-soldier of the Greek polis, even though he was a king and not an ordinary citizen; yet he acted out the duty which Sparta expected of each of her sons. Immerwahr finds that within a series of antitheses used by Herodotus to describe the battle, "the heroism of Leonidas and his Spartans stands out as an extreme of courage such as exists only in death."[30]

Herodotus' account is full of rhetorical parallels and polarities. The "realistic" strategy of the Athenians during the war is set off against the heroic (yet ultimately ineffectual) valor of the Spartans; the virtues of both are in sharp contrast with Persian *hybris* and cultural inferiority; and the victory at Plataea becomes the Greeks' retribution for Xerxes' treatment of

Leonidas. Within the story of the battle itself, Ephialtes is a foil to the king, as are the Thespians (who chose to remain with Leonidas) to the Thebans (who chose to leave when they were outflanked). So too are the two wounded men at Alpeni presented as foils, one asking to return to fight, the other choosing to save his life—but only for the moment, as he was soon to give his life to save his honor.[31]

Surely there is thoughtful planning in the telling of this story. The narrative itself develops through the deliberate juxtaposition of several contrasts which, taken together, argue for artfulness. The casualness of the Greeks on the eve of battle sharply points up the changing moods of Xerxes: at first he is over-confident, shown most strikingly when he fails to heed the warning from Damaratus; later, his threefold leap from his throne dramatizes his fear and frustration. Meanwhile, the Greek allies are slaying their thousands. The Greeks are at first successful and seem able to hold the pass indefinitely; their initial success allows Herodotus to show their superiority over the Persians, suggesting that finally not only treason but the great number of the invaders will be the deciding factors. Against them the greater skill and valor of the Greeks will finally be worn away, much as their spears are eventually splintered and shattered by the Persian swords in the final defense.

This argument is not a reproach of Herodotus' historical accuracy. He was, as his defenders point out, only as good as his sources. But close to forty years had elapsed between the time of the battle and that of his interviews with local informants. And who were those informants? Did the Thespians survive to tell tales of the last stand? Curiously, they are not mentioned as being with the Spartans in the last moments on the hillock or at the fight over Leonidas' body. The Thebans had withdrawn long before; Herodotus is not likely to have this story of a noble Spartan defense from the Persians or even from any Greeks who may have sided with them (none are mentioned). Neither are natives in the area mentioned in the narrative, and in any event folk memory is generally inaccurate.[32] Aristodemos is known to have fled before the end.[33] The heroic words of Dieneces about fighting in the shade of the Persian arrows also invite questions: who is the Trachinian stranger who told him of the Persian numbers? He might have been Herodotus' source for the story of Dieneces' brave reply, but he most likely would have been captured (if not killed) by the conquerors. How did he know the name of this Spartan warrior? Perhaps Herodotus heard of the anecdote on subsequent trips to Sparta, but if so the accuracy of his informants, so long a time after the actual battle, must be questioned. That Herodotus was writing history should never be doubted; but since much of it came to him through an oral tradition we can be certain that it had already assumed dramatic qualities that compromised its accuracy. And in that he carefully planned his narrative, aesthetic considerations gained even more importance. Why that happens—the ways in which "facts" become "fictionalized"—is one of the major concerns of this book, and a fuller discussion must await a later chapter.

The most famous of the epic heroes of the West is no doubt that nonpareil warrior of the Franks, Roland. Yet his fame is that of the largely (if not entirely) fictional character who emerges in the *Chanson de Roland* and other *Chansons de Geste*. Of the real Roland almost nothing is known; of the battle in which he fell, little more. Einhard's *Vita Caroli* chronicles the retreat of Charlemagne's army through the Pyrenees in 778. The narrowness of the valleys left the army vulnerable to ambush, for it had to string itself out through the mountain passes. While it was in this vulnerable position, hostile Basques chose to attack the army's rear, with the baggage trains and their small guard. The terrain is ideal for guerrilla ambushes; and when the main body of the army had descended the slopes of these steep mountains into France, the Basques attacked. Their rush out of the woods caught the Franks by surprise, and they were driven into a narrow valley. The Basques followed up on their initial success and killed the Frank guard to the last man; then, under cover of night, they stole away with their looted baggage. Because of the Basques' swiftness and knowledge of the land and the ensuing darkness, they were able to make their escape successfully. The heavily armed and battle-hardened Franks could do nothing to recover their property or revenge themselves for their personal loss.

By any standards the battle was a small, though galling one. It would never be considered one of "The Decisive Battles of the World" or even of France, yet it has achieved an international fame. Joseph Bedier thought that the monks at the monastery fostered the legend to encourage pilgrims to stop at Roncesvalles on their way to the shrine at St. James de Compostella; but even this pious legendizing, if true, could not account either for the extent of the legend's popularity or for its persistence. And yet all that is known of Roland the man is that one of the three named (and therefore noble) casualties in the pass at Roncesvalles was one *"Hruodlandus Brittannici limitis praefectus"*—Roland, a prefect of the Breton Marches. The Oxford manuscript has been dated as a product of the first quarter of the twelfth century. Charlemagne was thirty-six years old at the time of the battle, but he strokes a long, patriarchal beard in the poem. And, of course, the battle is no longer a

Roland, charging into the enemy at Roncesvalles, looks like a Custer in plate armor in this nineteenth-century French engraving.

minor defeat like the mosquito sting of some annoying pest, but an epic struggle of hundreds of thousands against a Frankish force of about 20,000, after which Charlemagne's revenge is thorough and devastating.

The story of Roland's defeat at Roncesvalles may have been in oral circulation for nearly three centuries, more than enough time for it to have become shaped and polished. Bedier thought that it had been glamorized and publicized by the monks at the site; Jan de Vries speculated that a Frankish warrior class perpetuated the story not only to commemorate one of their brethren but to serve as an expression of the ethos of the class and as an inspiration to knight-aspirants.[34] In any event, and regardless of the known facts of the battle, the created narrative is an engaging one, but one that Turoldus composed independently of Herodotus (who was lost to the Middle Ages) and the Samuels.

A summary of Roland's last stand might help to highlight some of its relevant features and demonstrate how close this story comes to our paradigm. The trap had been set by Ganelon's betrayal of the Franks' line of march to the enemy (in the epic they have become Saracens). In contemplating his march through the mountains, Charlemagne offered half of his army to his nephew, Roland, but the offer was refused, lest the young warrior be thought incapable of defending the army's rear with the usual numbers (laisse 63),[35] much like Custer's famous refusal to accept Gatling guns or reinforcements from the Second Cavalry. When the enemy revealed his seemingly endless array of armed men in the distance, Roland's chief lieutenant Oliver was concerned:

> ... "Jo ai paiens veüz:
> Unc mais nuls hom ên tere n'en vit plus.
> Cil devant sunt. C. milie ad escuz,
> Helmes laciez e blancs osbercs vestuz;
> Dreites cez hanstes, luisent cil espiet brun.
> Bataille avrez, unches mais tel ne fut."

> ... "I see the pagans.
> No man has ever seen a greater number.
> Those in front carry one hundred thousand shields,
> With helmets laced and hauberks shining white;
> Straight are the handles of the multitude of burnished spears.
> You have a battle such as you have never had before."

> (1039-44)

The warning seems to foreshadow the admonition of Custer's scouts that far more Indians were encamped in the valley of the Little Bighorn than he had anticipated, and probably more than the Seventh Cavalry could handle. Custer's general attitude was also as cavalier as Roland's reply:

> Respunt Rollant: "Ne dites tel ultrage!
> Mal seit del coer ki et piz se cuardet!
> Nus remeindrum en estal en la place;
> Par nos i ert e li colps e li caples." AOI.

> Roland answers: "don't speak such foolishness!
> Evil is the heart that cowers!
> We shall keep this ground!
> We will be prepared with sword and spear!"
> (1106-10)

Oliver is soon convinced, asserting that "gente est nostre bataille" (valor will give the battle to us [l. 1274]). As at Thermopylae, Maldon, and Kóssovo (and, according to Whittaker, at the Little Bighorn) the hero and his men are at first successful, as dozens, scores, then hundreds of Saracens fall before the Franks' onslaught. But eventually, and inevitably, the greater number of the pagans tells against Roland and the Frankish guard (at laisse 115), and their strength begins to wane. As the knights see the tide, up until then at the full, begin to ebb, they cry out to their leaders for help; Bishop Turpin replies by urging them to fight on yet more bravely:

> "Seignors Barons, n'en alez mespensant!
> Pur Deu vos pri que ne seiez fuiant,
> Que nuls prozdom malvaisement n'en chant.
> Asez est mielz que moerium cumbatant.
> Pramis nus est fin prendrum a itant,
> Ultre cest jurn ne surum plus vivant."

> "Barons, do not be fearful!
> For God, I pray you, hold your ground,
> So that no one sings evil songs of you.
> Better to die here with honor;
> Soon we will meet our destined end.
> We cannot live beyond today."
> (1515-20)

The tide of the enemy's strength rolls on inexorably, and though the Franks fight on bravely, they are hopelessly inundated. Near the end they are reduced to but a scant sixty, but like the Spartans at Thermopylae who preferred to fight in the shade (created by the density of Persian arrows), they vow that they will make the pagans pay dearly for every life lost: "Einz que li moergent se vendrunt mult cher" (1.1690), fulfilling Roland's earlier proclamation that it was better to die than live in shame: "Melz voeill murir que huntage me venget" (l. 1091).

When the battle against the Indians was all but finally lost Whittaker imagined that Custer called out to his men, "We can but die once, boys, but SELL YOUR LIVES DEAR." And at the same moment in the battle's course, Turoldus has Roland cry:

Ço dist Rollant: "Ci recevrums martyrie,
E or sai ben n'avons guaires a vivre;
Mais tut seit fel cher ne se vende primes!"

Then Roland says: "We will have martyrdom here,
And I can see that we have little time left
But he who sells his life cheaply be cursed!"
(1922-24)

Roland's final minutes were discussed in detail earlier. When the field at Roncesvalles had been deserted to the dead and dying, Roland staggered to a nearby hill and there, under two lofty trees, fainted away. A stealthy Saracen who was hiding among the bodies rushed forward to claim the hero's sword as his prize. Suddenly Roland revived and struck the interloper on his helmet, shattering it and the Saracen's skull in one swipe. But then he felt his sight fading; he struggled to smash his sword, Durendal, on a rock, but he could not. Sensing the imminence of death, he groped his way toward a lone pine tree, and lying down atop Durendal and his great horn, Oliphant, he prayed one last prayer and died. The enemy had not killed him, but his temples burst when he blew the Oliphant for help. According to the Oxford manuscript no survivor lived to tell the tale; for this detail we must look in the *Pseudo Turpin* (and later redactions) where Baudouin, Roland's brother, escapes to carry the news to Charlemagne.

If such a death as this is afforded only to a nation's greatest warrior, we have underestimated the role of Sir Gawain in the fourteenth-century alliterative *Morte Arthure*.[36] Let me recapitulate that great moment in this late

Middle English poem to give it some perspective. Arthur had conquered nearly all of civilized Europe, and he paused with his armies outside Viterbo. Then, at the height of his military successes, he was troubled by a dream in which Lady Fortune spun him to the bottom of her wheel (Charlemagne also had troublesome dreams presaging disaster on the eve of Roland's defeat). The omen was shortly confirmed to Arthur when he met Sir Craddock, fresh from England with news of Mordred's treachery. Acting with great haste, Arthur gathered up a large portion of his force and marched back to Normandy. There he and his men embarked in an invasion flotilla, defeated Mordred's forces at sea, and then attempted an amphibious landing to recapture his kingdom. Sir Gawain led the first assault.

With a galley full of knights he sailed up an inlet, and when the ship was beached, he and his men leaped ashore, ready for war. With a rousing declamation of encouragement to his men, Gawain and his standard-bearer led a charge up the strand and then up the slopes of a green hill toward the enemy's positions. In this first bold attack Gawain's forces were successful, and 300 of Mordred's men, who happen to have been Dancs, were thrust to the earth (11. 3754-55). And so victory at first seemed within the grasp of Gawain and the loyal English. But soon Gawain's impetuosity, or recklessness (he was "full of anger" [l. 3756]) drove him to lead his men down from the hilltop, where lay the shattered contingent of Danes, into Mordred's middle guard, commanded by the archtraitor himself. Gawain, as befitting his station, had been in the forefront of the action, slashing and hacking away, keeping a wary eye for the opposing commander. But the enemy troops, composed mainly of Danes, Lithuanians, mercenaries, and Saracens from various lands, numbering 60,000, soon proved too much for Gawain's scant seven score.

When Gawain realized that his small band was surrounded and hopelessly lost he wept with pity for his men (l. 3799), but he girded up his loins—and theirs—with this rousing speech:

> We salle ende this daye alls excellent knyghttes,
> Ayere to endelesse joye with angelles vnwemmyde.
> Thofe we hafe vnwittyly wastede our selfene,
> We salle wirke alle wele in the wirchipe of Cryste.
> We salle for ʒone Sarazenes, I sekire ʒow my trowhe,
> Souppe with oure Saueoure solemply in heuene...
>
> (3800-3805)

The force of Mordred's minions wore away the heroic resistance of Gawain's noble knights. Before the end Gawain slipped between the individual combats of the melee, seeking out the traitor to engage him in single combat to the death. Finally, hero and traitor met. Gawain's first thrust was with the lance, but it only injured Mordred. Gawain leaped in to finish off his enemy with his shortknife, but his aim was poor; Mordred evaded the thrust and parried with one of his own. His aim was the better, and Gawain's helmet was pierced and his brains spilled. With the battle then over, and Gawain lying dead at his feet, Mordred was moved to eulogize the man who had been England's greatest knight. Later, when Arthur visited the field and saw the same body lying amid a circle of knights with a ring of slain Saracens slumped around them, he also grieved for the one man alive, as he said, worthy to be king (11. 3960-61). With his heart still full of sorrow he rushed into that final combat from which he never returned. Revenge, which was Charlemagne's in Spain, which was the Athenian's at Plataea, which was to have been the Cavalry's in the spring of 1877, was in its fullest measure denied Arthur.

In trying to understand medieval narrative, we customarily look for sources, for it is axiomatic that every medieval author was retelling an old story anew, and never making up a new one. C. S. Lewis once imagined a conversation during the Middle Ages in which a naive interrogator asked Layamon or Chaucer, "Why do you not make up a brand-new story of your own," to which Lewis fancied they would have replied, "Surely we are not yet reduced to that."[37]

Parts of the alliterative *Morte Arthure* may have come from the *Chanson de Roland*, which was certainly well-known in England (Chaucer himself alludes to the traitor Ganelon). When scholars of Old French literature have sought for New Testamental archetypes for the death of Roland, however, it has been Christ, and not Saul, who has been their choice.

Charlemagne has been likened to that other priest-king, Abraham.[38] And the sacrifice, or the intended sacrifice of Isaac by the father of faith may in some way prefigure Charlemagne's "sacrifice" of Roland, as in medieval exegetical writing it was commonly believed to prefigure the Crucifixion. Isaac, then, who prefigures Jesus, would also be an antitype of Roland. Ganelon, like the infamous apostle, is known primarily for his treason. His cupidity (in accepting payment from the Saracens) further heightens his parallel with Judas. His victim, Roland, predicts the manner in which he will die, and the count appears strangely unwilling to oppose his destiny, almost seeming to choose every action that will ensure his death in battle. Christ-as-knight he may well be, dying on a hilltop, betrayed while nature stormily and darkly mourned for him in France, mourned for one who in turn lamented the loss of so much blood. Nevertheless, there is more than a faint and distant echo of Saul in this story of Roland's death—unintentional though it may be.

The *Roland* may owe much to the New Testament and some to the Old, but what is the debt of the *Morte Arthure*'s creator? Several chronicles have been suggested as partial sources, particularly *La Voeux du Paon,* but never the *Chanson de Roland*.[39] Yet it would seem clear that if the *Morte* had an earlier life in France—if it, like so many other Middle English romances, had a French original (in this case lost)—then the *Chanson de Roland* is a rather obvious choice as the inspiration for the account of Gawain's death. On the other hand, several versions of the ambush at Roncesvalles were known in England; the most obvious source for the *Morte* among these is the Middle English *Song of Roland*, of which only 1,049 lines have survived. Its date—1400—is about right if we are to consider it as a source, though such dating is always approximate (the *Morte* is usually put at 1360). The chronology of *Otuel and Roland* raises no problems as a source, since its genesis is conventionally given at around 1330; and one should at least consider this rather wretched poem as a possible source for the narrative of the death of Roland. A final possibility is Vincent of Beauvais' *Myrrour Hystoryal*, whose book 13 relates the battle of Roncesvalles.[40]

The more controversial possibility—that of independent genesis—is the one this book favors. Specifically, do we need a source of this traditional kind to explain the *Morte Arthure*'s inspiration? Is there any clear indication in the text of the *Morte* which suggests that it relies on another work for its account of Gawain's death? And how much more do we know about this poem when we conjecture that it may have derived from the *Song of Roland*, said to have been written forty years later? We are fairly sure that Herodotus was not familiar with the Old Testament, but rather got the details of this most famous of Greek battles from peasants in the area of Thermopylae. From these stories and anecdotes of the combat he reconstructed the battle and gave them a form that was most suitable to the event and to the meaning he felt it embodied. It seems just as unlikely that Turoldus was inspired either by Herodotus or by the books of Samuel. Rather, the *Chanson de Roland* was in oral tradition for over two centuries and acquired its shape and its details, as Jan de Vries thinks, from the countless mute inglorious Turolduses who told and retold the story of the death of their most luminous warrior hero.

In this sense it is the property of "das Volk" as much as it is of accomplished artists; note that in either instance the narratives are still strikingly similar. It will be argued shortly that independent genesis is the most likely option because given a very few basic facts—in this case the defeat of one's own forces—a narrative of that defeat is very likely to be presented in a certain way, with certain details that will soften the hard facts of defeat. The folk, as well as great artists, have their pride and their honor and a desire to mollify any blow to that pride. And as we have seen in very great detail, the heroic aspects of Custer's Last Stand arose quite naively in the imaginations of many Americans, some of whom actually participated in the battle itself and who should have known better, but none of whom had ever read Herodotus, Turoldus, or Flaubert.

Of all the martyred heroes on the hilltop, nowhere can we see so radical a transformation from event to narrative as in Flaubert's retelling of Polybius' account of the Libyan revolt from Carthage in the novel *La Salammbô*. For us the interest lies in what the great realist made of the leader of the revolt, Matho, after years of meticulous, almost compulsive research on the archeological and historical backgrounds of the "Inexpiable War," which included a visit to Africa and several of the battlefields. Polybius' account of the war[41] (which Flaubert read in the translation of Dom Vincent Thuillier) and of Matho's ultimate defeat was told rather succinctly and often with a Carthaginian bias, though the Greek historian considered the Inexpiable War one of the goriest of his acquaintance and did not greatly favor either side.

Having returned from fighting Carthage's war in Sicily, the Libyan mercenary army grew impatient over their wages. The Carthaginians, on the other hand, taxed almost to death, had trouble raising the promised stipends. Two mercenary leaders, Spendius and Matho, sought to increase the discontent of the soldiers by appealing to their fears and insecurities. Gesco, the Carthaginian who had been their wartime leader, was accused of withholding their compensation for horses and corn. Meetings were held during which Spendius and Matho created the atmosphere of a frantic mob; many were stoned if they spoke out against the leaders, and soon anyone other than Spendius was stoned if he spoke out at all:

> They used to behave thus mostly when they held meetings after their morning meal in a drunken condition, so that moment anyone called out "Stone him," the stones flew from all sides and so quickly that it was impossible for anyone who once came forward to address them to escape. (P. 189)

Gesco was quick to see the danger. The mercenaries were now disorganized and unruly, and they presented a clear and present danger to Carthage and its citizens. Gesco therefore took it upon himself to continue negotiations in the hopes of appeasing the rabble until their demands could be met. He addressed groups of the soldiers and at times met privately with their officers, at a "great personal risk" to himself, but to no avail. The Libyans quickly consumed their patience and went to Gesco to demand their pay "in a very insolent manner," and he, thinking to "rebuke their presumption," (p. 191), told them to go to their "General," Matho, for it.

That was the spark for which the keg had yearned. The Libyans' frustrations and fury exploded into a mindless riot: they seized all the money they could find and made prisoners of Gesco and other Carthaginians with him:

> As for Matho and Spendius, thinking that the most expeditious means of fanning the flame would be to commit some violation of law or good faith, they co-operated in the excesses of the soldiery, plundering the personal effects as well as the money-chests of the Carthaginians, and after subjecting Gesco and those with him to the outrage of putting them in fetters, sent them to prison. (P. 191)

Such was the beginning of the war which was to last for more than three years, during which Carthage was plagued by inadequate money and material, by the shifting alliances of her neighbors, by her own corruption and decadence, and by the famous personality conflict between her two generals, Hanno and Hamilcar Barcas. And so the ravages of the war drifted back and forth, neither side skillful or energetic enough to win. Finally, after many entreaties by their senators and countrymen, Hanno and Barcas agreed to a reconciliation of their animosities for the sake of the war effort. United they began to defeat the mercenaries in a series of engagements, though none of them was decisive. Matho was weary and eager for a decisive battle, having been unsuccessful in several fights around Leptis, and agreed with Barcas to decide the entire issue in a single general battle:

> Both sides then, with this purpose, called on all their allies to join them for the battle and summoned in the garrisons from the towns, as if about to stake their all on the issue. When they were each ready to attack, they drew up their armies confronting each other and at a preconcerted signal closed. The Carthaginians gained the victory, most of the Libyans falling in the battle, while the rest escaped to a certain

city and soon afterwards surrendered, but Matho himself was taken prisoner. (P. 235)

Polybius' narrative is crisp and the facts sparse; there is hardly any description at all, certainly not of the personalities involved, and the only fact we know of Matho is that he was captured. The terrain on which this battle was fought is not described; the course of the battle is omitted, and we are told only that the two armies faced each other and at a signal began fighting. We do not know if the mercenaries fought well or bravely in this last fight, but only that nearly all of them were killed or captured. (The Dom Vincent Thuillier translation adds no details, being for the most part quite literal.)

But Flaubert's fiction[42] "fills in" many of the details of the battle, not from the historical sources but from the author's imagination. Like the passions of all of the characters, that of Mathô for Salammbô is invented; as Lanson says, "bizzarres parfois en leurs effets, ou monstreuses,"[43] another facet of what Georg Lukács termed his "bestially savage character."[44] Hamilcar's daughter is referred to by Polybius but once, and then he does not name her; that her occasional lover and leader of the rebels is wild and passionate is certainly suggested by Flaubert's source, but at the end of the novel a considerable degree of dignity is granted him. Although Polybius was relatively unbiased in his contempt for both sides, occasionally despising the rebels more, Flaubert sided with Mathô: "in the struggle—or fusion—between civilization and barbarism, Flaubert's sympathies are plainly with the barbarians."[45]

Flaubert commences the rebel's last battle on a plain, but as the tide begins to run against Mathô and his men they are driven back to a hillock. There they defend themselves with desperate ferocity, but there they are slowly destroyed by the spears, swords, rocks, and anything the maddened Carthaginians can hurl at them. Near the end only Mathô and an unnamed Samnite are left alive, and in the last moments even the Samnite is slain. Mathô, his armor beaten away, his clothes tattered by the missiles and blows of his now rabid enemies, seeing all of his comrades slain, hurls himself at the mass of Carthaginian spears, hoping thus to end his life on the field. But as he leaps, the wave of weapons parts before him, depriving him of the death of his own choosing. Instead, he is seized and led in humiliating captivity through the town, mocked by the wretches he had for nearly four years terrorized, past the viewing of Salammbô. His humiliation is ended by his execution, and his heart is ripped from his chest.

The commonplace labeling of Flaubert is that of romantic and realist:

Entres les deux ecoles romantique et naturaliste se place Gustave Flaubert, qui procede de l'une et annonce l'autre, corrigeant l'une par l'autre, et melant en lui les qualites de toutes les deux."[46]

If these labels are at all helpful, we can certainly see their marks in *Salammbô*; but especially, I hope, we can see the romantic: a concern not with what is but what might or should be (in Cazamian's capsule definition[47]), writing that is imaginative and sentimental—an apt description of Mathô's last stand. *Salammbô* shows Flaubert's meticulous attention to archeological and historical detail at its most "scrupuleuse et savante."[48] Like *Madame Bovary*, it represents nearly five years of work. And the realist is there: in the brutality with which the war was fought, brutally described, and the unrelieved suffering of many of the actors and thousands of extras; Mathô's wild savagery and Salammbô, whom Sainte-Beuve thought so much like Emma Bovary, an unhappy and restless woman vaguely searching for some romantic release.[49]

Flaubert sought to write on a subject of splendor after the sordid experience of the publication of *Bovary* and its aftermath, to write on a subject that would be greatly distant from the modern world of which he professed to be sick. On the one hand he sought to apply the methods and principles of realism to the historical novel;[50] but the ending, so romantically heroic in its hilltop setting, is hardly "realistic." Flaubert actually disliked what he thought to be Realism; its proponents copied life photographically, whereas for him art implied choice. He was obliged to choose among reality's farrago for the materials of his art, and in the finale of *Salammbô* he made his choice. Fay found the end of the battle, with Mathô in his passionate desperation hurling himself at the victorious enemy, "an infinitely more epic situation" than Polybius' original.[51] And epic it is, as we have seen in the identical situations on Mt. Gilboa, at Thermopylae, and at Roncesvalles, though the total effect in *Salammbô* is strangely anti-epic: despite the excesses of the characters throughout, they are rather ordinary people. Flaubert did not create epic personalities but conventional people with conventional feelings expressed excessively. Harry Levin thought that they were "plastic."[52] Few, if any, are drawn at all carefully by the standard of Flaubert's own abilities; Mathô, the hero, "is as unshaped as an operatic tenor,"[53] and when he and the others are placed in the epic circumstances of the war between Carthage and Tunis they are unavoidably deflated.[54]

Flaubert's intentions in giving Mathô so heroic an end are not entirely clear. Perhaps he thought to give his "bestially savage character" a glorious finish as Shakespeare gave the sympathetic although villainous Macbeth a heroic death. I leave that evaluation to literary historians and critics of French literature. What is certain is that the ending derives from Flaubert's imagination, developed out of his own sense of what was appropriately heroic (however ironic his intent for that heroism), and not from any of his sources. Certainly he did not get the idea of the last stand on the hilltop from Polybius, and though he knew Scripture well it is extremely unlikely that he thought of Saul as a counterpart of Mathô. His good French education at Rouen (before studying law in Paris) no doubt included the *Chanson de Roland*, but if the medieval epic made any impression on him we do not know of it and no one, so far as I know, has suggested the *Chanson* as a source for *Salammbô*.

Flaubert himself is the most likely "source," and for our study of epic this is important. The other battle accounts we have reviewed so far in this chapter were based on oral traditions which developed years (40 for Thermopylae, perhaps 500 for Mt. Gilboa) before they were recorded. We know that oral traditions transform facts erratically; but that Flaubert the careful literary artist would tell his story much as the other last stands had been told in oral tradition is important to note. It suggests that there is a certain way of telling certain stories, in this case stories of heroic defeats. It suggests that particular narratives may naturally draw to themselves certain details and their arrangement, in our case the hilltop, and valorous defense, the inevitably victorious enemy, the fight to the last, and the rest. That these details should occur to Flaubert as well as to the nameless purveyors of tradition in Europe, on the Balkan peninsula, and in the Middle East suggest that we may be dealing with a universal of narrative, almost a deep structure of story-telling. In Flaubert we have the hero on the hilltop developing not out of any racial unconsciousness or out of the collective and anonymous creations of das Volk, but out of the (identifiable) imagination of a single artist.

In the Scandinavian *Bjarkamál* a number of interesting variations from our basic pattern illustrate clearly the flexibility of this heroic paradigm. No complete version of this poem survives, yet we know enough about its outlines to treat its action competently. Axel Olrik[55] remarks of it that no poem in Scandinavian history was so great a favorite, but this must surely be one of the most poorly preserved popular favorites in world literature. We have only two stanzas from *St. Olaf's Saga*, and two other fragments are preserved among the leaves of the *Gesta Danorum* (though Saxo's translation of the original skaldic verse into Latin hexameters has lost much); finally, a rather poor paraphrase found its way into the last chapters of *Hrolf's Saga Kraki*, but this is a very late compilation of the sixteenth century. Certainly this is a merciless fate for so great a favorite.

About the poem's legendary hero, Bothvar Bjarki, we know a bit more. His name, which means little bear, is for his great strength (of course!), but also revealing of his parentage. His nickname, Bothvar, also has an appropriate meaning—warlike. In *Hrolf's Saga Kraki* he slew a winged beast which had been impervious to all previous opponents. Another of his victims was the *beserkr* Agnarr; and Saxo records that at one time he had encountered a bear and killed it. In the *Bjarkarimur* his opponents were a she-wolf and a bear. This poem also records that Bjarki and Hjalti were among those warriors who helped Uppsala's king Athils in his struggle against king Ali of the Upplands.[56] And in the *Bjarkamál*, the poem which describes his death against hopeless odds, his opponents were the warriors of the traitor Hjarvarth's army of Swedes and Goths. Against them his incredible strength and skill are of little effect and he is defeated; yet in defeat (or because of it?) he becomes, in Olrik's estimation, the greatest favorite of the Scandinavian Middle Ages.

We are not even sure when Bjarki lived or when the *Bjarkamál* was composed. The sixth century is a reasonable guess, but whether the song was in the form Snorri gives to us or, as Jan de Vries has generalized, it was in the hands of the folk for several centuries, we do not know. Within the sagas we are told that on the eve of battle at Stiklestad (in 1030), in which St. Olaf was martyred and his army defeated, the skald Thormod sang the "Lay of Bjarki." The setting was much like the famous and apocryphal anecdote about the Norman invasion of England when the jongleur Taillefer sang the *Chanson de Roland* to enhance the courage and valor of his countrymen before the first charge:

> The day is breaking,
> The cock is shaking
> His rustling wings,
> His crowing rings!
> The hour is come
> When thralls at home
> Begin their toilsome task—
> Ye friends of Adils, wake at last!
> Wake up! Wake up!
> Nor wassail cup,
> Nor woman's cheer,
> Awaits you here,
> Rolf of the bow!
> Har of the Blow!

Brave men, the battle ne'er forsaking!
Til Hildur's game that bides your waking.[57]

The consequences are entirely different: though the *Chanson de Roland* is about an epic disaster, the retelling of its hero's valiant combat seems to have stirred its warrior-audience to victory. It is an anecdote told, after the fact, of a putatively real event. The recitation of the *Bjarkamál* and its tale of defeat is a literary device within a well-organized chronicle whose purpose is to lead us to anticipate, by analogy, the forthcoming defeat of St. Olaf.

The comparison is instructive, for Bjarki's greatest moment is nonetheless the moment of his destruction; it is Bjarki the loser whom we best remember (whom Thormod also best remembered), the defeated hero who became the Roland of the North, for in his fated battle at Lejre castle, in defense of his king against the foreign invaders, he became—with the other culture heroes we have admired on these pages—a type that is usually created only once in the history of a people, whose admirable qualities are most apparent in death.

And yet Bjarki is alluringly different. Although he shares with other folktale heroes his bear's son youth, as bears' sons they all are closer to the folk imagination than is Bjarki the king's champion, and his analogues on other hilltops. The story is told (in the *Hrolf's Saga*) about the wicked suggestions of his wicked stepmother to his father, Bjorn. She was his father's second wife; and when Bjorn refused her Phaedra-like advances she cursed him to live like a bear by day. At night he returned to human form, and as a man fathered three children upon his real sweetheart, Bera. The third of these triplets, Bjarki, was given a magic sword by his father, which he carried on his adventures throughout the world.[58]

The champion's arrival at the court of Hrolf also has familiar rings to it. Bjarki killed a winged dragon which had been terrorizing the neighborhood for some time, and as a result was welcome at court. When the king's *beserkrs* returned home from a warring expedition they offered, in their exuberance, to fight any man in the house. Beowulf, remember, was given an equally hostile, though verbal, challenge from Unferth; and Ulysses was forced to prove himself at the court of Alkinoos. When Bjarki brained the chief *beserkr* he was allowed to sit with Hrolf and to be his man. And then he was given Hrolf's only daughter, Drifa, in marriage.

Bjarki became the most trusted member of Hrolf's *comitatus*, for his valor, his strength, and his experience. Yet in the *Bjarkamál* the moment is charged with mortal danger: Hjarvarth and his entourage, including sorcerers, norns, Swedes, and Goths, had visited Hrolf and accepted the hospitality of the castle. This was in itself harmless enough, yet there was treason in the guest's heart; with the aid of his sorcerers he concealed his fighting men until they should be used. It seems that Skuld, Hrolf's half-sister, had for a long time been urging and prodding Hjarvarth, her husband, to this act of treason, in revenge for Hrolf's trickery in making Hjarvarth his vassal in the first place. Skuld's plight was that of a number of Teutonic ladies of the Middle Ages. Caught between the tugs of pride and her conflicting loyalties to her husband and to her kin, the action she would precipitate would inevitably lead to disaster.

At a prearranged hour Hjarvarth's Swedes and Goths attacked without warning and, gaining the momentum which surprise affords, quickly put Hrolf's guards to rout. Bjarki, literally caught napping, was slow to rise to the danger in this, his final battle; the *Bjarkamál*, which is realized through an extended dialogue with the younger warrior Hjalti, is the account of his defense of his lord.

The younger Hjalti comes to where Bjarki is sleeping and wakens him with the news that the Swedes are already attacking at the gates: "Whoso cherishes friendship for the king, let him take up arms.... Glory is now appointed for wages; each can be the arbiter of his own renown, and shine by his own right hand."[59] In *Hrolf's Saga* Hjarvarth's men are aided by a mighty bear who swipes aside the defenders as though they were straw; when Bjarki is ready to fight, an awesome boar, of oxen size, is leading the attack.

Bjarki awakes, but before proceeding further calls to his page to light the fire, as though he could not fight with cold hands. Several epics of defeat have the hero delay decisive action at crucial moments until death is inevitable. Roland waits until the battle is lost and most of his men are killed before blowing on the Oliphant; Leonidas allows his Greek allies to escape Thermopylae, choosing himself to stay with a small force; and—as we shall shortly see—Byrhtnoth successfully defends the ford at Maldon, but he chooses to allow the vikings to cross the river, where they then defeat him. Bjarki's behavior shows him most poised at the moment of greatest danger, suggesting that he knows the end is to come and so he need not hurry, thus his composure provides a sharp contrast with Hjalti's anxious energy.

This same Hjalti Bjarki had earlier rescued from a life of shame. When the champion arrived at Hrolf's court and found the land ravaged by the flying monster, none cowed more cravenly than Hott, who was the butt of the court. When Bjarki slew the creature Hott was with him; the champion made him drink the monster's blood and eat its heart, which gave the timid young man the strength and aggressiveness the beast had owned in life, the blood being thought to carry the soul and the characteristics of the possessor (for this same reason Rain-in-the-Face was thought to have eaten Custer's heart). When Hrolf and his men arrived at the field, Bjarki made it look as though Hott had been the dragon's slayer. In gratitude the king renamed him Hjalti after the sword he had wielded, Gullinhjalti (golden hilt).

At Lejre it is Hjalti who urges Bjarki to action. "My master is the greatest of Danes: let each man, as he is valorous, stand by him; far, far hence be all cowards." Meanwhile, the Swedes advance closer to victory. Hjalti curses Hjarvarth as the "betrayer of a noble king" and damns his wife's "everlasting guilt." Then he returns to Bjarki, taunting the aging warrior for his slackness, suggesting (perhaps) even cowardice: "It is right to spurn all fear with words of courage, and to meet our death in deeds of glory." To this taunt Bjarki responds, much as does Beowulf to the flyting of Unferth. He recites several of his past deeds, agreeing that "happy beyond all things is he who can mete out revenge for such a crime, and with righteous steel punish the guilt of treacheries." Together, then, the two warriors go forth to face the enemy and their own fates, but by this time the situation has become hopeless. Bjarki soon realizes how the fight will end:

> I do not remember any combat wherein swords were crossed in turn and blow dealt out for blow more speedily. I take three for each I give; thus do the Goths requite the wounds I deal them, and thus doth the stronger hand of the enemy avenge, with heaped interest the punishment that they receive. Yet singly in battle I have given over the bodies of so many men to the pyre of destruction, that a mound like a hill could grow up and be raised out of their lopped limbs.

The *Hrolf's Saga* has an ending even more terrifying than the *Bjarkamál*, as Gwynn Jones thinks.[60] Hjarvarth and his men are *draugar* who are no sooner killed than rise again to attack their slayer. Bjarki, shaken, sees no end to the enemy's number: "I fear now that the dead stir here, rise up again and fight against us ... and for all so many limbs as here are cloven, shields split, and helms and corslets hewn in pieces, and many a chieftain cut asunder, these the dead are now the grimmest to contend with."

Nevertheless, the *Saga* relates that Hjarvarth fell with most of his men in the attack at Lejre, and that among the very few survivors was the wretched Skuld. Of course there was vengeance; what teutonic tale of the Middle Ages could omit it? Bjarki's two older brothers, Elgfrothi and Thorir Houndsfoot, are told of the disaster by Vogg (Wigg) and return to finish Bjarki's bloody work. Saxo's ending is slightly different. Hjarvarth was left alive and held a victory feast to celebrate his triumph. Wigg (Vogg, Viggo) offers his allegiance to the conqueror, but when handed a sword (symbol of the service he would perform for his new master) Wigg ran him through up to the hilt, thus ending Denmark's shortest reign—about six hours.

Here are most of the details of the "Custer cluster,"[61] though in distinctive form. Hrolf, like Charlemagne, is betrayed by a vassal who owes him loyalty. In the battle that ensues, in which the treason is manifest, the king's finest warrior and a relatively small number of faithful retainers are overwhelmed by the enemy. All are killed except a relative unknown, Wigg (like Curly, Abronichus, and Baudouin), who escapes to tell the tale that will bring revenge upon the evil-doers. The variant details do not invalidate the paradigm: although the fight is usually in the mountains, in the *Bjarkamál* it is in the courtyard (like the Alamo); Ganelon's animus is against the hero himself, as is usually the case in the cluster, and Hjarvarth's is against the king. The *Bjarkamál* is unique in describing the action through the eyes of the slain hero. And a number of other details are not to be found anywhere else: Skuld's ambition, the treason within the hosts' dwelling (found in the *Finnesburgh Fragment*, which is not an exaltation of the defeated hero), the pause by the fireside; yet amid this welter of particularizing details, the basic frame of the martyred hero story is evident.

As in the other epics of defeat, the *Bjarkamál* has dramatic and character contrasts in plenitude: the young and eager Hjalti and the veteran, more phlegmatic Bjarki; the challenge to the valiant to stand with Hrolf, and the contempt for the cowards who will not; Hrolf himself, the "greatest of all the Danes," the treason of Hjarvarth, and the "everlasting guilt" of Skuld; the generosity of Hrolf and the stinginess of Rorik (alluded to by Hjalti), who was "stronger in gain than bravery, and thinking gold better than warfare, he set lucre above all things"; the fierce Goths at the gate, the resigned heroes within; the great hero meeting his end at the hands of traitors; the great men slain within Lejre's walls; and the escape of the insignificant Wigg.

One of the few legends of martyred heroes which does not place the action on a hilltop is that of the Texans at the Alamo (though the Alamo mission is on a slight hill). The outlines of the popular version of its defense are known to most Americans, and the story has long been a favorite of children's books. The account in *A Book of Brave Deeds* [62] is typical: the small Texas garrison of 140 "efficient men," who were "few in numbers and weak in resources" but nevertheless "mighty in spirit and in name," was attacked by several thousand Mexicans, many of whom were stimulated by hopes of plunder. The attackers launched a continuous bombardment on the old mission from all sides, yet—as Travis was at one point able to write to the outside world—"We have been so fortunate as not to lose a man from any cause, and we have killed many of the enemy."

In another letter he wrote that "victory costs so dear, that it will be worse for him than a defeat. God and Texas! Victory or death!" Death it was to be; the Reverend Newell proudly wrote that "they sold their lives as dearly as possible, and fell to a man." In the final assault all of the fighting men were killed; one man asked to surrender but was slain along with the rest by this "ruthless" enemy. Jim Bowie, lying sick in bed, was murdered there and his body was mutilated. Newell wrote that the end of David Crockett was "glorious": "He and his companions were found with heaps of dead around them, whom they had immolated on the altar of Texan Liberty." Yet just a few lines later, to emphasize the brutality of the enemy, Newell reviled the savages who denied the Texans their rites of burial: their bodies were "stripped, thrown in a pile, and burned! Thus was bigotry added to cruelty." Only Mrs. Dickerson and Colonel Travis' servant, Ben, were allowed to leave unharmed.

Newell's hero was neither Crockett nor Bowie, the usual selections, but Travis himself:

> The storming of the fort had lasted less than an hour. Colonel Travis had stood on the walls cheering his men, and exclaiming, "Hurrah, my boys!" till he received the shot of which he fell. A Mexican officer then rushed upon him, and lifted his sword to destroy his victim, who, collecting all his expiring energies, directed a thrust at his inhuman foe, which changed their fortunes,—for the victim became the victor; and the remains of both descended to eternal sleep—but not alike to everlasting fame.

In the Welsh *Gododdin* of the sixth century the conception of the poet is so substantially distinctive that nearly all of the generalizations we would like to make about heroic tales of defeat dissolve; and yet they dissolve only to produce a poem of great power. Bowra compared heroic poetry with elegy,[63] and in few poems does the connection between these genres appear more clearly than here. The *Gododdin* is not narrative in the conventional sense; most of the story emerges from the sequence of elegies rendering the tribute of poetic immortality to the warriors in the retinue of Mynyddog the Wealthy—and to the leader himself. There is no explicit chronology of skirmish, initial success, and ultimate defeat, but a number of individual tributes are interspersed with more general encomiums to the attacking column. Heroic poetry honors the dead and inspires the living; seldom have such promises been more movingly fulfilled than in this commemoration of the defeat at Catraeth.

Mynyddog the Wealthy feted and gifted the finest warriors of Celtic lands for a year before leading them into battle against the heathen English.[64] Like true heroes the men from the North went to battle against a force many times their number; among their ranks bravery was commonplace. Aneirin said of one of them:

> ... Wearing a necklet, in the front rank, bearing weapons in battle, a mighty man in the fight before his deathday, a champion in the charge in the van of the armies; there fell five times fifty before his blades, of the men of Deira and Bernicia a hundred score fell and were destroyed in a single hour. He would sooner the wolves had his flesh than go to his own wedding, he would rather be prey for ravens than go to the altar; his blood flowed to the ground before he could get due burial, making return for his mead with the hosts in the hall. Hyfeidd the tall shall be honored as long as there is a minstrel.

Like the thanes of *Beowulf* and *Maldon* Mynyddog's men owe him an unstinting loyalty; but unlike the retainers in those later poems, they do not flinch from giving it. In poignant contrasts—the mead was their delight and their death, and the furious din of battle was overcast by the silence of death—Aneirin honored his companions:

> The men went to Catraeth, strenuous was their army, the pale mead was their feast, and it was their poison; three hundred men battling in array, and after the glad war-cry there was silence. Though they went to the churches to do penance, the inescapable meeting with death overtook them.

For his audience just the name of Catraeth must have had power. Again and again Aneirin begins his stanzas with "the men went to Catraeth" or "the men hastened out" with the heavy sense of fateful and inevitable disaster that we might use today in speaking of the raid on Dieppe or the defense of Wake Island:

The men hastened out; they were feasted together for a year over the mead—great were their vaunts. How pitiful to tell of them, what insatiable longing! Fatal their resting place, not a mother's son succoured them. How long the grief for them and the yearning, after the fiery men from the wine-fed domain. Gwlyged of Gododdin, who met the swift foe, the feast of Mynyddog made him famous and precious, though paid for by the fight at Catraeth.

They met the foe as the finest heroes of any land always do, "charging forward in battle among broken shields; and though they were slain they slew, none returned to his lands." Yet at least one man did survive this futile assault upon the English fortress: "Of three hundred champions who set out for Catraeth, alas, but for one man none came back." They attacked the enemy "famous in battle dress, reckless of their lives," "seven times as many English they slew," and they were themselves slain. This is the quintessence of the heroic defeat, and in its poetic simplicity lies its acsthetic formidability. The *Gododdin* is not like any other tribute to the defeated; the rules of objectivity are broken, the modern poetic injunction that the poet merely tell his story and make us feel its implicit emotions is disregarded. Aneirin openly laments the dead, and he does not fail to arouse our grief as well:

> It is grief to me that after the toil of battle they suffered the agony of death in torment, and a second heavy grief it is to me to have seen our men falling headlong; and continual moaning it is, and anguish, after the fiery men lying in the clodded earth—Rhufawn and Gwgawn, Gwiawn and Gwlyged, men of most manly station, strong in strife; after the battle, may their souls get welcome in the land of Heaven, the dwelling-place of plenty.

The strength of the poem is cumulative. Information the modern reader prefers is only grudgingly forthcoming: we learn the "details" of the battle only as they emerge piecemeal in individual eulogies. Hyfeidd the Tall slew five times fifty of the enemy—the men of Deira and Bernicia. Rhufawn the Tall, who slew as many, had given gold to the altar and fine presents to the minstrel. Their chieftain provided for them sumptuously: the feast of Mynyddog made Gwlyged of Gododdin "famous and precious." Slowly, somberly the (implied) narrative proceeds, pausing with solemn deliberation on the heroes' departure ("The men went to Catraeth, strenuous was their army .../ The men went to Catraeth with the dawn, their high courage shortened their lives .../ The men went to Catraeth, they were renowned ..."). To the battle: "The warriors arose together, together they met, together they attacked...." To the lament: "It is grief to me that after the toil of battle they suffered the agony of death in torment...."

The *Gododdin* is a great poem which celebrates a battle no one remembers; the *Bjarkamál* no longer exists as a poem, though the battle it commemorates has been chronicled; the defeat suffered by the Serbs at Kóssovo in 1389 is both real and important, and though it is said to be present in the folk conscience to this day, no epic but rather only several ballads tell of the battle. The plains of Kóssovo, the "Plain of Blackbirds," nestle amid the mountains of Macedonia and Serbia around the present city of Priština. The Communist regime has heavily industrialized the area; when I visited Kóssovo in 1973, several heavy industries darkened the skies above the rich brown plains, and in those darkened skies air force jets spun and rolled playfully, sundering any fanciful recreations I might have about what the field was like "then."

A stone tower has been erected to honor the slain at Kóssovo but in May 1973 it was not attended. A carelessly paved path from the main road leads the 1,000 yards to the memorial, around which a small grass yard had been modestly landscaped and was casually tended. Empty wine bottles and food wrappings littered the entrance chamber, showing that someone had been there recently. The tower itself is about seventy or eighty feet tall, and approximately Romanesque. Its top commands a view of the fertile and heavily cultivated plains rolling toward Serbia; this is where the battle was allegedly fought. It is a fine place for a battle, really the only place in the region for medieval armies to make war. One has no trouble imagining that both armies, after their tedious marches through the rugged, forbidding mountains, would gladly encamp on the plains and welcome the battle with relief. If the fate of Serbia was to be settled for over four centuries, here was the place to decide it.

About a mile down the road, toward Beograd, is the putative tomb of Murad, under a mosque's dome, enclosed within a disappointingly small space by a stone wall. But the tomb is, at least, attended—by an old Moslem woman and an even more decrepit man. Neither attendant will vow that Murad is buried within the draped casket in the domed structure, and the plaques on the wall offer little more certainty. They tell of the likelihood that Murad was removed for burial at home and of the several plunderings of the area by different Balkan (especially Bulgarian) and Western (especially French) troops during the past century. Outside the wall a gypsy family cooked its meal over a fire and squatted in the mud. One thing had not changed: the legendary blackbirds of Kóssovo soared, and strutted, and chattered everywhere, the one living testimonial to the legend that began there nearly six centuries ago.

By 1386, the empire of Murad reached as far north as the present Jugoslavian city of Niš and westward to the Albanian border, probably near "modern" Pivski Manastir. Lázar Hrebeljanovich, a prince of north Serbia who had recently inherited his domain, soon found himself a vassal owing allegiance to the Turks. The empire was so vast that when Murad wished to quell the emir of Karaman to the east, he demanded military aid from the Serbs. Lázar thought to exploit the situation, and out of injured pride or political opportunism he renounced his vassalage. He organized a pan-Balkan alliance against Murad and in 1387 defeated a Turkish army on the Toplitsa River. When the fires in the east had been momentarily quenched, Murad wheeled his armies to settle matters on the western front, and on 15 July 1389 he marched to the Plain of Blackbirds.[65]

Early on the morning of the battle, as the sultan was dressing, a Serb was brought to him professing to be a deserter with information about the placement of the Christian forces. But as he approached the sultan he withdrew a knife which he had concealed and stabbed the leader of the Turks to death. He was himself promptly murdered, which was to be expected; the outcome was not. The sultan's two sons suppressed news of the calamity while the elder, Bayezit, took command of the army and moved at once into action. The Turks fought with confidence and poise; the Christians could not break their massive phalanxes and early in the fight began to waver. Almost immediately talk of treachery rose up; the Turks routed the demoralized Christian army by nightfall, Lázar was captured, brought to the tent of Murad's murder, and was himself put to death.[66]

Marko Kraljevič, revered as he was (and is) by the Serbian people, should have been the martyred hero of Kóssovo, but oral history, which has done so much violence to events, has fallen short of this outrage. Marko's father, Vukašin, had been ignominiously routed by a Turkish army on the Maritsa River in 1371. Vukašin was drowned in this swiftly running stream along with thousands of his men, leaving the way open for Murad's conquest of the Balkans. Marko succeeded his father as king of Prilep but was no more successful in containing the Turkish tide. In 1385, perhaps to retain his authority and his possessions, he declared allegiance to Murad and entered his service. Five years after Kóssovo Marko was still in the service of the Turks, and at Rovina, while in the army of Bayezit, he was killed fighting Romanian Christians.[67]

No document attests to his presence at Kóssovo,[68] yet the popular imagination has afforded him a most noble hilltop death elsewhere. In response to a vila's prediction of his death he rides to Urvina mountain, kills his mighty stallion Sharatz, breaks his saber (as Roland tried to break his) so that the Turks will not claim it as a trophy, and dies. Marko wills what no heathen sword nor mace could accomplish.[69] Another ballad places Vukašin at Kóssovo, wounded, within a folktale framework that sounds as though it could well have been borrowed from the first book of Samuel: Marko meets a Turkish merchant who, in explaining why he wants to sell a Serbian sword, reveals that it was taken from the dying Vukašin, whom the merchant decapitated and tossed into the Sitniča River. Marko repaid the Turk in kind.[70]

But we must leave Marko to his mountaintop; there are none at Kóssovo, where Lázar fought and died. These plains were once said to have exerted a great, almost magical power over the consciousness of the Jugoslav people; peasants were said to speak with reverence of it as though it were a holy place.[71] This view has been challenged recently: Albert B. Lord insists that this is not the case, and that though several ballads about the battle survive, no folk epic was ever composed, further evidence that the claims of preeminence in the folk consciousness have been exaggerated.[72]

The ballads and legends turn nearly all of the known facts inside out. We have seen some grounds for accusing the Serbs of treachery in the murder of Murad; in their popular ballads the battle was lost because of the treachery of Vuk Brankovitch who, at the crucial moment in the fighting, fled with his 12,000 men. In "The Banquet on the Eve of Battle"[73] Lázar's retainers broke bread together before their ordeal. The Last Supper is imitated: Lázar declares that someone present is about to betray him. Miloš Obilič is at first thought to be the traitor, but he in turn denounces Vuk—who at the real battle fought bravely and well. In "Tsar Lázar and Tsaritsa Militsa"[74] the Serbs are seen riding off to the battle, having vowed to shed their blood for Christ's honor. Lázar has been asked by a heavenly presence (in "The Fall of the Serbian Empire"[75]) whether he wishes an earthly kingdom or one in heaven. The tsar is told that he may have his choice, that victory will be granted him if he chooses it; but of course he chooses death at Kóssovo and life hereafter.

The battle is joined and at first the fighting goes well for the Serbs. But then the Serbian Judas, Vuk, deserts the field and his cause, and God's will is fulfilled. Later Milutin, a servant and thus a minor character in the drama, returns from the field, seriously wounded, to tell his countrymen of the treachery and the defeat he has seen.[76] Lázar is decapitated on the field—in this

The Turks often beheaded their defeated enemies. In this seventeenth-century
Serbian woodcut a sainted Lázar, the heroic loser of Kóssovo, contemplates the
severed yet miraculously preserved head of Lázar the warrior. For many centuries
the Serbs have been vigorous defenders of Christendom, and their land has been the
embattled frontier of countless struggles.

tradition—and his head is saved by a young Turkish boy, while his body lies miraculously undisturbed. Years later another miracle happens, and head and body are joined; the grateful and awed Serbs are said to have erected a statue of a blackbird on the plain.

A final note on Miloš: the earliest legends do not name the slayer of Murad, but by the nineteenth century this dubious honor passed to Obilić. Gibbon reported that as the conqueror walked across the corpse-laden fields, he was killed by a Serbian warrior who leaped up and stabbed him in the stomach.[77] This shifts the entire dramatic weight of the legend. Obilić becomes a hero, slaying the traitor Murad after his own people have been ingloriously routed. If he was thought to have been the pretended deserter, his act would be considered stealthy and ignoble trickery.

Fame has been at least as kind, and as perverse, in her manipulation of the reputation of James IV of Scotland, whose fall at Flodden in 1513 has about it much of the comic gallantry of warfare in the Middle Ages and early Renaissance.[78] The Scots, led personally by the heroically inclined James, arrived first on the battlefield. The soldiers were intelligently stationed on a hill whose only route of approach was across a narrow field which could be raked by their artillery. But they were soon to give up voluntarily this position of strength. Surrey, the English commander, did not relish an uphill assault across open ground covered by cannon, and he sent a herald to James requesting that the Scots remove themselves to Millfield so that both armies might engage on equal terms! The king's response is most revealing: he was annoyed to be addressed in this manner by a mere earl, but he nevertheless agreed to disdain the advantage of ground and moved his force down from its commanding position.

As was the practice of the day, each army was carefully arranged in position facing each other; on this day each was comprised of four phalanx groups with a fifth in reserve. The figures are necessarily approximate, as are the total manpower estimates of 20,000 for the English and about 5,000 more for their antagonists. Each phalanx had roughly 5,000 men; the Scots were armed primarily with long pikes, the English with somewhat shorter bills.

The battle opened around 2:30 P.M. when the Scots, urged on by drums and bagpipes, moved to advance. The English artillerymen on the right flank began an effective fire on the Scots' left, cutting swathes through their formation. The heavier Scots guns could not return this fire, however, because they could not be depressed, and so they continually overshot their targets. But the absurdity was only beginning. The noise of the English guns so awed their own crews that many of them—need it be said they were untried recruits—fled. Without a shot falling among his men, Lord Dacre lost about 500, or nearly half of them, to "the enemy."

Those who remained, however, kept up a galling fire that swept through the Scots' lines unanswered. By late in the afternoon James' officers lost patience, and a general attack was ordered. It was hardly carried out with precision or *eclat*; the Scots' left flank had easier going over relatively level ground and made contact first, while the phalanxes to their right were still lumbering toward the English lines. The resistance was stubborn at first, but the English were soon routed; Lord Dacre rode to their rescue with his reserve troops, and though he probably prevented the Scots from rolling up the English squares in flank one at a time, he did not press home the charge with enough vigor to regain momentum. Having checked the enemy advance he felt that he had done his part, and he played no further role in the battle. Three years later he would be executed for his inactivity.

Lord Dacre had "done his part," yet the Scots were no more aggressive in doing theirs, and the left wing spent much of its time in that traditional and characteristically medieval battlefield practice of stealing horses and robbing the dead. Meanwhile the Scottish squares to their right were making contact with the English pikemen. Some of the refugees from Edmund Howard's shattered phalanx were induced to stay and fight with the Lord Admiral, and thus strengthened he met the oncoming Scots on more equal terms. Next to them Surrey's men received their attackers, personally led by James, who stationed himself, with idiotic dash, in the front rank.

The slowest phalanx was on the extreme right of the Scots line; and as it wavered and lurched down the hill to the attack, English archers (from the far left of their own "line") fired a steadily pelting rain of steel shafts into their flank. The continuously crepitating barbs that fell among them, dropping their comrades to the ground one after another before any reply could be made, unnerved the Scots. Thus when the left wing of the English troops, led by Sir Edward Stanley, attacked up the hill, the Scots lost all control, threw down their pikes, and scrambled for their lives. Bellowing triumphantly, Stanley's men ran up the hill in pursuit, while hundreds of arrows flickered into the jumbled mass of the fleeing Scots.

The Scottish reserve, "safely hidden" in a hollow behind the attacking formations, were at their ease when their comrades from the now demolished right flank fled among them. Their terror was contagious; and with a steady hail of arrows falling among them, the reserve was almost instantly transformed into a hysterical mob of fugitives. Stanley was to be the hero of the day; no Lord Dacre he. With the Scottish wing and the reserve in full and confused retreat before him, his opposite number, the Earl of Bothwell, slain by a grey goose feather arrow, Stanley reined in his enthusiastic conquerors, regrouped them, wheeled, and crashed upon the Scottish rear, at that time still heavily engaged with the English to their front. What had been a relatively hard-fought battle to this point dissolved into a chaotic rout. When the English came crashing down upon their backs, the Scottish formations wavered and then disintegrated. Units lost their cohesion and terror spread like a plague as the soldiers abandoned their lords and their comrades, threw down their weapons so they might run the faster, and left the English standing alone on the field.

The extent of the debacle could be discerned by numbers alone: the Scots lost nearly 12,000 men, including the Archbishop of St. Andrews, 2 bishops, 8 earls, 13 barons, and 4 knights. All 17 of their guns were taken. And most important, they lost King James. The price to the English for their splendid victory was 4,000 casualties, of whom about 120 were prisoners.

Though Stanley's maneuver had been decisive, James' conduct had not been exemplary. He got himself killed in the melee without having designated a successor, leaving his army leaderless. Nevertheless, the legend arose, well-known to Scottish schoolboys,[79] that their gallant king died under the most heroic circumstances, amid a cluster of his most faithful knights, the last remnant of his shattered army, pierced through the eye by an errant English arrow (like Harold at Hastings and Janoš Hunyadi at Belgrade).

For Scott, the laureate of Scottish glory, the battle was as cosmic as Custer's against the devils of the plains; in "Flodden"[80] the armies clash in ignorant confusion so that anything is possible:

> They close in clouds of smoke and dust,
> With sword-sway and with lance's thrust;
>   And such a yell was there
> Of sudden and portentous birth,
> As if men fought upon the earth
>   And fiends in upper air;
> O life and death were in the shout,
> Recoil and rally, charge and rout,
>   And triumph and despair.

The English emerge from this cloud of dust triumphant. Scott blamed "Fortune"; some of the Scottish ballads blamed English "subtility," an "ambush," or simply their overwhelming numbers.[81]

James then braced himself for his last stand, according to Scott:

For still the Scots, around their King,
Unbroken, fought in desperate ring.
Where's now their victor vaward wing,
    Where's Huntly, and where Home?
O for a blast of that dread horn,
On Fontarabian echoes borne,
    That to King Charles did come,
When Roland brave, and Olivier,
And every paladin and peer,
    On Roncevalles died!

But there is no Charlemagne to come to the rescue of the Scottish Roland; the English hordes will win the day: "Front, flank, and rear, the squadrons sweep/ To break the Scottish circle deep/ That fought around their King." What though the field would be lost? To the Scots would go the greater victory:

But yet, though thick the shafts as snow,
Though charging knights like whirlwinds go,
Though bill-men ply the ghastly blow,
    Unbroken was the ring;
The stubborn spear-men still made good
Their dark impenetrable wood,
Each stepping where his comrade stood,
    The instant that he fell.
No thought was there of dastard flight;
Linked in the serried phalanx tight,
Groom fought like noble, squire like knight,
    As fearlessly and well;
Till utter darkness closed her wing
O'er their thin host and wounded King.
Then skilful Surrey's sage commands
Led back from strife his shattered bands;
And from the charge they drew,
As mountain waves from wasted lands
    Sweep back to ocean blue.

So the field was left to the Scots, beaten but unbowed. In this version the English were forced to yield Flodden and leave King James to die from his wounds—but in the Scottish hands, and not from an enemy's sword:

Tradition, legend, tune, and song
Shall many an age that wail prolong:
Still from the sire the son shall hear
Of the stern strife and carnage drear
    Of Flodden's fatal field,
Where shivered was fair Scotland's spear,
    And broken was her shield!

The Emperor Constantine Paleologus has fared as well in both oral and written history. This brave man was ruler of the Byzantine empire when no one man could save it from the Turks. He made a last stand of sorts, rushing to that point in the city's walls where the enemy had made a breakthrough and, fighting beside his common soldiers, fell with them and was swept away by the Turkish tide pouring through the St. Romanos gate. And although local folklore has it that Constantinople was built on seven hills (like several other cities, notably Rome), the gate of St. Romanos (the present Topkapi) was at the highest point of a ridge, through the emperor did not perish exactly there.

The conqueror of the God's holy city was an unlikely young man whose youth Steven Runciman has called "lamentable."[82] · Viscount Montgomery is more direct: "... tactiturn and cruel, a homosexual, inclined to drink...."[83] His early life may have been ridden with errors of judgment and impropriety, but he had an indomitable will. At one point in their negotiations Constantine too misjudged him, making demands which only strengthened the young sultan's determination, because he had judged Mehmet weak and inept.[84]

In 1452, a year before the city fell, a Hungarian engineer named Urban had gone to Constantine and offered his services to manufacture cannon. But his salary demands could not be met by the financially beleaguered Greeks, and Urban shortly after sold his talents to the Turks. Across the Bosphorus he was warmly welcomed, given double the salary he had requested and all the technical support he needed. Urban said that his gun could blast the walls of Babylon itself. When the first model was completed, it was placed on the castle walls of Rumeli Hisar, commanding the Bosphorus, and in its first action sank a Venetian merchantman attempting to sail up the straits. Mehmet then ordered a cannon made which would be twice its size. This second behemoth was cast in Adrianople and was ready in January 1453. Contemporary estimates put it over twenty-six feet long, with a bronze barrel eight inches thick and cannonballs weighing twelve hundred pounds. In its first test firing it hurtled its shot about a mile; and when the half-ton missile came to rest it had lodged itself six feet into the earth.[85] Pregnant women twelve miles away

Greek tradition claims that more than 300,000 Turks stormed the walls of
Constantinople. Actually, the intelligent use of cannon like that in the foreground
did the job. The breakthrough was at the St. Romanos Gate, shown here, which the
Turks have now widened to accommodate a broad boulevard.

were said to have had miscarriages. Montgomery remarks that sixty oxen drew it to the walls of the city where, ironically, it broke down; Runciman credits it greatly with bringing the walls of the city down.

The size of the Turkish armada varies according to the report. Byzantine historians were given to exaggeration, but Italian sources report it more reliably at 6 triremes, 10 biremes, 15 oared galleys, about 75 *fustae* (ships smaller and lighter than biremes), 20 heavy cargo barges with sails (parandaria), and a number of smaller sloops and cutters. In oral tradition the number of Turkish troops has been increased to a healthy 300,000 (supported by 300 ships); Runciman found Greek sources which swelled the attacker's number to 3 or 4 million and Venetians who put their force at about 150,000. But the Turks themselves spoke of about 80,000 regular ground troops supported by about 20,000 Bashi-bazouks. The number of the real force was great enough, opposed as they were by about 5,000 Greeks and about 2,000 Franks—the generic name for Westerners. At the inflated odds of the legends the Byzantine defenders were outnumbered by about fifty to one, though Professor Constantine Patrides (who very generously delved into Greek and Byzantine traditions for me) found other legends insisting that opposed to every Christian were more than 500 Turks. And a popular poem by Georgios Zalokostas credits the emperor alone with facing 1,000 of the barbarians.

At the beginning of the siege Constantine was supported by several Venetians who, despite the odds against the city, were too proud to leave. And shortly after they were reinforced by a small force of Genoese who sailed into the imperial city on their own, led by the Bocchiardo brothers and Giovanni Giustiniani Longo, but with a small contingent of about 700 men. In the last moments of Constantinople's life Giustiniani was to play a crucial part in the defeat, but until then he was a great source of strength. His military reputation had been gained in the defense of walled cities, and he was diplomatic enough to secure the cooperation of the Greeks, who disliked most Genoese.

Popular legends have supplied at least two candidates for the role of betrayer. The Hungarian engineer Urban has escaped this stigma, though his behavior would seem to make him the prime subject. Mehmet, not surprisingly, does receive part of the dishonor. On his accession to the Sultanhood he had sworn to respect the integrity of Byzantine territory. Later, despite agreements with Constantine to the contrary, he built fortifications near Constantinople. One of the more important fortresses still stands, several miles away from the city toward the Black Sea, on the banks of the Bosphorus, its walls almost as impressive as those of Constantinople. When Mehmet surrounded the city he was in violation of still other commitments.

Yet if these legends about Turkish betrayal arose because of the hatred of the conquered toward the conqueror, the betrayal of the city by the Genoese—the "Franks"—has a more solid foundation in the events of the last days. Giustiniani and his Genoese volunteers fought bravely and well throughout the siege, and their section of the defense perimeter, Mesoteichion and the Lycus valley, was under the heaviest attack. During the early stages of the battle Giustiniani was wounded, but he returned to his station promptly. On the day that proved final, however, he was seriously wounded by a culverin shot which tore right through his breastplate. Bleedly wildly, he asked to be taken from the field. And while some of his men thought that he had merely retreated, most of the others recognized that the battle was lost, and they streamed back through the city. The emporer was then alone with his own men to defend the walls. Professor Patrides tells me about a tradition which greatly heightens the accusation of "treason" on the part of Giustiniani: his courage is said to have failed him at once. "No," he is said to have cried out in despair, "God is not fighting with us but with the Turks: God leads the Turks."[86]

Constantine's death remains a mystery. Although an illustration in a nineteenth-century Austrian children's history book shows Constantine, in full plate armor, about to strike down some Turks as they rush up at him—outside the city's walls—he most likely perished within. When the Genoese withdrew from their positions, after Giustiniani fell, the emperor galloped to the Lycus valley positions. With Don Francisco, John Dalmata, and Theophilus Palaeologus he tried to hold the gate through which the Genoese had been carried. But the battle, the city, the empire had already been lost. The attackers poured through a breach in the walls and slaughtered the few Byzantines who could be brought from the flanks to protect this widening wound. The situation was hopeless; rampaging Janissaries, the Sultan's elite corps of warriors bred for combat from early childhood, poured through the walls in a torrent. Constantine, apparently not wishing to outlive his empire, rushed into the flood. He was never seen again.

The frightfulness of the slaughter that followed has been greatly exaggerated in oral tradition; that very much killing of civilians took place at all is historically doubtful. Yet the legend persists in the city that high upon one of the columns of the Hagia Sophia—about five miles from the St. Romanos gate—one can still find traces of blood. This stain was said to have been made by Mehmet himself with the palm of his blood-soaked hand when he entered this "eighth wonder of the world" to transform it into a mosque. His hand was able to reach so high because he had to step on the bodies of the Christian defenders, slain by the Turks as they forced their way into the sanctuary.

Constantine has been elevated to the level of the greatest of Greek heroes, historical or mythical. When the Ottoman armies burst through the St. Romanos gate, the emperor is said to have roared like a lion, and with his sword already broken from his many killing blows, to have rushed into the heart of the combat, tearing the enemy apart with his hands and finally with his teeth, killing great numbers of them.

He was certainly not the last defender to be slain, since the attack on the western walls was only the first breach of the city's defenses. Other sections were able to defend themselves until some time later. Several ships evaded the Turkish armada and fled with refugees out through the Dardanelles. A small contingent of Cretan sailors in a strong point near the entrance to the Golden Horn were not taken at all, but seeing the rest of the city capitulate early in the afternoon they offered to surrender their position as well. Their Turkish besiegers, in admiration of their bravery, allowed them free passage home.[87]

Emperor Constantine probably lay among a crowd of dead, all of whom the Turks decapitated. One story which later circulated in the Italian provinces told of Constantine's head on display atop a column in the Augustan Forum; later it was said to have been sent around to the leading courts of Islam. Saul's head was displayed by the Philistines; Byrhtnoth was said to have been buried headless; Lázar's head was preserved by a Turkish boy before it was miraculously rejoined to his body; and occasional stories of decapitation were told about the Little Bighorn mutilations. Another tradition held that the emperor was delivered from the battlefield by an angel (also like Lázar and something like Roland) and removed to a deep cave in the center of the earth where he waits, patiently, for the proper moment to come to the liberation of the holy city.

The legend of the expected return (or the "sleeping warriors") has been told in all times in nearly all parts of the world: it was told of Nero, of Thor waiting in the mountains of central Germany, of Odin in the Odinwald, of Siegfried, of Charlemagne, of Dietrich, of Thomas Paine, of King Arthur on Avalon, of Hitler alive and well in Argentina, even of Quantrill, who was said to have escaped death to become a farmer in Mexico after the Civil War. It has most recently been said of John F. Kennedy, reportedly alive on Onassis' island in the Mediterranean.

I would be careless of the memory of Constantine and his men, and of the brave Turks who slew them, if I closed this summary of events at and around the St. Romanos gate without mentioning its present state. The Middle Ages are said to have ended in 1453, with the fall of Constantinople, and although historical epochs do not terminate abruptly and cannot be precisely defined, the capitulation of this center of the Eastern Church is certainly one of the most momentous events in the history of the West. And so the St. Romanos gate is a spot of earth charged with significance. Even the Turkish government thinks so, and the old Byzantine walls of the city are widely advertised as one of Istanbul's major attractions. One is amazed, therefore, to find that it has been allowed to deteriorate into squalid dwellings for squatters. The towers that once were all that separated the Christian army from the Moslem have now been decorated with shipping cartons and corrugated metal. Near the spot where Constantine fell amid the streaming banners of the Janissaries, filthy rags droop on rusting wash lines, strung between the battlements. Where Byzantine archers crouched to protect themselves from Urban's mighty artillery while they readied another bolt for the heathen, excrement reveals what the present occupants crouch there for. The Topkapi gate is the one battle site of old where late at night the spirits of the defenders do not respond to the bugle calls, where the ghosts of the victors do not gather again for the charge, where the walls—chipped and pocked by the bolts and shafts of the inexorable Turks—are old stone and only stone.

I save a personal favorite for last, one of the finest heroic poems in English, that compact and luminous gem which deserves to belong among the greatest narratives of defeat in the West, *The Battle of Maldon*. Such praise may seem excessive; *Maldon* is, after all, one of the "minor" poems.[88] This fragment (only 325 lines survived the Cottonian fire of 1731, which consumed part of the beginning and end) has been so routinely considered merely a record of a battle with the vikings near Maldon that its artistry is often given short shrift. For instance, the first twenty pages of E. V. Gordon's edition discuss the poem as history;[89] the actual battle and its topography, which the poem is alleged to have accurately described; the possibility that Olaf Tryggvason was the viking chieftain; and a biography of the Saxon leader, Byrhtnoth. When these important matters have been completely disposed of, the "Composition and Art of the Poem" is finally approached.[90] So pervasive has been the bent to see *Maldon* almost entirely as a metered and alliterating chronicle, that recent replies have begun by addressing themselves to the poem's historicity. Both Jess Bessinger and George Clark went to the battlefield and found, for instance, that the verbal exchange between the viking messenger and the Saxon leader was not physically possible.[91]

The battle which the poem celebrates was fought in 991. A force of seaborne vikings, successful in other raids along the eastern coast of England, established a camp (presumably) on the island of Northey in the delta of the Blackwater, several miles southeast of the village of Maldon. Near the Blackwater River ("Pante" in the poem) the Essex ealdorman Byrhtnoth or-ganized a force of his retainers to resist the invaders. In the engagement that followed, the English were defeated.

Aside from *The Battle of Maldon* little is known of the course of the actual struggle, although the poem's most respected editor insists that "the account of the battle in the poem, in so far as its statements can be checked, is accurate in every particular."[92] The geography of the immediate area as it appears today has been squared with that of the poem, as has the age and general personality traits of Byrhtnoth. We are told that the poet was an intimate of the warriors and familiar with the terrain, and although he must have known the names of the viking leaders, he chose not to identify them; we are told also that he must have known the heroes of the poem personally; that the poem was written shortly after the battle (so fresh in the poet's mind are the details); and that "every detail" of the poem, particularly the "heroic words of the retainers who will not leave the battle," is "true and real."[93] On reading this last judgment, however, we must stop short, particularly when this same critic also concedes that the *Maldon* creator was a "practised poet" who was "well versed in the old heroic and aristocratic tradition of poetry."[94]

As with the account of the battle of Thermopylae, we should inquire about the historian's informants. From whom did the poet get his information about the fight? Not from the vikings, certainly, if for no other reason than that the narrative is told entirely from the English view; the English, and never the vikings, are exalted. Just as certainly the details of this defeat did not come from those warriors who, like Godric, fled from the field when they saw their leader slain midway through the battle. Who is left? The code of the Germanic warrior forbade his leaving the field in dishonor, and though the end of the poem is lost, most likely a last stand to the death was made.[95] Another account of the battle—the twelfth-century *Liber Eliensis*—although admittedly inaccurate in some respects, tells of two battles at Maldon: the first successful, the second a prolonged and heroic struggle in which the English took many viking lives before succumbing—with Byrhtnoth still at their head—to a final wedge-formation assault by the raiders, which destroyed everything in its path.

Very few discussions of *Maldon* consider the possibility that the story may have been in oral circulation for even a short time, yet this seems as likely a possibility as its commitment to vellum when the "memory of all that happened was still fresh."[96] In any event, we saw in the Custer legend what happens to certain events in men's imaginations, within days of the fact, in a society that was ostensibly more concerned with facts and the accurate reporting of them than was Anglo-Saxon England. And we know what chroniclers often did with history: witness—for just one instance—the discrediting of the *Liber Eliensis* because it is confused and exaggerated by the "makers of stories using oral tradition."[97] If we can admit the possibility that accounts and versions of the battle were being told by people in the area, perhaps even by a noncombatant eyewitness, we should also admit that we have been far too concerned with *Maldon* as a record of the battle to the shameful disadvantage of its artistry. Furthermore, the manuscript on which the poem has survived is not in the dialect of the area where the battle was fought but is mainly West Saxon. It was not even written until the late eleventh century,[98] and although one can invent all sorts of circumstances under which the poem may have been composed immediately following the battle, the distance of the manuscript—in time and space—suggests intermediaries. The conventional argument of "lost manuscripts" may be invoked, of course; but even if *Maldon*, as we now have it, accurately copies the first written version of the battle (and we know how even manuscript versions become elaborated and otherwise altered in transmission), we are back with the problem of the accuracy of the first written version. Under these circumstances we should consider the possibility—in my opinion the likelihood—that in oral or written tradition, or both, the "facts" of the battle against the vikings at Maldon, if they were ever known in detail, became altered for aesthetic and didactic purposes; that the narrative of the course of the battle became structured; and that our interest in this splendid poem should be not historical but aesthetic.

Maldon has been criticized for its unadorned language,[99] but clearly its strengths lie not in the ornateness of its rhetoric but in the manipulation of the narrative's events. Contrasts—of event, of mood and tone, of character—define the poem. In the first lines of the fragment, a young knight, identified only as Offa's kinsman, is hawking some distance off from the men who are preparing for the fight, when his game is interrupted by the realization that Byrhtnoth is preparing for battle in deadly earnest. Byrhtnoth had ordered every warrior to dismount and to let loose his horse; Offa's kin then turns loose his falcon, sending it flying from his wrist to a neighboring wood. As the bird finds the safety of the forest, so will the cowards later. The audience's focus thus shifts from the casual game to the serious business of war. The men are soon ready for battle, but the first clash is only one of words: the vikings demand a tribute of gold in exchange for the Saxon's safety; Byrhtnoth replies that his people will answer in steel and blood.[100]

Again we expect the battle to be joined, but it is delayed by the flow of the river separating the two forces. There is a pause; the vikings try to force the stream but are repulsed easily by Wulfstan, Elfhere, and Maccus. Still there is no general battle. Our expectations, relaxed for an instant by this stalemate, rise again when the vikings ask to be allowed to cross so that the battle may continue; Byrhtnoth grants them permission,[101] and the entire viking force crosses unopposed so that the battle may be decisive, much as Polybius said that both the Libyans and Carthaginians agreed to settle their difference finally in a single general battle, and as James IV and Surrey decided, by note, that one force should not have an advantage but both should meet on open ground.

Now the battle is joined. The poet's skill is never shown to greater advantage than in the descriptions of the fighting.[102] He alternates between the panoramic and the individual combats, so that we get the sense of battle of great scope being fought by individual heroes. Spears fly forth from fists; arrows leap out of the bows and are received in wooden shields; and warriors fall dead on either hand (ll. 108-12). From the general the poet moves to the specific: one of the slain is Wulfmær, while on another part of the field Eadweard slays a viking with his sword (ll. 113-19). The poet then returns to a general description for several lines; then back again to the individual heroes' fights, at this point that of Byrhtnoth.

Finally the old warrior is wounded; by his side stands a young warrior, a youth not yet fully grown (l. 152), who takes the viking spear which has wounded his leader and hurls it back into the body of the enemy. His missile thus expended, Byrhtnoth draws his sword, but then his arm is wounded, he drops to the ground the sword which he no longer has the strength to grasp, and the English chieftain stands helpless before his enemies. Here is another moment of expectation and tension while we await Byrhtnoth's inevitable end; our poet is too much of a craftsman to let it slip by easily, and in this moment of anticipation he imparts to Byrhtnoth a prayer of thanks to God (ll. 173-80); then, when the action can be delayed no longer, he tells us that the heathens hewed him down.

Maldon is a poem with a simple theme: the allegiance owed to one's lord is an easy matter to affirm over a tankard of mead, but the measure of the man and of his word is put to the test only on the battlefield. There, only two options are available to the warrior: to live up to his pledge and his code, follow faithfully or avenge the lord he has sworn to serve, or to flee.[103] To make this clear it is necessary that Byrhtnoth die before the end of the battle, for when his men are thus put on their own, with only their honor to support them, they are most critically challenged. The leader's death is important in itself, of course;

from the line in which we are told that a viking raised his spear and rushed toward Byrhtnoth until he lies dead on the strand, fifty-four lines have elapsed (ll. 130-84), almost exactly one-sixth of the entire surviving poem. And yet of equal importance are the reactions of his thanes. If Byrhtnoth's heroism was to be exalted above all else, his death would have to be at the poem's end.

Its placement at about the middle marks its role as fulcrum. Byrhtnoth's bravery has already been demonstrated; it was well-known before the battle, it was reasserted in his decision to fight the vikings, in allowing them to cross over the Pante, and in his personal conduct of war on the field. If he died last, the poem's priorities would have been shifted; and even though he dies before the end, unlike Leonidas, some of his men will run. As the vikings are the agents by which the English are tested at all, Byrhtnoth's death is the extreme, the supreme challenge to his men.

Ælfnoth and Wulmær choose to die by their master's side; at that same moment Godric flees from the field, riding—simulacrum of the heroic ideal—a horse which the ealdorman had once given him. Several others followed, forsaking their honor to save their lives. Ælfwine and Wulfmær became models of loyalty and social cohesion to those thousands of later Saxon warriors who heard—or possibly even read—of their acts. Godric, on the other hand, was a shameful lesson to succeeding generations of Saxons of the disgrace in which cowards were held. More than cowardice, which today we may dismiss more easily as a fear for one's safety, desertion of one's leader in the tenth century was nothing less than treason, as Offa says when reminding his comrades that they have been "betrayed" (*beswicene* [1. 238]).

The flight of the traitors evokes four speeches from among the survivors, each a declaration of his resolution. Ælfwine puts the matter directly: often had they boasted of their prowess while drinking within the safe halls of home; now they will have to prove those words. "No one," Ælfwine declares, "will ever have any reason to reproach me with the desire to desert this army and run home, now that my prince has been slain" (ll. 220-23). And as if to confirm the intent of his own words, he rushes forward into the fight and impales a viking with his spear. At this point the inevitability of defeat has not yet occurred to the survivors. Like Ælfwine, their concern is for upholding their honor.

Offa speaks next, telling Ælfwine that he was right to encourage the men at such a serious moment, now that their earl was dead, to fight as long as they could wield their weapons. Offa realizes that a catastrophe has befallen them (1. 243); the flight of the cowards has broken the phalanx, and the Saxon position is perilous. Leofsunu, in the next speech, replies to Offa, pledging his word that he will not retreat one inch. Whereas Ælfwine had sworn that he would not return home as did the cowards, Leofsunu adds that he will remain on the field until the end, when weapons take him (1. 252). And so saying, he strides forward angrily, fighting with enhanced fury.

Dunnere speaks last in this declamatory collocation, as is appropriate to his station as "lowly churl" (1. 256), and his words are the fewest, as is dramatically appropriate to his being last. The conclusion is fitting: Ælfwine has reminded the survivors of their oaths and has asserted his own intentions, Offa has praised his encouraging words because the flight of the cowards has endangered those who chose to remain and fight, and Leofsunu has responded (as with the voice of all the remnants) that not only will he not yield one inch but he knows that he will die on the field, and so it is fitting (logically and dramatically) that Dunnere point out that whoever intends to avenge their lord must neither flinch nor have regard for his own life (ll. 257-59). Words were followed by deeds: the Saxons rush forward once more, praying to God that they be granted vengeance.

But very quickly the tide turns against the Saxons, fatally weakened in numbers. We know that Wulfmær had been mortally wounded earlier (ll. 113-15), and that two men died by Byrhtnoth's side. Nevertheless, the battle went well as the Saxons carried the fight to the seafarers. But the waxing Saxon tide began to ebb. Eadweard smashed into the viking shield-wall and, selling his life dearly, was beaten to the earth. So too did Ætheric: his shield was fractured and his corselet "sang a terrible song," and he too was smashed down. Offa killed a viking and was in turn quickly brought down. So in the space of sixteen lines the fall of three Saxons is shown, and the vikings had clearly taken the initiative. The seafarers surged forward, Wistan advanced, struggling to stem the tide, and slew three of the enemy in the melee before he was also brought down. The battle had become hopeless; the viking's strength[104] had begun to tell on the steadily weakening English. Fierce in the fight, standing firm, one by one they nevertheless fell. When Byrhtwold gives his noble speech of defiance, further fighting is useless; the situation has already changed drastically from the moment of Ælfwine's declamation, when the outcome of the fight was in doubt. Because the fight is hopeless, Byrhtwold's courage is all the greater, his honor all the more enhanced:

> Hiȝe sceal þe heardra, heorte þe cenre,
> mod sceal þe mare, þe ure mæȝen lytiað.

Her lið ure ealdor eall forheapen,
ʒod on þreote. A mæʒ ʒnornian
se ðe nu fram þis piʒpleʒan pendan þence
Ic eom frod feores. Fram ic ne pille,
ac ic me be healfe minum hlaforde,
be spa leofan men licʒan þence.

Thoughts shall be braver, hearts shall be bolder,
Courage shall be greater, as our strength lessens.
Here lies our leader, all hewn to pieces,
The good man on the ground. May he grieve forever
Who now thinks to flee from this war-play.
I am old in years, so I will not,
But here beside my own dear lord,
So beloved a man, I intend to lie.

(312-19)

The speech poignantly complements the earlier vow of Ælfwine, that "winter-young" warrior. The young man had sworn to fulfill his obligation, though it entailed danger, with the outcome of the fighting still in the balance; the old thane, knowing how close they all were to defeat, nevertheless, in the face of that inevitable defeat, vows that he will fight until the might of the enemy allows him to share the fate of his lord. The early viking arrogance has been countered, poetically, by English determination and courage; the early success contrasts with the eventual defeat; the peril of the situation has been defied by the oaths of indomitable resistance; treason is countered by loyalty.

With such abundance of poetic drama it is hard for me to believe that the battle was fought exactly as the *Maldon* poet records it for us; reality is hardly ever so dramatic, so structured, so noble.[105] If it were, then the fight at Maldon would surely rank with the great martial (rather than poetic) feats of Western heroism, with Thermopylae, with the charge at Balaclava, far exceeding the real defense at Roncesvalles. We should be satisfied, however, with the heroic quality of *Maldon* as poetry and not try to pretend that it records real heroism; as heroic poetry it suffers little from comparison with any epic or lay in our civilization.

Nearly all of the dramatic elements of the heroic defeat are skillfully wrought in *Maldon*: the small band of men who determine to die fighting to the last ounce of their strength and to take as great a number of the enemy as possible with them to death; the traitor to his comrades, who causes their defeat; the greater strength of the enemy, who are so frequently racial or national aliens; and the heroism of the leader, around whom much of the action is focused. In *Maldon* there is no hilltop, probably because the actual field south of Maldon is flat marshland, possibly because hills are not common to the coasts of England, certainly not to the portions where the vikings raided: it is one of those details of the area's geography, so much admired in the poem, which was "realistic." And there is no "lone survivor" as in some of the other stories. Yet the poem is moving and successful without these elements other artists found useful: aesthetics are not bound by schematics. And although one of the arguments of this book is that certain kinds of stories are best told in certain ways, those "ways" are not so rigid and unwavering as to preclude variation and individuality. The inspiration for the narrative of Byrhtnoth's last stand has far too much in common with the accounts of the stands of Saul, Leonidas, Roland, Gawain, Mathô, and Custer for us to deny its similarities, and enough that is distinctive to insist on its individuality.

8

The Making of a Legend

Without the will to believe—not only in one set of circumstances rather than in another, but that some things did happen and others simply did not—we would have no legend of the Last Stand. The "causes" we have discussed (and will discuss further in the next chapter) would never come into being without will. It is not irrelevant to delve into the role of tradition or into the dramatic necessity of telling these legends a certain way, but each is like a safe deposit box, containing its store of contributions, which will remain inaccessible unless the key—will or desire—is turned. Binary contrasts give form and sometimes even meaning to our narratives, but without will, without the desire to remember, to retell the story in a way that justifies our mood, the shaping force of binary contrast would never come into play.

For instance, why does Graetz say that at Gilboa Saul and his Israelites fought bravely all day?[1] Or why, for that matter, in the absence of facts, does anyone think that any of our heroes made a creditable account of himself? We have no evidence for an estimation of Saul one way or another, either for "all day" or for "bravely." Yet most of us familiar with the story make this assumption, probably because we have come to think that a defeated army with which we sympathize will meet its fate, in Whitman's homey phrase, "wringing out every cent of the pay before they sell their lives." We all know of small armies disgracefully routed; but if the defeated unit is "ours," one with which we empathize, we will not want to believe its defeat disgraceful. At such moments will controls our perceptions.

Earlier in this book we saw that two substantially differing accounts of Custer's last battle—the "slaughter-pen" ravine and the "last stand"—were presented almost simultaneously to the American people. We saw how the public chose to accept the second account, that of the heroic "line behind line" defense of Custer Ridge. When news of the battle first fell like a tomahawk on the American people, they could not believe it; when a steady stream of confirmatory reports made the disaster undeniable Americans did not want to believe it. Actually, the newspapers had word of the debacle at least a day before

Terry's official communique reached General Sherman in Washington. During that interval Sheridan was openly dubious about the reports of defeat, pointing out that the "news" had not come from official sources; he insisted to a reporter of the *New York Herald* (7 July, p. 3) that such stories from scouts were not to be trusted. A defeat was possible, Sheridan concluded, but certainly not such a slaughter as the newspapers were already describing. And Sherman, also without Terry's confirmation, subsequently reacted to the news in a way that is far more significant than he or anyone at the time realized: "I don't believe it, and I don't want to believe it, if I can help it."[2] Americans did not want to believe this horrible news, and their revulsion at the reported events (the "slaughter-pen" version was publicized at least one day earlier) prepared them to accept a version they wanted to believe.

Nevertheless, regardless of what Sherman and the American people wanted to believe, the loss of over 250 cavalrymen in action and the successful escape of the entire enemy force with but slight loss—women and children, the aged, and household belongings included—could not merely be wished away. And regardless of Sherman's initial protests, the steady flow of rumors, reports from "reliable sources," and finally the official communiques and the headlines made disbelief on the part of the public impossible. The news was extremely galling, as *The Times* of London (7 July) remarked with great insight: "So heavy a blow has seldom, indeed, been struck at the regular troops of a civilized Power by a barbarous enemy.... It is inevitable that such a disaster should sting the American people almost more as an insult than as an injury." And so to ease the pain of so burning a sting, white America chose to believe this was a defense of heroic proportions, a defense so gallant and valorous that it surpassed and overshadowed the fact of the loss itself. This mechanism has been studied in detail by Leon Festinger, who terms it "cognitive dissonance."[3]

Festinger's most illuminating examples are domestic. He cites several studies which demonstrate that after we make major decisions such as the purchase of a car we will read, or watch (on TV) advertisements extolling that car. Once we have made up our minds we do not want to know about the advantages of owning a competitor's product, and so we "close our minds" to any information that might disturb our sense of the correctness of our choice—which would cause "dissonance." This phenomenon usually occurs when confusing or painful data are unresolved, when "an event occurs and impinges on [one's] cognition creating strong dissonance with the existing cognition." Under such conditions Festinger's subjects sought to reduce their dissonance "by acquiring new cognitive elements consonant with the original cognition."

In 1876 this could not have worked since the "new cognitive elements" all reinforced the dreadful news that Custer and his men were indeed dead. What happened then, however, was predictable: certain of the facts were challenged and others altered, details were invented—in fact nearly the entire course of the battle on Custer Ridge was invented—until the meaning of the event soon became entirely transformed. The Little Bighorn became not a defeat at all, but a great moral triumph, as great a display of heroism as the world had ever witnessed. Custer's fall was fortunate indeed.

In addition to the role in the legendizing process played by the Centennial Exposition and by national and sectional interests, as discussed earlier, two other "cognitive elements" made the news of the disaster hard to accept: Custer's reputation and the attitude of white America toward the Indians. Custer was the darling of the public and the press. The "boy general" who had won his first star in the Civil War at age twenty-three, "the intrepid Napoleon of the Plains," "the Murat of our service," and "the Marshal Ney of the American Army"—he was known to the public if not to the military as an experienced Indian fighter, although his only major encounter with hostile Indians had been his raid on Black Kettle's Cheyenne village in the dead of winter, which was modestly successful and handsomely reported in the press. When Russia's Grand Duke Alexis Alexandrovich toured the American West early in 1872, General Sheridan, "Buffalo Bill," and Custer were his escorts, as we have noted. And the Seventh Regiment enjoyed an equally high reputation, deservedly or not.

One of the major reasons why the public expected a speedy and easy victory over the Indians was the red man's reputation for cowardice. This had little basis in fact but was inspired by the Indian's frequently used tactics of hit-and-run and of ambush. Countless times the pioneer victims had been one or two prospectors in their cabin, a small detachment of cavalry, a farmer and his family. Indians never deployed for combat shoulder-to-shoulder (or flank-to-flank) as did European armies, and on the few occasions when large forces of them could be induced into battle against a sizable or a well-supplied army unit, the outcome as often as not went against the Indian—as in the Wagon Box fight or the Hayfield fight. On the morning of 25 June Custer's greatest concern was not the superior numbers of the enemy, but the likelihood—so he thought—that the Indians would try, as they had so often, to escape. And it was with these thoughts in mind that he ordered his fateful attack on that morning. Given this widespread attitude toward the Indian, that he was cowardly, savage, and fit only for slavery or death, that this was, in Captain Jack's words, "a race that knows no mercy.... For theirs is a life of falsehood, treachery, and heartless cruelty, from their birth to grave,"[4] the shock and disbelief of the American people at the death of Custer and his men is understandable.

Whether many of the reasons for the public's astonishment after the Little Bighorn disaster are applicable to other legends of the "Custer cluster" is a question not easily answered. We do not know whether Roland (the real one) and Lázar and Mynyddog were charismatic figures at the times of their deaths. Leonidas may have been; Bjarki perhaps was; Saul probably was, judging from the animosity he aroused among the scribes; and Byrhtnoth and Constantine most likely were. This detail seems insignificant beside the event for which the man, charismatic or not, is remembered and celebrated; yet from what we know of the utterly capricious turnings of Fortune, one is hard put to give prominence either to the man or the event. What we have said about "cognitive dissonance" and the other attempts to cope with painful news—as distinct from parochial considerations of specific times and particular places—certainly applies to the other "hilltop heroes" as well as to Custer. The Christian world hardly expected its best fighting men, laboring under God's aegis, to be defeated by Moors or Basques; Saul, who had been consistently successful in battle, would hardly be expected to lose battle, army, and life at Mt. Gilboa; and Lázar, fighting on his own ground against Murad, whom he had already defeated on the Toplitsa just two years before, must have inspired the confidence of his people when they attacked their Asian enemy at the plains of Kóssovo (more on this subject later).

The mid-1870s held many difficult times, particularly because of the way in which American life was swayed and staggered by its faltering economy. And regardless of economic problems, life on the frontier was always difficult from day to day, and it demanded of those vigorous men who lived there a commensurate toughness. Part of the attitude toward the Indian—that *he* was savage, that *he* was uncivilized, wild, and treacherous—was a projection of the fears of white Americans, particularly Westerners, who attributed to the red man what the white feared about himself; for example, white as well as red men took scalps. And to be effective on the plains against a quicker enemy who seemed to know the land perfectly the army had to be as ruthless as it felt the situation required.[5] Like the black man today, the red man was immediately visible. Unlike the Blacks, the Indians were ready scapegoats because they were "external"; as Hitler was able to marshal the insecurities and frustrations of the German people (and later the Austrians, Hungarians, and Romanians as well) against the non-Aryan "strangers" in their midst, so the Indians were a natural goat against whom white Americans could release their frustrations and thereby draw their own fury away from the numerous internal problems.

The emotional cycle is one with which we, as Americans, are too familiar: apparent freedom, opportunity, and near omnipotence is frustrated. The result is aggression, often expressed in violence, which is soon followed by guilt, which leads, in its turn, to further frustration; then the cycle is complete and self-perpetuating. The American people, from the nineteenth century (perhaps even earlier) to the My Lai massacre and beyond,[6] have often been the victims of the country's brightest promise. But for reservation Indians, or Blacks, or Japanese-Americans in 1942 (to specify just three of the most obvious examples), America was not the land of the free. And despite the supposed dream of European immigrants to American shores, the streets have not been paved with gold. The nation which lay before them like a land of dreams, so rich, so various, so new, was most of the time in reality filled with hard work, severe climates, and near poverty. But this is not the place to review European immigration attitudes in detail: this outline will suffice here to suggest how the frustrated expectations of immigrants could lead to violence.

So it was when gold was discovered in the Black Hills. Here was another opportunity to get rich quickly, and if the streets did not have nuggets in the concrete, the ore was to be found in the Dakota territory. But then, in addition to the recession and the embarrassment and anger over governmental corruption (which enabled a few to become wealthy while many were jobless), prospectors were painfully frustrated by the paucity of gold found and mined in the Black Hills. Many who were either optimistic or desperate persisted in believing that it was there. Two years after the first nuggets had been panned, the *Cheyenne Weekly Leader* still carried in each issue a detailed, two-page map showing access to the "gold" fields. To many it must have seemed that the only obstacle to the wealth the New World offered them was the Indian, whose frequent depredations made prospecting a dangerous business. This frustration, in addition to the rarity of actual gold discoveries, enhanced the Westerner's aggressions.

Frustration and aggression are not the exclusive possessions of villains or heroes; such hostility is shown by all men under stress. We are interested in it here because of the treatment it allows racial or hereditary aliens. In the *Chanson de Roland* it made the indiscriminate slaughter of Saracens not only possible, but noble. After Custer's Last Stand it fostered the government's

The most effective illustrations of the Last Stand give the Indians' perspective; here a small cluster of soldiers is staunch, yet forlorn, amid the smoke and dust of battle, which inundate them, while "the best light cavalry in the world" sweeps 'round them, in an ever high tightening circle.

extermination policy. The feeling of this particular kind of hostility may, at times, be shared by all men. Recently we have found it in a very unheroic context—in the Vietnam war—where the violence bred of aggression was made easier—perhaps even possible—because the victims of the Americans were racial aliens.

This is a motive quite apart from the desire for revenge, which has already been afforded several pages. One of the most infamous and widely publicized American atrocities[7] was tried by a Marine Corps court-martial during January 1967. Ostensibly on a night patrol, an entire squad of marines attacked the friendly hamlet of Xuan Ngoc, which was not even thought to be hiding or concealing the enemy, and several hours later when the Americans withdrew, five Vietnamese (two of them infants) had been brutally murdered and a sixth (a young woman) badly beaten and raped.

In the early stages of the pretrial investigation the squad leader said that at the ambush site one of the riflemen had told the other men in the patrol that he had received orders from their platoon leader, a lieutenant, that the patrol was to "go out and terrorize and find out where the V.C. were. Harass, destroy, beat up on people. Rape if there were some young girls around. And shoot anybody that got in the way and wreck their houses." When the lieutenant was confronted with this charge the investigating officer introduced a new and even more ominous perspective: "It looks as though you engineered this thing. By implication if nothing else. Or by saying, 'go to your ambush site and at a specific time go out and rape, rob, beat and terrorize these goddamned people and get these zipperheads or gooks, shoot them, and don't bring any prisoners.' "

What emerged at the trial about the condition of this squad was even more serious; another man in the platoon testified that "our platoon had been sort of fouling up in garrison, seemed like everything we did, and we wanted to get some V.C. so we could more or less prove that we were as good as anyone else because we had a lot of pride in our platoon and we wanted real bad to get some V.C. that day." Since no V.C. were in the vicinity, the marines took out their accumulating fury on the most convenient aliens. During the trial the platoon leader was asked about two of the ringleaders:

> "They've often been told before about maltreatment of the people."
> "You knew they had antagonism for the people?"
> "Yes sir."

"You knew that in the past they were guilty of antagonism and brutality toward the Vietnamese people?"
"I wouldn't say brutality."
"Pushing around?"
"Yes."
"Hitting on occasion?"
"I have never seen it but I had heard it."
"You knew the victims of their acts, roughhousing, were innocent people?"
"That's correct."
"And yet you let them run the squad?"
"They were both good troopers. Very good."

And then a final, wincing, cringing note to finish this horror story: one of the marines, deeply remorseful at the pretrial investigation, was asked about his role; at one point he said that "as we looked down at the baby I was glad this wasn't in the United States." The investigating officer replied:

> "What the hell difference does it make where it's at. You murdered five people!... What difference does it make where you did it at? You raped one woman and tried to murder her. Does it really make any difference where it happened?"

War crimes against the South Vietnamese people had become so common that early in 1971 Representative Ronald Dellums of California headed an informal congressional panel to investigate American conduct in the war.[8] The panel was unofficial: it had no legal standing, no power to subpoena, and the witnesses could not be sworn. The only formal action the Dellums panel could take would be to prepare a report recommending congressional action. Nevertheless, a number of volunteer witnesses told of suspects wired to telephone lines while the power was turned on; other informants recalled that Vietnamese were dropped to their deaths from helicopters aloft, in an attempt to frighten still other suspects into talking about the enemy's activities. One intelligence agent, who worked in plain clothes in Vietnam, recalled that when his Chinese interpreter angered a captain in their unit (the 525th Military Intelligence Group), the officer shot her in the neck and left her body in a yard. Osborn remembered his saying, "She was just a slope anyway.... What difference did it make anyway."

The Vietnamese war was acutely anguishing to many Americans; what happened there has happened in other wars and at other times, but this time Americans were involved, and all of America knows it. Yet the Franks of the eleventh and twelfth centuries surely felt many of the same passions about the Saracens that our soldiers now feel about Asians. The *Chansons de Geste* are filled with vengeance and the joyous shedding of Saracen blood.[9] Could it be otherwise with crusaders pledged on their sacred honor to wrest the Holy Land from the infidel who was to him little more than an aspect of Antichrist? Or with the Franks in Europe who had no real contact with the Saracens and whose impressions and hatred of them was nurtured by what they heard in church?[10]

We know of the Saxon's fear and hatred of the vikings, of Saul's fear of the Philistines, Constantine's of the Turks, Leonidas' awareness of how the Persians endangered his home and his destined role in defending it, of the Slavs' hatred of their Turkish oppressors. The writer of the alliterative *Morte Arthure* populated the traitor's army with Saracens, Danes. and various pagans. Danish Bjarki perished before the slashing steel of the traitor's Swedes and Goths. In all of these last battles we do not claim that "war crimes" or atrocities were committed by the fallen hero's comrades (though what records we have of the crusades would prove such a claim easily); rather, we feel that revenge is made easier, that violence is enhanced when the enemy is alien, particularly if he was what the Greeks termed those who did not speak their language—"barbarian."

The legend of the martyred hero, with its implied call for revenge, sets one people against another; in fact we have seen that this is often its purpose. In the case of Custer's martyrdom, the floodgates of hatred and resentment were opened all around the country. The South—to repeat a point made earlier—attributed the Seventh's loss to President Grant's foolish policies and the resultant shortage of troops in the West. Those territories in closest daily contact with the Indians saw in the defeat the inevitable outcome of Grant's "peace policy," and they used the event to urge the confinement or extermination of the Indians. And the nation at large acted swiftly, regardless of whom it felt was at fault, to avenge Custer. Some may have exploited the battle cynically to further their own interests—the railroads and miners and ranchers had the most to gain, certainly—but hatred of the Indians was so great on the frontier, and had been for so many years before the battle, that it is hardly necessary to claim that cynicism was a motive for the calls to avenge the slain troops.

But whatever the intentions of sectional, private, or corporate interests, the nation as a whole groped toward revenge. From literally every region of the country volunteers offered their services to fight the Sioux; the army in the Western Territories was strengthened (including a unit commanded by General Nelson Miles, an officer of unquestioned talents and accomplishments), and an offensive began against those tribes which had not escaped away to Canada or back to their reservations. These events have been noted earlier.

A role in Custer's glorification perhaps equal to these limited political and economic aims was played by American cultural jingoism of the last decades of the nineteenth century, an aspect of the "bosh and buncombe" of American exuberance. Elbridge S. Brooks imagined Captain McDougall on Reno Hill exclaiming, "There's Injuns to right of us, Injuns to left of us, Injuns in front of us—somebody's blundered."[11] By 1898, the Custer debacle was commonly compared with Cardigan's, as memorialized in "The Charge of the Light Brigade." The *New York Herald*, for instance, had not allowed the glitter of the Little Bighorn to be outshone; in its editorial of 12 July 1876 it insisted that "the charge of Cardigan was not as daring a deed as the charge of Custer.... The charge on the Yellowstone was victory or death." A persistent and aggressive chauvinism pervaded American attitudes in numerous respects. When Walt Whitman reported (in the *New York Tribune*, 15 August 1881)[12] on his impressions of John Mulvany's painting, *Custer's Last Rally*, he allowed his patriotism to sway his aesthetic judgment. He revealed that he knew little about the facts of the battle, but, more important, his review tried to make a virtue of the painting's sins by insisting that Europe had something to learn about the fine arts from the likes of John Mulvany. I quote only a few of the most embarrassing lines here:

> Went to-day to see this just-finished painting by John Mulvany, who has been out in far Dakota, on the spot, at the forts, and among the frontiersmen, soldiers, and Indians, for the last two years, on purpose to sketch it in from reality, or the best that could be got of it.... A dozen of the figures are wonderful. Altogether a western, autochthonic phase of America, the frontiers, culminating, typical, deadly, heroic to the uttermost—nothing in the books like it, nothing in Homer, nothing in Shakespeare; more grim and sublime than either, all native, all our own, and all a fact.... Custer (his hair cut short) stands in the middle, with dilated eye and extended arm, aiming a huge cavalry pistol.... Two dead Indians, herculean, lie in the foreground, clutching their Winchester rifles, very characteristic.... There is almost an entire absence of the stock traits of European war pictures.... I only saw it for

an hour or so; but it needs to be seen many times—needs to be studied over and over again. I could look on such a work at brief intervals all my life without tiring; it is very tonic to me; then it has an ethical purpose below all, as all great art must have. The artist said the sending of the picture abroad, probably to London, had been talked of. I advised him if it went abroad to take it to Paris. I think they might appreciate it there—nay, they certainly would. Then I would like to show Messieur Crapeau that some things can be done in America as well as others.[12]

America was proud to be America in 1881, and this no doubt accounted for much of the fame given Custer, yet the other martyred heroes often achieved their glory in somewhat similar conditions. The national pride of Saul's Israel may never be known, but we do know that it, too, was a young nation (Saul was its first king), and a relatively weak nation—unlike the United States in 1876—which had many powerful enemies to fear, but also, because of its monotheism, had reason to feel superior. Were not the Israelites God's chosen?

At Thermopylae Leonidas led an army that was in several ways inferior to its opponent, which heightened the heroism of his last stand, making it an inspiration to subsequent generations of Greeks. We have remarked how the *Chanson de Roland* was probably used to foster the crusading ethos, how the last stand of the Franks may have been recited to persuade men to leave their homes and their lands to go and fight the infidel beyond the Bosphorus. We think that some version of the *Chanson* was sung to steel men's courage on the eve of battle at Hastings. And the story of Byrhtnoth's death while defending his lands against the vikings emerged and grew during the time of the reign of Ethelred the Unready, when frequent raids by those superb warriors from the north threatened to tear apart the kingdom shire by shire. And the revenge motif for the defeat of Lázar at Kóssovo is one of the most persistent legends of Serbia.

The desire for vengeance after a defeat should not be underestimated. It is a great spur to action on the part of the survivor's countrymen, providing them with a greater incentive than would a victory. When the USS *Maine* was blown up in her Cuban slip, "Remember the Maine" immediately became the battle cry which swept away any lingering resistance to this war against the Spanish in Central America and the Pacific. No doubt the *Maine* affair was more an insult than a mortal offense to the American people; nevertheless, the reaction was immediate and severe. More serious, certainly to Texans, was the attack on and reduction of the Alamo. And the cry that resulted—"Remember the Alamo"—sprang from the throats and hearts of thousands who later mobilized to counterattack Santa Ana's army. It was the same after the 7 December 1941 attack by a Japanese carrier task force on Hawaii: Americans were told to "Remember Pearl Harbor" as the day that would live in infamy. In a war filled with propaganda and slogans and contrived bravado, "Remember Pearl Harbor" stands out among the most popular and moving cries of the era. For Israel, "Masada Shall Not Fall Again" has similar associations.

For some of the heroes—Bjarki against the Goths and Swedes, and Mynyddog against the heathen English—little is known about what political capital may have been made of their legends, but again one suspects that their stories may have been used the same ways, given the traditional hositlity of the martyr's people to their slayers. Constantine has never been revenged; when he died at the walls of his city his empire died with him, and revenge is historically irrelevant (though Greek hatred for the Turks lives on), unlike the events of the aftermath of Custer's defeat.

Turning defeat into firmer resolve, into an even greater determination to fight on until victory, was the effectively accomplished purpose of several of Winston Churchill's speeches following the defeat of the English armies in France and their evacuation from Dunkirk. Though many of these heroic words of defiance amid defeat are well known, they are well worth repeating here as instances of eloquence of the feelings we have been discussing.[13] After the fall of Dunkirk he addressed The House of Commons:

> The British Empire and the French Republic, linked together in their cause and in their need, will defend to the death their native soil, aiding each other like good comrades to the utmost of their strength.... We shall go on to the end, we shall fight in France, we shall fight on the seas and oceans, we shall fight with growing confidence and growing strength in the air, we shall defend our Island, whatever the cost may be, we shall fight on the beaches, we shall fight on the landing grounds, we shall fight in the fields and in the streets, we shall fight in the hills; we shall never surrender, and even if, which I do not for a moment believe, this Island or a large part of it were subjugated and starving, then our Empire beyond the seas, armed and guarded by the British Fleet, would carry on the struggle, until, in God's good time, the New World, with all its power and might, steps forth to the rescue and the liberation of the old.

Two weeks later (18 June 1940), before that same House of Commons, defeat was still on Churchill's mind, but so was the determination to remain, in adversity, resolute. The situation reminded him of the bleak days of the first great war:

> During the first years of the last war the Allies experienced nothing but disaster and disappointment. That was our constant fear: one blow after another, terrible losses, frightful dangers. Everything miscarries.... What General Weygand called the Battle of France is over. I expect that the Battle of Britain is about to begin.... The whole fury and might of the enemy must very soon be turned on us.... If we can stand up to [Hitler], all Europe may be free and the life of the world may move forward into broad, sunlit uplands. But if we fail, then the whole world, including the United States, including all that we have known and cared for, will sink into the abyss of a new Dark Age, made more sinister, and perhaps more protracted, by the lights of perverted science. Let us therefore brace ourselves to our duties, and so bear ourselves that, if the British Empire and its Commonwealth last for a thousand years, men will still say, "This was their finest hour."

And in the fall of that year, when the Battle of Britain had indeed begun, when wave upon wave of German bombers had crashed upon his island fortress, Churchill once again rallied his people in their darkest hour:

> Every man and woman will therefore prepare himself to do his duty, whatever it may be, with special pride and care.... These cruel, wanton, indiscriminate bombings of London are, of course, a part of Hitler's invasion plans.... Little does he know the spirit of the British nation, or the tough fiber of the Londoners.... This wicked man, this repository and embodiment of many forms of soul-destroying hatred, this monstrous product of former wrongs and shame, has now resolved to try to break our famous Island race by a process of indiscriminate slaughter and destruction. What he has done is to kindle a fire in British hearts, here and all over the world, which will glow long after all traces of the conflagration he has caused in London have been removed.

Thus in our own time a nation near defeat has been spurred on to vengeance and victory. Although here we are discussing real characters, in the preceding pages both real and fictional characters have been treated, often being subjected to the same kind of analyses. One of the points I have tried to establish is that imaginary people can be quite immediate to us, yet nearly all the people who have actually lived on this earth have no effect on us at all. Before I attempt to get at the heart of the matter of epics of defeat, this important point should be elucidated.

In describing the humiliating rout of Varus' legions before the savage assaults of Hermanus' "barbarian" Germanic tribes in the murky depths of the Teutoburgwald, Sir Edward Creasy[14] sketched the stumbling, groping movements of the Romans, the befuddled indecision of their commander, and the ease with which the disorganized and confused legionnaires were panicked and finally slaughtered. Later, like the American reaction to Custer's Last Stand, this nearly complete annihilation of their legions long held a morbid fascination for the Roman people. Yet from this gloomy day in the Empire's history one particular incident shines with at least a faint glow. We are told that one body of soldiers (neither Creasy nor his sources say how many) halted their retreat on a convenient hillock and, forming themselves in a defensive ring upon it, smashed back every attack on them all that day, making the barbarians pay a bloody wage for their victory. Years later, visitors to the scene found the place where some attempt had been made to form a defensive ditch, though the legionnaires did not have either time or opportunity enough to dig effective fortifications. On the second day of battle the end came for these men: exhausted from hunger and fatigue, defeated by their wounds and their sense of their inevitable helplessness, they were unable to resist any further the more vigorous Germans, who swarmed over the hill, slaughtering many on the spot, carrying off the others to be sacrificed to their gods elsewhere.

We can take this account to be reasonably accurate, although even here there are suggestions of the fictive imagination at work. It is true that years later visitors to the scene would have little way of knowing what ills beset these resolute Romans (though hunger, fatigue, and wounds would be a reasonable guess) or that the defense was successful on the first day but collapsed on the second. Nevertheless, the account has much in it that we accept without question: some men, even some defeated men, may at one point in their lives make a determined stand. Whether out of bravery or resignation or anger or frustation or despair does not matter. At some point in the midst of a disaster a few—or perhaps just one—will say, "This far and no further: here we will stand."

The resistance of these few legionnaires amid the general flight of their comrades differs in our minds in at least one way from the resistance of, say, Roland and his guard: we take Creasy's anecdote to be real, and we understand Turoldus' epic to be fiction. Nevertheless, our feelings for the "real" men are the same as for the fictional: we admire them both, and for the same reasons, for the "real" legionnaires are no more a reality to us than Custer's men (or contemporaries who have no direct and immediate impact on our lives), and Roland's barons may have a very dramatic presence in the lives of some scholars, perhaps for thousands of readers at the moment that they "experience" the *Chanson de Roland*. Fiction is easily made real for us, and events are readily fictionalized; the point does not need much argument. What should be recalled, however, at this place in our argument, is that the "aesthetic experience" is a concatenation of everyday emotions, and that history, well told, can inspire this experience as well as narrative art. The artist's facility with words makes all the difference, or else we would be forced to say that Whittaker's "Custer's Last Charge" was the equal of the *Chanson de Roland*. But for the moment let us put aesthetics aside; then we can see that the admiration we have for the Romans in the Teutoburgwald is the same as that for Roland (detaching his stand from the rest of the epic).

The price for not making such a stand may be shame, self-recrimination, guilt, remorse, frustration, and anger. I visited Czechoslovakia during the summer of 1969, several months after the invasion by the Warsaw Pact armies which suppressed the Dubček regime. Even then loyal Czech soldiers patrolled the streets of Prague with submachine guns. On the roads in the country one frequently met columns of armored cars and occasionally T-54's on maneuvers. MIG's were always in evidence, flying low over the cities and buzzing the country roads, the bright red star on their wings looking strange and chilling to Western eyes. The first shocks had been absorbed by the Czech people, and in the summer of 1969, after Jan Pollack had burned himself to death in St. Wenceslas Square in protest, the mood of many was angry. In the three cities I visited—Plzen, Prague, and Bratislava—the resentment and anger of many Czechs was overt. Sometimes it was manifested as self-hatred. The owner of one hotel at Bratislava interrupted an embarrassingly candid conversation with me to glance at a larger than life poster of Dubček papering the wall behind him and compared his leader to Quisling—for his order to the Czech people to passively capitulate to the Russian army. When I asked him what the Czechs might have done against so strong an invading force (which included East Germans, Poles, and Hungarians as well as Russians) he said, "We might have fought. Even if only for half an hour. At least we would have done *something*."

This Bratislava hotel manager, in his emotions at least, had reached that threshold of anger and frustration where submission to defeat is no longer tolerable—much like Varus' small body of legionnaires; and he said, "No more, here I stand." But for him and for Czechoslovakia it was too late. As in modern Czechoslovakia, so throughout history—and legend. For one of the traits of our fictions about martyred heroes which has given them a life of their own is our response to them as though to a real disaster. In many of the narratives we have discussed here, the accounts, and usually in detail, have, within the logic of the account, been believable. Almost always we celebrate the event more than the artist who superbly recorded it. We respond to such stories as though they happened and as we would, and do, respond to our encounters with reality. Only Flaubert perhaps taxes our belief, allowing us to feel that we are experiencing a fiction.

An immense statue of Leonidas now guards the site where the Spartans are thought to have fallen to their last man, though the line of march of the attacking Medes has been paved over by a four-lane highway. (Unfortunately for the feelings of antiquarians, this "Leonidas' " dress is that of a Homeric hoplite.) Thermopylae, and not Herodotus, is remembered in the names of clipper ships and Athens' streets, as well as by American reporters who glorified Custer's last fight. The plain at Kóssovo is commemorated by a tall stone tower, decorated with blackbirds (Kóssovo is the Plain of Blackbirds), although no Slavic *guslar* who sang of its glory is remembered. Literary historians and critics often praise "Turoldus," but the Association of Old French specialists devoted to his study is the Société Rencesvals; and the scores of statues of Roland and illustrations of his struggles pay tribute to a "reality" and not to the man who created that "reality."

In the *Chanson de Roland*, where the details of the battle are entirely fictional, many realistic elements have been incorporated. Armies do (and did) begin fighting at a distance, and for the Franks this meant with the lance while mounted; at Maldon the fight began with arrows and other missiles; for the Seventh Cavalry the weapon was the carbine. As the combat wore on the lances were shivered, and the enemy closed to fight at close quarters. Roland and his men then had to fight on foot, with their swords, as Byrhtnoth was forced to do with his Saxons. Gawain finally used his dagger and was himself killed by Mordred's. And in the end Custer drew his sword (!) to take three more of the red devils with him to cavalry Valhalla.

So seriously taken are the details of the stand at Thermopylae that archeologists and Hellenist historians have scoured the pass and the valley for geographical support for Herodotus: the battle site is appropriately commemorated. Mt. Callidromon is honeycombed with footpaths, a number of which could have been known to Ephialtes and used by him to lead the Persian troops onto the Greek flank. Perhaps the battle did happen (though almost co-incidentally) as Herodotus described it; yet despite the undeniable reality of the mountain paths, the convincing detail of the Greek warriors combing their hair before the battle, despite the explicitness of the description of Spartan tactics—despite these and many other "real" details—we are left to question much about the authenticity of the narrator's descriptions.

Historians, mythographers, and poets are not the only people who record life as though it were a well-planned fiction. What we have been observing is not history imitating art—the point cannot be stressed strongly enough—but history recreated, interpreted, and presented according to the same principles as art so that it becomes art. Custer himself did the same, in a letter written to Judge Kidder (dated 23 August 1867; Kansas Territory)[15] describing the death of Lieutenant Lyman Kidder in July of that year:

> Another proof of the determined gallantry exhibited by your lamented son and his little party, was the fact that the bodies, which were probably found as they fell, were lying near each other, thus proving that none had endeavored to flee or escape after being surrounded, but all had died nobly fighting to the last. No historian will ever chronicle the heroism which was probably displayed here.

And then in lines worthy of what Whittaker in his most inflamed moments might well have said about Custer's own disaster nine years later:

> We can picture what determination, what bravery, what heroism must have inspired this devoted little band of martyrs when surrounded and assailed by a vastly overwhelming force of bloodthirsty, merciless and unrestrained barbarians, and that they manfully struggled to the last, equally void of hope or fear.

In Custer's account of the Kidder massacre several imaginative elements are combined with what little was known to the general: Kidder's "little band of martyrs" (the phrase itself so much like that found in dime novels of the day) formed a circle when attacked, as did Custer's own officers and the men of F Troop for the Last Stand—as did Gawain and his knights, the determined veterans of Varus' shattered legions, the defeated thanes of James IV, perhaps even the Spartans who drew themselves close together as one body (though Herodotus does not describe whether their formation was circular or not).

From the "probability" that the bodies fell where they were found, Custer assumes—or wants Judge Kidder to think—that none had tried to escape. All of Kidder's party, we are told without much evidence, died fighting nobly to the last. Whether the men with Lieutenant Kidder fought with inspired heroism or cringed and fired their weapons into the air (as did the men with Elliott at the Washita) neither we nor any historian will ever chronicle. Yet we can believe Custer's account of this skirmish in outline (allowing for his purple rhetoric) because it does contain several "real" details: the greater number of Indians, the small detachment huddled together for their defense. Like many of the details of epic—as well as of heroic legend—these ring true, because we know that so many times, under similar or comparable circumstances, others did the same.

Hilltops, for instance, are obvious places from which to defend oneself: the enemy is obliged to attack uphill, fighting gravity (to a certain extent) as well as the defenders. So axiomatic is this principle of warfare that its exceptions are worthy of note and elaborate explanation. When Rommel captured the Mimeimat Ridge in his first assault on Montgomery's forces at El Alamein (to cite a recent instance), one of the battle's chroniclers[16] pointed out in some detail that the British staff was actually pleased: this vantage point enabled the Germans to observe deceptive moves Montgomery wished Rommel to see, and such deception was one of the decisive factors in the English victory.

Custer took no exception to the axiom to take the high ground: he sought the nearest ridge around when he was attacked, though he did not position himself at its crest. The Spartans retreated to a hillock, as did the legionnaires. Saul, like Roland, died on a mountaintop. Sir Gawain at first captured the "green hill," which he should have held, for abandoning his position of strength doomed him and his men. Flaubert placed Matho's last stand on a hill purely for reasons of drama, since Polybius implied that the battle was fought on a plain.

Besides the advantage which geography affords, encircled soldiers are in a better position to defend their chief or king. Tacitus summed it up well when he said that among the Germans the king fought for victory and the warriors fought for their king. Surely the same was true of Leonidas' Spartans and for most of the armies of the Middle Ages. After Leonidas was killed his men increased their efforts—to preserve his body. After Byrhtnoth fell and several traitors fled, Ælfwine and others declared their determination to stand by their fallen leader and to die with him. Near the end of that poem, we have seen Byrhtwold's declaration that though he is old in years he will not flee, but "beside my own dear lord ... I intend to lie."

Heroic poetry is, after all, for the amusement and edification of the living as much as the celebration of the dead; it is meant to apply to situations quite apart from the immediate marshalling of men's courage as they prepare themselves for war, as was true of Taillefer's song at Hastings and Thormod's at Stiklestad. Heroic songs of the tribe's or the nation's illustrious warriors from times past remind the listeners of the nobility and valor of their ancestors as well as, by analogy, their present responsibility. Thus the decision of Ælfwine and the others to stand by Byrhtnoth and to die with him is not only the poet's glorification of the past for its own sake, but an instrument of reinforcement of the immediate duty owed one's lord in battle. Poems like *The Battle of Maldon* reaffirm the existing ethics of the tribe or class for which they were composed. And, more than being just moralizing medicine for hesitant warriors, heroic poetry is an enjoyment among men who themselves sought fame and their portion of immortality by their strength and skill with arms in battle. After Beowulf had disposed of the Grendel family, Hrothgar's castle was the scene of much feasting and joyous drinking; and then the *scops* came forward to sing songs not only of the nation's heroic past but of Beowulf's freshly done deeds.

Further, the audience of heroic narrative is pleased by recitations of glories past. As Grönbeck observed, the dead are rejuvenated and honored, and the descendants are thus flattered. When the family or the tribe is praised in such songs, they are all returned to the present. And when the warrior hears his forebears honored in his presence and that of his peers, he realizes that some day he too may be so honored, and in that sense he will not die.[17] When the beleaguered Franks turned to Roland and Turpin for relief, the archbishop urged them to fight yet more fervently, lest "no one sing evil songs of you" (ll. 1516-17). The best songs are the good, old songs, telling of the most important things a warrior must possess: courage, martial skill, and unfailing loyalty to his chief.

Out of such realistic (and often historically accurate) details as the great number of the enemy, the circular formation on the hillside or top, and the undying devotion of the warriors to their leader comes a believable narrative of defeat—however bloated the glory of that defeat—and often the story is used to serve the nation's interest. This aspect is not the same as the heartening effect heroic poetry may have on the individual warrior; and for modern attitudes the nation's interest may be even more important.

National and sectional interests supply people with the will to believe in whatever serves those interests. Once a will is exercised, several modes are possible to accomplish the desired end. It has been argued here previously that the martyred hero legends did not derive from earlier texts, and that the people who lived these legends did not make them up because they had read them in the lives of other men. This brings up the question of independent genesis.

We know that Herodotus had no knowledge of the Old Testament account of the defeat of the Jews at Mt. Gilboa, and that Turoldus did not know Herodotus and ignored the Old Testament. The *Gododdin* and the *Bjarkamál* derive from entirely separate traditions, as do the popular ballads and legends of Lázar and Constantine XI. And although the death of the alliterative *Morte Arthure's* Gawain may be derivative, as may the death of Flaubert's Mathô, no one has suggested it, and I too doubt it. In all of these variants we may be faced with yet another archetype, but no such image has yet been declared. Or we may be dealing with some Indo-European narrative tradition; but such a tradition has only rarely been the subject of conjecture[18] and has never been described because it has never been demonstrated to exist.

Why then have these stories from unmistakably varied sources and transmission processes become so much alike? At least one possibility that must be considered is that there is a "best," most dramatic, most "natural" way of telling certain stories. To consider this alternative we have only to project ourselves into the minds—perhaps the imaginations—of those people, the *scops*, minstrels, *jongleurs*, troubadours, historians, scribes, and poets, though not necessarily the legend mongers: How are these artists, each in his own way and according to his own level of articulation and eloquence, how, given the social pressures that may be active upon them, given the paucity of verifiable facts, and given their own desires, are they to believe in some things and not to believe others? How are such makers to write of, sing about, descibe aloud? How are they to remember a defeat in battle of one of their countrymen? How, to put the question directly, may the losers be glorified?

The dramatic and descriptive range of possibilities for exalting one's own forces is actually limited: the heroes must be, in the circumstances that interest us, noble or brave or valiant—or all of these. That the "friendlies" should be brutal or savage or inept or cowardly is simply inconceivable. Such criticism of one's own army is possible, of course, in certain kinds of literature, particularly farce or satire. And such denigration is the likely device of political commentary, as when one section or faction wishes to criticize a particular war, its conduct, its leadership, or even war itself.[19] But we are thinking about the necessary attitude toward the home forces in heroic literature, the literature of praise for brave men and brave deeds. One cannot imagine Turoldus speaking of Roland's "rag-tag mob" or Herodotus taunting the Greeks first for wearing their hair long, and then for combing it so methodically when the most important battle in their nation's history was imminent. Such taunts must be directed at Xerxes because his initial contempt for the Greeks opposing him has great ironic impact when it turns first to surprise and concern, then later to worry and frustration. Xerxes' contempt for the Greeks is an important element in this well-told heroic narrative; had Herodotus for any reason shown the same feelings toward the Spartans, a heroic narrative could not have been possible.

The enemy can also be brave and skillful, as are the Saracen antagonists of Roland. Bjarki's complaint is of the aggessiveness of the Swedes; and not the Turks (at Kóssovo or at Constantinople), the Philistines, nor Mordred's forces seem particularly timid. Again, the reason is determined by the dramatic situation. The hero and his brave band cannot be defeated by a gang of cowards. Aside from the contradiction inherent in such a situation, the "friendlies" must be given worthy opponents. Where is the valor, what are the skills tested, the determination tried, in killing vast numbers of cowering sheep? But if the enemy is skillful, and preferably also cunning, or savage, or ruthless, defeat of the home forces is understandable; and when great numbers of such an enemy are slain before the hero's own fall, the greater is his accomplishment.

The enemy who defeats the hero may thus be described within a wider range of possibilities, but still the choices are not without severe limits. Perhaps most important, the enemy must be numerically superior. Only their great numbers can manage to overcome the fortitude and skill of the defenders. Even the greatest warriors tire, their weapons finally break or are otherwise exhausted, or they are betrayed, and the enemy with his irresistible and endless waves of fresh troops finally manages to inundate the hero's small band: Leonidas and his 300 against the 10,000 who outflanked the Greek position, Roland and his 20,000 against more than ten times their number, Constantine standing alone at the St. Romanos Gate succumbing to 1,000 Turks, Gawain and his seven-score surrounded by Mordred's mighty army, Bjarki against the Swedes and Goths who gave him more blows in return for each he dealt them in any previous melee—this detail of the last stand is essential to explain away the loss of the field, regardless of the genuine heroism of the home forces. In several actual last stands the enemy did really outnumber the hero's men, we realize. In the heroic literature celebrating such a defeat, however, this detail will certainly be emphasized and usually exaggerated.

In at least one poem, *The Battle of Maldon*, the number of the vikings is not specified,[20] yet we have always assumed—and for the best of reasons— that the English were badly outmanned by their conquerors. What kind of poem would we have if the larger Saxon army was put to rout by a small viking force? Certainly not a heroic poem. The actual number of Basques who attacked the Franks at Roncesvalles is not known, nor is the number of their victims. That the Basques appear to have fought as guerrillas suggests, if anything, that the Franks in the real battle were at least as numerous. Polybius does not give the numbers of the armies of Matho and Hanno, but Flaubert, following this tradition, makes certain to weigh the numerical odds heavily on the Carthaginian side. He knew what he was doing.

Outside the world of heroic poetry the same principles usually hold. We have come to think that the American forces were outnumbered at Bataan, overwhelmed by the Asian hordes who could not shoot straight (because their eyes were "slanted") and in any event whose bullets were so small they were little more than toys. Yet finally, exhausted by sleeplessness and wearied by wounds and malaria for which no more medicine could be found, the small American force capitulated. Actually, the Japanese landing force was the smaller. In Europe, at the beginning of World War II (after the resumption of hostilities following the "Sitzkrieg") the German army which flew over and drove around the Maginot line, which cut the French army to bewildered tatters and slashed through the English lines like a hot knife through lard (later to battle them at Dunkirk where they let them slip through their clenched fists)—this German army was the smaller of the two.[21]

To demonstrate the qualitative superiority of the hero's small band, their greater valor and skill, they must inflict upon the enemy far more casualties than they themselves suffer. This is the most convincing way of demonstrating martial prowess; it is also the least complicated and the one with which there can be little argument: a simple body count. Once again we should ask ourselves what the effect would be on the audience if the hero and his men inflicted only slight casualties on the enemy. What would we think of Leonidas and his 300 if only 25 or so Persians fell before their spears? An annihilated army that kills more than its own number of the enemy has, in the hardest terms of the professional soldier, accomplished something. This surely was in Benteen's mind when he wrote to his wife (a few days after the battle) that Custer's command had taken more than their own numbers of the Sioux. That he later wrote in his diary that he didn't think Custer's men did any "first-class fighting" is beside the point; his subsequent bitterness must not be allowed to confound his genuine will to believe, on Custer Ridge, that his comrades had acquitted themselves well.

The traitor performs several dramatic functions. Primarily, he is the rational-ized reason for the failure, or at least a major factor in the hero's defeat. Again and again the American people sought to apologize for Custer's loss by in-venting traitors and their alleged treason: Crow scouts who sent secret signals to (their enemies) the Sioux, or Billy Cross (how far did the name itself suggest a "double-cross"?) who led the column into an ambush. Finally, and perhaps inevitably, the onus fell on Major Reno, who is still, in some quarters, accused of allowing Custer to ride to his bloody fate while he sat safely atop another hill up-stream. The traitors at Maldon—Godric and the other cravens—weakened the English so much that death became inevitable.

During the astonishingly successful German conquest of Europe in 1938 and 1939, the humiliating Polish disasters were attributed to the superior numbers of Germans, even though Polish losses were usually three and occasionally ten times those of the invader.[22] Nevertheless, the allies continued to believe that despite their setbacks the Poles were really the braver and more dashing.[23] German successes were said to be due to their ruthless tactics: their Stukas at-tacked schools and hospitals, and from the sky they machine-gunned de-fenseless women and children. When the Polish army was hopelessly defeated, several colonels escaped with their lives, and little more, to Romania, and subsequently became the scapegoats of Poland's fall. On them was laid all the blame for the efficiency of the *Wehrmacht,* much as various German generals were blamed for "selling out" their country at the end of World War I.

When the Panzer units were unleashed on the Anglo-French armies in the West, their advance through Luxembourg, Holland, and Belgium was ex-ecuted with deftness and lightning speed. Erwin Rommel, later to acquire a legend which became attached to his heroic life in the North African desert, led the Seventh Panzer Division through to the French coast. But in the un-conquered West it was fashionable to blame the successes of the Panzers on the "fifth column." The Germans used paratroops for the first time in a major war (having developed the technique during the Spanish Civil War) and the astonished Danes and Dutch condemned this novel tactic as sinister and treacherous. Paratroops were imagined everywhere in civilian clothes and even in Dutch uniforms. Spies and traitors were "found" as often. Leopold of Belgium and Wilhelmina of Holland were in those first days of bewildering defeat branded as traitors and tools of the German conquerors. As Marie Bonaparte wrote:

> Doubtless it seemed less humiliating to attribute defeat to its treachery than to admit that we generally retreated because the enemy was

stronger, better armed, better led, and because no soldier, even the French, could eternally endure being bombed with no chance of reply.[24]

When defeat is the fault of such traitors as Ephialtes, Godric, Vuk, or the Polish colonels, the hero remains in spirit undefeated. He has triumphed morally, for even though he has been physically beaten it has not been in any way his fault. We will be left with the feeling that but for the traitor the hero might have been successful, and so he rises in our estimation above the overwhelming numbers of the enemy. Traitors make the job of assigning blame an easy one, and consequently they are handy people to have around. If no traitor is visible or obvious, we will invent our Reno or Hjarvarth or Mehmed.

In literature the traitor frequently is posed as a foil to the hero, whose commitment to some transcendent ideal is in sharp relief with the villain's petty lust. In contrast to Roland's willingness to die rather than shame his family is Ganelon's betrayal of his countrymen and his acceptance of lavish gifts from Marsile for his treason. Saul would die like a king, undefiled by the enemy; the skulking Amalekite robbed the crown and bracelet from his body in hopes of a reward. So too with Ephialtes, who sold out Leonidas when the Spartan made his determined stand to the death for his homeland. Godric fled for his life on a horse Byrhtnoth had given him immediately after his leader died with a prayer on his lips that his thanes continue their fight for God's sake. This motif recurs continually in Western heroic literature. Siegfried and Achilles are also slain treacherously by assassins they would have blown aside in an open fight. Beowulf is left to battle the dragon alone when his army flees to the woods. Even Jesse James was said to have been gunned in the back by "that dirty little coward," and Bonnie and Clyde (in the movie at least) were finally caught—and shot—by the police from ambush because of their accomplice's betrayal. The hero and his men have dedicated their lives to some transcendent loyalty: to country, to family, to king, to freedom, to God. The traitor's motivation—for money, for craven revenge, out of cowardice—heightens through this contrast the hero's noble motives.

The hero must fight to the last and in most cases will himself be the last to die. We know well the dramatic and moral lesson that is drawn from the behavior of those warriors who, by fleeing, survived Leonidas and Byrhtnoth. But again we should pose an alternative: What kind of hero would we be celebrating if he died first? What would we think of Roland if he fell in the first Saracen assault, or of Lázar if a Turkish arrow, casually arched merely to find the range, had felled him before the serious fighting began? The result would be a travesty, just as much as if Gawain had killed himself because he tripped over a discarded lance and then fell on its point, or if Constantine had been slain while consulting with his chief engineer about a blocked sewer. Leonidas and Byrhtnoth do not have to be the last to die. Their falls are close enough to the end to show the stuff they are made of.

Last or not the hero's fall is tragic, for by it he gives up his life to gain some higher spiritual reward. All the heroes we have discussed share this tragic aspect in some form, perhaps none so explicitly as in the ballads about Lázar. He is given the choice of victory in this world or an ultimate triumph in the next. His choice of the latter implies the Turkish victory; yet the Serbs will have it both ways, blaming the defeat on the treachery of Vuk as well. For others the choice is not always as clear as salvation or death; sometimes the alternative to death is dishonor or treason to one's country or to one's king. When the hero chooses death, then, he makes a tragic decision.

His flaws are varied, but again within a limited range. Roland is proud, even arrogant on the eve of battle, more concerned for his honor and that of his family than for the safety of his comrades: possibly his flaw is *desmesure*.[25] Sir Gawain falls victim to his rash anger and leads his men down from their secure position on the green hill to attack Mordred on his own ground. Byrhtnoth is usually accused of excessive pride (*ofermode*) in allowing the vikings to cross the Pante unmolested. And Custer was at first blamed, but later praised, for his recklessness.

And after he has fallen the hero is honored for his decision and his deeds. We have not seen the time when the French condemned Roland for oppressing underdeveloped nations, nor have the Greeks defamed Leonidas for his ruthless treatment of the "barbarian." What is happening now to the reputation of Custer is unique in heroic legend. In the nineteenth century the stories were rampant that the Sioux had spared Custer's body out of respect for the remarkable bravery shown by their fallen foe. David's lament for Jonathan and Saul has become more famous than the men it mourns. Charlemagne wept over the body of his bereaved nephew; Arthur mourned as profoundly over the man he once said was the only man alive worthy to be king. If anything, Gawain had been given even higher praise earlier when Mordred eulogized him as the king's most valiant knight. Sir Maurice Bowra has observed that panagyric is akin to heroic poetry, and that kinship is nowhere more plainly seen than in these moments of eulogy. Heroic poetry subsumes the panegyric; itself a poem of praise of the hero, it bestows its approbation as does all well-wrought narrative, through action. As Fitzgerald once scribbled across one of his manuscript pages, "Action is Character." Once the hero has fallen the narrative pauses to introduce a panegyric which further praises the nobly fallen. A great man should not go to the grave unsung.

Nor must his death be unrevenged, for that would trivialize his memory and what he had tried to accomplish; it would be an admission that he died for something inconsequential or irrelevant and that it was not worth the effort of his surviving *landsmänner* to perform. In heroic legend and song this could not happen. The point has already been made in at least two poems that aggression is often the greater when the motivation is revenge for a wrong, a defeat, or an insult: the defeats of Roland and Gawain galvanize the determination of Charlemagne and Arthur. The cases of these two are the clearest, though a strong case could be made for *Maldon* as well as the songs about Lázar and Constantine. We are not sure to what extent David's motives in warring upon the Philistines were retaliatory, especially since quite a time elapsed between Saul's death and the subsequent attack on his slayers. In this interval David's first task was to reorganize the Hebrew tribes and to bolster their morale. When he finally did move he rolled up an impressive number of victories over Israel's oppressors. In the *Hrolf's Saga Kraki* revenge is wrought by Bjarki's brothers Elgfrothi and Thorir Houndsfoot, aided by the men of Sweden's Queen Yrsa.

Hardly necessary to the heroic tale is the figure of the lone survivor. He is rarely a person of any consequence, certainly playing no major role in the events preceding the battle, and he is a minor figure in the fighting itself. He does not even enjoy the authority and importance of Ishmael, who alone escapes to tell the tale—whose version of the events aboard the *Pequod* is the one we know. Yet this character type appears so often that he deserves our notice. Wigg alone survives among all of Hrolf's men; Milutin the servant escapes from the slaughter of Kóssovo; the coward Tedbald flees his dying leader Vivien, forcing him to face the enemy alone; Godric does the same to Byrhtnoth at Maldon; the unnamed Amalekite tries to capitalize on the Israelite defeat at Gilboa; Abronichus escapes to his boat to bring the news of the Spartan defense to Athens; one or more anonymous warriors survive Mynyddog's defeat in the *Gododdin*.

The "lone survivor" may not be essential to heroic poetry per se, but when he does appear he plays an important part in the narrative. His most obvious function is to provide the outside world with an eyewitness account of the fighting. Innumerable newsmen used Curly to give authenticity to their imaginative accounts of Custer's Last Stand, and the young Crow was widely cited, especially in those first years, as an expert on the progress of the battle. His inaccessibility, in Montana, and his ignorance of English made him the ideal "authority" on the battle. The same is true of the survivor in fiction in that he gives the narrative a believability it might not ordinarily have.

In those legends where the "friendlies" lose a great many men, or where the entire force is destroyed, the escape of one man contrasts with the loss of hundreds, perhaps thousands. Leonidas and his 300 fought like tigers to the end, while an unobtrusive Athenian made his way to his small boat and escaped from one of the great heroic moments in his country's history. Or Bjarki, champion of countless victories over man and beast, and the finest of Denmark's warriors, perishes in a struggle from which only one insignificant man survives. And if the survivor is the traitor, like Godric or the Amalekite, then his function in the narrative is to further heighten the contrast with the hero. Godric escapes with his life, while Byrhtnoth and his faithful companions are slain on the field: the noblest and best die for their convictions; the unworthy escape with their lives, but only with their lives.

And when only one man survives the debacle, the idea of the totality of the loss is strengthened. If half of the defenders escape, or only a third, or even a quarter, regardless of the actual numbers involved, the dramatic impression made is far less than when all—save one—have perished. The "all" is devastating; it speaks worlds of the desperation of the struggle, of the total commitment of the slain to their cause and their leader, and of the terribleness of the loss. This is made especially poignant when the "one" who lives through it or escapes from it is an insignificant character. By his very existence he proclaims that all of those brave and great men have perished, while he, a rather ordinary and inconsequential man, has managed to elude their majestic fate. Everyone of importance has died; in effect, "all" are dead. And it makes little difference to the totality of our impressions regarding their end that this one puny spearcarrier has lived to tell the tale. His tale will be, in fact, far more important than the man himself.

The function of the hero's call for help, when the battle is already hopelessly lost, is more problematical still. The greatest difficulty in analyzing this detail, which occurs with surprising regularity, is the variety of forms it assumes. To be perfectly literal, only Custer and Roland are said to call for help. Sergeant Butler's mission in the real battle on Custer Ridge is unknown; he may possibly have been trying to flee, or he may have been shot from behind as the battalion withdrew from the river on its way toward the ridge. That would seem to leave the only certain call for help that of Roland blasting away on his Oliphant.

If we can be a little less literal and view the "call for help" in terms of narrative funtion (á la Propp) the situation is clarified: at some point in the battle the hero is faced with a choice which, if acted upon in time, may be able to save his life and the lives of his men. One of the several forms this choice may take is the literal call for aid. Roland's first refusal is put in sharp relief for us when he later decided to signal Charlemagne of his peril. But further, the tale is made more dramatic, and Roland's disdain of danger is further enhanced in our eyes, by the possibility that had he been less recklessly brave he might have escaped, though we could never have forgiven him for it. After his initial decision to lead the rear guard; when he refuses more reinforcements than is usual for one in this role; and finally when in imminent contact with the enemy he chooses to fight—in all the instants Roland had the opportunity, after seeing how perilous his situation really was, to summon aid. His tardy attempt, when we all realize that the moment of possible rescue has passed, only heightens our admiration for the decisions which have brought him to this magnificent desperation.

So too with Custer's last minutes as conceived by Whittaker. This is the reason for the conversation with Curly during a pause in the action: Custer, with his thoroughbred horse, has a chance to escape—like many of the other defeated heroes—but chooses to stay. Without this interlude the hero is merely a superb warrior; when he is given a choice to live or die and he chooses death, his heroism is by far the greater. An important dimension is added to his character. He is not merely a very brave man making the best of a hopeless situation, but he is a responsible agent in the making of his own glory. Given the freedom of choice, his decision to die demonstrates his nobility most compellingly.

Bjarki does not send for assistance, since his situation is beyond the intervention of any ally. He delays arming himself until death and defeat are inevitable: he warms his hands by the fire while the impetuous Hjalti urges and cajoles him to rouse himself to the task confronting them. The Scandinavians were not without their sense of irony: this same Hjalti was in earlier years the coward Hott whom Bjarki saved from ignominy, and who had changed his name to signify his new life role. Bjarki's casualness at Lejre highlights his poise and his resignation to the inevitable. Whatever chance Leonidas may have had at Thermcpylae (Grundy thought that he thought he might have won), he sent marching down the road south while he and his men stayed behind waiting for the Persians. Byrhtnoth might have held the ford forever, but for whatever reason (there is no need to review the motivation controversy again) he allowed the vikings to cross unharmed, and thus committed himself and most of this men to annihilation. The celebrants of Lázar, as noted previously, have it both ways: he at first chose heaven over victory on the plains, but he lost the battle because Vuk (possibly in a fit of jealously) at a crucial point in the battle led his 12,000 fighting men from the field. Had Gawain held the green hill he would have won immortality, but after his initial victory he tossed all of his men's lives away in his headlong charge down the slopes. He *might* have won, or at least held out until Arthur arrived to rescue him from his besieged hill. In his second assault he charged to his death, yet won quite another sort of immortality—if we are to take the word of the poet. In nearly all of these tales the effects are the same: whether the hero sends or calls for help after it is too late, stays to fight when he might easily escape, allows the enemy to advance onto more advantageous ground, is resigned at the moment of imminent defeat, or leaves the safety of a hill to charge into the midst of an overwhelmingly superior force, we have the sense that the hero might have saved himself, but at the crucial moment took it upon himself to choose the most perilous path.

Each of the events just considered was seen as a dramatic necessity within a narrative frame in which each contributed to the totality of impact of that narrative. I have, in this analysis, put myself in the position of the synthesizer of several individual particles related to one discrete story; so we would do well to remember that many more legends consist of merely a few fragments (which are like anecdotes) and that in any event dramatic necessity cannot satisfactorily account for all the story's details. The saber, for example, so important to the epics of defeat, appears very often, because of our traditional associations with it.

Custer is a good model here since he was thought, erroneously, to have carried and to have fought with a sword, specifically a saber. Not only Whittaker's but hundreds of accounts—newspapers as well as popular poems and fiction and illustrations—armed the Seventh and its commander with swords, though by 1876 they were no longer carried into battle. No doubt in the public's mind the saber had become intimately associated with cavalry. The horseman and his blade had ridden to countless battles in the past great war; indeed very few people in America grasped the fact that the Civil War was the first major conflict in which the primary weapons were projectile-firing: muskets and rifles, carbines and pistols, and artillery. Especially toward the last year of the struggle, 1864-65, battles decided by the saber or the bayonet were rare. The cavalry tactic of the next fifty years was conceived in the Civil War: horsemen rode to the edge of combat, dismounted, and then fought on foot. In 1914 the machine gun blasted away the combat effectiveness of horses, and consequently of horse cavalry tactics, yet at the Last Stand it was still in use: Reno's men dismounted to fight on foot in the valley and so, apparently, did Custer's men on the ridge.

But in the imagination of Americans in 1876, what kind of weapon could Custer have carried? The lance, which European cavalry had used with great effect all through the century, never found favor in America. The Seventh is seldom shown armed with carbines (the actual issue) because that weapon is too stubby and thus aesthetically unattractive, though its size, weight, and handiness made it ideal for soldiers on horseback. The rifle was often carried by officers; in those days officers were permitted to arm themselves, and Custer is occasionally painted with a rifle. Could one imagine that he had armed himself with a bowie knife? Hardly; and the nature of the weapon and our associations with it make any discussion of Custer's possible use of the bowie knife unnecessary. The saber would, in the public's mind, be the Seventh's inevitable armament because of our long-standing associations with it.

These very same associations of the saber with the life of honor and noble adventure are reversed by Bernard Shaw in *Arms and The Man*.[26] Without such romantic and sentimental attitudes, the famous verbal duel between Bluntschli and the Bulgarian cavalry officer Sergius would have no basis for its humor. Challenged to a duel with sabers, the pedestrian Swiss hotelkeeper replied that he had the choice of weapons, and, being in the artillery, he would take a machine gun.

These techniques when combined are the most effective for glorifying the defeated, for making not only the best but a rather handsome victory out of defeat. They insure that the disaster will not be seen as pathetic, or shameful, or even contemptible; instead, the hero and his small band of martyrs die a death more honorable than victory would have been. That would be glory enough, certainly, but men who fight with the same (or greater) fierce zeal in defeat are somehow more admirable than they would be in triumph. Beowulf engaged in mortal combat against the dragon is more poignant, more profoundly heroic, than Beowulf the young man quarreling with the Grendel family. "Death is better," said Wiglaf, "for any man than a life of shame." Roland's sentiments to the same effect have been cited. In a heroic defeat we feel that the hero (and his men, usually) have given everything of themselves. In defeat the hero struggles with every fiber of his muscle, every element of his skill, with more courage than ever he realized he could summon. Defeat is the ultimate test of skill and character, more taxing of the whole man than the most strenuous and exhausting triumph.

We have the same feeling about men in real combat. The great majority of Congressional Medals of Honor—the most honored recognition of martial valor in the United States—are awarded posthumously. No one has compiled statistics on the subject; my source was the recruiting sergeant assigned to the First Army's public relations display on this medal. His estimate, admittedly only approximate, was that seventy-five to eighty percent of these medal winners had died in combat. It was also his opinion that in most cases where the soldier survived his own heroism he would likely be awarded the next highest medal, the Silver Star, so pervasive is the feeling that heroism in defeat and death is the more heroic.

Something of these feelings survive in our domestic lives. I want to turn for a moment to an event in quite another battlefield, for an instructive model of the reaction to defeat. During 1971, the Penn State football team won its first ten games and had been invited to the Cotton Bowl, when it lost its last game rather decisively to the University of Tennessee, 31-11. The Penn State *Daily Collegian* reported:

> Penn State has always been known for its ability to lose a game as proudly as a victory. After Tennessee blackened the Lion's season, it was still a proud bunch. (6 December 1971, p. 1)

When the team returned to the field house that evening, they were applauded for fully three minutes. No such demonstration had ever been given a returning victorious team. Whether it was true or not that the team lost with as much "pride and poise" as it had often won with is not so important or interesting as the newspaper's and fans' feeling that they were proud—and that despite the defeat they ought to be proud.

Although this analogue is trivial compared to the great battles being discussed, it may help explain the reaction to heroic defeats. The reaction of the Penn State fans would not have been the same had 1971 been a losing or even a mediocre season: in that case the loss to Tennessee would not have stirred pride as it did. The reaction that we have been describing does not always occur following a defeat. The American people would not have looked on the Custer disaster as more of an insult than a defeat had they regarded the Indians as cultural equals or had they the respect for the Indian's "light cavalry" that his performance in combat deserved. The figure of Roland might never have emerged to its present stature had not Charlemagne's armies been so consistently successful. Nor would Saul have been given so heroic a death had he not demonstrated that the Philistines could be beaten. In all of these instances (and with the other hilltop heroes as well) a proud and resentful people, accustomed to victory or expectant of it, retained their pride and apotheosized their defeated hero because they had not lost their will, nor the reasonable expectation of triumph.

The desire for vengeance is blunted unless success has been reasonably expected, unless the hero and his men have in the past been victors. Custer's defeat was startling because of his spectacular record of previous successes;

Americans would hardly have been surprised had the Seventh's commander been a chronic loser. In fact, had that been the case, the public's reaction would have been of disgust or contempt or anger that an incompetent had been given command over so many men. So too with Sir Gawain, said to have been Arthur's most successful lieutenant; so it was also with Lázar, who had driven the Turks from Serbia; or the Greek army, which had been so successful at Marathon a short time before.

When the Polish army was easily routed by the Germans at the beginning of World War II, the Polish people were sickened by the unremitting string of defeats and humiliations. The Warsaw ghetto, which later held out for six weeks, is remembered with pride by Jews, but not by Poles who could think only of the poor showing of their army. This attitude, this bitterness born of so complete a defeat, made it possible for many to turn against their own countrymen—the colonels who escaped to Romania—and blame them for their national disgrace. The Germans should have been used to the phenomenon: weary and dispirited from the ghastly bloodbaths of the Western front of 1918, when the armistice was signed they turned against their own generals. Led by their propagandists to expect imminent victory, when defeat came they naturally accused their own leaders of betrayal.

The same emotions of pride in certain kinds of defeat permeate the play world even more deeply than collegiate football: one manufacturer of plastic models for children capitalized on the nostalgic interest in prewar America by producing a model of the USS *Arizona*. But this company's advertising staff had a problem: what could be said about the *Arizona* to make it attractive enough for young children to buy? The ship was commissioned in 1916 but spent World War I on training cruises in Chesapeake Bay. After the war she served as an escort for President Wilson's 1918 continental visit. So uneventful was the *Arizona*'s log book that the advertisements listed among her "major events" her modernization in 1929-31 when new tripod masts were fitted and her guns and boilers replaced. The *Arizona* later carried President Hoover on a West Indies cruise. Her first shots fired in anger were few in number when, on the morning of 7 December 1941, Japanese dive and torpedo bombers sent her to the bottom of Pearl Harbor. Most of her crew were breakfasting at the outset of the attack; at day's end over 1,100 of them had perished, close to half of all the fatal casualties at Pearl. The toy company chose to glamorize the *Arizona*'s destruction in her imagined defiance:

> Her flag still flew as Arizona settled into the murky waters of Pearl Harbor—a defiant banner at the scene of devastation. The ship still

lies submerged there, a memorial to the valiant men who shared her fate. During a simple ceremony in 1950 a fifty foot flagpole was erected on her superstructure. Admiral Radford, Commander-in-Chief of the Pacific fleet and speaker at the dedication said, "From today on, the Arizona will fly our country's flag just as proudly as she did on the morning of December 7, 1941."

So natural are the devices for glorifying the defeated that countless writers—and other carriers of tradition—have used them in innumerable narratives. In the *Njals Saga* the lone survivor Hrafen reports to Flosi that in the battle of Clontarf Brian, Sigurd, and all of the vikings were killed saved Thorstein Hallson (Flosi's brother-in-law), who alone was spared. The *Nibelungenlied* has its devasting fights and its lone survivor. Finn and his men were outnumbered at the ford by two-to-one, but after a long and hard fight Finn alone was left. Fer-Tai dealt the hero a mortal wound, and was himself mortally wounded. D.W. Griffith's *The Battle at Elderbush Gulch*, one of the first of the "Cavalry-to-the-rescue flicks," finds Lillian Gish with Lionel Barrymore and others in a group of farm houses surrounded by Indians on the warpath menacing them from outside. Many are killed (on both sides), the red men draw closer, we are about to have another Fetterman disaster (though surely the Indians will spare Lillian's helpless infant), when the pony soldiers gallop over the distant ridge, brandishing bugles, guidons, and sabers. The rescue, to be repeated thousands of times subsequently, drains the scene of its heroic quality but adds melodrama.

In all levels of narrative—in epics, romances, sagas, in novels and short stories, poems, and in movies—these events which glorify the defeated appear. Their occurrence outside of the "Custer cluster" legends is further demonstration of their efficacy as narrative techniques. One thinks also of Ottokar's defeat at Marchfeld, and his murder on that day with the consequent rumors of treason which made him the popular favorite for a century after. Or of Janoš Hunyadi, said in one account[27] to have been on the verge of victory at Varna in 1444, when a chance Turkish arrow struck him in the eye (like Harold, like James IV) and gave the victory to the heathens. Actually, this incredible man, for decades the savior of Christianity and the Western world in his incessant wars against the Turks in the Balkans, died of cholera at the siege of Belgrade in 1456.

Our responses are the same when the doomed are defiant in pure "history," or that brand of history which survives in legend: General Anthony McAuliffe's "Nuts!" in reply to German surrender terms at Bastogne echoes in spirit the cries from naval quasi-history, "Don't give up the ship" and "We have just begun to fight." So too with the defiant reply from beleaguered Wake Island to "send us more Japs." These examples could include vignettes from nearly all of our experience, "real" as well as literary; each motif has been used repeatedly in heroic poetry and narrative, in discursive prose, in the stories of popular and folk cultures, in films: they are part of the way we tell stories of the defeat of someone we admire, and they make their particular contribution to the narrative. To nearly all of us General McAuliffe is as unreal a "fiction" as is Count Roland: neither of them is likely to influence our grocery bills or our laundry lists. That one man lived within our lifetime and the other is almost entirely of the imagination has little effect on the way we respond to the heroism of each. Perhaps, just perhaps, this observation reveals why I have chosen to spend my life contemplating literature; yet I still do not believe that this attitude is that of one who has lost a sense of the real. Rather it reflects the sense of one who sees the actual in narratives that were thought to be real.

When we tell other kinds of stories we find that they too gather, almost irresistibly, other clusters of motifs to themselves. When Beowulf presents himself to Hrothgar's court to announce that he has come to put an end to the troll problem, he is questioned rather sullenly and brusquely by one of the resident courtiers, Unferth, who wants to know why the young stranger thinks he can accomplish what many older and more experienced warriors have not. Unferth misremembers that some time back Beowulf had been challenged to a swimming match by Breca, and that in this relatively simple contest Beowulf had been bested. The Geatish hero then defends himself with words, and during his justification of himself we learn (for the first time) of some of his youthful exploits: he, and not Breca, had won the match by swimming for seven days in the north sea, while killing nine sea monsters with his sword. Then, with Beowulf's vow that he will again triumph, this time over the Grendels, Unferth is silenced and does not again figure prominently in the action.

The challenge to the hero's skill or bravery, verbal or otherwise, occurs in many narratives, particularly epics, and the similarity—particularly between *Beowulf* and the *Odyssey*—was so striking that Albert Lord thought that both must be products of some "Indo-European oral narrative tradition."[28] In both the Old English and classical Greek stories the hero crosses a body of water and is challenged by the coastal watch who quickly bids the stranger welcome; at the foreign court the stranger is at first greeted warmly, but he is presently questioned rather harshly about his past exploits, to which he responds with an assertion, or (in Ulysses' case) a demonstration, of his abilities. Later all of the court, seemingly satisfied, retires for the night. In Homer the court is that of Alkinoos, the challenger Euralyus.

The first problem with the "Indo-European oral narrative tradition" is historical: though occasionally suggested, no one has convincingly demonstrated that the *Beowulf* poet knew Homer or his works. Moreover, the distance (spatial as well as chronological) between eighth-century England and Homer's Greece has seemed unbridgeable.[29] But when we consider Unferth's function in the narrative, his role in eliciting certain responses from the hero and particular information about his past, and the contrast he provides, we see that he has his counterparts the world over (in many places where direct attribution is, however, possible) and we see that his creation is the most natural and rhetorically obvious means of accomplishing his assigned role.[30]

A galling taunter the equal of Unferth and Euralyus is also found at the court of King Arthur: Sir Kay. His surliness and his readiness—even eagerness—to challenge, though usually verbally, the visitors to the Round Table appears fairly early in the history of Arthurian romances. In the *Gilgamesh* it is Enkidu, created by the goddess Aruru for the express purpose of being the equal of Gilgamesh and of challenging what the gods consider his insolence. When the two strong men meet they begin fighting almost at once: "so they grappled, holding each other like bulls. They broke the doorposts and the walls shook." Gilgamesh at last threw Enkidu to the ground, and then victor and vanquished immediately became close friends. Victory over the Unferth figure is by no means the most important task that the hero must accomplish; this initial combat is merely a preliminary round, and it merely postulates the hero's valor, and strength, and other heroic qualifications, establishing him as the most promising of the friendly forces, so that once we (the audience) and the hero's acquaintances (within the narrative) are suitably impressed he can get on with the really serious business of his mission.

For Beowulf this mission is the extermination of the Grendel family. For the several knights errant of Arthur's court it is the numerous tasks various authors and legends have assigned them: rescuing maidens, overcoming giants, crossing a sword-bridge, surviving in an enchanted castle, learning to ask the right questions. For Gilgamesh it is the perilous journey into the deep forest to confront the evil giant Humbaba. Such friendly enemies (as Enkidu and Sir Kay) provide the authors of epic and romance with an ideal means of realizing the hero.[31] As with Gilgamesh and Enkidu, specifically, the contrast is obvious: as a result of their titanic tussle our esteem for the hero rises even further. Gilgamesh proves himself, and we do not have to rely on his legendary reputation. Now he is ready for the truly epic struggle, with Humbaba, and our sense of the magnitude of this battle is sharpened because of the earlier match with Enkidu. Dinadin performs a role similar to Unferth's in Malory, as does Falstaff in *Henry IV*.

9

Laws of Contrast

The great Danish ethnologist and medievalist Axel Olrik had extensive experience with Scandinavian peasants and their *Märchen* as well as a profound knowledge of medieval literature, and this sagacity is apparent in his observations about the principles of oral narrative composition. The dozen or so "laws" that emerged therefore cover a broad field; and it is the more to Olrik's credit that his formulations concern the epic and saga as well as the folktale, for despite the vast gulf in economic and sophistication levels between the audiences of these genres, they share a vital common determinant: all are shaped by oral transmission. Yet "law" is a misleading term in criticism, since it implies fixity and inevitability, and for productions of the human imagination the implications would be boggling. Olrik's "laws" are better taken as "tendencies" and "characteristics" of traditional narratives.

The tendency to polarize and contrast people and events in narratives is of the greatest relevance to the Custer legend in that this tendency changes the traits of central characters, heightens certain features of others, and may even demand the creation of new ones[1] or the omission of those who are superfluous:

> The *Sage* [traditional narrative] is always polarized. A strong Thor requires a wise Odin or a cunning Loki next to him; a rich Peter Krämer, a poor Paul Schmied; near a grieving woman sits a joyful or comforting one. This very basic opposition is a major rule of epic composition: young and old, large and small, man and monster, good and evil.
>
> The Law of Contrast works from the protagonist of the *Sage* out to the other individuals, whose characteristics and actions are determined by the requirement that they be antithetical to those of the protagonist. An appropriate example is the Danish King Rolf who is so celebrated in our heroic sagas because of his generosity. He thus requires a stingy

opponent. However, in this example, the identity of the opponent changes. Now it is a Skoldung: Rörik; now it is a Swede: Adisl. But even if only one such contrasting person is found, this is sufficient to satisfy the demands of narrative composition.

   Some types of plot action correspond exactly to the Law of Contrast. (1) the hero meets his death through the murderous act of a villain (Roland, Rustem, Rolf Kraki, Siegfried); (2) the great king has an insignificant and short-reigning successor (Hjarward after Rolf, Hjarni after Frodi, "Shorthair" after Conchobar).[2]

The popular narrative of Custer's Last Stand, which has been transmitted to us and until recently was widely believed, shows at several points how it has been shaped by the "Law of Contrast." Custer, dashing to the point of recklessness, handsome, fearless, the "Napoleon of the Plains," has been balanced by the plodding, overcautious, and perhaps even cowardly Reno. We have seen how Reno halted his charge when near the Indian village; although many saw this step as an act of prudence, "overcaution" makes the contrast sharper. And Reno's subsequent disorderly retreat to the bluffs followed by his alleged failure to come to Custer's rescue was for many nothing less than cowardice. Given the nature of the events—Custer's reputation for valor and audacity, and Reno's defeat in the valley after halting his charge—the "Law of Contrast" suggests that Reno's condemnation was all but inevitable, and that this inevitability was totally unrelated to the subsequent need of many to find a scapegoat for the disaster.

   The antagonists on the Little Bighorn—red Indians and white soldiers—were by their natures polarized, but the popular culture of the nineteenth century (and to a certain extent of our own) has heightened that polarity. *The Times* of London wrote about the event as the worst defeat ever inflicted upon a civilized power by the savages and went on to contrast British policy in regard to "inferior races." In America the Indians were seen as savage, ruthless, treacherous, and pagan; Custer and his men, by contrast, were brave, valiant, unflinching, white, and Christian. "They" used barbaric weapons such as the hatchet, tomahawk, and bow and arrow, whereas the Seventh fought honorably with firearms—or gallantly, with sabers. Many who did not find Reno cowardly or traitorous made Sitting Bull a foil to Custer, representing the battle as a struggle between the two.

   The Indians swarmed through the valleys and crawled up ravines, while the troopers stood on the hilltops. To heighten the poignancy of an illustrious regiment riding fearlessly to its total destruction, among its ranks the veterans of the great battles of the Civil War, an insignificant actor in the drama, the Crow scout Curly, made his escape. Against the small, determined, combat-hardened band of heroes swarmed the hostile and undisciplined mob. And in defeat these gallant men were mutilated and stripped of their most personal belongings. These contrasts, Roy Harvey Pearce has shown,[3] were part of the myth of the West. The red man could be the noble primitive, the ferocious barbarian, or the drunken devil, and it was almost impossible for European settlers, regardless of their sympathies, to see him as other than one of these stereotypes. The westward movement of "civilization" depended on this contrast of the stereotyped Indian with the resolute pioneer farmer and the pious frontiersman.

When several of the more notable last stands were reviewed (in Chapter 7) I took care to emphasize the most obvious elements of contrast in the narratives. To repeat them all now would be superfluous; but a short analysis of one epic—the *Chanson de Roland*—would be useful. In this epic of medieval defeat we can see that the same dramatic necessities which shape many a popular story are also at work in great literature. For instance, a young Charlemagne (who in fact may well have been younger than the real Hruodlandus) would be inappropriate to the story. Roland, who is young and vigorous—and perhaps somewhat reckless—necessarily requires an older, more contemplative emperor. Ganelon, who sells out his comrades for his hurt pride (also accepting the enemy's gifts), is an appropriate antagonist to Roland, who would rather die than live in shame. The hero is accompanied into this last battle by other contrasting figures. His "secularity" is balanced by the Church's representative, Archbishop Turpin; and his ferocity contrasts with the wisdom of Oliver: "Rollant est proz e Oliver est sage." Many of the contrasts in the *Chanson* are also emphasized in the Custer story: the many against the few, Christian versus pagan, the refusal to call for aid and the resultant slaughter of all, valley and ridge, first success and then (inevitable) defeat.

Now it happened that Custer was the leader of the few against the many, that he actually labored through a "slack youth" (culminated by his dismal record at West Point), and it is no fiction that he refused the support of the Gatling guns. However, these convenient dramatic events must not be taken for an instance of how history sometimes imitates art; rather it is (once more) an illustration of the way in which these elements have been emphasized by Custer's mythographers. Other elements in the real narrative of the battle are seldom noted: anything from the march up the Rosebud to the thinness of Custer's rapidly balding hair. Nearly always only the dramatic elements are selected for retelling, because unlike the real history of the Little Bighorn campaign, the narrative of it must be made to have more of a structure; it must have the beginning, middle, and end that gives point to narratives. Custer did refuse the Gatling guns; but he also refused a battalion of the Second Cavalry, which few know about. He did have a slack youth; what is interesting is that so much has been made of it. And in so doing history has been retold as art and has been created according to many of the same principles.

In a recent article in the *Chaucer Review* the author argued convincingly that much of Old English poetry was composed on principles of opposition: lexical, syntactical, and thematic.[4] Unfortunately the author discusses this phenomenon only in terms of Old English poetry, implying that contrasts in poetry have been less important since 1200. Chaucer, after all, has Pandarus argue with Troilus that no man can comprehend what is white until he has experienced what is black; nor can we understand sweetness except by knowing what is bitter, nor can we know pleasure unless we know pain.[5] And much work has been done recently by Chaucerian scholars on the principles of contrast and opposition in the linking of *The Canterbury Tales*. One of the first of such studies demonstrated the ways in which the Miller "quited" the Knight: both pilgrims tell tales in which two young men court the favor of a fair maid, but the ways in which the events of each tale differ   to say nothing of the characters, the atmosphere, and the narrator's attitude—made all the difference in the medieval world. For example, the wife of Bath's romance gives an ascendancy to woman; the Clerk's tale of "Patient Griselda" puts its heroine completely at her husband's whim. To lighten the air after the Monk has droned on with tragedy after tragedy, the Nun's Priest relates a brisk and witty animal fable, though at its core it is no less weighty than the Monk's flabby and dreary *exemplars*. Or the Physician, that healer of bodies whose study was but little on the Bible, tells the *exemplum* of Virginia whose father destroys her body to save her from dishonor; the Pardoner follows— that one pilgrim hopelessly damned—with the story of the three treasure-finders who, in search of gold above all else, murder one another.

At least two essays in professional journals have discussed the principles of contrast and binary opposition which link the Tales of Fragment VIII.[6] In the *Canon's Yeoman's Tale* the clever but crooked Canon has as his foil the gullible priest whom he dupes; and the sins of both are in sharp contrast with the virtues of St. Cecilia, as those glittering gauds are illustrated in the *Second Nun's Tale*. The contrast in this fragment does not materialize through the story—that is, event—but rather through a polarity of ideas and the lexicon which transmits those ideas. To repeat the argument, even in outline, would delay the present argument needlessly, but a few examples will be helpful: "*Opus*," the alchemical "work," the "experiment," is a means by which the priest hopes to enrich himself; by the same means, since the *opus* is in this case bogus, the Canon fleeces the Priest. But for the Second Nun, "work" are the good works—the good acts and deeds—of her revered Saint, through which Cecilia attains her salvation. And as the alchemical fire is alleged to reduce the corpus of matter so that its "spirit" may be brought to perfection, so fire is the means of Cecilia's martyrdom: her Roman persecuters, themselves limited to an understanding of life as corporeal, sentence Cecilia to death by burning. Unlike metals in the Canon's damned crucible, Cecilia's spirit is freed, and sung by flights of angels to its rest.

The principle affects all of man's dramatic arts: for *Die Zauberflöte* to succeed the grandly serious Tamino needs the twittering buffoon Papageno as much as he needs his beloved; and as the princess in distress is named Pamina, so the birdcatcher's aviary mate is Papagena. The magic of the Queen of the Night is countered by the high priest; the pure Pamina is threatened by the evil Moor Monostatos. The scenes of *Das Rheingold* alternate between the Rhine's bottom and the hills above it. Wotan, once leader of the furious host, has become humanized; but his shadow, Alberich (the Nibelung king of the dwarfs), then threatens him. Throughout the Ring Cycle man battles monster, dwarfs counter giants, gods are succeeded by heroes, light beams interplay with the darkness. Even Wotan's blind eye symbolizes his inner wisdom. Tristan, discovered in his betrayal of his king, in turn accuses Melot of betraying him; and the lovers find that only in death can their love be meaningfully consummated. And Puccini balances the love of Rudolfo and Mimi against that of Marcello for Musetta. When the first pair meet the other has been separated through a quarrel; when Rudolfo loses his Mimi at the end, Marcello has been reunited to Musetta. The first scene is the artist's garret where a wretched meal has been gathered; Mimi enters a little later to relight her candle. In the last act we are again in the garret and there is not even enough food to call a meal. Mimi again enters, but soon her life is to be extinguished.

Nor are the contrasts of narrative unknown in the psychologist's laboratory. The experimental findings of behavioral psychologist Frederick C. Bartlett on the memorial qualities of a number of Cambridge University students, findings still in the main valid, are well known to folklorists. In one set of experiments Bartlett presented his subjects with brief narratives, and after specific intervals he had them rewrite the tales. At another time he gave a tale to one subject to observe the dynamics of transmission to another. In every case the transmitted versions subsequent to Bartlett's original, whether repeated by the same subject (repeated reproduction) or by a series of transmitters (serial reproduction), were carefully noted, particularly as to the number and kinds of changes. The findings have been of limited value to folklorists because Bartlett's subjects were university students from rather diverse backgrounds, and not the homogeneous carriers of a genuine oral tradition; and the laboratory mode of transmission was written, not oral. Nevertheless, at least one of his findings is of particular interest to us because, quite coincidentally, Bartlett confirmed the tendency Olrik noted for story-tellers to polarize and to heighten certain contrasts in their stories:

> As a general rule, visual imagery tends to become more active the longer the interval preceding reproduction, and, at least in the case of stories containing the report of a number of incidents, increased visualization provides conditions which favor transformation. Relations of opposition, similarity, subjection and the like, occurring in the original, are very commonly intensified. This forms one illustration of a deep-rooted and widespread tendency to dramatization, and in particular, all those types of relation about the apprehension of which feeling tends to cluster are readily exaggerated or emphasized.[7]

Bartlett's student-subjects were not chosen for their artistic or their writing ability; they were not folktale raconteurs in any formal sense, yet it may be assumed that as young adults they had, like most of us, at one time or another told innumerable jokes and anecdotes, and they had probably heard as many. During this experiment as they continued to hold Bartlett's tale in their minds, their "visualization" was heightened; and the longer they thought about the story, or simply "stored" it in memory, the more they sharpened such "relations" as opposition, similarity, and subjection. In a word, their tendency was to dramatize even further the story given them.

That Bartlett observed this phenomenon among "ordinary" university students; that Olrik found it among the peasants in the farming communities of Denmark; that it is the basis for the compositions of the illiterate as well as for the schooled, and for folktales as well as for *Canterbury Tales* suggest unanswerably that the inclination toward opposition and contrast is natural to the story-telling propensity of man—not only medieval man, or classical man, or educated man. The tendency is common to the blacksmiths, goosegirls, and yokels who were the subjects of the asperity of Roger Sherman Loomis[8] (in denying that their stories could ever be the source of the medieval romance), as well as to courtly poets, academic novelists, tellers of legends, and Miltons, mute and inglorious; and it is found among the educated as well as the ignorant, the urban as well as the rural, the industrialized as well as the agrarian.

That the "Law of Contrast" is also found quite apart from story-telling—whether oral or literate—and appears to be inherent in information processing and in remembering, explains why people who never wrote a single line of poetry, perhaps never even read a single line, would dramatize such events as Custer's Last Stand in ways similar to those chosen by poets of some schooling. This phenomenon may be related to the binary contrast long noted by psycholinguists:

> The operation of binary contrast appears to be a linguistic fundamental to which the human mind is uniquely adapted. Binary pairs of adjectives appear in all languages, and there are in English as well as related languages formal devices for inventing new adjectival contrasts. When we list the attributes which apply to a given concept, we nearly always imply that these attributes are to be thought of as being contrasted with an opposite state.... The notion of opposition is a linguistic fundamental, and despite its dubious logical character, permeates all languages of the world.[9]

Deese is not describing exactly the same propensity as was Olrik (or Bartlett), yet the same mental processes seem to prevail. The language which conveys our feelings and thoughts is permeated with the "notion of opposition," and in narratives contrast and opposition are enhanced. And although Deese is describing linguistic rather than narrative contrast, more is involved here than two coincidentally analogous processes.

In citing these passages from Olrik and Bartlett I am implying that the form of certain narratives is necessarily structured. The materials of the narrative (the events of the story, the characters and their relations, and so on) in part come from the creator's sense of reality, but after what we know has happened to men and events in legend we may well wonder to what extent reality accounts for the narrative's form. The Count Roland who slays Saracens by the thousands in the leaves of Digby 23 bears only the most tenuous and superficial resemblance to the Prefect of the Breton borderlands whose name he happens to carry. So too with most—probably all—of the hilltop heroes and their entourages, Custer not excepted.

Tradition, but only in a very special sense, is also involved in providing the materials of narrative. Consider the way in which we store information—

process the details of our lives into memory, if you will—so that it is subject to recall.[10] The current fashion of comparing the human mind to a digital computer is sometimes heuristic and instructive, but it is as often misleading. Human memory is not literally or even primarily reproductive, calling upon some image which it has stored somewhere in the brain and which it brings, complete and unaltered, to use. Electronic memory cores are much better at storing data and then retrieving the precise information. Nor do humans store single impulses or images singly (cortical islands); they combine and cluster with related images—the individual making the relation and the connection— so that the "past" is for us not a collection of singular items, each retaining its particularity, but an organized mass.

Among Bartlett's most striking conclusions was the observation that memory was not a process of reproduction of stored data, but an entirely new construction. Memory is "creative," or at least constructive. What is remembered is not the single element of experience, but the "schema" to which individual impulses become attached. "A new incoming impulse must not become merely a cue setting up a series of reactions all carried out in a fixed temporal order, but a stimulus which enables us to go direct to that portion of the organized setting of past responses which is most relevant to the needs of the moment."[11]

When a subject was asked to remember a complex situation rather than a single fact, image, or detail, the process of recollection did not involve any attempt to reconstruct the situation in all its particularity, detail by detail, then to construct the entire situation from the individual elements:

> In all ordinary instances he has an overmastering tendency simply to get a general impression of the whole; and, on the basis of this, he constructs the probable details. Very little of his construction is literally observed and often, as was easily demonstrated experimentally, a lot of it is distorted or wrong so far as the actual facts are concerned.[12]

When the first news of the Custer disaster was out, millions of Americans thought of ravines (or, like Whitman, of "Far Dakota's Canyons") and of the weapon most people other than cavalrymen associated with the cavalry, the saber. Only a very few facts were known at first: a presumably large number of Indians had wiped out a relatively small unit of federal troops led by Custer. Such were the schematic responses cued by these sparse facts that an entire battle-drama was soon constructed, made up, formed by the principles described by Olrik and Bartlett. When the wire services carried the version of the heroic defense on the hilltop, yet other responses were evoked, and these responses were determined by the desire of the American people to believe in their soldiers' gallantry. Desire and attitude had played a crucial function when Bartlett's subjects "remembered": what they constructed ("remembered") was usually strongly slanted toward their attitudes and predilections at the moment of memorial construction:

> The construction that is effected is the sort of construction that would justify the observer's "attitude." We say that it is characterized by doubt, hesitation, surprise, astonishment, confidence, dislike, repulsion and so on. Here is the significance of the fact ... that when a subject is being asked to remember, very often the first thing that emerges is something of the nature of this attitude. The recall is then a construction, made largely on the basis of this attitude, and its general effect is that of a justification of the attitude.[13]

In many instances of what Bartlett called "repeated reproduction" (in which one subject repeated the same story several times after specific time intervals) the stories were preceded by some such characterization as "exciting," "adventurous," or the kind of tale the subject had read as a boy. The story was first labeled, then built up—"remembered"—in a way that justified the label, in effect the subject's emotional state. For the American public, for the public of every hero whose martyrdom has been discussed here, as for Bartlett's university students, remembering can be a matter of seconds as well as decades. In the letter to his wife Benteen "remembered" Custer Ridge and the Indian casualties and Curly; later he would "remember" that the five companies with Custer had not done any "first-class" fighting.

In Chapter 2 of this book the account of the battle on the Little Bighorn was related in large part in the words of the men who were there. Obvious as is such a narrative technique, it had never (to my knowledge) been presented this way before. I endeavored there to give a sense of what it may have felt like to have been at the battle, even if only through the often limp prose of the participants who, after all, were soldiers and not writers. A certain feeling may have been communicated, but with how much accuracy? How precise were the recalled perceptions of trooper William Slaper when he later admitted that "this was my first experience under fire. I know that for a time I was frightened, and far more so when I got my first glimpse of the Indians riding about in all directions, firing at us and yelling and whooping like incarnate fiends...."[14] The editor does not say when Slaper gave this account to him, but the book in which it appears was published in 1952. How had the intervening years altered Slaper's perceptions of the battle, initially made while he was under fire for the first time and admittedly frightened? Consider just two details. First, although Slaper clearly remembered that when fleeing across the river during Reno's retreat Lieutenant Hodgson clung to the stirrups of trumpeter Henry Fisher, several other men who saw the incident remember that it was not Fisher but quite another trooper to whom Hodgson clung. And we might ask whether the phrase "incarnate fiends" was originally Slaper's or language which he acquired since, as popular as it became in newspaper accounts of the battle.

Sergeant Charles A. Windolph of Company H remembered the battle some seventy years after the event, and though the editors of his account, Frazier and Robert Hunt, claimed that "his mind was still clear and alert,"[15] how unclouded could it have been about the events on that day? Are we to believe that Windolph never read about the battle after his experience in it? Of course he did, and almost as assuredly he was influenced—in however subtle the manner—by such narratives. They, almost by definition and certainly by necessity, were ordered, planned, and structured. The battle, like all events in life, was not. How far, then, can we trust Windolph, particularly when the account he gave of the position of the bodies on Custer Ridge sounds much like the wire service "line behind line" account: "from the way the men lay, it was clear that that one troop had been ordered to dismount and fight as a skirmish line. Then a second troop had been posted a little farther on and to the east. Then a third and fourth troop. And finally on the knoll of the hill lay some thirty bodies in a small circle. We knew instinctively that we would find Custer there...."[16]

From the way these same men lay it was clear to Benteen that the "battle" (though one can hardly call it that given Benteen's description) was a panic and a rout. The situation of the marble markers today suggests that more of a defense was made than Benteen thought, but certainly it was nothing like the organized resistance implied by Windolph. And it is absolutely certain that four troops had not dismounted one at a time, in the orderly and precise manner of the sergeant's version. The briefest glance at the U.S. Department of the Interior's map shows that—quite clearly.

It is not a matter of bad will here, of mendacity, or of pious fraud. No one has, so far as I know, seriously questioned Windolph's integrity, or that of Slaper, or of Benteen—or of any of the participants whose accounts are utilized here. Nor is their intelligence inadequate. But none of their accounts is to be trusted implicitly and without supporting evidence because all of these men are fallible; they have remembered their reality in ways that make of it an anecdote, a legend, a *heldensage*. What they remembered of the battle was determined extensively by their feelings—many of them subsequent to the fact—of the fight and their own role in it. We may trust Bartlett's judgment when we apply it to these accounts: their recollection of it was a justification of their attitudes.

When the *Chicago Tribune* "remembered" Custer, he was the "brave, brilliant soldier, handsome and dashing," which did not obliterate his "rashness" and "love of fame." Defeat in battle cued responses of an "ambuscaded ravine" which was much like a "slaughter pen." Its fury momentarily spent, its frustrations momentarily appeased, the public (again, in the *Chicago Tribune*'s and wire service's language) no longer blamed Custer but blamed President Grant and perhaps, even at that early time, Reno. The will to believe in a heroic defense cued schemata of defensive positions tenaciously held line behind line and of companies of men lying where they had fought, shoulder to shoulder. If tradition is involved in any of the stories here, it is the tradition which implanted those images of heroic defense, overwhelming enemy, loyalty and treason, the fight to the last, the lone survivor, and all the other aspects, in the minds of Western man so that when a few of the facts were known an entire cluster was brought forth.

As Bartlett concluded:

> Remembering is not the re-excitation of innumerable fixed, lifeless and fragmentary traces. It is an imaginative reconstruction, or construction, built out of the relation of our attitude towards a whole active mass of organised past reactions or experience, and to a little outstanding detail which commonly appears in image or in language form.[17]

We have all had countless experiences with "remembered" events which, though we are not even conscious of the alteration, alter with each retelling; when we hear a repeated narrative from someone else, however, we may be more aware of the variations. And each time the past is recalled and recounted it becomes more visual, more precise, more dramatic, and certainly it is remembered in terms of shaped and more clearly defined contrasts. What is true of our lives is true of our literature; what we do with our fiction we do also with our "facts."

Difficult as it is to distinguish fact from fiction, the situation is hopelessly muddled by such books as *Showdown at Little Big Horn* by Indian apologist

Dee Brown. *Publisher's Weekly* (11 October 1971, p. 59), reviewing this early work after the much later publication of *Bury My Heart at Wounded Knee,* said that "the novel can be read either as a straight western adventure or as nonfiction to appeal to the vast number of new Dee Brown fans who prefer that form." But is it Western adventure or nonfiction? For this work and others like it, it is important to try to know. *Bury My Heart* ignores, alters, and exaggerates history, for example, by describing flashing sabers at the Little Bighorn but then it claims only to be an "oral history" and thereby excuses itself from strict adherence to facts. Yet no doubt many have understood it in those terms—as "fact."

"Oral history" is not found only in books: television news is a source for millions of people every day. The *Report on Network News' Treatment of the 1972 Democratic Presidential Candidates*[18] argues that network newscasts are competitive and so must entertain to draw viewers; thus theatrical demands cause distortion of the news. For example, planned news narratives maintain the audience's interest by involving it in the situation's drama, usually by building the news around certain narrative configurations the authors of the report call "themes." One such theme used in the 1972 Presidential campaign is that of the "frontrunner."

When Senator Edmund Muskie of Maine announced his candidacy for the Presidency in the fall of 1971 he became the frontrunner, appearing to hold a commanding popular appeal. To build drama into such a situation, reporters may raise questions about the frontrunner's ability to sustain his advantage. Often reporters pick a percentage of the primary vote which a candidate "must" win to be considered successful, so that the frontrunner is running against an arbitrary standard imposed by newscasters. Since Muskie failed to meet this arbitrary standard the newscasters gradually transformed him from a frontrunner to a man "fighting an uphill battle" against the new frontrunner, Senator George McGovern. Finally Muskie was subordinated to a subplot foil, while McGovern became the hero suddenly emerging to slay the dragon, surprising everyone because of his unpromising youth.

Thus the 1972 Presidential campaign illustrates how newscasters turn facts to fiction. The report's conclusion is that the networks, in stressing the dramatic aspects of the news, and shaping the news as though it were a narrative, tend, probably unconsciously, to favor a certain kind of politician: the new, pro-citizen, anti-politician politician.

The danger of using contemporary political analysis of this kind is obvious, and it is necessary to point out continually that the use of such materials here is not intended as any sort of involvement in the political issues, for or against any candidate or, for that matter, the press. What is germane is that we recognize a tendency to dramatize the "news" on the part of America's TV networks, and that the findings of the *Report* complement one of the major arguments of this book.

Another case in point—and far more controversial—is the fictionalizing of the 1945 Yalta conference by opposing political blocs in the United States, first by the right and recently by the revisionist left. To the late Senator Joseph McCarthy, and other anti-Roosevelt forces, Yalta was an instrument of defeat where the Western Allies lost much of what they had gained on the battlefield. For the revisionist left, Yalta inevitably prepared the way for the cold war at a moment when détente was possible. For still others, like former ambassador Charles Bohlen, the conference was a success: it established that no member of the U.N. Security Council—then in planning—could exercise a veto over procedural matters; it secured a commitment from Stalin concerning Russia's role against Japan; and what Roosevelt "gave away"—Soviet sovereignty over Eastern Europe—was no more than had in fact been accomplished by the presence of the Russian armies. As we have seen so often of other historical events, each person saw in the Yalta agreement what he wanted to see; as C. L. Sulzberger of the *New York Times* concludes, citing Bohlen:

> Moreover ... it is an American tendency to feel that if things don't work out some villain must have sold us down the river. This kind of thinking even inspires some revisionist historians to adduce the argument that Washington tricked Moscow at Yalta and finally reneged on its pledges. The hardest thing to remember about Yalta is the truth.[19]

These discussions of Presidential campaigns and international agreements share with the *Chanson de Roland*, and even with Custer's Last Stand, the fictionalizing of reality—a common aspect more important by far than their obvious differences as historical events. And as each of us interprets events far less complicated than the Yalta conference in his own way, as individual cues call forth particular schemata which construct details not supplied and provide some new details, so do we interpret literature. Two examples from medieval literature illustrate this point.

Earlier, when we reflected upon *The Battle of Maldon*, we noted that although neither the number of the vikings nor their relative strength regarding their Saxon opponents was stated, readers always made the assumption that the English were outnumbered and, especially after Byrhtnoth's fall and the ensuing flight of Godric and his cronies, the greater number of the norsemen overwhelmed Maldon's defenders. Recently, however, this assumption has been questioned. Pointing to the poem's vagueness on the size of both forces, George Clark insists that no conclusion can be made on this point.[20]

As a scholarly close reading Clark's observation is admirably precise; to avoid careless habits and foolish mistakes we often need to check carefully certain assumptions we make almost unconsciously about literature that is extremely familiar to us. But what other reading is possible here? What kind of heroic battle poem would we have if the English were not outnumbered at Maldon? What would happen to the poem (and to our responses) if a smaller number of vikings had attacked and defeated a larger English force? What would this say about Byrhtnoth's leadership, to say nothing of the fighting quality of the Saxons? Such a poem might be possible as a cartoon, a satire, or a political attack of some sort, but not as a heroic poem in which the English are the heroes.

Heroic literature such as *Maldon* triggers certain responses in us, and through the schemata which are evoked we interpret—we read into the text—certain details that may not be explicitly stated. In this case we are technically wrong in making assumptions about the number of vikings, but without question we are right, poetically, in assuming that the English were outnumbered; any other "reading" all but renders the poem, qua heroic poem, impotent. Viewed another way, our schemata comprise a personalized Motif-Index carried within each of us. Many elements within stories which we hear and read will "register" somewhere in the brain (the cue), and bring forth a response which may be more complicated or in any event somewhat different from the stimulus. Concerning *Maldon*, the general situation of the poem suggests other details (relevant schemata) that may then become part of our interpretation, such as the number of the vikings. That so many readers have understood Byrhtnoth's men to be outnumbered is significant in itself.

Roland is for thousands of readers—perhaps even millions by now—the grandly defeated hero of the battle of Roncesvalles. We have all responded to the *Chanson* with many of the same feelings as we have the defeat of Bjarki or Leonidas or Saul or Custer. Yet many of these reactions to the poem would have to be changed if we accepted the careful reading of one distinguished scholar who holds that Roland is, after all, the victor in the battle.[21] He is, this argument points out, undefeated in his personal combats with the enemy, for before his slashing Durendal the Saracens flee as thickly as bees; he falls not from the bite of a hostile sword but only when his own temples burst after blowing the Oliphant for help. And at the end of the fighting Roland is left in charge of the field, while the tattered remnants of the Saracens slink away westward to nurse their wounds and their pride. Again, this close reading is interesting, but it is more important to consider the ways such a reading shifts the proportions of the rest of the poem. If Roland is the victor in some sense other than that of a moral triumph, then Ganelon's treason—so infamously heinous because in large part it led to so many deaths and to the "defeat"—loses much of its criminality. The acting out of his animosity against Roland and 20,000 of his countrymen would not be the substance of heroic tragedy but of irony. Roland's would truly be a fortunate fall: Ganelon would have unwittingly given him the opportunity to win a great battle. Why does Roland try to smash his sword (like Marko) if victory is his? Why then is Charlemagne's grief so deep, and his vengeance so swift? Not so that he can further punish the Saracens who, in this interpretation, had been beaten once already. He sets out to avenge himself upon the pagans, but one's sympathies would not be with him as profoundly if he is merely striking down the already defeated Saracens: Charlemagne is a vengeful but not a sadistic man.

But the quality of our feelings about Roland would be altered. A great deal of the admiration that we have for his reckless courage is exemplified by his vow to sell his life dearly when he knows that death is inevitable. Roland knows that his death is imminent; but is his defeat? Unlike the victorious Lord Nelson, Roland does not die with, "Thank God, I have done my duty" on his lips. If Roland is the victor at Roncesvalles then his martial skill has been heightened further than we have realized, but certainly his spiritual triumph has been diminished. In victory he is not quite so brave, so resolute, so noble as in defeat.

The reader has his right to his pleasures and they should not be taken from him by quibbles. We are not empirically certain of Turoldus' intentions in this case, since he is not explicit on the point; but one is inclined to say that even if he meant for Roland to triumph, then he made a serious mistake in judgment, and the centuries of readers and listeners who have thrilled to the gallant loss at the pass at Roncesvalles have responded to something within them—cued schemata, perhaps—and have interpreted it "aright." Like the thousands of anonymous creators of the Custer legend, they have sensed rightly what heroic epic is all about, just as they knew what they were doing when they gave the Last Stand its name.

They did what we do—and what Frederick Whittaker did when he heard that Custer and a large segment of the Seventh had been destroyed. Whittaker placed him on the top of the hill with a saber in his hand, refusing to desert his men merely to save his own life in one minute, cutting down three Indians with his saber in the next. Whittaker did not need Curly or anyone to tell him that Custer's men died unflinching to the last, selling their lives dear; he "knew" it at once, just as thousands of Americans "knew" it as soon as they heard the awful news. And it did not take Whittaker very long to "realize" that if Custer was even half the man the novelist thought he was, then something even more ominous than the enemy was required to explain the defeat: treason.

Heroic legend is the property of its creators, whereas heroic songs are usually the creative "property" of a single recognizable artist, even though we may not be able to identify him. The distinction has been made most cogently by Jan de Vries in *Heroic Song and Heroic Legend*; and one of the demonstrations of its validity is its capacity to subsume the Custer legend, which in turn can be used to answer some of the questions such a division of epic is meant to deal with. On the formation of the Custer legend, at least, and its relation to the historical events that inspired it, enough has been said here.

But Custer's legend can tell us something about an equally important question, the length of time necessary to create a legend. Until now we have thought this gestation period a long one. Don Rodrigo Diaz de Vivar was one of Christendom's more vigorous and successful champions against the Moors in the last half of the eleventh century. His countrymen gave him the name *Campeador*, meaning "conqueror," out of their love and respect for him; the Moors honored him as highly, calling him *sidi* (lord), by which name he is known to all the West as *Cid*. The epic which honors him, *Cantar de mio Cid*, was written down (in the form we know now) in 1140. De Vries remarks that "the short lapse of time between the historical events and the poem about the hero explains why the broad outlines of his life and deeds have been preserved unaltered in the epic; they have only been given in greater relief."[22]

So too with Herodotus' life of Cyrus, king of Persia, who died in 529 B.C. The Greek historian traveled through Persia around 450 B.C. and probably heard stories of the Cyrus legend then, though for reasons he does not specify, de Vries thinks that they were in oral circulation for at least thirty years. The legend is the familiar one of the young child whose life is threatened and who is spirited away from the realm which will some day be his. He is reared secretly by strangers, but soon his noble character is manifest and he eventually regains his due honors. If the life of Cyrus is to be our model, then the gestation of a heroic legend is about half a century. Lord Raglan agrees with both of these estimates,[23] allowing the hero about fifty years after his death to become the subject of legend. He is precise about his selection of fifty, and he makes the curious mistakes of the man who speculates without having a certifiable model to work with. First, he says that the person about whom myths are to be told cannot be too recent, "or the true facts of his career will be remembered." And the man cannot have lived too many years before the first stories are told about him, else "he will have been superseded and forgotten."

But Custer shows that this is far too long; the legend-making process begins within days, perhaps hours of the event. In those very early hours the legend is fragmentary: one reporter has the idea that the regiment fought to the death, "line behind line"; a letter-writer to the newspapers is convinced that Custer's command must have been betrayed; an amateur poet imagines Custer standing alone and defiant on the hilltop, all his brave men lying around him, dead; and with the same dizzying speed dozens of men are convinced that a Crow scout has seen the battle and has said that many more Indians than troopers fell on Custer Ridge.

First dozens believe it, then thousands, then millions—this geometric progression is as rapid as the steam press. But this marvelous machine and the telegraph are only part of the explanation: they do not create legends, they only help to disseminate them. Still, these machines do not make all the difference between a few days and the fifty years of de Vries' conjecture. Before mechanical dissemination of "news" and narratives, oral transmission was rapid enough. The reasons for our vagueness about the dissemination speed of information in oral transmission in medieval and classical societies is obvious enough, yet what we know about oral transmission today in traditional cultures suggests that a lot less time would be needed to develop heroic legends on an extensive scale. This speed would be particularly true of situations in which the hero of the legend was actually a hero—whether warrior or king—to his people.

At the end of the movie *Viva Zapata* the revolutionary hero, who has been lured down from the mountains for a treacherous meeting with his mortal opponent, is ambushed and mercilessly riddled by a hundred guns. Moments later his killers drag his body to a well in the village square and throw it in the dust. At once several peasants emerge from their adobes and rush forward to adore their hero. But on seeing that he is really, and irretrievably, dead, one of the actors turns toward the faraway hills and cries, "This is not Zapata; *he* is still alive in the hills; they will never be able to kill him" (or words to that effect). But of course this is a movie, and John Steinbeck, known for his continuing interest in legend and myth, had a role in preparing the dialogue and probably in introducing the idea of Zapata alive and well in the hills. Though it is a movie, though Steinbeck wrote it, this is still the way people really react: spontaneously, a reflection of what they must believe, and what they must believe immediately.

Although I just wrote "what they *must* believe" as though it had the inevitability of a law of physics, the mind has not yet been shown to be predictable. Yet a reasonable degree of predictability about legends has been assumed in much of what this book says, for if no predictability exists at all, then (to reverse the order of speculation) no principles of legend-making are valid. The first test of this theory came in the spring of 1972 when, during a lecture on Byzantine art, Professor Constantine Patrides of York University mentioned, quite parenthetically, that the Emperor Constantine's task in defending his city against the Turks was hopeless. On the basis of just these facts—that Constantine and a small garrison were defeated by a large Turkish army in 1453—I thought it likely that the full epic of defeat might have developed. I spoke to Professor Patrides later about the possibility. He knew enough of such legends to confirm my suspicions, and when he returned to Athens that summer he discovered enough material to demonstrate completely the phenomenon in the Holy City. This was an important part of understanding the process of legend formation, for it showed that given a very few details of an event, one could predict how they would be elaborated, expanded, and structured, and what the result (in outline) would be.

If we know a little about "how," we know quite a bit more about "when." We have seen that the legend *can* begin immediately; there is no proof that it always does. Einhard's life of Charlemagne was written about forty years after the ambush at Roncesvalles, and he makes no mention of the legend. His biography itself may have been the source for the legend of Roland; but the suggestion of de Vries that stories of the Prefect of the Breton Marches received their first legendary form among the warrior class from the Breton borderland is more likely. Nothing can be proven, however, one way or another; Einhard may not have written a legendary account of Roland simply because he did not know of one, which may say something about the breadth of the legend's distribution, if not its transmission speed.

In the Custer legend it is not the fault of the people that no great poet seized upon the legend which they had bequeathed him and made of it a *Chanson de Custer*. Whittaker fused nearly all of the legendary elements of the Last Stand in "Custer's Last Charge" and in the final chapter of his biography. But neither work has had any life of its own as art, though the biography has been influential—with generations of pulp writers. The times have been wrong: for the genre of epic, lately for the admiration of military heroes, for any "oppressors" of such racial minorities as the American Indian. Perhaps, too, we know now a bit too much about the real Custer. The mechanical press, which did such splendid service in the cause of spreading the Custer legend, has now been used with equal vigor to defame him. And that is not the fault of all the people either; they have given us the materials for a fine heroic epic; they lack now only a poet of talent to give their story a form that will keep a drowsy populace awake. The Custer epic exists *in potentia*; it too is alive and well, awaiting the right moment to be reborn.

We also learn from studying this legend that more than one traditional pattern, one legendary life, becomes attached to the man. Not everyone has the same idea of the hero, and so it is with Custer. One gathering of traditions about him suggests the life of the hero outlined by Raglan. In the early stages of the legend's growth it may not have either shape or direction. Innumerable people will have a great variety of ideas about the hero and will have heard many varied, often conflicting, stories about him. To put several of these legend-fragments together, to see a pattern out of the welter of motifs which are circulating, requires a certain talent—not necessarily a great talent such as Turoldus had, but nevertheless a flair for dramatic narrative, such as Whittaker's. It is a tribute to Custer's fame that so many stories were told about him that a number of them would make of him the Raglanite hero.

In America we like to think that we have passed the age of belief in myth. The form the Custer legend has assumed surprises us because its development is so late and has taken place in so literate, technological, and reasonably sophisticated a society. Yet more surprises are to come. Francis Lee Utley several years ago "demonstrated" in a brilliant *tour-de-force* of learned wit that Abraham Lincoln could not have lived. The basis of this examination of the alleged "life" of the Illinois rail-splitter was Lord Raglan's theories on the legendary quality of more than a score of the world's culture heroes.[24]

Raglan was able to identify twenty-two biographical events in the lives of the heroes he studied:

1. The hero's mother is a royal virgin;
2. His father is a king, and
3. Often a near relative of his mother, but
4. The circumstances of his conception are unusual, and
5. He is also reputed to be the son of a god.
6. At birth an attempt is made, usually by his father or maternal grandfather, to kill him, but

7. He is spirited away, and
8. Reared by foster-parents in a far country.
9. We are told nothing of his childhood, but
10. On reaching manhood he returns or goes to his future kingdom.
11. After a victory over the king and/or a giant, dragon, or wild beast,
12. He marries a princess, often the daughter of his predecessor, and
13. Becomes king.
14. For a time he reigns uneventfully, and
15. Prescribes laws, but
16. Later he loses favor with the gods and/or his subjects, and
17. Is driven from the throne and city, after which
18. He meets with a mysterious death,
19. Often at the top of a hill.
20. His children, if any, do not succeed him.
21. His body is not buried, but nevertheless
22. He has one or more holy sepulchres.

The incidents fall conveniently into three groups: those related to his birth (1-10), his accession to the throne (11-15), and his death (16-22). In fairness to Raglan we should remember that he saw in the hero's "life" a verbal re-creation of a ritual, in these cases the principal *rites de passage*: birth, initiation, and death.[25]

Not all heroes' lives will accumulate all twenty-two "events," of course: Raglan has thrown his net wide enough to catch nearly everything that swims, and some catfish may be found among the trout. Some events are given a liberal interpretation to fit them into the scheme. But even so, his comparisons tell us much about the popular "lives" of such diverse figures as Moses, Heracles, Romulus, Robin Hood, Oedipus, and Siegfried. It may be that part of Raglan's book "sometimes makes the reader suspicious because of its amateurish character";[26] Utley's objections were congealed around Raglan's assertion that the legendary hero could not have been at any time a real man. Since so many of the events of the hero's life were patently fictional, Raglan assumed that none of the subjects he studied could actually have lived. If true, this theory would be disturbing to what (we think) we know about legend: its genesis, its development, its *raison d'être*.

As a test, Utley compiled a popular "life" of Lincoln, derived mainly from oral sources, and applied the Raglanite thesis to it. With a little cutting and trimming, a little pinching and squeezing, and some good will, Lincoln was shown to fit Raglan's scheme on all twenty-two counts. The most salient features of Lincoln's heroic life include the ambiguity of his precise birthplace, the humble childhood, the defeat of a fierce enemy (the South—or slavery), and the momentous and mysterious death after he had become a law-giver to his people. Lincoln's assassination, Utley points out, was on a less conventional high point of ground: Capitol Hill.

One of the more serious problems with Utley's approach is that all of his sources—biographies, essays, newspaper articles, and the records of various oral traditions in even more various places—are fragmentary, none of them presenting a complete popular "life" of Lincoln, or anything approaching completeness. Therefore, except in Utley's mind (a formidable enough locus, to be sure), there was no popular "life" in any meaningful sense. Neverthe-less, his demonstration is valid, for he marshalled a convincing amount of docu-mentation, and he has taken an important step in understanding that intricate relationship between lives and legends. So here is yet another instance of the universality of the legendizing process: it arises among the literate as well as the urban and the cynical. It shows us that the Custer phenomenon is not unique in America except for the personality of the hero; it shows that the American peo-ple could create old legends of several kinds, and that they are still in the making.

In a brief epilogue to his monograph, written when the project was nearly finished, Utley noted that some of the same legendary fragments were being told about the (then) recently murdered President John F. Kennedy. But between that time and 1968 I collected a number of legends (one student labeled them "rumors all") which were even then in oral currency. Utley's prediction was being borne out in the legends about Kennedy, which were making of him a twentieth-century King Arthur. Nearly all of the many versions I collected from students at the University of Virginia made some mention of Raglan's obser-vations about the death of the hero—or his imagined death—and his subsequent destiny, yet none of these informants, all of whom were undergraduates, had read *The Hero*. All were surprised to learn that the same stories which they had heard about Kennedy had already been told about others.

Hardly had the president's remains been buried when the rumor came alive that he was not really dead, but only critically wounded and under intensive care away from the prying eyes of the madding crowd. Yet the location of his retreat was never clear. Various people have offered various locations where they said they "knew" he was sequestered, but there was nothing like unanimity in their locations. All of these stories did agree, however, on the essential fact: that Kennedy was alive and well—somewhere. Later, when his widow remarried, with the anguished cries of the naive for her epithalamium, a new rumor took flesh: JFK was to be brought to Onassis' island in the Mediterranean to recuperate from his wounds and to spend the rest of his days in peaceful isolation.

To many the story was shocking; yet it should not have been, for it is the same tale told of many times and many places. Long after his death, Charlemagne's tomb in Aachen was venerated because it was expected that he would some day return and free the Holy Sepulchre from the heathen. Similar stories about the hero who is only apparently dead have been told about Friedrich Barbarossa, Nero, Thomas Paine, Siegfried, and Abraham Lincoln—who walks at midnight. Zapata is not really dead, but still hiding away in the hills. Vlad Tepeš (who is known to his countrymen not as the vampire Dracula but for his many victories over the Turks) lives still in the Carpathians. And villains can also be honored: Hitler is alive and well in Argentina. But the closest predecessor of America's former king is Arthur, not really slain by that arch-traitor Mordred, but merely wounded and spirited away to an island in the vast reaches of the sea, the isle of Avalon. There he waits and watches still, to return at the hour of his country's direst need.

Typical of the Kennedy stories was the account given me by one young man who heard it from a fraternity brother, who heard it in turn from a "Candy Striper" volunteer at Bethesda Naval Hospital, a Miss Bitten Bender (!) of Baltimore. The story had circulated among some of the employees at Bethesda Naval that Kennedy had not sustained a fatal wound, but was still alive "in a vegetable-like state." This infelicitous phrase was used in many of the accounts of Kennedy's survival. According to the Candy Striper (by way of the informant's friend and through him as well), the top floor of the hospital was "sealed off from the rest of the building" and protected by two armed guards positioned at the elevators and staircases of the floor below. Two other guards were stationed on the top floor itself, where admission was strictly prohibited. According to the "head nurse" (who told the volunteer, making the story at least fourth-hand at this point), Jacqueline Kennedy went to the hospital "one day" and was taken directly to the top floor where she remained for several hours. Miss Bender did not know about Jacqueline Kennedy's visit personally, but said that she had herself seen the guards. If not Kennedy, who or what else could they be guarding?

The fraternity brother thought it at least possible that Kennedy was still alive. He certainly believed other accounts of the alleged assassination to the effect that the coffin had never been opened after it left Parkland Hospital, and that Kennedy's "body" had been seen by a very few people, and they, for obvious reasons, weren't talking. Furthermore, my informant's friend was suspicious of the interval between the assassination "attempt" and the announcement of the president's "death"; it was too long for the kind of wound he was said to have sustained. If Kennedy had died almost immediately, this reasoning goes, why wasn't the announcement made sooner, "instead of three days later."

The mystery enshrouding this version, reeking of innuendo and subterfuge (the cynical might even say paranoia), resembles the mystery surrounding the death of that equally handsome, youthful, and gifted jewel of the Habsburgs, the Crown Prince Rudolf. Nearly ten years passed, according to an Austrian friend, after his body had been discovered (in 1889) before suicide was publicly mentioned as a possible cause. The royal remains had long since been buried in the family's country estate at Mayerling; the young Baroness Maria Vetsera who was involved in the affair had been simultaneously—and distantly—interred in an unmarked grave according to this legend. By the time rumors of suicide were taken seriously, Rudolf had been reinterred in the Capuchin crypt of the Emperors in Vienna's *Neuer Markt*, an honor which could not be afforded suicides. In the meantime the Imperial family had given the world no choice but to forget the entire affair: the police records of their investigation were said to have been "lost" or destroyed when actually they were published by the Vienna police in 1957; and everyone connected with Rudolf's death, including the physician summoned to make a determination of death, a Dr. Hermann von Widerhofer, went to their graves with their secrets, if there were secrets to be kept at all.

Such stories always thrive best amid secrecy and anonymity. Another Virginian, a former marine who asked not to be identified, had heard yet other variants of the Kennedy legend while a guard with the "Eighth and I" (for the streets) guard company. He claimed to be familiar enough with Bethesda Naval Hospital to know that President Kennedy, in whatever condition, was not there. However, this man repeated the story—which he did not entirely disbelieve—that Kennedy was then (1968) at Camp David, a story which was "widely accepted" by other marine guards in Washington and at the Marine Corps base in Quantico, Virginia. This former marine's "evidence" was the alleged frequent visits to Camp David by Kennedy's widow when no one (again, according to my marine informant), not even cabinet officials, was allowed access. He added that normally not even the wives of former presidents were permitted on the grounds.

Parkland Hospital in Dallas was not above suspicion either. The stories involving Parkland, however, came to nation-wide prominence in a rather intricate way. The 3 April 1969 issue of the *Milwaukee Metro-News* ran a headline "news" story which attributed to writer Truman Capote the assertion that John Kennedy was, in fact, still alive. Capote was well-chosen as the victim of the fabrication, since for several years he was known to be a friend of the Kennedy family. This report, with Capote represented as its author, had been widely circulated earlier to newspapers around the country, and was even read on the air by disc jockeys in New York City and Chicago. That was a month before the *Metro-News* broke its story. One radio account had cited *Time* magazine, noting that Mrs. Kennedy had visited the "grave" of her husband only five times in the four and one-half years since his "death," but that since 22 November 1963 she had visited Dallas' Parkland Memorial Hospital over 340 times. A spokesman for *Time* quickly denied that the magazine had ever published, or had ever considered publishing, such a report. Ironically, the scenario was an old one at Parkland Memorial, where a hospital spokesman said, "We have heard these reports about President Kennedy being alive. Of course they are utter nonsense. But, still, many people have phoned and written about it."[27]

The fourth location often given as John F. Kennedy's present home highlights the Kennedy-King Arthur parallel. This version has it that the Kennedy family made a "deal" with Aristotle Onassis to provide a secluded home for John, away from the stress of public life. The "deal" included a mock wedding, which—according to this version—no outsider saw. The purveyors of this fantasy point to the alleged opposition by the Catholic Church to remarriages and the apparent incongruity of the match (in the minds of many): how could Jackie, the naive at heart have asked, be attracted to so old a man? How could she want him to be the father of her and John Fitzgerald Kennedy's children?

The rationale for these silly and rather offensive theories is that Jackie did not want the public to know of John's pathetic condition, and she needed seclusion, among untrodden ways, to nurse him back to complete health. One variant of this rationale has it that the American people would have been shocked to learn of the lamentable condition of their hero, and that the shock would be too great for the nation's morale; another is that in such a condition he would soon be remembered only as an object of pity, and that to save him from fame's oblivion Jackie was leading the world to believe that John really died from Oswald's bullets.

But why bring Onassis into the plot? Surely the Kennedys are wealthy enough to buy their own island, in the Mediterranean or anywhere else, if it was seclusion they wanted for their son. Onassis is introduced into the story because he happened to have married the president's widow—really an inescapable detail—even though he only complicates people's fantasies. And so, according to the theory of the "deal," Kennedy, like King Arthur, lives on an island across the reaches of the sea on an American Avalon, where perhaps he too is awaiting the hour of his country's greatest need and from whence he too will one day return.

Capote vehemently denied any implication in the "Kennedy is alive" story. On the Johnny Carson "Tonight" show (15 April 1969) he denounced the *Milwaukee Metro-News* article as "a very vicious hoax. It's a nasty, cruel and disgusting thing. When I first saw it I thought it so stupid that nobody in the world would ever believe anything about it for one instant." But Capote did not see that this hoax, however preposterous, appealed to the desire of Americans to believe in it. To his "total amazement" Capote found himself the victim of "60 to 70 letters a day." Most interesting (as an analogue of this phenomenon to the reaction to Custer's death) were the "extraordinary number of letters from young women who say they hope it's true because no matter in what shape or form President Kennedy survives, it means so much to them."

Utley was probably the first to notice how the Kennedy legend was developing along the patterns which he found in the "life" of Lincoln, but shortly after that black November day in 1963 a great many comparisons were made between the two presidents, all of them facile and childishly superficial:

> Both "Lincoln" and "Kennedy" have seven letters.
> Lincoln was elected in 1860; Kennedy in 1960.
> Both presidents were succeeded by a man named Johnson: Andrew and Lyndon have six letters.
> Both presidents were slain on Friday.
> Lincoln was the first, Kennedy the last (!) president to be assassinated.
> Both were killed in the presence of their wives.
> "Oswald" and "Boothe" both have six letters.
> Both assassins were thought insane; both were murdered before their trials.
> Both served in the Senate.
> Both successors were southern Democrats.
> Lincoln and Kennedy were carried by the same caisson.
> A theater was involved in both deaths.
> Boothe and Oswald were born a century apart.
> Both murderers were known by all three of their names.
> "Lee Harvey Oswald" and "John Wilkes Booth" each has fifteen letters.
> Lincoln and Kennedy were shot from behind.

And William Manchester,[28] if anything, added a few other "parallels" which, though silly in themselves, must have fostered, and furthered, the Kennedy legend: on *that* day in Dallas Kennedy was riding in the back seat of a Lincoln; and later, as was the case with "The Great Emancipator," the medical report was "baffling."

And so an American King Arthur was born, or reborn, when John F. Kennedy died. Although these rumors are offensive to many, they are also a high tribute, for to wish so hard that a man were still alive, even in a "vegetable state," that one believes he is still existing, is a manifestation of veneration bordering on worship. And we should consider that these same "disgusting" stories have elevated Kennedy, in the popular mind, to the pantheon where few Americans but Lincoln dwell, to that vasty chamber where sit in perpetual council Charlemagne, Siegfried, Alexander, Odin, Friedrich Barbarossa, the Cid, and, among other notables, Vlad Barbaraš (Vlad the Impaler, the original Dracula), and Arthur, the once and future king.

Perhaps—it will be argued—these legendary recreations in America are not at all the products of reverence, but the conscious copying of old stories and their intentional application to new heroes. Let us consider this possibility briefly and then move on. My students at the University of Virginia, like the millions of others who were perpetuating the "Kennedy is alive" legends, believed in what they were saying. Those who did not believe them did not pass on what they heard. The believers lived their beliefs, and they did not try to make Kennedy appear like some other king in some other land at some other time. Few of my students recalled that King Arthur (to name just the most famous of the "alive-and-well" heroes) was said to be living on the Isle of Avalon. Rather they thought that Kennedy was alive because they wanted him very much to live again, and this desire nurtured a legend that happened to have been the same as a very old one. People wanted badly to believe that Arthur not only once lived, but was still alive: and so were David and Zapata and Quantrill and Charlemagne and Hitler—alive and well in Argentina. This belief is not to be muddled with cynicism, but is nothing less than the will to believe that an important part of one's own emotional and ideological life had not died: naiveté perhaps, but not premeditated cynicism.

A case could also be made for Kennedy as a Raglanite hero: his family (said to be America's first royal family), the dangerous adventures in the South Pacific during the war, and the great mystery said to enmesh his death. But his memory is too fresh with me to indulge in such a game here; I leave that to someone else and return to Custer. Custer, the hero on the hilltop, is also—in another legendary syndrome—Raglan's giver of laws. At least sixteen of the qualities which *The Hero* enumerates are appropriate to the general, giving him a higher status than the likes of Jason, Apollo, Zeus, Elijah, Siegfried, and Robin Hood, but only tying him with Bellerophon.

The hero is reputed to be the son of a god (incident 5); Custer's father was named Emanuel, meaning "God with us." His son's divinity was suggested by Whittaker, who claimed that as a child Custer never told a lie, and by a recent writer whose thoughts of the battle recalled an old saying: "Take the shoes from off thy feet—you stand on sacred ground."[29] More serious is the fact that when he was eight years old he did leave home to live with his sister and her husband for several years, much like the hero who is reared by foster-parents in a far country (incidents 7 and 8). But this is really about all we know of Custer's childhood, which seems to have been uneventful and bland (9).

The hero goes to his future kingdom (10); in Custer's case this is probably the West, and his first assignment there was at Fort Leavenworth, Kansas. It was there that he achieved a victory over a "king and/or a giant, dragon, or wild beast" (11). Surely this is his triumph over the "fiends incarnate" of the plains, and their "king," chief Black Kettle. This success was a sharp contrast to his unpromising days at West Point: he did actually finish last in his class, but the fact is stressed too often and is given too much emphasis for its importance.

He had married Libbie during the Civil War (12), but the sequential order of the hero's life is not crucial, as Raglan himself shows in several of his own illustrations. Then the hero becomes king (13): Raglan takes this title rather liberally, saying of Asclepios that he became merely "a man of power"; Moses became "a ruler"; and Robin Hood became "King of May and ruler of the forest." Custer as regimental commander, then, is in their company. After the Washita campaign Custer's life was for a time uneventful (14); during this period he "prescribes laws" (15). Custer's "laws" were the usual commands and general orders of a regimental commanding officer, but this is as much to the point as Raglan's Pelops, who "regulates the Olympic games," and Dionysos, who "prescribes the laws of agriculture." Robin Hood, we might also note, "prescribes the laws of archery," and Arthur "prescribes the laws of chivalry."

But after a while the hero loses favor with the gods or his subjects (16). We need only point to Custer's court-martial at Fort Leavenworth, both for leaving his assigned duty post, Fort Wallace, and for ordering deserters summarily shot. The trial was held during September and October 1867;[30] Custer was found guilty of all charges and specifications. He and Libbie stayed on at Fort Leavenworth for several months after sentence had been imposed, but then they returned to Monroe, Michigan, until the sentence was suspended by the request of General Sheridan. This corresponds with event 17, the hero driven from the throne and the city. Again Raglan is quite liberal in his interpretations: Moses is merely "removed from leadership" and Elijah simply "flees."

The rest we know: his death is on a hill—not the summit, perhaps, but a genuine hill all the same (19). And in the best tradition of the Raglanite hero, confusion enshrouds his resting place (18). When the 1877 burial party returned to the field to reinter the dead more securely, and to remove the officer's remains for private burial, the group of bones thought to have been Custer's caused some problem. Sergeant M. C. Caddle noticed that although they were placed in one coffin, a blouse under another body bore Custer's name. Caddle reported that yet other remains were then put in the Custer coffin, and in an aside he added, "I think we got the right body the second time."[31]

The Custers had no children (20) and so none could succeed him in his country's service. There are memorials to him in Monroe, Michigan, New Rumley, Ohio, and Hardin, Montana. Custer is ostensibly buried in the chapel yard of West Point, but a number of shrines have his relics, and owing to the confusion mentioned by Sergeant Caddle we are not really sure where Custer's bones are buried (22). For over a year his remains lay exposed to the winds and the wolves under Montana's big sky (21).

At this point we may begin to speak of the Custer "myth" at least as it was defined by Eliade:[32] that he is not really dead, he is a modern avatar analogous to the Son of God, who is to return at the end of the world. He is also, in this aspect, the conqueror of the pagans, fertilizing the American plain with Christianity and Progress, and as such the events of his death recapitulate the cosmic struggle told in several poems of his struggles with the forces of Satan, the fiends incarnate. As hero-redeemer he escapes from Time because, as his magical sword and his situation prove, he is not only of the year 1876. Custer, finally, recreates for us the initiation into death.

Epic heroes of the past have their cults and their rituals. Rituals and myths are inseparable, again as Eliade has shown: rituals are acts that recapitulate an event said to have taken place in the earlier world of the gods; myths are the recreations of those events.[33] In the lives of the heroes of old—and we must include the Saints of the Middle Ages among them—people saw more than just a mortal life. For the popular imagination the ancient hero comes to embody some transcendental quality which is actually the basis for his adoration; Ajax is typical, worshipped as a god at Salamis and admired as a great warrior at a Hellespont memorial. In time the epic heroes—the actual men whose "lives" are the basis of the narratives we study—acquire and thus will share many of the same attributes with others and will be credited by stories which are already extant but become attached to them. They are remembered and revered for some transcendental quality (Leonidas' civic devotion, Roland's pride and fighting skill, Lázar's piety), and a cult keeps their memory alive; if anything, the cult improves upon their hero's memory, not only perpetuating it but enhancing it. Stories about heroes very understandably acquire many of the same traditions and gather to themselves many of the same motifs as the tales of the gods. In many cases they will be the same stories which have become attached, indiscriminately, to gods, demigods, culture heroes, and the Custers of this world. As de Vries says, "priests, cult and myth are inseparable. The heroic legend growing and living in such a *milieu* cannot but assume the character of a myth. A myth, not of a god, but of a man who raised himself to the level of the gods."[34]

The legend of the hero survives, outliving all of the cultists, as long as its meaning continues to have validity. To leave Custer for just a moment, the "Wild West" is itself an elaborate and potent myth widely accepted by Europeans as well as most Americans. Some think of it as a world in a primordial, perfect state, but it is also a world where problems, themselves unambiguous, were solved quickly, unambiguously, and usually violently. This is the idea perpetuated by the movies and television; and the "lesson" of this myth of the West is that violence can be controlled by more violence, and that in the name of "right" violence is admirable. Most Americans would now agree with Dr. Kent E. Robinson[35] that such a charter for a violent morality is no longer acceptable; more significantly, the charter is based entirely on this myth, which bears little resemblance to life in the American West during the last century. To cite just one instance of how the popular media have legendized ordinary men, Wyatt Earp was shown in a successful weekly television series taming the wild frontier, a series in which the "Wyatt" must have averaged more than one shooting a week. Actually, in the forty months that Earp was marshal of Dodge City he killed only one man (at the famous "showdown" at the OK corral) and was himself never wounded. In the series Earp's motivation is a devotion to law and order; the real marshal was probably more strongly motivated by the $2.50 bounty he received for each arrest under Dodge City's law.

The myth might be harmless, but many people believe in myths that are the bases for their action, perhaps seeing in this imaginary concept of the frontier a charter for swift and unambiguous justice in modern urban society. Legends and myths are believed; we act on the basis of them. Legends are "usable myths"[36] in a very practical and immediate sense. The dissent of many United States citizens, the persistent belief that the United States must act as a moral leader in world politics, and the disillusion when this does not happen—these are various ways in which we all, "silent majority" and ob-streperous minority, believe that America is, morally and ethically, a New World which still maintains (or ought to maintain) a position of moral leader-ship. The historical basis for this complex of beliefs is indisputable, and despite the radical change in America's world role the popular belief in her destiny remains. It persists because not only Americans, but many others, find meaning and some level of satisfaction in the belief, and they continue to choose to believe.

The myth of Custer's Last Stand may also suggest to us something more than a sacrifice to manifest destiny; if that were all, this legend would have died with the ethos. Like Roland, Leonidas, Saul, or the alleged last message from Wake Island to "send us more Japs," Custer is the embodiment of our defiance—against those people, societal forces and coercions, institutions, obligations, and destinal traps that seem to envelop and at least partially smother the lives of those of us who live in modern, urban society. Custer on the hilltop, waving his sword defiantly at the red faces of the enemy who he knows in his heart will eventually overwhelm him, is that part of all of us which resists capitulation, and it is that part of us that defies, or wants to defy, our society, our surroundings, our situation in life. The Custer of our dreams is much like Camus' existential man who rises slightly above the inevitability of his life and of his death, by bravely fighting his inescapable fate to his last breath. He is Sisyphus, smiling as his boulder crashes down the slope of the hill once again; he is Tevye ordering the Imperial officer from his land, which the czar has just decreed will be his for only three days more; he is Macbeth knowing that he must soon die, yet resolving to die with the dignity of a Scot-tish king. Such a Custer is of course one of America's greatest heroes (as was Leonidas to the Greeks, Roland to the Franks, Lázar to the Slavs, Constantine to Renaissance Greece), and despite renewed Indian assaults, this time upon his memory and his fame, he will remain heroic to most of white America.

Recently a friend asked me how I presented the story of Custer's Last Stand to my sons. He wanted to know how he could tell his daughter, only six years old, about the Last Stand so that it could be demythologized, so that it could be understood in the light of our recent appreciation of the plight of the

American Indian, our compassion for him, and our realization that during the eighteenth and nineteenth centuries in conquering a wilderness and building a mighty nation we also oppressed a people. This is no simple matter. Should we point out that Custer—indeed no white man—had any right being on this land which had been granted the Sioux by treaty? We all know this now, just as many Americans knew it in 1876. Should we say that in Karl Menninger's professional opinion[37] Custer was psychopathic, characterized by "excessive vanity, complete disregard for the feelings and safety of others, a lack of loyalty either to cause or to friends, either to the principles of humanity or to the established code of ethics, and a conspicuousness of achievement at times passing for success under circumstances where ruthlessness and boldness are to some advantage." We admire the hero for some quality that, however coincidentally, may have been his in life; if we were to deny all the great men and women in our culture because they were psychopaths or egomaniacs or had other personality and character defects which rendered them socially inept or objectionable, we would have few outstanding leaders—anywhere, at any time.

Should we tell the story from the Indian's perspective, depicting the tranquillity of the villages Custer attacked in both Oklahoma and Montana, and should we dwell on the women and children who were struck down by the cavalry's charge? This is being done now, by Dee Brown in his "oral history" of the Plains Indians and historical novels, by the movie and novel *Little Big Man,* by many concerned citizens including movie stars and television personalities. Yet this effort does not seem to have been eminently successful, because (among many reasons) Custer is an unlikely symbol of white oppression of the Indians. He is, after all, the loser of the battle of the Little Bighorn, and to see his death and that of all of the five companies with him symbolizing the most destructive aspects of white racism takes a greater suspension of disbelief than most Americans are able to muster.

If one wanted a single photograph of Nazi brutality—to use an extreme and superficially dissimilar illustration of the use of such symbols—one might display that of the women and children of the Warsaw ghetto, hands upraised, surrounded by insolent, posturing German soldiers brandishing their guns; perhaps a news photo of a burial ditch at Dachau, strewn with naked and emaciated corpses. But Nazi brutality is not cogently demonstrated by the picture of Hitler and his aides picking their way through the rubble of Berlin after an Allied air raid.

We have yet another problem in presenting the Last Stand to white children from the Indian perspective: identification. Should we say that not only were the Indians "right," but when Custer and his men attacked, the cavalry fought badly? Benteen said as much, but to no avail. Should we ignore all references to the hilltop from which the men of the Seventh defended themselves; should we forget that they *were* a small band surrounded and outnumbered by a greatly superior force of the enemy? Perhaps. But with whom will our children, the children of white Europeans, identify? If they are so disaffected with the society of the United States—as those who carried or displayed the Viet Cong flag here claim to be—if they are so alienated that they want the "other side"—whatever that side may be—to win, then little can be said or done to prevent them from identifying with the Sioux. But I think that most Americans feel that Custer is in some way, however vague, a hero; and this feeling will persist because of the circumstances of his death, despite what we think we now know about the man, despite our compassion for and guilt over the Indians, because the story of the Last Stand seems to reach imperceptibly deep into some profound and impalpable region of our psyche, and there it is united with those impulses that aroused our grandparents, and theirs before them.

If Custer died for our sins, then perhaps that impulse is guilt, a need to kill something within us; so we continually, even ritually, relive the death of Custer at the Little Bighorn. In a ritual sacrifice some good is sought, some evil forestalled.[38] But perhaps we recreate his death because we want that golden boy, that boy general who did so much, who lived so fully in just thirty-six years, to die; we may not want to "permit" anyone to live a life that we ourselves are incapable of. In Custer's death we see some cherished yet never realized aspect of our lives die.[39] We may be glad for that symbolic death and return to it persistently for the comfort it affords us to know that he died young; or in our sorrow we may be drawn to the event to purge our emotions in a tragic catharsis of our own imagining. In either case the legend of the hero survives within us.

Why this happens is no simple matter. When we denigrate Custer we sacrifice some ideal within ourselves, and it is quite beside the point that this ideal does not correspond to the reality. There is some feeling in the United States that revisionist theories of the conquest of the plains are not what adults want their children to know: it is taught as a rape of the environment and of the Indian. Many Americans, perhaps most, think that it is one of the most heroic real-life epics in world history.[40] And since it is popular literature, popular history, and the popular mind that we are talking about, it is a good bet that among "the people" this concept, this legend, will prevail.

Debriefing a nation of its legends is a difficult process; probably it is impossible. Marie Bonaparte in the late 1930s collected various legends about Hitler, analyzed them, "exposed" them, but could never hope to destroy them. Her analogue for Hitler was Napoleon; neither the retreat from the debacle in Russia nor the catastrophe of Waterloo nor the defeats at Leipzig and Aspern could expunge the legend of a glorious Napoleon from the memory of the French. And she was forced to conclude that despite the vastly different qualities of Napoleon and Hitler, despite the mass murders with which the Germans will forever be associated, to the German imagination Hitler will remain the Siegfried who conquered the dragons of Europe and destroyed their "treacherous" coalitions with the Judaic Nibelungs:

> Possibly even, despite the announcement of his death, some new legend, like that of Barbarossa, will place him in the caves of some similar Kyffhauser, whence to emerge one day of vengeful glory?
>
> For it is not enough to kill an enemy to obliterate him: he will survive in legend.[41]

Custer was no Hitler, of course; that is not at all the point. But as this evil man lives on in legend, so too have the Indians immortalized their enemy when they slew him on Custer Ridge.

And the myth itself lives on: in the Iadrang Valley in 1966 where two companies of the First Cavalry (air mobile) Division were badly mauled and where stories of a heroic last stand almost immediately appeared; in the Golan Heights in 1973 where stories of a tank crew fighting to its bitter end displayed nearly all of the motifs of the last stand.

And the legend of Custer lives on: Custer the buffoon-hero of *Little Big Man*, but also the attraction at the only national park which bears the hero's name—and draws nearly 200,000 visitors each year. Nor has the worst defeat in the plains wars discouraged the modern Seventh Regiment from retaining as its motto the title of that favorite melody of soldier-and-Indian movies, Custer's regimental march, "Garry Owen."

The question posed in the first pages of this book may now be answered simply. Who is this hero and who are his men? He is the embodiment of the aspirations and ideals of his tribe or nation, a man whose failure his kinsmen revere as some old legend, an avatar of an ancient myth. Or he is all of these. His men are extensions of these qualities which the hero personifies. Their enemy may be of today, either physical of psychological; or the enemy may be of all time: cosmic, like the legions of Satan. The "battle" is fought in this particular form because we will it so, just as its hero is a product of our will. That is why, when the guns have rusted to crumbs and the dead have disintegrated, we will remember him—hardly as he was—when all the facts and details of his last stand have evaporated. If he fought badly, we will nevertheless say that he was valiant; if he never fought at all, we will say that he was valorous; and if he fought well, we may ignore him altogether. Our hero of epic defeat is what we would want to be ourselves, as long as we couldn't win.

Notes

Notes to Chapter 1

[1] For our interests, the alliterative *Morte Arthure* differs from similar accounts of Arthur's life and death—in Geoffrey of Monmouth, in Wace, in Malory—primarily in the form given Gawain's last battle.

[2] Frederic F. Van de Water, *Glory-Hunter—A Life of General Custer* (New York, 1934).

[3] The estimate is that of Don Russell in *Custer's Last* (Fort Worth, Tex., 1968), p. 1. *Custer's Last* is a brief history of Custer art with several reproductions of the more famous works.

[4] Don Russell, *Custer's List* (Fort Worth, Tex., 1969). *Custer's List* is a bibliography of paintings and illustrations.

[5] Most accessible in William A. Graham, *The Custer Myth* (New York, 1953), pp. 382-405.

[6] Philip M. Shockley, "Sabers of the 7th," *Little Big Horn Associates Research Review* 5 (1971), 1-5. See also the statement by survivor Lieutenant E. S. Godfrey in Graham, *Myth,* p. 127.

[7] A Cheyenne squaw, Kate Bighead, remembered seeing several troopers alive after those in the ring were dead in Edgar I. Stewart, *Custer's Luck* (Norman, Okla., 1955), p. 461.

[8] From a letter to his wife dated 4 July 1876 "... our men killed a great many of them—quite as many, if not more, than was killed of ours" (Graham, *Myth,* p. 300).

[9] David Humphreys Miller, *Custer's Fall* (New York, 1957), p. 255, put the loss at thirty-two.

[10] See Stewart, *Custer's Luck,* p. 458; Graham, *Myth,* p. 91; or the evaluation of the Seventh's survivors in William A. Graham, ed., *Abstract of the Official Record of Proceedings of the Reno Court of Inquiry* (Harrisburg, Pa., 1954), p. 274.

[11] See Graham, *Abstract.* Among those who still believe in Reno's treason are the guides at the Monroe, Michigan, Historical Society.

[12] Graham, *Myth,* p. 9: Curly reported to Lieutenant Bradley aboard the steamboat *Far West* that "I did nothing wonderful—I was not in the fight."

[13] Such as in the article by G. W. Schneider-Wettengel, "Custer's Laying Out," *Little Big Horn Associates Research Review* (1970), 7-9.

[14] Mari Sandoz, *Cheyenne Autumn* (New York, 1965), p. xvii.

[15] Thomas B. Marquis, *She Watched Custer's Last Battle, Her Story Interpreted in 1927* (Hardin, Mont., 1933).

[16] Quoted in Philip Young, "The Mother of Us All: Pocahontas Reconsidered," *Kenyon Review* 24 (1962), 403. Much of my information about the Pocahontas analogues comes from this provocative study.

[17] Philip Young's thesis is that the Pocahontas figure is "all the 'Dark Ladies' of our culture—all the erotic and joyous temptresses, the sensual brunette heroines, whom our civilization ... has summoned up only to repress" (*ibid.*, p. 415).

[18] Charles A. Eastman, "Rain-in-the-Face, The Story of a Sioux Warrior," *The Teepee Book* (1916), 31-32, 99-101. See also Thomas B. Marquis, *Which Indian Killed Custer?* (Hardin, Mont., 1933).

[19] Milton Ronsheim, *The Life of General Custer* (Cadiz, Ohio, 1929), n.p., Newberry Library, Ayer Collection.

[20] *The Complete Poetical Works of Henry Wadsworth Longfellow* (Boston, 1880), p. 272. Only stanzas 3, 4, and 6 of the original eight are quoted here.

[21] Cited in *Americana Magazine*, n.d. (Newberry Library, Ayer 228/ H 18 b), p. 57; the material has been collected by Eugene D. Hart in a scrapbook entitled "The Battle of the Little Big Horn: A Miscellaneous Group of Published Accounts."

[22] A concise discussion of this belief in classical and medieval literature is in Bruce A. Rosenberg, "The Blood Mystique of Gottfried and Wolfram," *SFQ* 4 (1963), 214-22.

[23] Quoted in Graham, *Myth*, p. 376.

[24] From the *Bismarck Tribune*, 6 August 1938, n.p. (Newberry Library, Ayer 228/ S 43).

[25] Recounted by Lieutenant Godfrey; reprinted in Graham, *Myth*, p. 135.

[26] The *Chicago Tribune*, 18 July 1876, p. 1.

[27] This message, written by Adjutant W. W. Cooke, is kept in a vault and is not on display to the public.

[28] Frederick Whittaker, *The Life of General George A. Custer* (New York, 1876), p. 599.

Notes to Chapter 2

[1] Reprinted conveniently in William A. Graham, *The Custer Myth* (New York, 1953), pp. 132-34.

[2] Custer had been ardently defended by Charles Kuhlman, *Did Custer Disobey Orders at the Battle of the Little Big Horn?* (Harrisburg, Pa., 1957), and attacked professionally by Colonel T. M. Coughlan, "The Battle of the Little Big Horn," *The Cavalry Journal* (1934), 13-21.

[3] Robert M. Utley, *Custer Battlefield*, Historical Handbook Series No. 1 (Washington, D.C., 1969). The movements of the columns are described on pages 19-20. For more details of the battle see William A. Graham, *The Story of the Little Big Horn* (New York, 1959); the best written account of the battle is by Mari Sandoz, *The Battle of the Little Big Horn* (Philadelphia, 1966).

[4] Utley, *Custer Battlefield*, p. 25.

[5] Frazier Hunt and Robert Hunt, *I Fought With Custer* (New York, 1947), p. 152.

[6] *Ibid.*, p. 153.

[7] *Ibid.*, p. 74.

[8] *Ibid.*, p. 154.

[9] Earl Alonzo Brininstool, *Troopers With Custer* (Harrisburg, Pa., 1952), p. 46.

[10] William A. Graham, ed., *Abstract of the Official Record of Proceedings of the Reno Court of Inquiry* (Harrisburg, Pa., 1954), p. 147.

[11] Brininstool, *Troopers*, p. 89.

[12] Loyd J. Overfield, II, *The Little Big Horn 1876* (Glendale, Calif., 1971), pp. 39-40.

[13] Brininstool, *Troopers*, pp. 76-77.

[14] Hunt, *Fought With Custer*, p. 80.

[15] Utley, *Custer Battlefield*, p. 50.

[16] Brininstool, *Troopers*, p. 48.

[17] *Ibid.*, p. 101.

[18] Utley, *Custer Battlefield*, p. 56.

[19] *Ibid.*, p. 57.

[20] Graham, *Myth*, p. 102.

[21] Hunt, *Fought With Custer*, p. 166.

[22] Brininstool, *Troopers*, p. 52.

[23] *Ibid.*, pp. 82-83.

[24] Hunt, *Fought With Custer*, pp. 103-4.

[25] So designated because of this identification given it on a map by Lieutenant Edward Maguire, Corps of Engineers, in September 1876; a photograph of it appears in Graham, *Myth*, p. 132.

[26] Hunt, *Fought With Custer*, pp. 213-14.

[27] See the Fred Dustin, "Some Aftermaths of the Little Big Horn Fight in 1876: The Burial of the Dead," in Graham, *Myth*, pp. 368-72.

[28] Although my summary of the battle follows those of Graham, Utley, and Sandoz, I have relied more heavily upon Graham for the disposition of troops on Custer Ridge: he is far more detailed than Utley and more of a historian (rather than a story-teller) than Sandoz. See especially Graham, *Myth*, p. 88.

[29] Jerome Greene, "The Custer Disaster," M. A. diss. (University of South Dakota, 1969).

[30] Hunt, *Fought With Custer*, p. 29.

[31] *Ibid.*, p. 30.

[32] From a typescript copy in the Newberry Library (Ayer C 92).

[33] Hunt, *Fought With Custer*, p. 190.

[34] *Ibid.*, p. 141.

Notes to Chapter 3

[1] William A. Graham, ed., *Abstract of the Official Record of Proceedings of the Reno Court of Inquiry* (Harrisburg, Pa., 1954), pp. 145-47, 155-56.

[2] *Ibid.*, p. 32.

[3] Although this passage was taken from the *Brooklyn Eagle* (12 July 1876, p. 2), its wording is essentially the same as the account carried around the nation.

[4] In Robert M. Utley, *Custer Battlefield,* Historical Handbook Series No. 1 (Washington, D.C., 1969), p. 51.

[5] Thomas B. Marquis, *She Watched Custer's Last Battle* (Hardin, Mont., 1935), n.p.

[6] Frederick Whittaker, *The Life of General George A. Custer* (New York, 1876), pp. 596-98.

[7] Quoted in William A. Graham, *The Custer Myth* (New York, 1953), p. 62.

[8] Quoted in Graham, *Abstract,* pp. 259-60.

[9] Philip M. Schockley, "Sabers of the Seventh," *Little Big Horn Associates Research Review* (1971), 1-4.

[10] Ernest Hemingway, *A Farewell to Arms* (New York, 1957), p. 20.

[11] Don Russell, *Custer's Last* (Fort Worth, Tex., 1968), pp. 31-35.

[12] These and other accounts have been accumulated, unfortunately without reference data, in the Newberry Library (Ayer 228/ C 921).

[13] In Graham, *Myth,* p. 355.

[14] From an article by Wallace Coburn (no other data) (Newberry Library, Ayer 228/ H 18 cus).

[15] Graham, *Myth,* p. 46.

[16] *Ibid.*, p. 92.

[17] John F. Finerty, *War-Path and Bivouac: The Big Horn and Yellowstone Expedition* (Norman, Okla., 1961), p. 133. Originally published in 1890.

[18] William A. Graham, *The Story of the Little Big Horn* (New York, 1959), p. 118.

[19] All the preceding estimates are from Graham, *Myth.*

[20] David Humphreys Miller, *Custer's Fall* (New York, 1957), p. 255.

[21] Graham, *Myth,* p. 354. This is a slight variation of Ronsheim's text.

[22] Reported in the *New York Herald,* 1 August 1876, p. 3.

[23] Published in Billings, Mont.

[24] A long-overdue defense of Reno was only recently published: John Upton Terrell and George Walton, *Faint the Trumpet Sounds* (New York, 1966).

[25] Graham, *Abstract,* pp. 230-31.

[26] Graham, *Story,* p. 58.

[27] Graham, *Abstract,* pp. 5-6.

[28] [Anon.], *Frank Leslie's Illustrated Newspaper,* 29 July 1876, p. 338.

[29] Delegate McGinnis of Montana thought that Custer was "smarting," as quoted in the *Chicago Tribune,* 9 July 1876, p. 1. The editorial condemning (praising?) Custer's "rash gallantry" is on p. 2 of this edition.

[30] *Ibid.*, p. 2.

[31] Elbridge S. Brooks, *The Master of the Strong Hearts* (New York, 1898).

[32] These obituaries are from the Newberry Library, Watson Collection.

[33] The Finkel and Ryan papers are in the historian's files of the Custer Battlefield National Monument.

[34] Graham, *Myth,* p. 7.

[35] Joseph Mills Hanson, *The Conquest of the Missouri* (Chicago, 1909).

[36] *New York Herald*, 6 July 1876, p. 5; the article and wording were everywhere the same.

[37] Whittaker, *Life*, p. 598.

[38] *Ibid.*, pp. 599-600.

Notes to Chapter 4

[1] Jan de Vries, *Heroic Song and Heroic Legend,* trans. B. J. Timmer (London, 1963), pp. 210-26.

[2] Rudolf Angerer, *Angerer's Nibelungenlied* (Vienna, 1972), p. 9.

[3] "General George A. Custer," *Galaxy* 32 (1876), 362-71.

[4] *La Chanson de Roland,* Joseph Bedier edition (Paris, 1964). Translations are my own.

[5] *Battle of Maldon,* ed. E. V. Gordon (New York, 1966).

[6] Quotations are from Frederick Whittaker, *The Life of General George A. Custer* (New York, 1876).

[7] All five novels referred to here are Beadle and Adams publications: *The Mustang-Hunters* was published in 1871; *The Grizzly-Hunters* and *The White Gladiator* a year later; and *The Death's-Head Rangers* and *Dick Darling* in 1874.

[8] "Custer's Last Charge," *Army and Navy Journal* (15 July 1876), special sheet.

[9] David Levin, *History as Romantic Art* (New York, 1963).

[10] *Ibid.*, p. 164.

[11] *Ibid.*, p. 10.

[12] William Hickling Prescott, *The Conquest of Mexico* (New York, 1909), 1:52.

[13] Whittaker, *Gladiator*, pp. 9-12.

[14] W. T. Dugard and Frank Smith, "The True Story of Custer's Last Stand," *Frontier Stories* (1938), 46-52 (Newberry Library, Ayer 228/ C 921).

[15] *Morte D'Arthur,* book 21, chap. 4.

[16] T. M. Newson, *Thrilling Scenes Among the Indians* (Chicago, 1889), pp. 186-87.

[17] Francis Brooks, "Down The Little Big Horn," in Burton Egbert Stevenson, ed., *Poems of American History* (Boston, 1908), pp. 580-81.

[18] Notes to "Custer's Last Fight," deposited in the Library of Congress, 20 April 1886 (copyright number 9562, awarded to John Furber of St. Louis).

[19] J. W. Buel, *Heroes of the Plains* (St. Louis, 1881), p. 391.

[20] Laura S. Webb, *Custer's Immortality* (New York, 1876), pp. 9-14.

Notes to Chapter 5

[1] Three officers, seventy-six enlisted men, and two civilians. The most authoritative account of the battle, and the best written, is Dee Brown, *Fort Phil Kearny: An American Saga* (New York, 1962). Much of the story retold here is drawn from Brown's work.

[2] *Ibid.*, p. 150.

[3] Jerry Keenan, "The Wagon Box Fight," *Journal of the West* 2 (1972), 63.

[4] Dr. Norman Vincent Peale, "Why Parents Fail," *Family Circle* (October 1969), 54.

[5] Albert B. Friedman, "The Usable Myth: The Legends of Modern Myth-makers," in *American Folk Legend: A Symposium,* ed. Wayland D. Hand (Los Angeles, 1971), pp. 37-46.

[6] Horace P. Beck, "The Making of the Popular Legendary Hero," in Hand, *Folk Legend*, pp. 121-32.

[7] Newberry Library (Ayer 228/ B47; typescript).

[8] John Upton Terrell and George Walton, *Faint the Trumpet Sounds* (New York, 1966), pp. 6-8.

[9] Henry Nash Smith, *Virgin Land* (Cambridge, Mass., 1971); George H. Williams, *Wilderness and Paradise in Christian Thought* (New York, 1962); Roderick Nash, *Wilderness and the American Mind* (New Haven, Conn., 1967).

[10] Smith, *Virgin Land*, p. 52.

[11] *Ibid.*, p. 54.

[12] *Ibid.*, pp. 84-85.

[13] Nash, *Wilderness and Paradise*, pp. 98-137.

[14] Cited in Nash, *Wilderness and Paradise,* pp. 107-9.

[15] Nash, *American Mind*, pp. 16-28.

[16] Chief Buffalo Child Long Lance, "The Secret of the Sioux," *Hearst's International Cosmopolitan* (June 1927), 40.

[17] Brian W. Dippie, "The Southern Response to Custer's Last Stand," *Montana* 21 (1971), 18-31.

[18] Signed by W. H. Eddys, *Chicago Tribune*, 8 July 1876, p. 3.

[19] *Galaxy* (22 September 1876), 362-71.

[20] Printed in the *Chicago Tribune*, 11 July 1876, p. 8.

[21] For a detailed explication of this general thesis see Richard M. Dorson, *America in Legend* (New York, 1973).

Notes to Chapter 6

[1] Brian W. Dippie, "Bards of The Little Big Horn," *Western American Literature* 1 (1966), 180; Burton Egbert Stevenson, *Poems of American History* (Boston, 1908).

[2] See Jan de Vries, *Heroic Song and Heroic Legend*, trans. B. J. Timmer (London, 1963), pp. 219 ff.

[3] Mircea Eliade, *The Myth of the Eternal Return* (New York, 1959), pp. 44-45, mentions the happy experience of Romanian folklorist Constantin Brailoiu who found a legend which had, in only forty years, supplanted the facts of an event. Unfortunately, Eliade gives no other particulars.

[4] De Vries, *Heroic Song*, p. 242.

[5] My summary of American taste in the 1870s is taken from James D. Hart, *The Popular Book* (New York, 1950), pp. 125-53. The poem "On through the smoke of

battle" appeared in the *Chicago Tribune*, 16 July 1876, p. 2. Originally printed in the *New York Tribune*.

[6] Laura S. Webb, *Custer's Immortality* (New York, 1876), p. 8.

[7] Also collected in Stevenson, *Poems*, p. 583.

[8] Hart, *Popular Book*, pp. 144-45.

[9] Cecil Woodham-Smith, *The Reason Why* (London, 1953), p. 7; the page citations in the following paragraph are from this book.

[10] Francis Chamberlain Holley, *Once Their Home; Or, Our Legacy From the Dakotas* (Chicago, 1890).

[11] Ella Wheeler Wilcox, *Custer; and Other Poems* (Chicago, 1896), pp. 94-134.

[12] Captain Jack, "Custer's Death," on the program of Buffalo Bill's play, "Life on The Border," 13 June 1877 (Newberry Library, Ayer Collection).

[13] John Neihardt, *The Song of The Indian Wars* (New York, 1925), pp. 194-95.

[14] William Gesell, "The Battle of Little Big Horn, June 25, 1876," in the *Monroe County* (Michigan) *Weekly*, 20 February 1936.

[15] Thomas Beer, *Hanna, Crane, and the Mauve Decade* (New York, 1941), p. 21.

[16] John Greenleaf Whittier, "On The Big Horn," *Atlantic Monthly* 59 (1887), 433.

[17] Walt Whitman, "From Far Dakota's Canyons," in *Leaves of Grass*, ed. Harold W. Blodgett (New York, 1965), pp. 434-35.

[18] Frederick Whittaker, "Custer's Last Charge," *Army and Navy Journal* (September 1876), special page.

[19] Cf. *Chanson de Roland*, 1. 1924.

Notes to Chapter 7

[1] H. Graetz, *History of the Jews* (Philadelphia, 1891), 1:102.

[2] These impressions of the Mt. Gilboa area were derived from a visit there in May 1973.

[3] Albert Edward Bailey and Charles Foster Kent, *History of the Hebrew Commonwealth* (New York, 1935), p. 97.

[4] Ernest Renan, *History of the People of Israel* (Boston, 1905), 1:329; see also Bailey and Kent, *Commonwealth*, p. 97.

[5] Bailey and Kent, *Commonwealth*, p. 96.

[6] Graetz, *The Jews*, p. 103.

[7] *The Interpreter's Bible*, however, thinks this exaggerated.

[8] See Louis Ginzberg, *The Legends of the Jews* (Philadelphia, 1913), 4:76, for the legend that Saul's armor-bearer, the son of Doeg, was the slayer of Saul. This would make him the traitor and he would then contrast dramatically not with the Amalekite but with Saul himself.

[9] Graetz, *The Jews*, p. 103.

[10] Ginzberg, *Legends*, pp. 65, 68.

[11] In Jewish legend David kills the armor-bearer, who is Saul's slayer (*ibid.*, p. 76).

[12] See, for example, Sir James G. Frazer, *Folk-Lore in the Old Testament* (London, 1918); W. O. E. Oesterly and T. H. Robinson, *An Introduction to the Books of The Old Testament* (London, 1934).

[13] Yehuda T. Radday, "Chiasm in Samuel," *Linguistics Biblica* 9/10 (1971), 21-31.

[14] Ginzberg, *Legends*, p. 67.

[15] Again in Jewish legend, a voice proclaimed to Saul, "Be not overjust." (*Ibid.*)

[16] Saul is reputed to have asked Samuel, "Can I still save myself by flight?" And Samuel answered, "If thou fleest, thou art safe. But if thou acceptest God's judgment, by tomorrow thou wilt be united with me in Paradise." (*Ibid.*, p. 71.)

[17] Of the battle God later said to the angels, "Saul goes to war knowing that he will lose his life, yet he takes his sons with him, and cheerfully accepts the punishment." (*Ibid.*, p. 72.)

[18] Josephus, *The Jewish War*, trans. H. St. John Thackeray (New York, 1928), 3.30.577.

[19] *Ibid.*, 3.30.619.

[20] *The History of Herodotus*, trans. George Rawlinson, II (London, 1933); all page references to Herodotus are from this edition. I also relied on a pamphlet which is sold at the battlefield: Konstantino P. Kontorlis, *The Battle of Thermopylae* (Athens, 1972). Unfortunately, only the nearest approximation to English has been rendered; for instance, on p. 6: "In 481 Xerxes to make the marching he had decided against Greece the easiest possible took the following measures...."

[21] Peter Green found Herodotus' figures "flatly incredible," estimating the Persians' numbers at about one-tenth of that given by him (*Xerxes at Salamis* [New York, 1970], p. 58). Yet 2 million, a more formidable number of the enemy, was repeated by redactions in grade school readers of the last century as well as the popular children's *A Book of Brave Deeds;* see "The Battle of Thermopylae," in *The National Fifth Reader* (New York, 1884), p. 444; Marcius Willson, *The Fifth Reader of The School and Family Series* (New York, 1861), p. 55; and Charlotte M. Yonge, "The Pass of Thermopylae," in John T. Trowbridge, Thomas Bailey Adrich, et al., eds., *A Book of Brave Deeds* (Boston, 1901), p. 33. And one account of the battle numbers the enemy host at 2,641,610 (Edward Kirk Rowson, Walter Camp, et al., eds., *Great Men and Famous Deeds,* Library for Young People, Vol. 8 (New York, 1903), p. 98.

[22] Green, *Xerxes*, summarizes these arguments on pp. 96-103.

[23] Herodotus, p. 203. Kontorlis described it thus: "At this heroic resistance of all the fighting Greeks the Spartans fought in a quite distinguished way and the more they applied the following strategic device. During the struggle they feigned a panic-stricken flight. The Immortals were fouled. They all turned and started pursuing competitively the Spartans in a rush, producing a big noise. Yet, the Spartans, as soon as the Persians came near, they suddenly turned round and keeping together in a close line drove back the stormy torrent of the rushing enemies decimating them in a hand-to-hand fighting, while they themselves suffered but little damage" (p. 18).

[24] G. B. Grundy, *The Great Persian War* (London, 1901), pp. 316-17.

[25] Each Spartan had three helots with him, making the field a bit more crowded

and the Spartan band less pathetically small.

[26] Green, *Xerxes*, p. 142, refers to him as Leonidas' "liaison officer."

[27] This observation is in opposition to the view of Green, who says, "even today it is an easy proposition for the average walker, and an army of ten thousand men could easily traverse it during a single night" (*Xerxes,* p. 116). Green elsewhere (p. 138) speaks of the "thick oak-woods" on the mountainside through which those ten thousand marched, and also notes that recent storms had shaken down leaves which loudly cracked under foot; but still, we are told, the Phocians were surprised.

[28] Henry R. Immerwahr, *Form and Thought in Herodotus* (Cleveland, 1966), pp. 255-66.

[29] J. F. C. Fuller, *The Decisive Battles of the Western World* (London, 1954), 1:32.

[30] Immerwahr, *Herodotus*, pp. 262, 263.

[31] *Ibid*., pp. 256-62.

[32] See Lord Raglan, *The Hero* (London, 1949), pp. 16-45.

[33] Many of these questions are asked by Reginald Walter Macon, *Herodotus: the Seventh, Eighth, and Ninth Books* (London, 1908) 1:332-37.

[34] Jan de Vries, *Heroic Song and Heroic Legend*, trans. B. J. Timmer (London, 1963), p. 207.

[35] All quotations and line references used here are from Joseph Bedier, ed., *La Chanson de Roland* (Paris, 1964).

[36] All quotations and line references used here are from the EETS (OS) edition of the *Morte Arthure* (London, 1865), Edmund Brock, ed.

[37] C. S. Lewis, *The Discarded Image* (Cambridge, England, 1964), p. 211.

[38] Gerard J. Brault, "Structure et Sens de *La Chanson de Roland*," *The French Review* 45 (1971), 8-9.

[39] See William Matthews, *The Tragedy of Arthur* (Los Angeles, 1960). Wace, which seems a more likely source, has been argued by John Finlayson's unpublished dissertation, "The Sources, Use of Sources, and Poetic Technique in the Fourteenth-Century Alliterative *Morte Arthure*" (Cambridge University, 1963), pp. 1-90.

[40] J. Burk Severs, ed., *A Manual of the Writings in Middle English* (New Haven, Conn., 1967), pp. 80-94.

[41] All quotations and page references used here are from Polybius, *The Histories*, trans. W. R. Paton (New York, 1922), 1:189-91, 235.

[42] Gustave Flaubert, *La Salammbô* (Paris, 1893).

[43] G. Lanson, *Histoire de la Litterature Francaise* (Paris, 1951), p. 1083.

[44] Georg Lukács, "Salammbô," in *Flaubert: A Collection of Critical Essays*, ed. Raymond Giraud (Englewood Cliffs, N.J., 1964), p. 149.

[45] Harry Levin, *The Gates of Horn* (New York, 1963), p. 282.

[46] Lanson, *Histoire*, p. 1078.

[47] Louis Cazamian, *A History of French Literature* (Oxford, 1955), p. 339.

[48] Lanson, *Histoire*, p. 1079.

[49] See Maurice Z. Shroder, "On Reading *Salammbô*," *L'Espirit Createur* (1970), 25-26.

[50] See Lukács, "Salammbô," p. 141.

[51] Percival Bradshaw Fay and A. Coleman, *Sources and Structure of Flaubert's Salammbô*, Elliott Monographs in the Romance Languages and Literatures, Vol. 2 (1914), 35.

[52] Levin, *Gates,* p. 267.

[53] *Ibid.,* p. 278.

[54] See Lukács, "Salammbô," p. 147; Shroder, "Reading *Salammbô,*" pp. 32-34.

[55] Axel Olrik, *The Heroic Legends of Denmark,* trans. Lee Hollander (New York, 1919), p. 66.

[56] A convenient summary of Bjarki's "life" is to be found in Gwyn Jones, *Kings, Beasts, and Heroes* (London, 1972), pp. 128-37.

[57] Snorri Sturluson, *Heimskringla,* trans. Samuel Laing (New York, 1964), 2:360-61.

[58] Magic swords are also in the possession of Arthur, Siegfried, Marko Kraljevič, Saul, Beowulf, and Custer.

[59] From the Saxo Grammaticus translation by Oliver Elton (London, 1894), pp. 69-89. Saxo's version is in the *Gesta Danorum,* book 2, chap. 56.

[60] Jones, *Kings,* pp. 149-51.

[61] The blame for this insolent epithet lies with Professor Samuel Bayard.

[62] Reverend C. Newell, "The Story of the Alamo," in Trowbridge, *Brave Deeds,* pp. 926-307.

[63] Sir C. M. Bowra, *Heroic Poetry* (London, 1964), pp. 9-17.

[64] Kenneth Hurlstone Jackson, *The Gododdin* (Edinburgh, 1969); see also the Olafsdrápá, in Margaret Ashdown, *English and Norse Documents* (Cambridge, England, 1930), pp. 109 ff.

[65] Steven Runciman, *The Fall of Constantinople, 1453* (Cambridge, England, 1965), pp. 37-39. Runciman apparently relied upon two Greek historians, Ducas and Laonicas, thought to have lived within seventy-five years of the battle.

[66] See D. H. Low, trans., *The Ballads of Marko Kraljevič* (New York, 1968), pp. xxv-xxvii, for a variant of this account.

[67] H. W. V. Temperly, *History of Serbia* (London, 1917), p. 95.

[68] Low, *Marko Kraljevič,* p. xxii. Low nevertheless thinks that Marko must have played "some part."

[69] In Sir John Bowring, *Servian Popular Poetry* (London, 1827), pp. 97-106; also see Low, *Marko Kraljevič,* pp. 174-78.

[70] "Marko Kraljevič Recognizes His Father's Sword," in Low, *Marko Kraljevic,* pp. 74-77.

[71] Helen Rootham, *Kossovo: Heroic Songs of the Serbs* (Boston, 1920), pp. 13-14.

[72] In a paper read to the Annual Meeting of the American Folklore Society in Washington, D.C., November 1971. Attempts have been made at stringing ballads together to create "epics"; see Owen Meredith, *Serbski Pesme; or, National Songs of Serbia* (London, 1961).

[73] Rootham, *Kossovo,* pp. 46-51.

[74] *Ibid.,* pp. 32-45.

[75] *Ibid.*, pp. 24-31.

[76] In "Tsar Lázar and Tsaritsa Militsa," *ibid.*, pp. 32-45.

[77] The version is given credence by Low, *Marko Kraljevič*, p. xxv.

[78] The historical summary of the battle of Flodden was taken largely from Peter Young and John Adair, *Hastings to Culloden* (London, 1964), pp. 96-103.

[79] According to Tom Scott, *Dunbar: A Critical Exposition of the Poems* (Edinburgh, 1966), p. 9.

[80] Sir Walter Scott, "Flodden," in Rowson, *Great Men,* pp. 453-61.

[81] See David Herd, *Ancient and Modern Scottish Songs* (Glasgow, 1869), p. 47 of the Heroic Ballads.

[82] Runciman, *Constantinople*, p. 91.

[83] Field-Marshal Viscount Montgomery of Alamein, *A History of War-Fare* (Cleveland, 1968), p. 248.

[84] Runciman, *Constantinople*, p. 97.

[85] *Ibid.*, p. 78; Montgomery, *War-Fare*, p. 248.

[86] Although the story is told by Runciman (*Constantinople*, p. 138), he does not include Giustiniani's last words, which argue strongly for cowardice; those words were given me by Professor Patrides, who got them, in turn, from an anonymous anthology, *Konstantinoupolis kai Hagia Sophia* (Athens, n.d.). This anthology draws heavily upon the collections of the Greek folklorist N. G. Politis.

[87] Runciman, *Constantinople*, p. 143.

[88] It is even included in E. V. K. Dobbie, ed., *The Anglo-Saxon Minor Poems* (New York, 1942).

[89] E. V. Gordon, ed., *The Battle of Maldon* (New York, 1966).

[90] The following essays and books are concerned at least in part with *Maldon*'s historicity: Bowra, *Heroic Poetry*, pp. 466-67; E. D. Laborde, "The Site of the Battle of Maldon," *EHR* 40 (1925), 161-73; Edward B. Irving, Jr., "The Heroic Style in *The Battle of Maldon*," *SP* 58 (1961), 457-67 (as the title indicates, Irving's primary interest is the poem's style); Edward A. Freeman, *The History of the Norman Conquest* (Oxford, 1870), 1:268-77; and Frank M. Stenton, *Anglo-Saxon England* (Oxford, 1947), pp. 371-72.

[91] J. B. Bessinger, "*Maldon* and the *Óláfsdrápa*: An Historical Caveat," in *Studies in Old English Literature in Honor of Arthur G. Brodeur*, ed. Stanley B. Greenfield (Eugene, Ore., 1963), pp. 23-35; George Clark, "*The Battle of Maldon*: A Heroic Poem," *Spec* 43 (1968), 66-67.

[92] Gordon, *Battle*, p. 4; see E. D. Laborde, *Byrhtnoth and Maldon* (London, 1936), p. 56, for the even stronger statement that the heroes' exhortations were copied down "word for word."

[93] The quotations are from Gordon, *Battle*, pp. 22-27; Bowra, *Heroic Poetry*, p. 467, thinks that the poet "records recent events carefully and accurately."

[94] Gordon, *Battle*, p. 22.

[95] See Clark, "*The Battle of Maldon*," p. 57.

[96] Gordon, *Battle*, p. 21; but see Clark's sage (and now obvious) observation that "oral transmission and historical accuracy are incompatible" (*ibid.*, p. 55).

[97] Gordon, *Battle*, p. 8.

[98] *Ibid.*, pp. 38-39.

[99] Kevin Crossley-Holland, trans., *The Battle of Maldon and Other Old English Poems*, ed. Bruce Mitchell (New York, 1966), p. 28; and Bowra, *Heroic Poetry*, p. 268.

[100] See Clark, "*The Battle of Maldon*," pp. 64-65. This otherwise excellent and perceptive essay is marred by some vintage scholarly overreading; for example, the viking messenger addresses Byrhtnoth in the second person singular form in order to "isolate" him from his men. The purpose is to induce him to pay tribute to the vikings because he is thus "grammatically insulated." The grammar of Byrhtnoth's reply closely identifies the men with their leader, so that he makes clear, through the use of "we" and "us" that he speaks for all. But isn't the messenger's grammar determined by the fact that he is addressing a nobleman whose decision to fight or capitulate is his alone; and doesn't Byrhtnoth reply as he does because, recognizing his position as leader, he can speak for all his men?

[101] A controversy has arisen among scholars whether this act is to be understood as Byrhtnoth's "tragic flaw" or not, or at least analogous to Roland's alleged *desmesure*: see W. P. Ker, *Epic and Romance* (London, 1908), p. 54; Stanley Greenfield, ed., *A Critical History of Old English Literature* (New York, 1965), p. 100; G. C. Britton, "The Characterization of the Vikings in 'The Battle of Maldon,' " *Notes and Queries* n.s., 12 (1965), 86-87; F. J. Battaglia, "Notes on 'Maldon': Toward a Definitive *Ofermod, English Language Notes* 2 (1965), 247-49; J. R. R. Tolkien, "The Homecoming of Beorhtnoth Beorhthelm's Son," *Essays and Studies*, 6, n.s. (1953), esp. 13-18; R. W. V. Elliott, "Byrhtnoth and Hildebrand: A Study in Heroic Technique, *Comparative Literature* 14 (1962), 23-35; A. D. Mills, "Byrhtnoth's Mistake in Generalship, *Neuphilologische Mitteilungen* 67 (1966), 14-27.

[102] Gordon, *Battle*, p. 28: "It is possibly true, as has been alleged, that the poet was not capable of giving a picture of the battle as a whole."

[103] See Clark, "*The Battle of Maldon*," p. 57: "In *The Battle of Maldon*, the Anglo-Saxon poet intends to praise heroes and condemn cowards, to divide men— Englishmen that is—into the classes of sheep and goats according to an unambiguous criterion: those who advance against the enemy are the good, those who flee from him are the bad."

[104] Gordon, *Battle*, p. 28, imagines the "wings" of the vikings possibly enveloping the English at the battle's end.

[105] Raglan, *The Hero*, p. 226: "... when we say that a story is dramatic, we mean that the characterization is well marked, that the dialogue is pertinent, that the interest is sustained, and that everything works up to a climax; we mean, in other words, that it is something very different from a description of scenes fom real life."

Notes to Chapter 8

[1] H. Graetz, *History of the Jews* (Philadelphia, 1891), 1:103.

[2] Sherman was quoted in the *Chicago Tribune*, 7 July 1876, p. 1.

[3] Leon Festinger, *A Theory of Cognitive Dissonance* (Palo Alto, Calif., 1957), esp. p. 199.

[4] Mary Noel, *Villains Galore* (New York, 1954), p. 243.

[5] Not that the cavalry was as brutal as Arthur Penn wants us to believe in his filming of Thomas Berger's novel *Little Big Man*, which turns all the racism of the nineteenth century around in favor of the Indians but is only modestly closer to reality than were Captain Jack's biases.

[6] See *Look Magazine* (1 June 1971), pp. 76 ff.

[7] Norman Poirier, "An American Atrocity," *Esquire* (August 1970), 59-63, 132, 135, 136, 138, 140-41.

[8] Associated Press news release; in the *Pennsylvania Mirror*, 28 April 1971.

[9] W. W. Comfort, "The Literary Role of the Saracens in the French Epic," *PMLA* 55 (1940), 629, 659.

[10] W. W. Comfort, "The Character Types in the Old French *Chansons de Geste*," *PMLA* 21 (1906), 323.

[11] Elbridge S. Brooks, *The Master of the Strong Hearts* (New York, 1898), p. 249.

[12] In Henry Nash Smith, *Popular Culture and Industrialism 1865-90* (New York, 1967), pp. 458-60.

[13] All of the quotations of Churchill's speeches are from *Churchill In His Own Words* (New York, 1966).

[14] Sir Edward Creasy, *The Fifteen Decisive Battles of The World* (London, 1915), p. 143.

[15] In Earl Alonzo Brininstool, *Troopers With Custer* (Harrisburg, Pa., 1952), p. 323.

[16] Fred Majdalany, *The Battle of El Alamein* (London, 1965), p. 56.

[17] Cited by Jan de Vries, *Heroic Song and Heroic Legend*, trans. B. J. Timmer (London, 1963), p. 169.

[18] But see Albert B. Lord, "Beowulf and Odysseus," in *Franciplegius: Medieval and Linguistic Studies in Honor of Francis Peabody Magoun, Jr.*, eds. Jess Bessinger and Robert Creed (New York, 1965), pp. 86-91.

[19] In such cases, however, one's own forces are seen as the "enemy"—of peace, of one's sectional biases, or of something else.

[20] See the comment of George Clark, "*The Battle of Maldon: A Heroic Poem*," *Spec* 43 (1968), 56.

[21] Maj. Gen. F. W. von Mellenthin, *Panzer Battles*, trans. H. Betzler (New York, 1973), p. 16: "The German Army was actually inferior to the Allied armies, not only in numbers of divisions, but particularly in numbers of tanks."

[22] This observation, as well as several of those in the following paragraphs, were taken from Marie Bonaparte, *Myths of War*, trans. John Rodker (London, 1947), pp. 78-90.

[23] See von Mellenthin, *Panzer*, p. 4: "Their best formations were undoubtedly their cavalry brigades, which fought with magnificent gallantry—on one occasion they charged our panzers with drawn sabers. But all the dash and bravery which the Poles frequently displayed could not compensate for the lack of modern arms and serious tactical training."

[24] Bonaparte, *Myths*, p. 86.

[25] A much discussed concept among scholars of Old French language and literature, we may here simplify it as "pride."

[26] George Bernard Shaw, *Complete Plays with Prefaces* (New York, 1963), 3:183.

[27] Anon., *Geschichte Ungarns* (Budapest, 1848), p. 92. This book was published during a revolution, and its pervasive nationalism gave rise to many of its errors.

[28] Lord, "Beowulf," pp. 90-91.

[29] See Bruce A. Rosenberg, "The Necessity of Unferth," *JFI* 6 (1969), 56-60.

[30] See Gwynn Jones, *Kings, Beasts, and Heroes* (London, 1972), pp. 114-15: "It would be an incursion into folly to argue for sources, influences analogues, consequences, borrowings, deviations. Our business is rather to observe how the common theme—the hunting of a great beast not wholly of this world—makes common demands on who would handle it."

[31] The idea of "realization" was suggested to me by Francis Lee Utley; but the brief analysis of *Gilgamesh* is my own. Utley felt that Humbaba himself (itself?) was the Unferth of the Sumerian epic.

Notes to Chapter 9

[1] An example of character addition is Absolom in the *Miller's Tale,* whom Chaucer created to contrast not only with Nicolas' brusque eroticism but with the rough virility of the smith. Alisoun is described in such a way as to preclude doubt over whom, Nicolas or Absolom, she will choose.

[2] Collected conveniently in Alan Dundes, *The Study of Folklore* (Englewood Cliffs, N.J., 1965), p. 135.

[3] Roy Harvey Pearce, *The Savages of America* (Baltimore, 1965).

[4] Jerome Mandel, "Contrast in Old English Poetry," *Chaucer Review* 6 (1971), 1-13.

[5] The theory of contraries appears in *Troilus and Criseyde*, 1:631-51.

[6] Joseph E. Grennen, "Saint Cecilia's 'chemical wedding': The Unity of The Canterbury Tales, Fragment VIII," *Journal of English and Germanic Philology* 65 (1966), 466-81; Bruce A. Rosenberg, "The Contrary Tales and the Second Nun and the Canon's Yeoman," *Chaucer Review* 2 (1968), 278-91.

[7] F. C. Bartlett, "Some Experiments on the Reproduction of Folk Stories," in Dundes, *Folklore,* p. 249.

[8] Roger Sherman Loomis, "Arthurian Tradition and Folklore," *Folklore* 69 (1958), 1-25.

[9] James Deese, *Psycholinguistics* (Boston, 1971), p. 103. Binary contrast is also the basic principle by which Claude Lévi-Strauss analyzes myth; see especially *The Raw and the Cooked* (New York, 1969).

[10] The theory of schemata is from pages 197-213 of F. C. Bartlett, *Remembering* (Cambridge, England, 1950). The distinction between the mind and a computer is my own.

[11] Bartlett, *Remembering*, p. 206.

[12] *Ibid.*

[13] *Ibid.*, pp. 206-207.

[14] Earl Alonzo Brininstool, *Troopers With Custer* (Harrisburg, Pa., 1952), p. 48.

[15] Frazier Hunt and Robert Hunt, *I Fought With Custer* (New York, 1947), p. xii.

[16] *Ibid.*, p. 110.

[17] Bartlett, *Remembering*, p. 213.

[18] James R. Ferguson et al., *Report on Network News' Treatment of the 1972 Democratic Presidential Candidates* (Bloomington, Ind., 1973).

[19] *The New York Times* News Service; from the *Pennsylvania Mirror*, 16 February 1971, p. 6.

[20] George Clark, "*The Battle of Maldon*: A Heroic Poem," *Spec* 43 (1965), 56-57.

[21] George Fenwick Jones, *The Ethos of the Song of Roland* (Baltimore, 1963), pp. 50-51.

[22] Jan de Vries, *Heroic Song and Heroic Legend*, trans. B. J. Timmer (London, 1963), p. 196.

[23] Lord Raglan, *The Hero* (London, 1949), p. 219.

[24] *Ibid.*; also Francis Lee Utley, "Lincoln Wasn't There; Or, Lord Raglan's Hero," *CEA Chap Book* (Washington, D.C., 1965).

[25] Raglan, *Hero*, pp. 179-99.

[26] De Vries, *Heroic Song*, p. 210.

[27] The involvement of Truman Capote in the Kennedy legend was reported by Thomas Porter in an article for the *National Enquirer*, 18 May 1969, p. 32.

[28] These comparisons were collected at the University of Virginia during 1969 from several students; William Manchester, *The Death Of A President* (New York, 1967), pp. 162-63, 222.

[29] Fred S. Kaufman, *Custer Passed Our Way* (Aberdeen, S.D., 1971), p. 353.

[30] See Col. John O. Shoemaker, "The Custer Court-Martial," *Fort Leavenworth Museum Series* (Fort Leavenworth, Kans., 1971), 1-12.

[31] Quoted in William A. Graham, *The Custer Myth* (New York, 1953), p. 364.

[32] Mircea Eliade, *Myth and Reality,* trans. Williard R. Trask (New York, 1963), pp. 175-76.

[33] De Vries, *Heroic Song*, pp. 228-29.

[34] *Ibid.*, pp. 240-41.

[35] From a paper delivered on 7 May 1971 to the American Psychiatric Association; released in advance by the Associated Press, 22 April 1971.

[36] As in the title of Albert B. Friedman's essay, "The Usable Myth: The Legends of Modern Mythmakers," in *American Folk Legend: A Symposium*, ed. Wayland D. Hand (Los Angeles, 1971), pp. 37-46.

[37] Karl Menninger, "A Psychiatrist Looks at Custer," *Surgery, Gynecology and Obstetrics* 84 (1947), 1012.

[38] Marie Bonaparte, *Myths of War*, trans. John Rodker (London, 1947), pp. 15-20.

[39] See Norman Maclean, "Custer's Last Fight A Ritual Drama," *The Westerner's Brand Book* 15 (1958), 57-58.

[40] Stephan Kahn, "Misunderstanding America: An Interview With Herman Kahn," *The Washington Post,* 1 July 1973, pp. C 1, C 4.

[41] Bonaparte, *Myths*, p. 11. These thoughts were expressed by Dr. Bonaparte before the popularity of stories that Hitler was in "exile" in Argentina.

Index

Abronichus (Habronichus), 169-70, 192, 242-43
Achilles, 16, 85, 134, 143, 240
Adams, Cassilly, 60, 103-4
Adventures of Daniel Boone, The, 117
Ælfwine, 88, 213-15, 234-35
Agag (Amalekite king), 162
Agnarr, 188
Ajax, 281
Alamo, the, 2-3, 192-93
Alcibiades, 86
Alexander the Great, 86, 278
Alexis, Grand Duke, 112, 219
Alkinoos, 189, 251
Alpeni, 169, 174
Amalek, 160, 162; the "unnamed Amalekite," 158-59, 166, 240, 242-43
American Home Missionary Society, 120
Aneirin, 194
Anheuser-Busch Co., 60, 103
Anopaea Track, 166, 172-73
Anthela, Plain of, 165, 170
Arapahoe (Indians), 23, 33, 110, 152
Arikara (Indians), 27, 67
Aristodemus, 169, 174
Arthur, King, 85, 101, 180-81, 208, 241-42, 245, 248, 251, 274, 276-79, 287 n. 1
Athens (and Athenians), 165, 167, 173, 181, 242
Athils, King, 188
Atrocities (in wartime), 222-25
Attitudes, toward aliens, 221-25; toward Indians, 96-97, 99, 122-28, 136, 138, 141, 143-47, 152, 219-20, 247, 254-55, 271, 282-83
Avalon, Isle of, 274, 278

Bailey, Albert Edward and Charles Foster Kent, 157, 293 n. 3

Balaclava, 140, 215
Balkans, the, 4, 13, 22, 165, 187, 197, 249
"Banquet on the Eve of Battle, The," 198
Barbarossa, Friedrich, 85, 274, 278, 285
Barney, Joshua, 131
Bartlett, Frederick C., 257-61, 263, 300 n. 7, 301 n. 17
Basque (Pyrenees guerillas), 175, 220, 238
Bathsheba, 160
Battle at Elderbush Gulch, The, 249
Battle of Britain, The, 229
Battle of Maldon, The, 2, 87-88, 154, 194, 209-16, 235, 238, 242, 265-66, 297 nn. 89-98, 298 nn. 99, 102-4
Baudouin, 179, 192
Bayezit, 197
Becker, F. Otto (painter of *Custer's Last Fight*), 56, 60, 108
Bedier, Joseph, 175-77, 291 n. 4, 295 n. 35
Beit Alpha, 155
Belknap, William W., 46, 121
Benteen, Captain Frederick, 9-10, 12, 28, 30, 32, 38-39, 44, 47, 49-50, 54-55, 65-66, 68, 70, 72, 78, 79, 101, 115-16, 129, 238, 261-62, 284
Benton, Thomas Hart, 116
Beograd (Belgrad), 196, 202, 249
Beowulf, 85, 189, 191, 235, 240, 246, 250-51
Beowulf, 160, 194, 250-51
Bessinger, Jess, 209
Bighead, Kate, 13, 63, 287 n. 7
Binary contrasts, 217, 259
Bismarck, D. T., 23, 62, 78
Bismarck Tribune, 17, 23, 78-79, 288 n. 24
Bjarkamál, 187-92, 196, 236
Bjarkarimur, 188
Bjarki (Bothvar Bjarki), 2-3, 188-92, 220, 225, 228, 237, 242-44, 266, 296 n. 56

Bjorn, 189
Black Hills, 21, 23, 126, 131, 221
Black Kettle, 11, 29, 112, 219, 279, 283
Blackbirds (of Kóssovo), 196-97, 200
Blackfeet (Indians), 29
Blaine investigation, the, 22
Blood, folk belief in, 15-16, 190-91
Bloody Knife, 28, 69
Bluntschli (in *Arms and the Man*), 56, 246
Bob Hampton of Placer, 7
Bocciardo brothers, 206
Bohlen, Ambassador Charles, 265
Book of Brave Deeds, A, 192, 294 n. 21
Boone, Daniel, 117-18, 131-32
Bonaparte, Marie, 239-40, 285, 299 nn. 22, 24, 301 n. 38, 302 n. 41
Bonnie and Clyde, 240
Bosquet, General (French observer at Balaclava), 73
Bouyer, Mitchell, 29-30
Bowie, Jim, 193
Bowra, Sir C. M., 193, 241, 296 n. 63, 297 n. 90, 298 n. 99
Bozeman Road, 109
Bozeman Times, 78
Bradley, Lieutenant James H., 47
Brady, Matthew, 8
"Branded" (TV series), 7
Brault, Girard, 295 n. 38
Brininstool, Earl Alonzo, 289 n. 9, 299 n. 15, 301 n. 14
Brisbin, Major James S., 45-57
"Broken Lance," 7
Brooklyn Eagle, 290 n. 3
Brooks, Elbridge, S., 226, 290 n. 31, 299 n. 11
Brooks, Francis, 101-3, 291 n. 17
Brown, Dee, 111, 263-64, 283, 291 n. 1
Brown, Captain Frederick, 111
Bryan, Daniel, 117
Buel, J.W., 104, 291 n. 19
"Buffalo Bill," 112, 219, 292
Bureau of Indian Affairs, 21, 27, 123
Bury My Heart at Wounded Knee, 264
Butler, Sergeant James, 9, 64, 66, 243
Byrhtnoth, 2-4, 6, 87-88, 154, 190, 209-12, 220, 227, 232, 234-35, 240-44, 265-66, 298 n. 100
Byrhtwold, 214, 235
Byron, Lord (George Gordon), 86, 153

Cadiz (Ohio) *Republican,* 67
Caddle, Sergeant M.C., 280
Calhoun, Lieutenant James, 9, 43, 50, 53-54, 103
Camus, Albert (and the Sisyphus myth), 163, 282
Canterbury Tales, The, 256-58
Capote, Truman, 275-77, 301 n. 27
Captain Jack, 144-45, 220, 293 n. 12, 299 n. 5
Cardigan, Lord, 73, 139-40, 153, 226
Carland, Lieutenant John, 46
Carlisle, Willard, 62-63, 108
Carrington, Colonel Henry B., 109
Carson, Kit, 117-19, 131-32
Carthage (and Carthaginians), 183-84, 186, 212, 238
Catraeth, 194-96
Cazamian, Louis, 186, 295 n. 47
Centennial, America's, 22, 121-22, 130, 136-38, 147, 219; the Philadelphia Exposition, 22, 121-22
"Centennial Meditation of America, The," 121
Century magazine, 46
Chanson de Roland, 2, 4, 5, 154, 175, 181, 182, 187-89, 221, 227, 231-32, 255, 265, 283, 291 n. 4, 295 n. 35
Chansons de Geste, 225
Charge of the Light Brigade, The, 73, 94-95, 106, 108, 130, 134, 139, 140, 153, 215, 226
Charge of the Light Brigade, The, 108, 130, 139, 153, 226
Charlemagne, 85, 175-77, 179, 181, 192, 203, 208, 241-42, 244, 247, 255, 267, 270, 274, 278
Chaucer, Geoffrey, 181, 256-57
Cheyenne (Indians), 14, 23, 27, 30, 33, 35, 41, 63, 65, 83, 104, 110; Northern Cheyenne, 24
"Cheyenne" (TV program), 7
Cheyenne Weekly Leader, 21, 122-23, 221
Cheyenne, W. T., 23, 76
Chiasm, 160-61, 294 n. 13
Chicago Daily News, 76
Chicago Tribune, 22-25, 50-51, 68, 70, 79-82, 116, 120-21, 123, 124, 126, 128-29, 137, 141, 263, 290 n. 29, 292 nn. 18, 20, 298 n. 2

Choice of death, the, 18-19, 82-83, 89-90, 108, 143-44, 158-59, 163, 167, 190, 198, 207-8, 212, 244-45, 268

Churchill, Sir Winston, 228-29, 299 n. 13

Cid, El (Don Rodrigo Diaz de Vivar), 268, 278; *Cantar de mio Cid,* 268

Civil War, American, 6, 8, 66, 70, 112, 131, 136, 141, 148, 208, 219, 245, 255

Clark, George, 209, 266, 297 n. 95, 298 nn. 100, 103, 299 n. 20, 301 n. 20

"Cognitive Dissonance", 218-20, 298 n. 3

Coleman, James, 78

Colonel Crockett's Texas Exploits, 115

Comanche (Indians), 94, 96, 115

Comfort, W.W., 299 nn. 9, 10

Comitatus, 189

Congressional Medal of Honor, 19, 246

Conquest of Mexico, The, 97, 99

Constantine Paleologus, 2-6, 204-9, 220, 225, 228, 236, 240, 242, 270, 282

Constantinople, 2, 4-5, 204-8, 228, 237, 296, 297

Contrasts (in characterization), 160-61, 174, 192, 211, 240, 253-60

Cooke, Lieutenant William W., 66, 288

"Concord Bridge," 136

Corlett, Representative W.W., 71

Cosby, Bill, 8

Crazy Horse, 22, 28, 56, 66, 121

Creasy, Sir Edward, 230-31, 299 n. 14

Crimean War, 140

Crittenden, Lieutenant John J., 50, 53

Crockett, Davy, 113-15, 193

Crook, General George, 23-24, 48, 52, 124

Cross, Billy 67, 239

Crow (Indians), 9, 18, 25, 27, 29, 63, 79, 83, 239; scouts with Custer (Hairy Moccassin, Goes Ahead, White-Man-Runs-Him), 77

Crow King, 66

Crow Scout Who Killed Custer, The, 68

Crow's Nest, the, 29, 153

Curly, 10, 18, 62, 65, 75, 77-83, 89-92, 143-44, 192, 242, 255, 261, 268-69

Custer: campaign of 1876, 21-32; charisma, 113-16; court-martial of, 112-13, 279; cult of, 17-18; early career, 112-13; fame, 2-3, 6-11, 14, 50, 57, 60, 62, 72-73, 113-14, 116, 128-30, 219, 271; as idealization of defiance, 19, 282; identification with, 284; influence on popular culture, 7, 101-8, 113-14, 133-54; last message from, 18, 66-67, 288 n. 27; legend, persistence of, 285-86; at the Little Big Horn, 8, 26-48; as model of epic hero, 4-6, 155, 245; "mysterious death" of, 280; as mythic hero, 280, 282-85; refuses escape, 18-19, 82-83, 89-90, 143-44; relics of, 18; standing with fellow officers, 44-48, 115-16; suicide, alleged, 16-17; symbol of ethos, 120-23, 131-32, 282; at the Washita, 11-14, 40, 112, 279

"Custer" (TV program), 7

Custer Battlefield National Monument, 7, 285, 290 n. 4

Custer of the West, 7

Custer Ridge, 9, 11, 15, 18, 41, 43-44, 49, 53, 60, 74, 83, 112, 120, 130, 217, 219, 238, 243, 245, 261-62, 269, 285

"Custer: To The Heroes of The Custer Tie," 141

Custer, Captain Thomas W., 15, 43, 74, 91

Custer, Elizabeth, 13, 17, 62, 144, 279-80

"Custer's Farewell," 141-42

Custer's Immortality, 105-8, 137

"Custer's Last Charge," 93, 95, 151-54, 231

Custer's Last Fight, 7

"Custer's Last Stand" (TV series), 7

Custer's List, 7

Cyrus (Persian Emperor), 268

Czechoslovakia, Russian invasion of, 231-32

Dacre, Lord, 201

Dakota Territory, 21, 122, 126, 221, 226

Danes (Mordred's soldiers), 180, 225

Darling, Dick, 93, 95-97

Darius, 169

David, 157-63, 241-42, 278, 293 n. 11

De Vries, Jan, 85, 135, 151, 177, 182, 188, 268, 270, 281, 291 n. 1, 292 nn. 2, 4, 295 n. 34, 299 n. 17, 301 nn. 22, 23

Deese, James, 259, 300 n. 9

Deloria, Vine, 8

Demaratus, 166, 174

Diaz, Bernal (historian), 100

Dieneces, 167-68, 174, 179

Dietrich, 208

Digby 23, 5, 86-87, 175, 179, 259

Dime novels, 53, 93-97, 99-100, 232, 291 n.7

Discovery, Settlement and Present State of Kentucke, The, 117

Dorson, Richard M., 292 n. 21

Dreadful Decade, The, 67

Dubček, Alexander, 231

Dugard, W. T., 101, 291 n. 14

Dunnere, 214

Durendal, 179, 266

Dustin, Fred, 7, 289 n. 27

Eadweard, 212, 214

Earp, Wyatt, 131, 281

"Eaten Heart, The," 15-16, 190

Ecclesiastical History of New England, The, 119

Ein Dor (Endor), 155, 162

Einhard, 5, 175, 270

El Alamein, 234

Eleazar, 162-63

Elegy (as genre), 193

Elgfrothi, 191, 242

Eliade, Mircea, 280, 292, 301 n. 32

Eliot, John, 119

Eliot, T. S., 14-15, 105

Elliott, Major Joel, 11-12, 40, 234

Emerson, Ralph Waldo, 136

"Enamored Moslem Princess, The," 13

Enkidu, 251-52

Ephialtes, 166, 174, 233, 240

Ethelred the Unready, 227

Euralyus, 251

Eurytus, 169

"Fall of the Serbian Empire, The," 198

Far West (steamboat), 24, 47, 78-79, 82, 89, 120

Female poets, 136, 137

Festinger, Leon, 218-19, 298 n. 3

Fetterman, Captain William Judd, 109-12, 249

"Few against the multitude, the," 3, 94, 155, 157-58, 163, 165, 177-79, 180, 185, 191-93, 203, 206, 214-15, 233-35, 237-38, 246, 255, 263, 294 n. 17

"Fight to the death, the," 1, 3, 60-64, 91-92, 136, 159, 169, 179-81, 185, 187, 192, 193, 207, 210, 215-16, 232-34, 240-41, 268

Filson, John, 117

Finerty, John, 65, 290 n. 17

Finkel, Frank, 76, 82, 290 n. 33

Finnesburgh Fragment, 192

Fisher, Isaac, 109-10

Fisher King, the, 16

Fisher, trumpeter Henry, 37-38, 262

Flaubert, Gustave, 4, 183, 185-87, 232, 234, 236, 238, 295 n. 42, 296 n. 51

Flint, Timothy, 117

Flodden, battle of, 2, 88, 200-204, 297 n. 78

Flynn, Errol, 8, 60-61, 113, 136

Ford B, 31, 40, 63, 74, 130

Fort Ellis, 24, 45, 78

Fort Fetterman, 24

Fort Laramie, 22, 23, 24; treaty of, 21, 127, 131

Fort Leavenworth, 23, 126, 279

Fort Lincoln, 17

Fort Phil Kearny, 17, 109-11

Fort Ticonderoga, 115

France, 1939-40 conquest of, 239

Frank Leslie's Illustrated Newspaper, 72, 128, 290 n. 28

Franks, 175-78, 225, 227, 232, 235, 238, 282; Byzantine name for Westerners, 206-7

Fremont, Jessie Benton, 118

Friedman, Albert B., 292 n. 5, 301 n. 36

"From Far Dakota's Canyons," 133, 148-50, 260

Fuller, General J.F.C., 173, 295 n. 29

Galaxy magazine, 53, 85-86, 93

Gall, 9, 40, 56, 74

Ganelon, 177, 181, 192, 240, 255, 267

Gatling guns, 9, 24-25, 46, 255-56

Gawain, Sir, 2-3, 154, 180-82, 216, 232-34, 236, 240-42, 244-45, 248, 287 n. 1

Germanic warrior's code, 210, 213

Gesta Danorum, 187, 296 n. 59

Gesta Romanorum, 13-14

Gibbon, Colonel John, 24-26, 45-47, 49, 67, 78

Gibbon, Edward, 200

Gilgamesh (epic and hero), 251-52, 300 n. 31

Gilpin, William, 116-17

Ginzberg, Louis, 293 n.n. 8, 10-11, 294 n.n. 14-17

Girard, Fred, 33

Giustiniani, Giovanni, 206-7, 297 n. 86

Glory-Hunter, 6, 287 n. 2

Godfrey, Captain E.S., 17, 46, 116, 287 n. 6, 288 n. 25

Gododdin, 2, 193-96, 236, 242, 296 n. 64

Godric, 210, 213, 239-40, 242-43, 266

Goldin, Sergeant Theodore, 115

Gordon, E.V., 209, 297 nn. 92-94, 96-98, 298 nn. 102, 104

Goths (Bjarki's foes), 188-92, 225, 228, 237

Graetz, H., 158, 193, 217, 293 nn. 1, 6, 9, 298 n. 1

Graham, Colonel William A., 40, 67, 69-70, 287 nn. 8, 11-12, 288 n. 23, 289 nn. 20, 25, 1, 290 nn. 7-8, 13, 15-16, 18-19, 21, 25-27, 34, 301 n. 31

Grant, President Ulysses S., 46, 68, 72, 121, 123-25, 129, 131, 225, 263

Great Sioux Massacre, The, 7

"Green Mountain Boys," 115

Green, Peter, 294 n. 21, 22, 295 n. 26

Greene, Jerome, 44, 289 n. 29

Grendel, 235, 246, 250-51

Griffith, D.W., 249

Griswold, Rufus, 136-37, 154

Gros, Baron, 57

Grummond, Lieutenant George Washington, 109-10

Grundy, G.B., 167, 244, 294 n. 24

Hagia Sophia, 207, 297 n. 86

Hamilcar Barcas, 184-85

Hanno, 184, 238

Hardin, Montana, 7, 280

Harold, King, 202, 249

Harrington, Lieutenant Henry M., 64-65

Hart, James D., 292 n. 5, 293 n. 8

Hastings, battle of, 202, 227, 235

Hawkins, Lieutenant Dean, 131

The Hayfield fight, 219

Heavy enemy casualties, legend of, 1, 9, 65-67, 84, 101, 166, 174, 178, 180, 191, 193, 203, 214-16, 230, 237-38, 269

Hector, 134, 141-42

Helena Herald, 78

Hemingway, Ernest, 56, 290 n. 10

Henry IV, 252

Henry, Frederick, 56

Heredeen, George, 26, 46

Hermanus, 230

Hero, The, 273, 279-80, 295 n. 32, 298 n. 105, 301 n. 23

Herodotus, 4, 165, 167, 169-70, 172-74, 177, 182-83, 232, 234, 236-37, 268, 294 nn. 20-21, 23

Heroes of the Plains, 104-5

Heroic song (compared with heroic legend), 5, 235, 242

"Hilltop, the," 1, 10, 84, 90, 157, 163, 169, 179, 182-83, 185, 187, 216, 230, 234-35, 261, 269, 284

History as Romantic Art, 97, 291 n. 9

Hitler, Adolf, 208, 220, 229, 274, 278, 283, 285, 302 n. 41

Hjalti (Hott), 16, 188, 190-92, 244

Hjarvarth, 2, 188-92, 240, 254

Hodgson, Lieutenant Benny, 38, 262

Holiday, "Doc," 131

Holley, Francis Chamberlain, 141-42, 150, 153, 293 n. 10

Holmes, Oliver Wendell, 136

Homer, 160, 226, 251

Hopkins, Gerard Manly, 142

"Horse For Mrs. Custer, A," 7

Howard, Edmund, 201

Hrolf, 189-90, 192, 242, 253-54

Hrolf's Saga Kraki, 187, 189-91, 242

Humbaba, 251-52, 300 n. 31

Hunkpapas, 29, 33

Hunt, Frazier and Robert, 262, 289 nn. 5-8, 14, 21, 24, 26, 30-31, 33-34, 301 nn. 15-16

Hunyadi, Janos, 202, 249

Hydarnes, 166-67, 172-73

Hyfeidd the Tall, 194

Immerwahr, Henry R., 173, 295 nn. 28, 30-31

Independent genesis, 236

Indian Ring, The, 122-23

"Inexpiable War," 183

Information processing, human, 259-60

Interpreter's Bible, The, 157, 293 n. 7

Ishmael, 242

Iwo-Jima, 6, 57

James IV, 2, 88, 200-203, 212, 233, 249

James, Jesse, 240

Janissaries, 207, 209

Jesus Christ, 56, 119, 134, 181, 198

"Johnny Appleseed," 120

Jonathan, 157, 162-63, 241

Jones, Gwynn, 191, 296 nn. 56, 60, 300 n. 30
Josephus, 162-63, 294 nn. 18, 19
Judas (as the arch-traitor), 181, 198

Kahn, Herman, 302 n. 40
Kanipe, Sergeant Daniel, 66
Kay, Sir, 251
Kellogg, Mark, 120
Kennedy, President John F., 208, 273-78, 301 n. 27-28
Keogh, Captain Myles W., 7, 9, 43, 50, 53-54, 63, 74, 101, 103
Kidder, Lieutenant Lyman and Judge (Sr.), 233-34
Kill Eagle, 66
King, Rev. Martin Luther, Jr., 57
Kolonos, 169-70, 173
Kontorlis, Constantine, 170, 172, 294 n. 20
Kóssovo, 2-3, 178, 196-98, 220, 227, 232, 237, 242, 296 nn. 71, 73
Kudrun, 16

La Salle, 99
Lanier, Sidney, 121
Lanson, G., 185, 295 nn. 43, 46, 48
"Last man alive, the," 60, 84, 135, 158, 240-41, 269
Last stand, the, as fiction, 6, 8-10, 20, 53-60, 67, 82, 88-92, 101-8, 133-54
"Law of the West," 16; Code of the West, 159
"Lay of Bjarki," 188-89
Lázar, 2, 6, 197-98, 208, 220, 227, 236, 240-42, 244-48, 281-82
Lee, Lieutenant Jesse M. (court recorder), 55, 86
Lee, General Robert E., 73, 131
Legendizing process, the, 5, 112-32, 210-11, 219, 235-52, 268-81, 285
Legends (as "usable myths"), 282
Lejre, 2, 189, 191-92, 244
Leofsunu, 214
Leonidas, 2-3, 6, 72-73, 86, 153, 165, 167, 169-70, 173-74, 190, 213, 216, 220, 225, 227, 232, 234, 237-38, 240-41, 243-44, 266, 281-82
Levin, David, 97, 29
Levin, Harry, 186, 295 n. 45, 296 nn. 52-53
Lewis, C.S., 181, 295 n. 37

Liber Eliensis, 210-11
Life and Adventures of Daniel Boone, The, 117
Life magazine, 62
Life of General Custer, The, 67
Life of General George Armstrong Custer, The, 4, 18-19, 53-54, 79-83, 89-92, 288 n. 28, 290 n. 6, 291 n. 6
Lincoln, President Abraham, 272-74, 277-78, 301 nn. 24-25
Little Big Horn Associates, 18-19
Little Big Man (novel and movie), 7, 283, 285, 299 n. 5
Little Bighorn River, 24-25, 29-30, 35-38, 44-45, 47-48, 50-51, 76, 130
Little Big Man (novel and movie), 7, 283, 285, 299 n. 5
Lodge Tail Ridge, 109-10
Logan, General Joshua, 23
London Times, 125-26, 218, 254
Lone survivor, the, 3, 10, 62-64, 73-84, 89-91, 158, 169-70, 179, 192-93, 198, 216, 242-43, 255, 263, 269; lone survivor claimants, 74-75
Longfellow, Henry Wadsworth, 14, 133, 136, 147, 288
Loomis, Roger Sherman, 258-59, 300
Lord, Albert B., 198, 250, 299 n. 18, 300 n. 28
Lounsberry, Colonel Clement A., 23, 78-79
Low Dog, 33, 53, 63, 66
Lucan, Lord, 140
Luce, Captain Edward S., 77
Lukács, Georg, 185, 295 n. 44, 296 nn. 50, 54
Lycus Valley, 206

McAuliffe, General Anthony, 249-50
McDougall, Captain Thomas M., 66, 226
McGovern, Senator George, 264
McGuffey Reader, 105
McKenzie, Ranald, 131
Macbeth, 159, 187-87
Madame Bovary, 186
Maldon, 3, 178, 190, 209-10, 215-16, 232, 239, 242
Malis, Gulf of, 165, 170
Malory, Sir Thomas, 101, 252, 287 n. 1, 291 n. 15
Man Without a Country, The, 136

Manchester, William, 278, 301 n. 28
Mandel, Jerome, 300 n. 4
Markers, marble, at Custer battlefield, 10, 41-43, 56
Marko Kraljevič, 197-98, 267, 296 nn. 58, 68, 70, 297 n. 77
Marquis, Thomas B., 53, 288 n. 15, 290 n. 5
Marsh, Grant, 78
Martini, trumpeter Giovanni, 66
Masada, 162-63
Massacre Hill, 111-12
Mather, Cotton, 119
Mathey, Lieutenant Edward, 115
Matho (or Mathô), 3, 183-87, 216, 234, 236, 238
Medicine Crow, Joe, 63
Medicine Tail Coulee, 66
Mehmet, 204, 206-7, 240
Meissonier, 57
Melampygou rock, 166, 172-73
Memory, 6, 260-63
Menninger, Dr. Karl, 283, 301 n. 37
Mexicans, 3, 94-96, 192-93
Michmash, 162-63
Miles, General Nelson A., 126, 226
Miller, David Humphreys, 287, 290 n. 20
Miloš Obilič, 198, 200
Milutin, 242
Milwaukee Metro-News, 275-77
Miniconjou (Indians), 29
Modoc (Indians), 50
Mo-Nah-Se-Tah, 11, 13
Monroe County Historical Association, 72
Monroe, Michigan, 7, 18, 280
Montana, 7-8, 19, 21, 43, 45, 57, 60, 72, 108, 120, 156, 242, 283
Montgomery, Viscount Field Marshal of Alamein, 204-5, 234, 297 nn. 83, 85
Mordred, 101, 180-81, 232, 237, 241, 274
Morte Arthure, 2, 154, 179-82, 225, 236, 287, 295 n. 1
Morton's Hope, 98
Moses, 56, 272, 279
Motley, John, 97-98
Mt. Callidromon, 165, 233
Mt. Gilboa, 2, 155-59, 162-63, 165-66, 172, 186-87, 217, 220, 236, 242, 293 n. 2
Moyland, Captain Myles, 115
Mulvany, John, 226-27
Murad, 196-97, 200, 220

Murat, Marshal Joachim, 86, 129, 219
Muskie, Senator Edmund, 264
Mutilation, 11, 14-15, 41, 49
My Lai, 221
My Life on the Plains, 53, 113
Mynyddog the Wealthy, 2, 193-95, 220, 228, 242
Myrrour Hystoryal, 182
Myth (as basis for action), 281-82

Napoleon, 86, 219, 254, 285
Nash, Roderick, 292 nn. 9, 13-15
Nausicaa, 13
"Naval Inquiry," the, 121
Neihardt, John, 145-46
Nero, 208
New Rumley, Ohio, 7, 280
New York American, 117
New York Herald, 62, 68, 72-73, 78, 128, 135, 218, 226, 290 n. 22, 291 n. 36
New York Times, 72, 127-28, 129, 265, 301 n. 19
New York Tribune, 226
Newberry Library, 228 nn. 19, 21, 289, 290 n. 12, 292 n. 7
Newell, Rev. C., 193, 296 n. 62
Newson, T.M., 101, 291 n. 16
Newspapers (in legend dissemination), 5, 15, 53, 73, 76, 78, 135, 217, 232, 269; the "line behind line" version, 52-53, 79, 101, 103, 217, 262, 269; the "slaughter-pen" version, 52-53, 79-80, 128, 138, 148, 217-18, 263
Ney, Marshal, 219
Nibelungenlied, 249
Njals Saga, 249
Norfolk Virginian, 125
Norton, W.H., 78
Nye-Cartright Ridge, 40, 44

Odin, 208, 253, 278
Odysseus, 13
Odyssey, The, 250
"Of Fidelity," 14
Offa (two Offas fight at Maldon), 211, 213-14
Oglallas, 29, 152
"Old Ironsides," 136, 141
Old Testament, 4, 157-59, 160, 163, 173, 182, 236

Oliphant, 16, 87, 179, 190, 243, 266

Oliver, 86-87, 177-78, 203, 255

Olrik, Axel, 187-88, 253-54, 258-60, 296 n. 55

Omnipotence, psychic, 64-65

Onassis, Aristotle, 208, 274, 276

Onassis, Jacqueline Kennedy, 273-76

Oral history, 197, 204, 264, 283

Oral tradition, 4-5, 20, 135, 160, 174-75, 177, 182, 187, 197-98, 200, 206-7, 210-11, 236, 250, 268-69, 271-73

Ottokar, 249

Otuel and Roland, 182

Paine, Thomas, 208

Pante River (Blackwater), 209-10, 212-13, 241

Parkland Memorial Hospital, 274-76

Parkman, Francis, 97-99

Passage to India, theory of, 116-18

Patrides, Constantine, 206-7, 270, 297 n. 86

Patroclus, 170

Paul Revere's Ride, 136

Paxson, Edgar, 57-58

Peace Policy, the, 123, 126-28, 145, 225

Peale, Dr. Norman Vincent, 112, 292 n. 4

Pearce, Roy Harvey, 255, 300 n. 3

Pearl Harbor, 248-49

Penn, Arthur, 30, 299 n. 5

Penn State football, 247-48

Peno Creek, 109-11

Persians (Medes, Cissians), 2-3, 139, 165-74, 225, 233, 238, 244, 294 n. 21-24

Peters, DeWitt C., 118

Philistines, 155-57, 159, 162-63, 208, 225, 237, 242, 247

Phillips, Wendell, 129

Pilgrims, 119

Pivski Monastir, 197

Plataea, 169, 173, 181

Poland, 1938-39 defeat of, 239, 248

Polybius, 88, 183, 185-87, 212, 234, 238, 295 n. 41

Powder River, 21, 24, 68, 121

Powell, Captain James, 112

Prescott, William, 97-100, 291 n. 12

Propp, Vladimir, 243

Pseudo Turpin, 179

Quantrill (Kansas guerilla), 208, 278

Quisling, 231

Raglan, Lord (English commander at Balaclava), 140-41

Raglan, Lord (folklorist and mythographer), 56, 268-69, 271-73, 295 n. 32, 298 n. 105, 301 n. 23

Rain-in-the-Face, 14-15, 74, 91, 104, 133, 147-48, 191

Ralston, J. K., 9

Rape of the Lock, The, 133

Reality as fiction, 3, 6, 159-61, 171-75, 183, 231-33, 262-65

Reason, The Only Oracle of Man, 115

Red Cloud, 109, 112

Red Cloud Agency, 22-24, 121

Red Horse, 54

Red Top, 63

Reno, Major Marcus, 9-10, 12, 15, 24-26, 28, 30-35, 37-38, 40, 44, 49-50, 54, 65-66, 68-72, 77-78, 89, 92, 116, 129, 239-40, 245, 254, 262-63, 290 n. 24

Reno Board of Inquiry, 10, 30, 54-55, 72, 86

Reno Creek, 8, 33

Reno Hill, 28, 116, 226

Repeated reproduction, 261

Report on Network News' Treatment of the 1972 Democratic Presidential Candidates, 264-65, 301 n. 18

Revenge motif, 1-2, 14, 138, 181, 191, 225-28, 230, 242, 247

Revenge of Rain-in-the-Face, 15, 133, 147

Reynolds, Charlie, 28, 34

Richmond Whig, 125

Rise of the Dutch Republic, The, 98

Ritual (and myth), 272, 280-81, 284

Robinson, Dr. Kent E., 281

Roland, 2-3, 5-6, 16, 72-73, 86-87, 154, 159, 170, 175-82, 189-90, 198, 203, 208, 216, 220, 231-32, 234-35, 237, 240-44, 246-47, 250, 254-55, 259, 266-67, 270, 281-82, 298 n. 101

Roman soldiers, 162, 230-32, 234

Rommel, Field Marshal Erwin, 234, 239

Roncesvalles, 4, 175-77, 179, 182, 186, 203, 215, 238, 266-67, 270

Ronsheim, Milton, 67, 288 n. 19

Rórik, 192, 254

Rosebud River, 24-25, 47, 69, 255

Rosser, General T. L., 70

Rudolf, Crown Prince, 275

Runciman, Steven, 204-5, 296 n. 65, 297 n. 82, 84-87

Russell, Don, 7, 287 nn. 3-4, 290 n. 11

Ryan, "Old Ed," 76-77, 290 n. 33

Ryan, Sergeant John, 34-35, 69

St. James de Compostella, 175

St. Olaf, 188

St. Olaf's Saga, 187, 189

St. Paul Pioneer-Press and Tribune, 74, 78-79

St. Romanos Gate, 2, 204, 207-9, 237

Salammbô, La, 4, 183, 185-87, 295 n. 49

Salt Lake City Tribune, 78

Samuel, 155, 158, 162-63, 294 n. 13

Samuel, Book of, 2, 4, 157-59, 160, 162, 173, 177, 182, 198, 296 n. 54

Sanderson, Captain C. K., 41

Sandoz, Mari, 13, 287 n. 14, 288 n. 3

Sans Arc (Indians), 29

Santa Ana, General, 228

Saracens, 86-87; foes of Gawain, 179-81; foes of Roland, 177-79, 221, 225, 237, 240, 259, 266-67

Saul, 2-3, 155-62, 170, 181-82, 187, 208, 216-17, 220, 225, 227, 234, 240-42, 247, 266, 282, 293 n. 8, 11, 294 n. 15-17

Saul's Throne, 155

Saxo Grammaticus, 187, 192, 296 n. 59

Saxons, 88, 209, 212-15, 225, 232, 238, 266; at the Pante ford, 211-12

Scapegoating, 68, 123, 220-21, 239, 254

Schemata, 260, 266-67

Schreyvogel, Charles, 101

Scotland (and the Scots), 200-203

Scott, Sir Walter, 153, 202-4, 297 n. 80

Second Cavalry Regiment, 9, 24-25, 46, 109, 111, 177, 255

Seitz, Don C., 67

Serbia, 196, 296 nn. 67, 72

Serbs, 197, 198, 200

7th Cavalry, 7

Seventh Cavalry Regiment, 6, 8, 10-12, 20, 24-25, 28, 38, 46-50, 53, 66, 68, 71-73, 76, 79, 129, 133-34, 154, 219, 225, 232, 245, 254, 267, 284-85

Shakespeare, 159, 187-87, 226

Shaw, George Bernard, 56, 246, 300 n. 26

Shaw, legendary English guardsman at Waterloo, 92-93

Shenandoah Valley Campaign, 73

Sheridan, General Philip, 24, 45, 112, 128, 218-19

Sherman, General William T., 24, 47-48, 128-29, 131, 218, 298 n. 2

Sherrod, Robert, 131

Showdown at Little Big Horn, 263-64

Siegfried, 16, 85, 208, 240, 254, 272, 274, 278-79, 285

Sioux (Indians), 6, 9, 14, 16, 21-23, 27, 28, 30, 35-36, 40-41, 50-51, 54, 56, 62, 64-65, 67, 80, 82-83, 89-90, 96, 100, 102, 105, 108, 110, 112, 120, 123-24, 127, 136, 152, 226, 238-39, 241, 284

Sitting Bull, 8, 14, 21-23, 28, 33, 36, 68, 74, 102, 127, 147, 151-53, 254

Sitting Bull, 7

"Sitzkrieg," 238

Skuld, 190-92

Slaper, Private William 30, 33, 37-38, 261-62

"Sleeping warriors," legend of, 208, 274, 278

Slogans, 194, 227-28, 249-50

Smith, Captain E. W., 26

Smith, Henry Nash, 117, 292 nn. 9-12, 299 n. 12

Smith, John, 13

Smith, Lieutenant Algernon E., 43

Société Rencesvals, 232

"Song of Custer and His Men, The", 140-41

Song of Roland (English version), 182

Spartans, 2, 165-67, 169-70, 173-74, 179, 233-34, 242, 294 n. 23, 295 n. 25

Spendius, 183-84

Spotted Trail Agency, 22-23

Springfield (carbine), 27, 39

Stanley, Sir Edward, 201-2

Stedman, Edmund C., 137-38

Steinbeck, John, 269-70

Stewart, Edgar I., 287 nn. 7, 10

Stiklestad, 188, 235

Stuart, General James Ewell Brown, 112

Sturluson, Snorri, 188, 296 n. 57

Surrey, Earl of, 88, 200-201, 203, 212

Sullivant Hills, 109

Swedes (Bjarki's foes), 188-91, 225, 228, 237

Sword(s) (sabers), 56, 63, 84, 193, 195, 245-46, 254, 260, 264, 287, 296, 299; Bjarki's,

189, 191; Byrhtnoth's, 89; Constantine's, 208; Custer's, 8, 55-56, 60, 62, 91-93, 101, 104-105, 112, 137-38, 141-50, 232, 254, 267-68, 280, 282; Marko's, 198, 267; Roland's, 179, 267; Saul's, 158, 162

Tacitus, 234
Tactics, cavalry, 34, 65-66, 83, 111, 219, 245; Indian, 34, 40, 65-66, 219-20
Taillefer, 188, 235
Tarawa, 131
Taylor, Muggins, 78-79
Telegraph (in legend dissemination), 5
Ten Eyck, Captain Tenodor, 110-11
Tennyson, Alfred Lord, 139-40
Terry, General Alfred, 10, 24-25, 44-47, 68, 72, 78, 125-26, 129, 131, 218
Teton Sioux (Indians), 29, 33
Teutoburgwald, 230-31
Texas (and Texans), 94, 192-93, 227-28
Thebans, 165, 174
Thermopylae, 2, 86, 108, 113, 130, 134, 139, 165-74, 178-79, 182, 186-87, 190, 210, 215, 227, 232, 244
Thespians, 165, 167-68, 174
They Died With Their Boots On, 7-8, 60-61, 113
Thor, 208, 253
Thorir Houndsfoot, 191, 242
Thormod, 188-89, 235
Thuillier, Dom Vincent, 183, 185
"Time Tunnel" (TV program), 7
Tongue River, 23-26, 68
Topkapi Gate, 204, 209
Toplitsa River, battle of, 197, 220
Tragic flaw, 19, 241, 298 n. 101
Traitor, the, 1, 3, 9-10, 67-68, 71, 84, 160, 166, 177, 180, 190, 192, 197-98, 206-7, 213, 216, 239-40, 263, 267-68, 293 n. 8
Transmission, oral, 257-59
Travis, Colonel, 193
Troy, 141-42, 143
Tryggvason, Olaf, 209
"Tsar Lázar and Tsaritsa Militsa," 198
Tullock's Creek, 26, 46
Turkey, 13, 22
Turks; as Constantine's foes, 204-8, 225, 228, 237, 270; as Hunyadi's foes, 249; as Lázar's foes, 197-98, 225, 237, 240-41, 248

Turoldus, 86, 177, 182-83, 231-32, 236-37, 267, 271
Turpin, Bishop, 178, 235, 255
Two Flags West, 7
Two Moon, 35-36, 40-41

Ulysses, 189, 250
Unferth, 189, 191, 250-52, 300 n. 29
Urban (Hungarian engineer and cannon founder), 204, 206
Utley, Francis Lee, 271-73, 277, 300 n. 31, 301 n. 24
Utley, Robert M., 288 nn. 3-4, 289 nn. 15, 18, 290 n. 4

Van de Water, Frederic F., 6, 287 n. 2
van Humboldt, Alexander, 116
Varnum, Lieutenant Charles A., 29, 34
Varus, 230, 233
Vetsera, Baroness Maria, 275
Vietnam War, 223-25
Views on the Last Stand: in the East, 123, 127-28; in the South, 124-26, 225; in the West, 122, 125, 126-29, 225
Vikings, 3, 88, 190, 210-16, 225, 238, 241, 244, 265-66, 298 n. 101; in Njals Saga, 249
Vincent of Beauvais, 182
Virginia, University of, students (as informants), 273, 275, 278
Viva Zapata, 269-70
Vlad Tepes ("Dracula"), 274, 278
Voeux du Paon, La, 182
von Widerhofer, Dr. Hermann, 275
Vuk Brankovitch, 198, 240-41, 244
Vukašin, 197-98

Wagner, Richard, 121, 257
"Wagon Box fight, the," 112, 219
Wainwright, Reverend, 17
Wake Island, 194, 250, 282
Wallace, Lieutenant George D., 17, 50
War Department, 21, 24, 129
Warpath, 7
Warsaw ghetto uprising, 248, 283
Washita (location of Black Kettle's village), 11-13, 40, 55
Waterloo, 92, 285
Webb, Laura, 105-8, 137, 153, 291 n. 20, 293 n. 6

Weir, Captain Thomas B., 38, 41, 70, 115-16

Weir Point, 38

West Point, 7, 70, 112, 255, 279-80

Weston, Jessie, 14

Wheatley, James, 109-10

Whitman, Walt, 133-34, 137, 141, 148-50, 217, 226-27, 260, 293 n. 17

Whitney, Asa, 116

Whittaker, Frederick, 4, 10, 18, 53-54, 60, 69, 72, 82-83, 85-86, 89-97, 99, 100-101, 129, 133, 135, 143, 178-79, 231, 233, 245, 267-68, 270-71, 279, 291 nn. 37, 6, 13; "The Column of Death," 150; letter to Representative W. W. Corlett, 71; "Custer's Last Charge," 93, 95, 151-54, 231, 291 n. 8, 293 n. 18; dime novels of, 53, 93-97, 99-101, 291 n. 7; eulogy in *Galaxy*, 85-86, 291 n. 3; *The Life of General George Armstrong Custer*, 4, 18-19, 53-54, 79-83, 89-92, 288 n. 28, 290 n. 6, 291 n. 37

Whittier, John Greenleaf, 121, 147-48, 293 n. 16

Wigg (Vogg, Viggo), 191-92, 242

Wilcox, Ella Wheeler, 142-44, 153, 293 n.11

Williams, Roger, 119

Wilson, Sergeant James, 78

Winchester (carbine), 34, 226

Windolph, Sergeant Charles A., 28-29, 32, 39, 262

Witch of Endor (Ein Dor), 157, 162

Woodham-Smith, Cecil, 139, 293 n. 9

"Wreath of Immortelles, A," 137

Wulfmær, 212, 214

Xerxes, 113, 165-70, 173-74, 237

Yalta conference, legends and beliefs about, 265

Yates, Captain George W., 43, 52, 74

Yellow Tavern, 112

Yellowstone River, 24-25, 73, 78, 131, 147, 226

Young, Philip, 288 n. 17

Zalokostas, Georgios, 206

Zapata, 274, 278

Zauberflöte, Die, 257

Ziklag, 163